CONSUMING JAPAN

STUDIES IN UNITED STATES CULTURE

Grace Elizabeth Hale, series editor

Series Editorial Board

Sara Blair, University of Michigan
Janet Davis, University of Texas at Austin
Matthew Guterl, Brown University
Franny Nudelman, Carleton University
Leigh Raiford, University of California, Berkeley
Bryant Simon, Temple University

Studies in United States Culture publishes provocative books that explore U.S. culture in its many forms and spheres of influence. Bringing together big ideas, brisk prose, bold storytelling, and sophisticated analysis, books published in the series serve as an intellectual meeting ground where scholars from different disciplinary and methodological perspectives can build common lines of inquiry around matters such as race, ethnicity, gender, sexuality, power, and empire in an American context.

CONSUMING JAPAN

Popular Culture
and the
Globalizing of
1980s America

Andrew C.
McKevitt

THE UNIVERSITY OF
NORTH CAROLINA PRESS

Chapel Hill

This book was published with the assistance of the Authors
Fund of the University of North Carolina Press.

Designed by Jamison Cockerham
Set in Arno, Bodoni, and Graveny by codeMantra
Cover illustrations: classic car by Blade-kostas, cassette player by
adventtr, and sushi rolls by vitalssss; © iStockphoto.com.

Manufactured in the United States of America

The University of North Carolina Press has been a member
of the Green Press Initiative since 2003.

LIBRARY OF CONGRESS CATALOGING-IN-PUBLICATION DATA
Names: McKevitt, Andrew C., author.
Title: Consuming Japan : popular culture and the globalizing
of 1980s America / Andrew C. McKevitt.
Other titles: Studies in United States culture.
Description: Chapel Hill : The University of North Carolina Press, [2017] |
Series: Studies in United States culture | Includes bibliographical references and index.
Identifiers: LCCN 2017003595 | ISBN 9781469634463 (cloth : alk. paper) |
ISBN 9781469634470 (pbk : alk. paper) | ISBN 9781469634487 (ebook)
Subjects: LCSH: Popular culture—United States—Japanese influences. |
Globalization—Social aspects—United States. | United States—
Relations—Japan. | Japan—Relations—United States. | Japan—Foreign
public opinion, American. | Consumer goods—United States.
Classification: LCC E169.12 .M39 2017 | DDC 327.73052—dc23
LC record available at https://lccn.loc.gov/2017003595

Contents

Illustrations

Acknowledgments

Surely someone will scold me for beginning a book with an apology, but I'm compelled to apologize to the inevitable someone, or someones, I will forget to thank below. Over the years many people helped shepherd this book from unwieldy idea to publishable manuscript, and I'm grateful to all of them. Unfortunately, my memory is as limited as the space I have to record their names.

I enjoyed the support of a wonderful community in the Department of History at Temple University. Nobody was more supportive than the tireless Richard Immerman, who encouraged my imagination, even when it ran far afield of his comfort zone and common sense, and challenged me to make every bad idea better. I wouldn't be a professional historian today if it weren't for him. I also owe thanks to Petra Goedde, Bryant Simon, and Will Hitchcock for providing feedback and opportunities to present this work at various stages. I received generous support from Temple's Center for the Study of Force and Diplomacy and the Center for the Humanities at Temple. Friends I must thank include Richard Grippaldi (who deserves credit for an endless stream of eighties robot-cartoon jokes, if not for reading just about all of this project at various stages), Kate Scott, David Zierler, Kristin Grueser, Kelly Shannon, Michele Louro, Wendy Wong, Eric Klinek, Jay Wyatt, Paul Baltimore, John Oram, and Holger Löwendorf. I received invaluable feedback on parts of this project from Naoko Shibusawa, Shoko Imai, Sayuri Guthrie-Shimizu, Jennifer M. Miller, Tom Zeiler, and Brent Allison.

In 2012 I was lucky to land in the Department of History at Louisiana Tech University, one of the hidden gems of our historical profession. The department graciously supported travel and research that were necessary to finish this project. I'm thankful for the support of my colleagues Steve Webre, Elaine Thompson, Jeff Hankins, and Ken Rhea and also for political science colleagues Jeremy Mhire and Jason Pigg. Dave Anderson deserves special mention for always being available to bounce ideas off of while I walked the dog around the neighborhood.

I want to thank Mark Simpson-Vos and the staff at the University of North Carolina Press for editorial guidance and for making this book a reality. Though the book is based on an analysis of lots of published (and subsequently forgotten) material, I nevertheless owe thanks to the many librarians and archivists who helped track down occasionally unorthodox sources over the years. I owe a special thanks to the staff at the Walter P. Reuther Library at Wayne State University and also to librarians in central Ohio—Stephen Badenhop at the Union County Records Center and Archives and Becky Hatton at Logan County Libraries were especially helpful. For permission to reprint illustrations, I'm grateful to Bruce Garfield at Honda, Vincent Piscopo at the UAW, Kevin Behrens at the *Marysville Journal-Tribune*, and anime fans Saul Trabal and Michael Pinto. I also appreciate the assistance of the editors of *Diplomatic History*, where an early version of chapter 7 appeared.

Finally, I must thank my family for putting up with me while I worked on this book. My parents, Linda and Henry McKevitt, were always supportive, even when they didn't know what I was doing (because I didn't know what I was doing). My partner, Jennie Flynn, and our son, Ian, deserve the biggest thanks of all for having my back when I somehow managed to be the crankiest person in a house with a newborn.

Acknowledgments

CONSUMING JAPAN

Resurrecting the Ordinary in U.S.-Japan Relations

"Culture is ordinary," Raymond Williams once wrote. The influential Marxist critic was reflecting upon daily life in the rural farming valley in Wales where he grew up.[1] I suspect that, like Williams's studies of British culture and society were for him, this book will be as personal to most Americans born after World War II as it has been for me. It is not exceptional—it is ordinary, in fact—that the material presence of Japan has always been a tangible reality in my life. I recall being ferried around in my grandfather's 1984 Toyota Corolla and my father's late-1980s Toyota pickup truck; for my seventh birthday, I received a Nintendo Entertainment System, an interactive device that came to dominate after-school activities, weekends, and relationships with friends; my family regularly gathered around our first VCR, a hulking Panasonic, to watch the latest movie releases in the comfort of our home; reared on American food heavy in calories and light on subtlety, it required a herculean effort of epicurean open-mindedness to get me to try, and enjoy, sushi as an undergraduate; today I drive a Subaru (after a decade of driving a Toyota), I own several electronic gadgets imprinted with the Sony label, and, like the 25,000 people with whom I occasionally attend the annual Otakon anime convention and the millions more who watch anime daily on television, I find Japanese cartoons to be more compelling than just about anything the U.S. entertainment industry offers. For me it has never felt unnatural to consume the many material manifestations of Japan, and I am not alone.

Of course, none of this is extraordinary, and measured against the stories of international change that have dominated headlines since I was born—from the Iran hostage crisis to the end of the Cold War and implosion of the Soviet Union to the world-changing events of 11 September 2001—my recollections seem positively mundane, if not trivial. Yet that so many people could identify with such a personal anecdote begins to make my point: since roughly the mid-1970s the consumption of Japanese products has been a central facet of U.S. social and cultural life. We lack a place for this story, however, in our narrative of U.S. history in the twentieth century. Current understandings of U.S.-Japan relations during this period, which focus on state-level economic conflict and Cold War security debates, also fail to acknowledge the depth and complexity of this important transpacific exchange, which foreign policy critic Chalmers Johnson once called "the most valuable transoceanic economic relationship that ever existed."[2] I argue that in the nuances of economic and cultural consumption, in the acquisition and use of Japanese goods and the attendant ideas about and images of Japan, Americans' engagement with the processes of contemporary globalization intensified. Consuming all things Japanese helped create a globalized America, a condition that became so natural—so ordinary—that Japan's role in that process has been overlooked. The chapters that follow resurrect Japan's contribution to the transformation of American life in the last quarter of the twentieth century.[3]

When many Americans of the twenty-first century's second decade think of Japan and the 1980s, they remember trade disputes, high-profile real estate purchases, the consumer culture—the food, the cars, the VCRs—and, accompanying it all, the "Japan-bashing," the name for anti-Japanese rhetoric spewing from the mouths of politicians, intellectuals, business leaders, and talking heads of many stripes. Buried within one of the founding documents of Japan-bashing, which peaked in the late 1980s and early 1990s, lay the idea—or better, the fear—that consumption could define communities. "The Danger from Japan" was not Pulitzer Prize–winning journalist Theodore H. White's best work, but it nevertheless helped establish the tone for criticism of Japan's meteoric economic rise of the preceding two decades. Before he made his name chronicling presidential campaigns, White had served as a war correspondent in the Pacific. He stood on the deck of the USS *Missouri* in August 1945, watching as General Douglas MacArthur signed and accepted the Instrument of Surrender on behalf of the Allied Powers, ending the four and a half years of vicious warfare White had chronicled for *Time* magazine. During the conflict White acquired his views of Japan and its people through the prism of racial propaganda that the United States mobilized to acculturate soldiers to the slaughter of allegedly subhuman Japanese people.[4] When he wrote forty years later of Japan's "locked and closed civilization," then, White made no distinction between the Japan he had seen during the war—a society at its very worst—and the Japan of the 1980s, a staunch U.S. ally and emerging economic powerhouse. He cautioned his readers that the Japanese were once again on the offensive, this time using televisions and Toyotas instead of Zeroes. In an article ostensibly about Japan's "dismantling of American industry," he mentioned Pearl Harbor four times. In the final instance he urged Japan to remember the end result of their surprise attack; "their trade tactics," he warned, "may provoke an incalculable reaction."[5]

White's article has been cited repeatedly as the first dissonant note struck in an eventual chorus of anti-Japanese voices, an early manifestation of what two media scholars a decade later called the "Japan Panic," a moment of intense, uncertain, and ultimately fleeting fear of and fixation on Japan.[6] Yet lost in the attention paid to his attack on Japan's economic expansion was his critique of consumerism and Americans' penchant for buying what Japan was selling. After all, the shape of U.S.-Japan relations in the 1980s was contingent on Japanese companies selling products Americans wanted. "No nation that thinks of itself as an assembly of consumers can resist Japanese penetration," White admonished his readers. "But a nation that thinks of itself as a community has reason for alarm."[7] By 1985 White's readers were conscious of the flood of Japanese goods into the United States but not yet fearful of its political and economic consequences. The "danger from Japan" lay in Americans becoming enslaved to shiny things sold by an untrustworthy foreign power. Ultimately what was at stake in unrestrained global consumption, White believed, was the sense of community that had empowered Americans to build the world's most important democracy, a democracy that, as White saw firsthand, had been unified in defeating the global threat of fascism.

White reproduced a common idea among intellectual elites in the United States in the twentieth century: consumer societies were antithetical to authentic communities. That idea found its first significant articulation at the turn of the century in sociologist Thorstein Veblen's critique of "conspicuous consumption." In *The Theory of the Leisure Class* (1899), Veblen argued that Americans used consumption as a means of communicating social status, and like other intellectuals of his class he could hardly contain his disdain for this trend. At midcentury influential Frankfurt Schoolers like Max Horkheimer and Theodore Adorno applied Marxist understandings to the notion of consumer choice, developing the "mass culture" theories that portrayed the trappings of consumer society as alternative means of class repression and shaping a generation of intellectuals to follow.[8] While the postmodern or cultural "turn" in the humanities in the 1980s critiqued elitist attitudes toward popular culture, empathetic approaches to consumption have not gained traction at the popular level.[9] A generally critical intellectual attitude persists, particularly in the wake of the economic upheavals of the first decade of the twenty-first century—upheavals, many have argued, rooted in Americans' material desires outreaching their means, as millions took out mortgages on homes they could not afford. Critics have mobilized the mountains of data and sweeping conclusions of Robert Putnam's *Bowling Alone* to demonstrate the existence of a time when Americans were civic-minded and community-oriented, a time before the iPod and the Caramel Frappuccino—icons of the "treacherous rip current" of the consumerist individualism of the last three decades of the twentieth century.[10] Contemporary critiques of Americans' consumerist tendencies link the rise of the shopping mall to everything from that loss of community to the decline of U.S. global power and the death of masculinity.[11]

But if recent trends among historians and other scholars are any indication, then Americans have always used consumption—as I define it, the production and reproduction of cultural meaning through the acquisition and/or use of goods—as a means of defining local and national communities.[12] Historians like T. H. Breen and Lizabeth Cohen have told new stories about communities built around the consumption of goods, ranging from the nation's founding to the postwar era.[13] Kristin Hoganson has sparked conversations about how Americans have used goods to define themselves against the foreign while also incorporating the foreign into their domestic spaces. Her exploration of "white, native-born, well-to-do American women" who "produced the globe" by decorating their homes in the late nineteenth century with "an assortment of decontextualized things" guides historians toward an understanding of the domestic (in both senses of the word) impact of the "incoming tide" of global goods.[14] It also points to the historically gendered nature of consumption. Foreign relations historians, for example, who frequently write about questions of diplomacy and international power— so often coded as masculine subjects—have neglected consumption, consciously or not, because of its non-masculine associations.

Gendering consumption belies the reality of how most people in the United States actually engaged with the rest of the world in the second half of the twentieth century. The vast majority of Americans related to Japan during this period not as policy makers, diplomats, trade representatives, or even soldiers but as consumers. What White missed in correlating increased Japanese production and export figures with American industrial decline was the fact that Japanese goods were in American homes because Americans chose to put them there; consumers liked how those goods changed their lives in small and big ways. Had White visited Marysville, Ohio, in 1985, for instance, he would have witnessed a community transformed in the aftermath of a devastating recession by the infusion of capital and culture from a Japanese corporation. Or had White been a member of the Cartoon/Fantasy Organization, the first club in the United States dedicated to promoting the consumption of Japanese animation, he would have found a budding cultural community, one using the consumption of Japanese goods to link local communities to transnational networks of shared cultural interests. Beyond the popular conversation about what the flood of Japanese goods into the United States meant for national rivalries and trade balances, those goods helped to rework the lives of individuals and communities in local, ordinary spaces.

One of those seemingly ordinary spaces was Bill and Ivena Palm's driveway. The "quintessentially American" white suburban Los Angeles family of five posed in 1989 for a special issue of *Life* magazine commemorating the end of the eighties. In a striking photograph spanning two full pages, the family stands unsmiling in their doorway, tucked into the distance—easy to miss, in fact. Drawing the reader's attention away from the Palms and toward the foreground is a remarkable collection of consumer products displayed on the family's front yard and driveway; the scene resembles a treasure-filled yard sale. An assortment of objects familiar to millions of homes by the late 1980s, these were the common belongings with which middle-class Americans filled their lives in the late twentieth century. For this piece called "Foreign Exchange," *Life* had asked the Palms to showcase "one family's shopping in the international mall." As Bill, Ivena, and their three children worked to gather items for the photograph, they "were surprised to discover products from so many foreign countries in their home." The photographer organized products by country of origin, placing a small national flag among each group. Seventeen countries were represented; some only contributed one product, like Colombia (coffee) and West Germany (kitchenware), while others provided noticeably more, like China (13) and South Korea (17).[15]

The truly palpable global presence in the Palms' front yard and driveway that evening, and by extension in their everyday lives, was Japan. The world's second largest economy accounted for 37 of the 124 foreign goods the Palms owned, ranging in value from a bottle of rice vinegar to a Honda Accord sedan. The Palms estimated the value of everything they collected to be over $50,000, and although *Life* did not mention it, readers could hardly miss that Japanese products accounted for at least 80 percent of that total. In addition to the Accord, the Palms owned other sophisticated, high-value Japanese products like a Honda Civic; three motorcycles—two from Honda, one from Yamaha; a Honda lawnmower; cameras by Canon and Minolta; a

Sanyo stereo system; a television; a Sharp VCR; a Casio watch; a Nintendo Entertainment System; and a Sony Walkman. So dominant was the Japanese material presence that, unlike the rest of the products, which were grouped with others from the same country, Japanese goods were spread across the driveway and yard, and readers would have had more luck locating the bespectacled, stripe-shirted eighties creation Waldo than the small Japanese flag.

The Palms' Japanese purchases also portrayed a deeper engagement with Japan than their other foreign goods. There was nothing particularly Korean, for example, about the General Electric electronics, Adidas sneakers, and Mickey Mouse doll that originated in South Korea. On the other hand, a geisha doll in "traditional Japanese costume," a kimono, decorated lacquer trays and a pottery bowl, and even the rice wine betrayed an interest in the "Japaneseness" of Japanese things. Perhaps such goods were the result of Bill Palm's job as an advertising executive for Honda, a company that in the previous decade not only sold cars in the United States but also started making them there, employing tens of thousands of Americans, from assembly line workers to designers and ad executives, like Bill, in the process. The Palms' Honda Accord, the article observed, was "assembled in Marysville, Ohio," where the very first U.S.-assembled Honda automobiles rolled off the line in 1982. Displayed in front of the Palms' home that night was evidence of both the quantitative and qualitative impact of the consumption of Japanese goods on Americans' ordinary lives.

It would be inaccurate, however, to call *Life*'s attention to the "international shopping mall" celebratory. A sense of unease remained about the broader impact of the flood of foreign goods into the United States—indicative of a decline in U.S. manufacturing and exporting—and the last half-page of the feature hinted at a lingering anxiety. A small photograph featured the Palms' Japanese counterparts, the Kuchiki family of Tokyo, who displayed their own foreign goods in the family room of their five-room apartment. In the land "Where Imports Are Alien," as *Life* dubbed it, the apparently typical family owned only about $3,000 worth of foreign goods, including French perfumes, Italian leather goods, and "Batmanabilia" from Canada for Kazunori and Nobue Kuchiki's two young sons. The anemic list of U.S.-made goods the Kuchikis owned—three children's books, a plaque, a toothpick holder, sunglasses, a few t-shirts, and a bottle of ketchup—implicitly yet pointedly drew readers' attentions to record annual trade deficits and perennial U.S. pressure on Japan to "spend more while working less, thereby becoming more like us," as the economist Irwin Stelzer urged.[16] In a feature otherwise rejoicing in Americans' expanded access to a world of convenient and fascinating goods,

Life reminded readers of the ambiguities inherent in Japan's contributions to global exchange in the late twentieth century.

The national story as White told it, then, is not the only story to tell. The chapters that follow begin by examining the national conversation on Japan but then refocus the aperture on the local level, on the lives of non-elites like the Palms, to reveal that the material impact of Japanese goods complicated stories about the "danger from Japan." Chapter 2 puts White's warning in a broader intellectual context, outlining the different explanations for Japan's success that commentators and pundits provided. Beneath the belligerent nationalist din, a number of observers saw Japan not as a threat but as an exemplar, a globalized nation pointing the way toward a more prosperous, borderless future in which new actors would rewrite the rules of international power. Chapter 3 then looks at how the national conversation manifested in popular film and literature. Popular media often reflected the ambivalence and anxiety about Japanese power that intellectual debates produced as entertainment reached out to larger audiences.

The remainder of the book explores local encounters with Japan to demonstrate how the consumption of Japanese products throughout American society linked individuals and local communities to developments in global commerce and culture, complicating simplistic notions of national power and identity. Chapters 4 and 5 detail the case of Marysville, Ohio, a small rural town outside of Columbus. In 1982 the Honda Motor Company opened the first Japanese-owned U.S. automobile production facility in Marysville, effectively transforming the economic and cultural landscape of central Ohio in the following decade. Chapter 6 examines how individual U.S. consumers engaged global cultural change by consuming a variety of personal gadgets, including the most prominent early icon of contemporary globalization, the VCR. Chapter 7 explores Americans' first encounters with sushi, which demonstrated how Americans came to learn about and assimilate cultural otherness. Chapter 8 then highlights fans of Japanese animation, or anime, in their first dozen years of organizing U.S. communities. Anime fans created local clubs of shared interest in a foreign cultural product and connected their communities to global cultural flows in ways unique for the late 1970s and 1980s. The epilogue brings the globalizing of America, courtesy of Japan, up to the present.

In all of these contexts, I argue, the consumption of Japanese things served as a catalyst for the material and ideological globalizing of America. Arguably, Americans consumed more goods from Japan in the 1970s and 1980s than they had from any other foreign country in all of U.S. history, save perhaps Great Britain in the eighteenth century.[17] They stocked their domestic spaces, driveways, and store shelves with an immeasurable number of material representations and manifestations of Japan—a conservative estimate might put it in the billions. Sometimes they considered the economic and cultural implications of this, as when they bought a Honda automobile or smashed a Toyota with a sledgehammer at a union protest, or when they ate sushi in search of an "authentic" Japanese experience; at other times, like when they watched Hollywood movies on Sony VCRs and televisions, they did not. Consumers' purchasing decisions were implicit or explicit statements not only about Japan's changing place in the world but also about that of the United States. Whether they knew it or not, Americans, in choosing to buy Japanese goods, chose a side in what eventually would be debates about the impact of globalization on the country.

The concept of globalization emerged from intellectual struggles to come to terms with the dramatic shifts in economy and culture in the United States and around the world from the early 1970s on. The seemingly endless flood of Toyotas and Walkmans forced observers to reconsider the concept of international power in the late twentieth century. Many interpreted the United States' post-Vietnam political and economic woes as part of a larger pattern of decline. What did it mean, then, that a Cold War client-state constitutionally prohibited from military aggression seemed poised to surpass a superpower based solely on the global appeal of its consumer goods? Consumption at the popular level thus generated ideological change among political and intellectual elites. Some of those elites, predictably, revised older nationalist scripts of racial and cultural demonization. Others, though, reconsidered the meaning of international power, adapting the novel concept of globalization to explain the transition to a new post–Cold War era. As they did so, they placed Japan and its corporations at the center of the first debates over this contentious new idea.

In short, the globalized future looked much more Japanese in the 1980s than we acknowledge three decades later. Workers at Honda's plants in Ohio, members of anime fan clubs like the Cartoon/Fantasy Organization, and cultural producers like Ridley Scott, the director of the dystopian, Japan-influenced film *Blade Runner*, could all attest to this, though it would not be until the early 1990s that globalization became a buzzword to describe processes set in motion years, decades, and centuries earlier. By then the Japanese economy had entered a tailspin, bringing down with it the perceived economic threat from Japan. Coupled with declared victory in the Cold War and a rebounded U.S. economy in the late 1990s, Japan's "lost decade" made Theodore White's anxiety seem like a curious anachronistic specter. At the end of the century, Japan's presence in everyday material life in the United States was so ubiquitous—so ordinary—that Americans seemed to have forgotten a time when businesspeople and students lined up to learn to speak Japanese, when consumers lined up to buy the newest Sony gadgets, and when observers across the political spectrum lined up to tell Americans what it all meant. In what follows, then, to borrow again from Williams, I aim to resurrect the ordinary "structures of feeling," the "meanings and values" as they were "actively lived and felt," which were suffused with ideological and material representations of Japan in the last quarter of the twentieth century.[18]

When at the end of Ronald Reagan's presidency Joan Didion wrote stingingly of the storytelling surrounding Reagan as the "Fisher King," the "keeper of the grail" possessing a "magical quality" to which devoted pilgrims were drawn, she could have been writing of the quarter century of historical accounts that followed the end of his tenure. If there was anything innovative about the Reagan administration, it was its emphasis on shaping the narrative of policy making rather than on actual policy making, in crafting myths about the enigmatic president through anecdotes intended to be allegories. Historians have often been guilty of reproducing rather than challenging the narrative of the "Reagan Revolution," a story about the alleged transformation of American society that participants constructed so consciously while it was (or was not) happening.[19] Historians have fallen under the spell of the Fisher King.

A glance at a list of U.S. history titles on the 1980s demonstrates an unhealthy fixation with the so-called Great Communicator: *Reagan's America; Morning in America: How Ronald Reagan Invented the 1980s; The Age of Reagan; Reagan and Gorbachev: How the Cold War Ended; The Rebellion of Ronald Reagan: A History of the End of the Cold War*; and the unabashedly hagiographic *Ronald Reagan and His Quest to Abolish Nuclear Weapons*. These works belong to a second generation of scholarship on the 1980s, one that followed a first generation that was more the work of critical journalists and partisan Reagan insiders than historians.[20] The conservative political apotheosis of Reagan in the wake of his death in 2004 influenced the second generation to reassess the "Gipper" in a favorable light, emphasizing the "feel-good" politics of the decade, giving weight to surface over substance.

Recently a third generation has started to take shape, one that finds deeper and more long-term economic and cultural processes at work to produce the 1980s, the conservative wave of politics on which Reagan rode into power, and the decades that followed. In this new generation of literature, historians like Jefferson Cowie, Judith Stein, and Daniel T. Rodgers locate the economy and culture of the 1980s in patterns established in the previous decade.[21] Their works break down the artificial demarcation between "the seventies" and "the eighties," derived from a tendency not only to naturalize divisions in the turn of decades but also to see Reagan's election as a political-cultural caesura. If the second generation of 1980s historiography delineated how Reagan created an age, this crucial third generation counters with how an age created Reagan.

I plant this book firmly in the third generation, and I see it contributing in several important ways. First, *Consuming Japan* aims to help scholars locate globalization in this era. Although intellectuals have been articulating the contentious idea of globalization for at least three decades now, scholarship generally fails to historicize the material and ideological origins of this ubiquitous buzzword. A kind of reverse Euro-, Western-, and Americentrism dominates globalization studies in the sense that scholars are more often concerned with the ways that Western or American economic, political, and cultural power have radically reshaped global material conditions and mentalities than with cleavages or changes within that center of power. While globalization scholars often proceed with the worthy intention of drawing attention to the plight of the underdeveloped world, paradoxically such an approach actually ends up being Americentric in that it reaffirms the hegemony of the United States in a world of diffusing power.

One prominent example comes from sociologist George Ritzer, whose "McDonaldization" thesis asserts that capitalist forms that are American in origin have penetrated societies across the globe and transformed not just their cultural representations but the very structures of production and consumption.[22] This thesis was itself a response to the "clash of civilizations" argument prominent in the Cold War's immediate aftermath. Civilizations rooted in fundamental differences, like religious ones, argued the Harvard political scientist Samuel Huntington, would inevitably clash around the world along the fissures created by those differences.[23] A third scholarly approach to globalization emerged in the 1990s and remains popular today—the "hybridization" thesis, following the work of anthropologists like Arjun Appadurai and Ulf Hannerz, holds that the globalization of culture has resulted in mixed, heterogeneous, and hybrid forms of culture, frequently with indigenous cultures adapting powerful global (typically, Western) cultures to local needs.[24]

I am less interested in engaging in contemporary debates about what globalization is—is it homogenization or hybridization? Is it waxing or waning?—and more interested in historicizing the concept, locating many of the first scholarly conversations in the United States about this idea in the encounter with Japan in the 1970s and 1980s. Some observers imagined

Japanese corporations like Sony as responsible for the forthcoming homogenization of global culture. Americans who tasted sushi in the 1970s, on the other hand, or anime enthusiasts who built fan clubs around their fascination with Japanese culture were participating in a hybridized form of global culture, which adapted its Japanese original to local American practices. What the encounter with Japan points to, then, is not a single definition of globalization but the varied local experience of many globalizations, an era in which we observe "an intensification of multiple forms of global interconnectedness."[25] In writing this book I wanted to know not what globalization definitively was at any given time or in any given place but rather how people in the United States started to conceive of globalization as an agent of change. In this regard I find historian Frederick Cooper's perspective on globalization most persuasive. As a concept now more than three decades old, globalization has the power to unite "diverse phenomena into a singular conceptual framework and a singular notion of change." Historians struggle against the gravitational pull of such a powerful explanatory metaphor. "Good historical practice should be sensitive to the disjunctures between frameworks of past actors and present interpreters," Cooper writes, which I read as a call to historicize the seemingly hegemonic presentist ideas we use to explain the dizzying changes at the local, national, and global levels in the late twentieth century.[26]

If it is time for historians to begin historicizing the idea of globalization, it is also time to find a place for the concept of postmodernity in our historical narratives of the late twentieth century. Here, too, the encounter with Japan is instructive. Popular memory has forgotten Japan's impact on the United States in the late twentieth century in part because of the pervasive attitude that domestic social life and international relations must be governed by conflicts between big ideas—liberalism against authoritarianism, capitalism against communism, white against black, rich against poor. Storytellers of all stripes are drawn to such metanarratives. Political, economic, and intellectual elites in the early Cold War successfully sold the U.S.-Soviet clash on big ideas. Theodore White's attempt to rally U.S. citizens against the consumption of Japanese goods, an effort to be repeated with increasing intensity and urgency over the half-dozen years that followed, failed to mobilize Americans in a long-term struggle of big ideas. Japan "is a threat to our wallets, and not to our ideology," observed the writer Charles Paul Freund in 1989 as he surveyed what the 1990s might look like. "That kind of opponent is a lot less culturally useful to us than have been such threats as Nazis and communists."[27] Japan lacked the big story, the metanarrative, to challenge American-style liberalism and capitalism once both had seemed to recover by the early 1990s.

In the United States the concept of postmodernity, emerging in the 1970s, was a product of the sense that the modern period of American hegemony was at an end. It was not just the debacle in Vietnam, though that helped give shape to a feeling of "malaise." It was also the end of the idea that American-style liberal democratic capitalism represented the future, one of the grand promises of the first two postwar decades. The Kitchen Debate made sense in 1959 because Americans and non-Americans alike could reasonably believe that life in the United States foretold the shiniest, most prosperous future that any society had ever imagined. By contrast, a debate between Vice President Walter Mondale and Soviet general secretary Leonid Brezhnev about the respective merits of the capitalist and Communist systems would have provided comic fodder for a sketch on *Saturday Night Live* in the late 1970s.

It was a French intellectual, Jean-François Lyotard, who first detailed the "postmodern condition" in 1979. He succinctly described it as "incredulity toward metanarratives"—that is, the failure of grand stories of the liberation of the human condition.[28] Lyotard's famous pronouncement was more than an abstraction. It was grounded in the international economic and political realities of the 1970s and referred to the end of the most endearing Western narrative of the modern era: the promises of American liberal democratic capitalism. After racial conflict, Vietnam, Watergate, energy crises, and stagnation, it was harder to believe the story of American modernity. As historian David Farber writes, "The torch had fallen."[29] By the 1970s the other grand narrative of the twentieth century, the social justice promises of socialism, embodied in the other global superpower, the Soviet Union, had proven equally dubious. Thus postmodernity by the end of the 1970s was a vacuum devoid of believable stories about the promises of human liberation.

Into the vacuum stepped Japan—the "Empire of Signs," as theorist Roland Barthes called it, a land of ever-changing, floating signifiers attached to no fixed meanings and thus no metanarratives.[30] Barthes, a seminal semiotician, developed the notion, first popularized in 1946 by Ruth Benedict in *The Chrysanthemum and the Sword,* that there was no such thing as moral absolutism or universalism in Japan. Ideas and behaviors were a product of circumstances, and the Japanese were acculturated to the constantly shifting "signs" of proper social behavior. As chapters 2 and 3 show, cultural elites as diverse as Harvard University political scientist Joseph S. Nye and author Michael Crichton pushed this idea one step further: lacking any sense of moral absolutism, Japanese culture had no core values or big ideas to offer the world. In Nye's case this meant that Japanese economic power ultimately could not challenge the global allure of American values, or American "soft power"; for Crichton the vacuity of Japanese culture was the very thing Americans should fear most.[31] In both instances, it was Japan's lack of a metanarrative that made it postmodern, or at least beyond-the-modern, to American thinkers and opinion makers.

This ambiguous but fully historicized understanding of postmodernity is as close to a definition as I provide. That sounds like an attempt to eschew responsibility for defining a slippery yet central analytical referent. It is not. Essential to this work's understanding of postmodernity is that by the time Japan assumed a dominant position in the way that Americans saw a changing world—say, by the end of the 1980s—it was a commonly debated notion within intellectual circles that the developed world had entered a qualitatively new phase in the relationship between commerce and culture. The two were divorced from stories of human liberation. While there was never a consensus on what exactly this meant or if it even was something truly unlike anything that had come before it, leading intellectuals incorporated the concept into their own study of the human condition. The idea mingled, I argue, with the notion that Japan represented a globalized future. Japan's rise to the status of global economic superpower coincided with increasing awareness of the concept of postmodernity; that much is empirically verifiable.[32] Attributing the development of thought about postmodernity directly to visions of Japan is admittedly more tenuous, particular compared with the widespread connections between the origins of the concept of contemporary globalization and Japan's globalizing. In 1998 Fredric Jameson, one of the central intellectual figures in outlining postmodernity, described the post-1973 period, in his characteristic way, as "some new or third, multinational stage of capitalism, of which globalization is an intrinsic feature and which we now largely tend, whether we like it or not, to associate with that thing called postmodernity."[33] Jameson's ambiguity makes articulating a clear definition for both globalization and postmodernity difficult, but it at least makes clear that the two concepts have been inextricably connected since their origins.

As historians begin to flesh out these complicated questions, they must consider how changing conceptions of the United States in the world after 1973—tied to Japan's rise to power—influenced vanguard intellectual currents. Thus when I use postmodernity in what follows, I historicize it to the extent possible. I make no claims about what it means today or how it functions in contemporary intellectual or popular discourse. Just like globalization, it is a word whose meaning is temporal and spatially contingent.

I have organized the book thematically between two chronological bookends: roughly the mid-1970s and the early 1990s. The first bookend was the product of a confluence of events that gave rise to the steady growth of anxiety about Japan that culminated in the panic of the early 1990s.

The era began with a series of policy-making initiatives known as the "Nixon shocks," which collectively aimed to stabilize a troubled U.S. economy's international position at Japan's expense. The first and most alarming initiative, Richard Nixon's 1971 decision to visit China to begin normalizing relations between the two Cold War rivals, seemed to threaten a Japan that had thrived under the U.S. nuclear umbrella precisely because it served as a bulwark against the spread of communism in East Asia. The second shock hit Japan's economy—Nixon ended the Bretton Woods monetary system whereby foreign currencies were pegged to the U.S. dollar, allowing those currencies to float freely against each other. The very inexpensive Japanese yen of the postwar era was valued at 360 to 1 U.S. dollar; overnight it grew in value to 308, which Japanese leaders justifiably interpreted as a threat to exports essential to Japanese prosperity. Nixon's third shock came when he demanded that the Japanese government act decisively to open its notoriously tight domestic markets to U.S. products. A series of lawsuits followed targeting Japanese industries, like textiles and later steel and televisions. Critics of Japan claimed those industries blocked the importation of U.S. goods into the country while flooding consumer markets in the United States with their own products. Taken together the Nixon shocks served to put Japan on notice that the United States would not abide Japan's seemingly limitless growth at American expense. Historian Walter LaFeber calls the shocks the "terminus" of postwar U.S.-Japan relations, marking the end of nearly three decades during which the United States protected and nurtured the Japanese economy, even to its own detriment.[34] The threats and challenges U.S. and Japanese policy makers perceived in the moment, however, belied the impact of the shocks over the following two decades. As historian Thomas Zeiler writes, "Japan's emergence as the world's second-largest economy testified, ironically, to the ultimate futility of Nixonian strong-arm tactics."[35] The Nixon shocks were certainly a turning point in the tone if not the substance of U.S.-Japan political relations, and thus they serve as a useful starting point for a new era.

The Nixon shocks were part of the decade's broader "shock of the global," as a recent book labels the subjective feeling in the United States that a series of crises around the world were responsible for the growing sense of "malaise" at home.[36] These other shocks included the 1973 oil crisis, which ushered the oil powers of OPEC onto the global stage; the increase in international terrorism, including high-profile incidents like the attack on Israeli athletes at the 1972 Munich Olympics; and the catastrophe-filled year of 1979, when the Soviet Union invaded Afghanistan, a Communist regime seized power in Nicaragua, and an Islamist political movement in Iran overthrew that country's U.S.-backed government and took fifty-two Americans hostage, generating a second oil crisis. Whether it was on television or at the gas pump, Americans felt the "shock of the global" in the 1970s more powerfully than they had before in the postwar era.

The decade of the 1970s also functions as a starting point because it was during that period that the impression of Japanese goods in the United States changed dramatically. The workers making Betamax cassettes at Sony's gleaming new plant in Dothan, Alabama, in 1979 had a privileged perspective on this transformation. "I can remember when I was young," said one foreman, "if you bought anything that said 'Made in Japan' it was a joke." It was a common refrain in the 1970s. But by 1979 he and more than a thousand other Alabamians were manufacturing high-end Japanese consumer electronics for sale both in the United States and in Japan. "The Japanese," said another foreman, "I've never seen a country that's changed their [sic] image as drastically as they have." The prestige of Japanese goods across the United States and the changes for which they were responsible in southeastern Alabama gave a *Washington Post* reporter the "sense that the world has been stood on its head."[37] Understandings and representations in the United States of the Japan that emerged from the 1970s contrasted sharply with those of a decade earlier, and in those ideas we find the beginning of our story.

What happened to the "danger from Japan," then, and why the second bookend? In short, Japan's major economic recession in the early 1990s—the bursting of the Japanese financial bubble—was responsible for the country's cultural recession in the United States. Whereas before the 1980s American and European banks dominated global finance, by the end of that decade the four largest banks in the world, and eight of the ten largest, were Japanese. Assets in all Japanese banks were worth more than double those in all U.S. banks, and by one estimate, the total value of real estate in Tokyo alone was worth more than all the land in the United States, a country twenty-six times larger than Japan.[38] But Japan's "economic miracle" through the 1970s had rested on state guidance of the country's innovations in industrial production—textiles, steel, automobiles, electronics, and so on. Japanese corporations built the finance system of the 1980s on speculation and the creation of paper value. Banks made bad loans that companies like Matsushita used to buy overvalued real estate, most notoriously in the United States—by 1998, by one estimate, the value of bad loans accumulated was worth 80 trillion yen, or 12 percent of Japan's entire GDP.[39]

When the Ministry of Finance tightened credit markets in order to curb speculation at the bubble economy's peak, it triggered a collapse of the Nikkei, the largest stock index in the world. From the fall of 1989 to the summer of 1992, the index plummeted from a high around 40,000 to a low near 14,000. The value of the losses, around $7 trillion, was staggering. The ministry justified its actions by claiming that it was weeding out bad debt created by speculators. But by 1991, the Nikkei collapse spilled over into other sectors of the economy. Banks hesitated to make loans. Industrial production between 1991 and 1994 declined 11 percent, consumer spending shrank, and the country's gross domestic product leveled at zero growth by 1994.[40]

It is instructive that the years in which Japanese bank assets swelled before the bubble burst, roughly 1989–91, correlated to the years of the most virulent anti-Japanese representations in the United States. A "cultural lag" dragged out intense anti-Japanese representations into 1993, but at that point the material conditions of the Japanese economy no longer presented an immediate economic threat to the United States. "When the bubble burst in 1990," writes Zeiler, "three years of [Japanese] national income was wasted." Americans were attuned to this collapse, and 1992 was a crucial year for changing attitudes toward Japan. A national poll by the *New York Times* and CBS News found that in just the span of a year, perceptions of Japan had shifted dramatically, with 45 percent of Americans at the end of 1992 believing the United States would be "the No. 1 economic power in the world" in the twenty-first century, while 30 percent felt Japan would claim that title; only a year earlier, the percentages had been reversed.[41] By 1996 the Japanese economy's rapid decline "erased most of the value artificially generated in the 1980s," and total assets were equivalent to those of a decade and a half earlier.[42] Cultural representations of Japan in the United States followed suit, distancing themselves from the heated rhetoric of five years earlier and returning to a discourse of guarded respect for Japanese industry and culture. Another East Asian financial crisis in 1998 exacerbated Japanese economic woes, and almost two decades later the Japanese economy remains a shadow of its former self.

Japan also suffered its own "shock of the global" in the 1990s. In the 1980s Japanese corporations showed Americans one powerful vision of a globalized future. While those corporations were exporting global ideas and products abroad, the domestic Japanese economy nevertheless remained insulated and structured in ways profitable for the national economy system of the 1960s and 1970s but vulnerable in the globalizing world of the end of the century. The Japanese state and the cronyism of domestic capitalism could shelter corporations from the impact of globalization only for so long.[43] Investors in

U.S. corporations benefited tremendously from the globalizing economy precisely because, as was the case when Japanese corporations bought real estate and set up production facilities in the United States, free-market ideologies, institutionalized during the Clinton administration, won out over protectionism. Anti-globalization activists never succeeded in erecting barriers to trade from countries employing exploited, inexpensive labor, so corporations from Nike to Walmart expanded rapidly on the profits from cheap imported goods. American jobs went overseas, but Americans paid less for just about everything—hardly an equal trade-off, but the allure of increased consumption, facilitated by access to inexpensive credit, stifled widespread dissent. In the process U.S. corporations, not Japanese ones, came to symbolize globalization, and narratives of that phenomenon have consequently excluded the Sonys and Hondas that pioneered its forms. The globalized image of Michael Jordan spoke of the triumph of post–Cold War American capitalism.[44] The story of American capitalism triumphant filled the vacuum left by Japan's economic collapse, exacerbated as it was by the very same processes its corporations helped create.

Also, while Japan's cultural presence is not as detectable today as it was three decades ago, it still exists in less pronounced ways. VCRs and the first Sony Walkman have faded into obsolescence, but their descendants—small, sleek tablet computers made in China and Apple iPhones "Designed in California / Assembled in China," as the back of each device claims—are cultural icons of leisure activity, global production and consumption, and media transformation. Seemingly all of them are manufactured in China, yet nothing ever bears a Chinese name, likely because "Chineseness" is not associated with luxury, quality, or cosmopolitanism. (If the Japanese case is any precedent, though, that day indeed lies in the future, and not coincidentally, China has replaced Japan atop the list of economic bogeymen.) Wherever they come from today, however, the forms originated in Japan.

While the encounter with Japan in the late twentieth century helped generate new thinking about the United States' place in the world, older stereotypes and clichés dating to the first transpacific encounters of the nineteenth century remained persistent and influential. American popular discourse continued to represent the Japanese in racialized and gendered terms, even as ideas a century old mutated to reflect an altered international landscape, one that would have looked unfamiliar just a quarter century earlier.

"Yellow peril" imagery, white reactions to the first waves of East Asian immigration to the United States in the mid-nineteenth century, pervaded late twentieth-century representations of Japan.[45] Emigrants from East Asia, according to this ideological construction, arrived in successive waves of "invasion," bringing unassimilable alien languages and cultures and threatening economic opportunities for working-class white Americans. Representations in the 1980s would draw on the invasion metaphor, whether the invasion was consumer goods (televisions, VCRs, or automobiles) or people (Japanese businessmen, flush with cash, swarming to U.S. shores to buy up the country's most cherished assets). The harshest representations, such as Michael Crichton's novel *Rising Sun*, imagined a racial dichotomy between Japanese invaders bent on conquest and vulnerable white Americans oblivious to the threat.

Anti-Japanese attitudes peaked during World War II, when the Japanese and Americans fought a "war without mercy," a vicious "race war," as historian John Dower has described it.[46] Though it ended three decades before the era I consider, World War II and its popular memory inevitably pervaded thinking about Japan's newfound economic power, and in that memory older yellow peril fears mixed with images and ideas about the treacherous, sneaky "Japs" who attacked the United States at Pearl Harbor. The generation of Americans leading government, business, and academic institutions by the 1970s had fought in the war or worked to support the war effort. For instance, all of the U.S. presidents from this period—Nixon, Ford, Carter, Reagan, and George H. W. Bush—had served in some military capacity during wartime (though Carter graduated from the Naval Academy too late to see the Pacific, and Reagan fought by making pro-war Hollywood films). Decades after the defining experience of their youth, during which they had learned to hate the Japanese with an intensity unknown in the European war, these leaders now had to meet the challenge of economic competition from an important Cold War ally, and many invariably drew upon old stereotypes and clichés learned during the war. They also tiptoed around race-based explanations for Japanese behavior that had been popular during the war, cognizant that such thinking was controversial in the 1970s and 1980s in ways it had not been in their youth. In countless public and private venues, the war would not go away, and each decennial anniversary—the thirtieth, the fortieth, the fiftieth—was another opportunity to reassess the war's continued resonance in U.S.-Japan relations.

In the years immediately following the war, Americans adjusted their representations of Japan to meet the political demands of the moment. As historian Naoko Shibusawa describes, the wartime image of the murderous Japanese simian transformed into a beautiful, subservient, vulnerable geisha during the postwar U.S. occupation of Japan. Using the language of gender and maturity—portraying Japan both as a woman defenseless against communism and as a child in need of guidance toward modernization—served to rally popular support in favor of U.S. policies aimed at quickly rebuilding a devastated former enemy. As Shibusawa observes, however, "Negative stereotypes of Japan remain embedded in American culture, ready to be pulled out as the political and economic situation changes."[47] Thus when Japan once again appeared to threaten U.S. hegemony, Americans had a deep well of negative ideas and images, more than a century in the making, from which they could draw to buttress shifting attitudes about their own standing in the world. Stereotypes floated in the 1970s from the harmless geisha to the dangerous samurai. American popular representations of the Japanese corporate *sarariman* ("salaryman"), so devoted to his company that he would work himself to death on its behalf, echoed Western fascination with stories of samurai dying for feudal lords, even committing seppuku—ritual suicide—if honor demanded it.[48]

Images of a premodern Japan of geisha and samurai mixed with fears of a postmodern Japan of amoral capitalist accumulation to efface the Japanese present. Persistent racialized images of the Japanese made it difficult for Americans to see Japan as a country full of millions of people similarly trying to solve problems many modern societies shared. This effacement could even be quite literal, as when surveys demonstrated that Americans had trouble identifying a single Japanese person, despite the widespread anxieties in the late 1980s that Japan was poised to overtake the United States economically.[49] Japan had no Hitler or Stalin to establish a cult of personality and embody a threatening ideology; it produced only faceless, alien armies of samurai or *sarariman* on the march. American representations continued to exoticize Japan as they always had, to define it as an "other," but those representations evolved in response to economic and cultural shifts that felt new in the 1970s and 1980s. In that sense Japan's very real economic power during this period tested the culture of "Cold War Orientalism" that historian Christina Klein describes, an ideology in which postwar representations of Asia "helped to construct a national identity for the United States as a global power."[50] What happened to popular American ideas about Asia when an Asian nation threatened U.S. hegemony in the region at a moment when the era of global superpowerdom appeared to be at its end? I try to answer that question in what follows.

Finally, by focusing on subjects that historians have largely ignored, I have unavoidably neglected other issues. I do not discuss U.S.-Japan security relations, for example, not because I think they are unimportant but because I do not think that the exciting drama in the relationship occurred in that sphere after 1973. The few historical works that do address U.S.-Japan relations during this period show just how stifling the official relationship was.[51] For most of that period Washington and Tokyo remained in a holding pattern of Cold War complacency. Occasional uproars over U.S. military bases or news of a military technology sale to the Soviet Union aside, there is no evidence that any policy maker in power in either country ever considered acting on the notion that the other was anything less than a steadfast ally. As the Cold War gasped its final breaths in the late 1980s, more than a few commentators believed that East Asia's great economic power would establish itself as the next threat to U.S. global political hegemony. But there was no indication that any high officials in the Reagan, Bush, or Clinton administrations ever thought or behaved in a way that reflected such attitudes. Tough talk on trade or demands for "voluntary import restraints" reflected negotiations between bickering allies rather than preparations for war. Despite Theodore White's concern, 1985 was not 1941, and powerful actors in Washington never moved to translate such rhetoric into policy. Fears and concerns instead more often played out in the public sphere—in the realm of discourse, in the realm of culture. Autoworkers in Detroit, cattle farmers in Texas, and rice growers in Louisiana had more reasons to be upset with Japanese trade practices than anyone in Congress or the White House. Such people rarely had access to institutions of international political or economic power.

Thus the subjects that usually occupy histories of bilateral relations prove inadequate for exploring a relationship that was complicated by the ideas and attitudes of discerning consumers and the multifaceted nature of contemporary globalization. A more nuanced picture of U.S.-Japan relations, and of U.S. history during this period and across the centuries, demands attention to the ways local actors engaged with global economic and cultural developments to bring about the globalizing of America. It demands resurrecting the ways in which the local and the personal—the ordinary—are transformed by the extraordinary global developments of our times.

At the outset, I said that this was personal. The countless conversations I have had over the years about this work proved as much, from colleagues who recounted family comings and goings across the Pacific for work, to the senior Japanese scholar, born perhaps during or even before World War II, who approached me at a conference and quietly, almost in a whisper, described how my project reminded him of one of his favorite songs—Styx's 1983 prog-rock classic "Mr. Roboto." I hope that every reader finds a little of his or her own story in the "structures of feeling" I have attempted to recreate in the following.

ONE

Japan Won the Cold War, and Other Strange Ideas from an Era of Ideological Change

President George H. W. Bush's approval rating was riding high in 1991 in the wake of victory in the popular Gulf War. But a year later the U.S. economy struggled to recover from a brief recent recession, and with a presidential election on the horizon, Bush lay in the political crosshairs. Democratic candidate Bill Clinton's strategists knew that the recession would be the incumbent's weakness, and, following a strategy devised by Clinton's cartoonishly charismatic campaign manager, James Carville, they sought to exploit it with a simple message: "It's the economy, stupid!" Clinton was hardly the only, or even the first, candidate to train his sights on Bush's economic Achilles' heel. Early in the primary campaign, former Massachusetts senator Paul Tsongas emerged as the front-runner and won the crucial New Hampshire Democratic primary in February 1992. His campaign brochure, *A Call to Economic Arms*, adapted the familiar language of war metaphors to economics, describing his "battle plan" to counter the "attack" from the "foreign ownership of industry" and real estate. It linked U.S. economic decline with the free trade system's failure to account for "unfair" foreign competition. More than Clinton, Tsongas emphasized the changing international context of American economic woes, and he found fault with one nation in particular. "The Cold War is over," he told audiences on the campaign trail, "and Japan won."[1]

And then came the infamous "tossing of the cookies." As he dined alongside Japanese prime minister Kiichi Miyazawa at a formal state dinner in Tokyo in January 1992, the president suddenly vomited and fell to the floor. The scene, reproduced on the nation's television screens and panned by every manner of columnist and comedian, reflected rather than created a moment of political crisis within the White House—that week, for the first time since he took the oath of office, more Americans disapproved than approved of Bush's job performance, according to the polls.[2] For Tsongas and Clinton it was an auspicious moment to go on the offensive against Bush's Japan policy, and the image of a prostrate president lingered in audiences' minds as Tsongas told them that their victory over the Soviet Union was, in fact, illusory.

Tsongas's quip reflected a painful paradox the United States confronted in the early 1990s: it had "lost" a trade war while winning a cold one. Japan's rise to the status of an economic superpower—one constitutionally prohibited from projecting military force beyond its own borders—forced Americans to rethink the nature of international power. Tsongas's awkward but sincere statement illustrated that he could access only the anachronistic vocabulary of the Cold War to explain the transformed state of international affairs. In the early 1990s Americans used "old words for new problems," as one Japanese historian put it.[3] For decades political and economic elites across the political spectrum had conceived of international affairs as a struggle between two economic and ideological camps. Events in Eastern Europe and the Soviet Union from 1989 to 1991 signaled a "victory" over communism and, in Francis Fukuyama's words, the "end of history."[4] Nevertheless, "in the aftermath of this triumph," wrote one think-tank president, echoing Tsongas's perplexity, "many Americans have a nagging sense that they somehow missed the victory party."[5]

Victory was fleeting indeed. While American-style capitalism seemed poised to triumph in Eastern Europe, Japanese companies were buying some of its more recognizable symbols. In 1989 Mitsubishi purchased New York City's Rockefeller Center and Sony bought Columbia Pictures just a year after acquiring CBS Records, which owned Columbia Records and the music of icons like Bruce Springsteen, the troubadour who penned the decade's most iconic (if misunderstood) rock anthem, "Born in the U.S.A." While Springsteen sang about the tribulations of unemployed autoworkers, the U.S. automobile industry, the most enduring symbol of American industrial might, continued to cede ground to Japanese automakers producing small fuel-efficient vehicles more attuned to a world of repeated oil crises. A consumer looking to purchase a U.S.-made television, stereo, or VCR would find shelves stocked with Japanese products. Policy makers stoked public fears with abstractions like the "trade deficit" to explain the consequences of Americans' desires for the hundreds of millions of products Japan sold in the United States during the decade. This chapter explores American intellectual efforts to come to terms with Japan's many economic successes in the rapidly changing international climate of the 1980s.

Japan Won the Cold War, and Other Strange Ideas

Political tensions ran high between Japan and the United States in the 1970s and 1980s. Yet the tone of official relations never rose above the level of a heated trade spat between committed allies. Cultural tensions, however, reached a boiling point in the last years of the George H. W. Bush administration, demonstrated by a spate of explicitly anti-Japanese publications.[6] Many political and economic elites recognized the dissonance between official policy and popular discourse. A sizable segment of the U.S. population agreed with the economist Pat Choate when he warned that "America is selling its economy to Japan and surrendering the political and economic control that always accompanies such ownership."[7] Nearly seven out of every ten respondents to a 1989 *Business Week* survey believed that the "economic threat from Japan" posed a "more serious threat to the future of this country" than the "military threat from the Soviet Union," and 41 percent of respondents believed that "eventually Japan will take America's place as the world's leading economic and political power."[8] Yet while such ideas permeated the pages of popular newspapers and magazines, officials in the U.S. government never acted in ways that made these popular ideas determine policy.

Observers of U.S.-Japan relations wrote in a context of increasing pessimism about the United States' role in the world. The defeat in Vietnam preceded two oil crises and further international debacles in Afghanistan and Iran in 1979. On the domestic front, the 1970s was the era of "stagflation," a dangerous economic brew of stagnating growth and continued inflation, which translated into increasing unemployment and decreasing consumer capacity. The increased presence of Japanese products on store shelves, the ever-present concern about a ballooning "trade deficit," and high-profile real estate acquisitions provided Americans with one convenient explanation for who was gaining at their expense. The perception that the balance of international power had changed considerably created a need for intellectual explanations, which a cohort of pundits and their publishers stood at the ready to provide.

As Americans purchased Sony televisions and Toyota automobiles by the millions, then, publishers spilled oceans of ink to satiate the public's demand for explanations and clarifications of all things Japanese. Today's university libraries serve as museums for the era of Americans' Japan fixation. Hundreds of books about Japan published in English during this period collect dust; due dates stamped on inside covers betray a flurry of activity after the mid-1980s and a marked decline in popularity beginning about a decade later. On these shelves lies the archive of a curious moment in the history of American self-reflection and self-doubt. When American intellectuals looked in the mirror in the late 1980s and early 1990s, they saw Japan, with the reflection representing all the ambiguity the mirror metaphor carries.[9]

Yet in less than half a decade after Tsongas's campaign of anti-Japanese economic nationalism, Japan vanished. To be sure, the cars and VCRs remained. Nevertheless, the all-pervasive ideological construct of Japan was no longer an important feature of U.S. social and cultural life. What happened? Japan's powerful state and business institutions, so often labeled the source of its postwar "miracle," resisted any transformation. Japanese corporations had not stopped selling products to Americans or buying real estate in the United States. Japanese "culture"—another important contemporary explanation for Japan's success—had not experienced any substantive change. What happened to the Japan obsession?

What happened is that Americans rewrote the story of international power. The intellectual framework for understanding Japan's position in the world changed. Quite simply, globalization "happened," and the adaptation of this new concept to the contingencies of the moment helps explain the end of the "era of bilateral acrimony" between the United States and Japan.[10] Of course, globalization was nothing new. Even the most shortsighted observers date its arrival to the early 1970s, and historians can justifiably argue for eras of significant globalization in the sixteenth and "long nineteenth" centuries. But in terms of the ways that Americans wrote and spoke about the relationships between the world's many nations, globalization became the new popular organizational metaphor in the 1990s. It replaced Cold War–era definitions of international power that relied on the language of bipolarity, strategic forces, and army divisions. Economic power now mattered, and specifically the sort of economic power that could transcend the artificial borders built by centuries of political and military conflict and decades of ideological and geopolitical struggle. Globalization was a new word for seemingly new problems.

Cultural power mattered too. As the chapters that follow illustrate, the consumption of Japanese goods in the United States garnered Japan a great deal of cultural power, though few observers at the time articulated it this way, and the exercise of cultural power looked very different from the exercise of military power. By the early 1990s observers labeled the exercising of such transnational economic and cultural power "globalization." Globalism, an ideology promoting neoliberal trade practices and perceiving the capitalist world as a single interconnected market, emerged in tandem with the evolving concept of globalization. The Clinton administration replaced the Cold War strategy of containment—in its broadest sense, a grand strategy that drew boundaries and ensured that they remained fixed and monitored—with

Japan Won the Cold War, and Other Strange Ideas

a strategy of globalization, which recognized the increasing irrelevance of borders and positioned the United States to benefit most from such a development. In the American imagination, the world had changed. Narratives of power in a globalized world replaced Cold War ways of thinking. New problems meant new words but also new opportunities.

I am thus interested not in defining globalization authoritatively but in historicizing its intellectual origins, locating the concept in the specific context of U.S.-Japan relations in the 1980s. Japan was central to the earliest articulations of the concept of globalization in the United States. Only later did the country recede from the U.S. global imagination once its "long decade" of the 1990s halted its unbroken upward trajectory. U.S. business elites and intellectuals espousing globalism throughout the 1980s first conceived of the concept of globalization with Japan as the model of a dramatic world economic revolution that would transform relationships between peoples and states; in fact, it would alter the very nature of power. Japan seemed to prove that a nation could reach the heights of international power without significant military capabilities. In the wake of the Japanese recession that began in 1990, however, Americans rewrote the narrative of globalization to position not Japan but the West, and the United States in particular, at the center of the late twentieth century's international transformations. As a result, by the end of the century Tsongas's claim that Japan had won the Cold War rang of a different time, place, and optic on the world.

REVISIONISM AND THE "JAPAN PANIC"

The Cold War had taught Americans to fear gaps and deficits. Director Stanley Kubrick tapped into this anxiety in 1964 when he created the character General Buck Turgidson, played by George C. Scott, for his Cold War parody, *Dr. Strangelove*. The film mocked the Kennedy-era fear of an alleged "missile gap" with the Soviet Union, which had enabled Kennedy to outmaneuver Vice President Richard Nixon on foreign policy in the 1960 presidential election. With global nuclear annihilation imminent, Turgidson's Cold War mindset assesses the United States' odds in a postwar rivalry with the Soviet Union, as both superpowers lie buried deep underground. Like a stumping candidate (quite literally—he stands up on a chair), Turgidson implores his president and fellow national leaders, "We must not allow a mineshaft gap!"

In the 1970s Americans learned to fear a new kind of gap—a trade gap. After maintaining a favorable world trade balance between $2 billion and $6 billion throughout the 1960s and reaching a high of roughly $12 billion in 1975, the United States would never again export more goods and services than it imported. Journalists regularly used the term "trade deficit"—implying something dangerously lacking—instead of the more neutral "balance of payments" to describe the changing dynamics of international trade. After the mid-1970s, posturing against this new kind of gap played well in the political arena.

While even the relatively meager deficit of $6 billion in 1976 alarmed some critics, concern over the gap peaked in the second half of the 1980s.[11] The figure reached an all-time high of $152 billion in 1987, a record unsurpassed until 1998. (By then another Asian economic power, China, commanded the deficit.) Of that $152 billion, Japan accounted for almost $60 billion, or roughly 39 percent, a share reminiscent of the goods displayed on the Palms' driveway in suburban Los Angeles.[12] The U.S. Department of Commerce's monthly reports on the deficit reminded Americans like clockwork just how far their torch had fallen and, according to the popular metaphor, just how quickly the Japanese sun was rising. To put it simply, were there no "trade deficit," there would have been no Japan Panic.

Observers' efforts to evaluate Japan's success increased in proportion to Japan's actual economic growth. By the mid-1980s dozens of books had already appeared, along with countless newspaper and magazine articles, assessing Japanese power and its implications for a weakened America. Making sense of the voluminous writing about Japan from the late 1970s into the early 1990s is crucial to understanding how Americans related to Japan through the consumption of its products. As historian David Engerman argues for the early Cold War, "The production and dissemination of knowledge both constituted a form of foreign relations and at the same time shaped American foreign policy as traditionally defined."[13] Just as they did when they consumed cars or VCRs, Americans engaged with a changing world by composing and reading hundreds of books and thousands of articles about U.S.-Japan relations by the early 1990s, trying to make sense of Japan's new role in a dynamic and confusing international environment.

What would come to be called "revisionism" by 1989 would dominate published writings on Japan throughout this period.[14] Revisionists asserted that economic setbacks engendered a perilous loss of U.S. international political power—the power to influence the actions of other nations either through force or persuasion. This diverse group of academics, journalists, business leaders, and policy makers attributed Japan's power to a number of causes. Their explanations fell into two general categories: the first, which I call structural revisionism, focused on Japan's economic and political institutions, and

Japan Won the Cold War, and Other Strange Ideas

the second, cultural revisionism, posited that Japan's "unique" culture provided its people, businesses, and government with unfair advantages in the economic and political competition for international power.[15]

Structural revisionists like Harvard's Ezra Vogel and Chalmers Johnson of the University of California at San Diego dominated the tone of the national conversation on Japan through the early 1980s only to be marginalized later in the decade by the more headline-grabbing claims of the cultural revisionists. Structural revisionists often worked in the academy and had extensive and rigorous research experience in Japan. Consequently their conclusions tended toward moderation and level-headedness, even among those writers, like Johnson, who identified Japan as an economic threat. Cultural revisionists as a rule were more scathing; their critics often accused them of racism, and they walked a fine line between intellectual discourse and "Japan-bashing."[16] The cultural revisionists eschewed the vocabulary of race (consciously so, in many cases), however, opting for a caricatured version of the anthropological language of culture to describe the differences that enabled Japan to triumph economically at a time when the United States was suffering its worst economic slump since the 1930s. The categories of structural and cultural revisionists, though artificial, allow for a distinction between intellectuals with legitimate and thoughtful critiques, like structuralists Vogel and Johnson, and nationalists relying on a century-old "yellow peril" script, stoking racial fears of an East Asian other.

What revisionists aimed to revise was the post-1945 orthodox interpretation, rooted in modernization theory, of Japan as a free market capitalist, liberal democratic Cold War ally. Prominent proponents of this view included Harvard University historian and former U.S. ambassador to Japan Edwin O. Reischauer and U.S. ambassador and former senator Mike Mansfield, who served in Tokyo from 1977 to 1988.[17] Orthodox interpreters like Reischauer, who spoke not only to U.S. scholars of Japan but also to a Japanese academy heavily influenced by Marxism, argued that as Japan grew wealthy it would become more like the United States.[18] Both structural and cultural revisionists felt betrayed by this promise of modernization theorists, instead popularizing an idea that was historically easy for Americans to accept: Japanese thinking and behavior differed fundamentally from that of "the West." Revisionists could disagree, however, on whether those differences were social, political, economic, or cultural. Dutch journalist Karel van Wolferen, who lived in Japan and wrote frequently for American publications, summarized the general revisionist position when he noted that there were two orthodox illusions that Americans (and Europeans) maintained: first, "Japan is a sovereign state like any other," and second, "Japan belongs with [the U.S. and Europe] in that loose category known as capitalist free-market economies."[19] Though structural and cultural explanations differed, they both countered the vision of Japan that modernization theorists offered.

The first important text of Japan revisionism, Ezra Vogel's 1979 work, *Japan as Number One*, lacked the sharply critical tone of revisionist texts to come in the 1980s. Nonetheless, it was important in launching Japan revisionism because it was the first popular text to describe systematically how Japan had succeeded while the United States had failed at confronting the social and cultural dilemmas of modern life. Vogel, a sociologist at Harvard with decades of experience studying Japanese society, claimed that "Japan has dealt more successfully with more of the basic problems of postindustrial society than any other country." Vogel wrote at a moment when Americans were primed to hear his message—that July, Jimmy Carter delivered to the nation his "crisis of confidence" speech, in which the president exhorted Americans to overcome the "growing doubt about the meaning of our own lives and in the loss of purpose for our nation."[20] The sociologist Vogel urged Americans to address the crisis by taking note of Japan's triumphs.

Vogel was certain that "Japanese success had less to do with traditional character traits than with specific organizational structures, policy programs, and conscious planning."[21] In other words, he believed that Japanese achievements were universally portable and not contingent on a mythical notion of the Japanese people's inherent uniqueness. Successful policies and practices were not based on any characteristics particular to a culture or race. Therefore, those practices could be adapted to cure the ills—unemployment, declining productivity, class conflict, "stagflation"—of any "postindustrial" society. This approach to Japan's postwar success defined structural revisionism.

In the years following the publication of Vogel's celebratory book, several developments in U.S.-Japan relations contributed to a more critical U.S. perspective on Japanese growth. A series of automobile assembly plants closed their doors, laying off tens of thousands and drawing attention to Japanese competition. The Reagan administration consequently requested that Japanese companies impose "voluntary" export quotas. A high-profile lawsuit accused Japanese television manufacturers of "dumping" on the U.S. market—selling goods at cost or at a loss in order to eliminate market competition. The "trade gap" nearly doubled from 1980 to 1981. In this context, Chalmers Johnson, a political scientist, published the innocuously titled *MITI and the Japanese Miracle: The Growth of Industrial Policy, 1925–1975*. The book provided ammunition to an army of journalists and policy makers by introducing them to the structural and institutional differences between Japan and the United States. His well-researched book furnished critics with a bounty of empirical evidence that Japan's economic and political institutions were structured unlike those of any modern state. Johnson turned "MITI," Japan's Ministry of International Trade and Industry, into a dirty word in the press and made it synonymous with the shadowy "Japanese bureaucrats" to whom Americans attributed so much agency in the governing of Japan's institutions.

Like Vogel, Johnson aimed to promote Japanese solutions to American (or modern) problems. The sooner revisionists dispelled American policy makers of modernization theory myths about postwar Japan, the sooner they could adjust to the conditions responsible for the trade imbalance and declining industrial competitiveness. According to Johnson, the most important explanation for Japan's economic "miracle" was the unique relationship between the Japanese state and the market. He labeled it the "state-guided market system," or the "capitalist developmental state," embodied in the institution of MITI.[22] MITI was responsible for defining Japan's "industrial policy," that is, it used state power to target specific industries for protection and growth. The ministry ensured that the nation's corporations had advantages over foreign competition, critics claimed. The Japanese state aided the steel industry, for example, by providing it with subsidies for exporting and protectionist barriers against imported steel.[23] These were, Johnson emphasized, hardly free market practices, and they left American producers at a disadvantage. Government policy continued to abet the deterioration of U.S. industry by allowing Japanese producers to sell in the U.S. market according to the tenets of free trade, while the Japanese refused to do so at home—a relic of the early Cold War, when the United States acquiesced to such practices in the name of ensuring prosperity for a crucial ally. In the changed landscape of the 1980s, Johnson asserted, such an approach was anachronistic and economically disastrous, and, as other critics had been saying since the downturn of the 1970s, the United States needed to respond to foreign competition with its own strategic industrial policy.[24]

Vogel and Johnson stand out as rarities during this period because Japan studies scholars rarely engaged in popular debates about Japan. Most revisionists did not have Vogel's or Johnson's academic training or experience, and there seemed to be a direct relationship between the aggressiveness of a revisionist's assessment of Japan and that revisionist's scholarly experience (or lack thereof) with the country and its people.[25] A special issue of the *Journal of Japanese Studies* in 1987 was one academic attempt to "provide better leadership" and "reach a wider audience," but it was nevertheless a specialist publication.[26] Vogel and Johnson helped to establish important themes early in the debate, but their academic colleagues largely dismissed the developing public discourse as media banter and crude nationalism, especially as humanities scholars turned increasingly toward the esoteric concerns of cultural studies. Furthermore, it was unlikely that prominent U.S. scholars of Japanese history and society would rush to the country's defense when they too found fault with contemporary Japan, though they worried little about economic nationalism and instead leveled their leftist critiques at Japan's continued reactionary political and social conservatism.[27] Consequently, a host of dubiously qualified authors usurped Vogel's and Johnson's ideas about the differences of postwar Japan and coupled them with persistent cultural stereotypes dating back to at least the World War II era, if not the nineteenth century. From the mid-1980s until the Japan fixation abated, the conversation would be dominated by the cultural revisionists, consisting of journalists, business elites, and the occasional scholar working outside his or her expertise. Cultural revisionists were uninterested in nuance and historical contingency; instead they sought and constructed a representation of Japan that could be mobilized to meet nationalistic political ends.

"JAPAN 2000" AND REVISIONISM UNLEASHED

"For those of you with a yen for 172 pages of mindless hype, artless drivel, shameless racism and fathomless idiocy," wrote University of Chicago historian Bruce Cumings in 1991, "I highly recommend *Japan 2000*."[28] Cumings had uncovered a remarkable revisionist document, produced secretly by the administration of the Rochester Institute of Technology (RIT) in conjunction with the Central Intelligence Agency, that identified Japan as nothing less than a menace to the American way of life.[29] "Japan 2000" reflected virtually all of the pervasive revisionist-inspired cultural understandings of Japan and therefore serves as a window onto the most critical U.S. perspectives during this period. "Our nation and its underlying values are threatened," the document warned. "Above all, the answer lies in understanding the threat and developing a national will to preserve that which is so rapidly slipping away. It need not!"[30]

The production of "Japan 2000" was embedded in a larger story of the relationship between RIT and the CIA. Throughout 1991, a local newspaper, the *Democrat and Chronicle*, revealed how the institute's president, former Nixon staffer M. Richard Rose, misled the Rochester community as to the nature of a recent sabbatical. He claimed to be assisting the George H. W. Bush administration with preparations for the Gulf War, but he was really in Langley, Virginia, assisting CIA operatives to "prepare . . . to deal with the post–Cold War period."[31] After this surprise the *Democrat and Chronicle* continued to publish revelations about RIT's CIA connections dating back to the late 1960s. Rose would resign in 1992.[32] In May 1991 the *Democrat and Chronicle* first published brief excerpts from an unpublished report, "Japan 2000: DEFCON 1."[33] The document was the product of discussions held at a weekend conference at RIT in October 1990, which brought together intellectuals, business leaders, former government officials, and unnamed representatives of the CIA.[34] The collusion between industry, academia, and figures close to government, along with intimate involvement from the CIA, made observers uncomfortable as details of the conference and resulting report emerged.

"Japan 2000" serves as a singular window on the popular attitudes of cultural revisionists. The document also reveals the shifting discursive boundaries of cultural attitudes in the United States generally. Very rarely did "Japan 2000" address the Japanese "race." In fact, in several instances it explicitly self-identified as nonracist, reflecting sensitivity to the accusations of racism often leveled at Japan revisionists. Instead the document repeatedly references the uniqueness of Japanese "culture" and the advantages it provided Japan in international relations. The explanatory power of racial difference lost legitimacy in the United States after the civil rights movement, the U.S. war against the Vietnamese people, and the emergence of the Holocaust in popular memory.[35] These social and military conflicts delegitimized race as an analytical category and pushed "culture"—disconnected from the physical body, the product of exposure to educational and social systems, and thus seemingly independent of race—to the forefront of popular attitudes toward relationships between different groups of human beings.

The document's emphasis on culture rejected explicit racism but nevertheless reproduced common American understandings of a Japanese "other." Much as the category of race served to dehumanize the Japanese during World War II, highlighting culture also implied that the differences between the two countries were unbridgeable. The document stated, "A general adherence to [the Imperial Oath of 1868] over the past 123 years speaks simultaneously to the culture and commitment and explains Japan's contemporary behavior."[36] (For those in need of reminding, the Charter Oath, which outlined Japan's modernization goals at the outset of the Meiji Restoration, was reproduced at the end of the document.) Fixing Japan permanently in 1868 permitted liberal use of clichéd imagery like the samurai and feudalism to describe Japanese ideas and behavior. This analytical choice also made clear that whatever changes affected Japanese society in the century and a quarter after 1868, the cultural universe its people inhabited remained resolute.

The book most responsible for these attitudes toward culture—and listed in the document's short bibliography—was Ruth Benedict's *The Chrysanthemum and the Sword*.[37] Benedict's influence on postwar American thinking about culture, especially Japanese culture, was commanding. Not only did she provide Americans with a framework for understanding their enemy-turned-ally, but she generally employed culture as an explanatory model to an extent greater than any previous popular writer as well. A student of Franz Boas, one of the pioneers of modern anthropology, Benedict explicitly rejected biological conceptions of race as a behavioral determinant. "Rather," as scholar Mari Yoshihara explains, "integrated cultural patterns, the unconscious logic of sentiments and assumptions, and the processes of enculturation were the keys to understanding people's behaviors."[38] This way of thinking about culture pervaded American thought in the postwar era and by the 1970s had trickled down to the popular level. The influential "linguistic turn" in cultural studies of the 1970s, spurred by such diverse scholars as Michel Foucault and Clifford Geertz, was dominant in the academy but hardly made a scratch on the surface of popular understandings of culture in the United States. For the document's authors and other revisionists, culture explained Japanese behavior; in many cases it simply replaced the word "race."

Consequently "Japan 2000" reproduced common orientalist tropes, repeatedly drawing a dichotomy between the cultures of East and West. The document argued that Westerners struggled to make sense of the Japanese because the latter's "culture does not recognize the existence of transcendental or absolute truths." Further, while the "ethical/moral underpinnings of Western business are held to be immutable," the "Japanese Paradigm . . . disallows the existence of any set of absolute rules." The document faulted "centuries" of Buddhist, Shinto, and Confucian tradition for imposing "strict hierarchical arrangements" and "political and intellectual suppression." The struggle between Western and Japanese cultures was emerging, and Americans would be mistaken to believe that these two cultures were compatible—"the cultures of the West and East are worlds apart and share very few values," the document stated in a caricatured echo of Rudyard Kipling's poem "The Ballad of East and West."[39]

In short, "Japan 2000" emphasized the stark disparity between U.S. and Japanese cultures. Cultural revisionists believed the differences between these two cultures became greater and more consequential because of the close relationship between the two countries. "Rarely in history," wrote William J. Holstein, a *Business Week* editor, in 1990, "have two societies of such vastly different values allowed themselves to become so interdependent."[40] Robert Christopher claimed that "the thought processes of Germans, Russians, Saudis or Nigerians resemble our own sufficiently closely that when we put our minds to it we can usually deal with them. . . . Between Americans and Japanese, however, the gulf is both wider and deeper. . . . Americans have no idea how Japanese think and feel."[41] This idea was another of Benedict's legacies. Though she wrote about Japan (for which she had neither formal training nor language skills—her study began as a World War II imperative), she was acutely interested in how its culture differed from that of the United States, as the opening line of her book expressed: "The Japanese were the most alien enemy the United States had ever fought."[42]

Revisionists adopted much of their observations about Japanese uniqueness from, ironically, the Japanese themselves, part of a transpacific dialogue about race, culture, and power. Revisionists frequently pointed to the concept of *nihonjinron*, which literally translates as "discussions of the Japanese," to turn the accusation of racial and cultural exclusivity against Japan. The term broadly characterizes a popular writing and publishing industry in Japan that promotes cultural nationalism and the alleged uniqueness of different aspects of Japan, ranging from the homogeneity of the "Yamato race" to the distinctiveness of the Japanese islands—not unlike, to be sure, American notions of "a city upon a hill," French ideas about "*civilisation*," or other forms of nationalist exceptionalism. Like other forms of cultural nationalism, *nihonjinron* downplayed divisions of ethnicity, class, and gender in society by emphasizing the characteristics allegedly universal to all Japanese people that explained the nation's successes.[43] In that sense *nihonjinron* was also prescriptive—it interpreted current achievements as a product of shared traits and values necessary for continued harmony and prosperity in the future. As such, other Japanese citizens were the intended audience, and by the 1980s the genre was quite popular among Japanese readers.[44] But in the globalizing media environment of the postwar era, *nihonjinron* ideas would inevitably escape Japan and enter Western imaginations, whether unintentionally or deliberately. For example, Kyonosuke Ibe, president of Sumitomo Bank, one of Japan's largest, wanted to assure American readers of *Business Week* that "it took the Japanese to build Japan." "So far, our strength has been in our homogeneity," he wrote. "As a people, we could predict the reactions of 100 million people of a single race."[45] A *Business Week* reader in 1982 echoed this sentiment, almost as if he took it straight from Ibe: "What most Americans don't comprehend is that

Japan is a homogeneous society that relies on a complete lack of friction from any of its parts. . . . They all act in a concerted fashion to 'beat the gaijin.'"[46]

Japanese cultural nationalism gave Americans license to exorcise their own racial demons. In the context of Japan's economic success and long-standing U.S. perceptions of the Japanese as the most "alien" of all peoples that Americans encountered, the language of *nihonjinron* struck a dissonant chord. It provided revisionists with an opportunity to argue that the heterogeneity of American society proved its greatest democratic and pluralist asset and that Americans were in a privileged position to highlight Japanese racism. Unlike the United States, "Japan 2000" stated, "Japan has no commitment to assimilate people of diverse cultures, ethics, or opinions. It is in these ways that Japan is racist. It is in these ways that Japan is not democratic." The journalist James Fallows, one of the more popular revisionists, wrote of the Japanese, "their fixation on the factors that make them unique in the world goes miles beyond what we normally think of as prejudice." What was unique about the United States, he insisted in a direct challenge to *nihonjinron*, "is its assumption that race should not matter, that a society can be built of individuals with no particular historic or racial bond to link them together."[47] That the liberal-leaning Fallows could efface the legacy of centuries of American racism to make a point about the superiority of U.S. society over Japanese was a testament to the ways in which Japanese power threatened American national identity.

"Japan 2000" also exposed debates about the changing nature of international power. The authors claimed that Japanese culture was above all concerned with power—assessing it, achieving it, manipulating it, and basking in it—and devoted an entire chapter to it. [48] Japan's rise portended "a revolution that will alter the very nature and use of power." While vast natural resources and mighty industrial production once bankrolled U.S. international power, it was Japan's ability to manipulate information technology and global systems of symbols that ideally positioned it to benefit from global transformations. As the authors wrote, "Japan has rewritten the rules of both international relations and international trade. It has sufficient power to make the world play by its rules."[49] Japan had not merely become powerful; it had redefined international power in a global age.

The document's discussion of "the nature of power" suggested the influence of recent debates in international relations. In 1985 Richard Rosecrance, a political scientist then at Cornell University, published a provocative work for a popular audience, *The Rise of the Trading State*.[50] Rosecrance argued that "a new 'trading world' of international relations offers the possibility of

Japan Won the Cold War, and Other Strange Ideas

escaping . . . a vicious cycle [of conflict] and finding new patterns of cooperation among nation-states." In a new international environment, "states, as Japan has shown, can do better through a strategy of economic development based on trade than they are likely to do through military intervention in the affairs of other nations."[51] He asserted that Japan's power did not derive from traditional military and political relationships, and therefore the nation was not likely to seek traditional military and political power because it had no need for such anachronisms. "It is not the American model that Japan will ultimately follow," he stated provokingly. "Rather, it is the Japanese model that America may ultimately follow."[52]

Two years later Yale University historian Paul Kennedy joined the decade-old discourse on American decline by introducing popular audiences to debates about international power in a historical context. His massive tome, *The Rise and Fall of the Great Powers*, sold 225,000 copies in 1988 alone.[53] The book recounted the major shifts in international relations since the sixteenth century, stressing that states had to balance economic resources and military capabilities to remain in the great power club. Readers might have judged the book by its cover—it weighed in at more than 600 pages, after all, so many readers likely stopped at the cover—to get a sense of its presentist concerns. Three cartoonish figures stood astride a globe shaped like a pedestal with three levels. At the front of the line, yet about to step offstage, was a Churchillian John Bull carrying the Union Jack. Behind him, at the very top of the world, but descending onto the second tier, looking old, weary, and worn, was Uncle Sam holding an American flag. Behind the American, a Japanese figure best described as a bespectacled *sarariman* (salaryman—the quintessential image of the faceless Japanese white-collar worker), appearing young and eager, prepared to scale the summit and hoist a Japanese flag atop the globe.

Those readers able to make their way through a massive and meticulously detailed history of European empires found that Kennedy's lesson was a lengthy allegory for American power in the late twentieth century. Historically, great powers fell when they succumbed to what he called "imperial overstretch": when military ambitions outweighed economic capabilities. The United States, he warned, sat on the brink of imperial overstretch because of the demands of the Cold War. Japan, on the other hand, did not have military commitments all over the planet and instead could dedicate its resources to domestic improvements and continued economic expansion overseas. If history proved a guide for great powers, then Americans should be vigilant about the Japanese sun rising over their shoulders, about the *sarariman* intent on dethroning them.[54]

Kennedy's book inspired an international relations scholar of equal stature to respond in 1990 with his own survey of the changing international system, and the result would be an influential new concept—"soft power"—rooted in the U.S. encounter with Japan. In *Bound to Lead*, Harvard political scientist Joseph S. Nye Jr. countered Kennedy: "In a world of growing interdependence among nations . . . U.S. decline is the wrong question." Instead, Americans should have been asking, "How is power changing in modern international politics?"[55] "Power is becoming less fungible, less coercive, and less tangible," he wrote. It was also becoming more diffuse—nongovernmental and transnational actors were taking advantage of new communications technologies and economic institutions, in the process contributing to the "diffusion of power away from all the great powers." As a result, "soft power resources—cultural attraction, ideology, and international institutions," or "co-optive power," were beginning to define a nation-state's power as much as the traditional categories of military capabilities and political control.[56] The United States may have declined, but no country had more co-optive power. Therefore the United States was "bound to lead."

Japan, however, was not. "Japanese consumer products and cuisine have recently become increasingly fashionable on a global scale," Nye noted. "They seem less associated with an implicit appeal to a broader set of values, however, than in the case of American domination of popular communication." He explained continued U.S. superiority by drawing on arguments for Japan's uniqueness, claiming that Japanese culture had an "inward orientation" and rejected foreigners outright anyway.[57] A couple of years later, Nye reiterated that while the Japanese had emphasized internationalization, "the United States and Europe have more universalistic cultures and more inclination to proselytize."[58]

Nye's way of representing Japanese power revealed a curious turn for understandings of international power. For Japan's orthodox interpreters, steeped in modernization theory, the country was a solid ally and a loyal imitator. For structural revisionists, it was a challenge to American policy makers; for cultural revisionists, Japan was a clear and present danger, a threat to American values. Nye had weighed these claims and found Japan, quite simply, unappealing, or at least not as appealing as "the ethnic openness of the American culture and the political appeal of the American values of democracy and human rights."[59] Nye was not the first observer to judge Japan this way. Almost a decade earlier, journalist Lance Morrow had the same concerns in mind. "The deepest questions of the Japanese future revolve around Japan's capacity to transcend the limits of its identity," he wrote in

Japan Won the Cold War, and Other Strange Ideas

Time magazine. The United States and the Soviet Union "stand for something in the world," he continued. "What does Japan represent? Does Japan have a universal meaning?"[60] Nye and Morrow both speculated that Japan lacked a big story—a metanarrative like U.S. liberal capitalism or Soviet social justice communalism—that could appeal to people across spatial and temporal borders. Without a metanarrative to serve as an answer to the universal problems of modernity, Japan existed in a localized postmodernity. Without a big story, the Japanese threat was toothless.

Revisionism, then, took the public conversation about race, power, and Japan to new places, where intellectuals and commentators experimented with novel ideas about a changing global landscape. "Japan 2000" articulated revisionists' most intense fears and more curious innovations on the narrative of international power. For cultural revisionists those ideas were troubling, revealing not only concern about a once pliant ally but also anxieties about the direction of American hegemony. Other observers, however, found not peril but promise in visions of a postmodern Japanese future.

INVENTING GLOBALIZATION

By 1984 the future looked Japanese. In that auspicious year for dystopian visions, science fiction author William Gibson echoed George Orwell's effort to imagine a future derived from the present's more unsettling characteristics. His landmark novel *Neuromancer* brought to life a society in which the borders between the real and the virtual blurred. Individuals and corporations struggled for the power to control the complex "matrix" of data that linked important financial centers around the globe. "Power," Gibson wrote, "meant corporate power. The zaibatsus, the multinationals that shaped the course of human history, had transcended old barriers. Viewed as organisms, they had attained a kind of immortality."[61] Gibson chose the word "zaibatsu"— referencing the pre–World War II giant industrial conglomerates that powered Imperial Japan's war machine—to convey that the sort of corporations that "transcended old barriers" and "shaped the course of human history" in the future had a distinctly Japanese flavor.

Ridley Scott shared Gibson's vision. In the 1982 film *Blade Runner*, the director visualized Los Angeles nearly fifty years into the future as a truly global city. The presence of a cacophony of ethnicities and languages, with Japanese, Chinese, and Russian signs and advertisements as ubiquitous as English, signaled that cultures and economies in the future could traverse borders as they had never done in the past. Giant video screens floated across the city, flashing images of geisha in advertisements. As in Gibson's world, corporations ruled: the Tyrell Corporation, a manufacturer of human-like robots called replicants, had the power to marshal the forces of law and order at its whim. In fact, state power is conspicuously absent in Scott's dystopia.

In Gibson's and Scott's futures, unprecedented power at the international level rested in the hands of corporations. They were unrestrained by "old barriers" like government regulations or the borders of nation-states. Looking back from the twenty-first century, the Japaneseness of these visions of the future appears strikingly original: Japan rarely figures as the central national player in stories of the unfolding late twentieth-century drama of globalization, driven by corporations amassing wealth and power on the scale of nation-states. Popular and academic conceptions of globalization almost universally position the United States or the "West" as ground zero for a series of dramatic, worldwide economic, social, political, and cultural transformations. In his provocative *Michael Jordan and the New Global Capitalism*, for instance, eminent historian Walter LaFeber describes the rise of the "Jordan-Knight-Murdoch-Turner phenomenon," which made Western corporations like Nike, News Corp., and CNN as powerful as nation-states.[62]

The historical genealogy of "globalization" betrays a different story. As intellectuals and business leaders in the United States began to conceptualize "globalization" in the 1980s, no country was more central to their thoughts than Japan. It was the remarkable worldwide expansion of Japanese corporations in the 1970s and 1980s that first introduced Americans to the characteristics they would come to associate with contemporary globalization. Globalization was not just a new way of explaining old processes; it was a way of conceptualizing the perceived shifts in power at the international level in the 1970s and 1980s, and at its heart was Japan. Some of the most important popular and intellectual understandings of globalization—the transnational turn of capitalism, the worldwide proliferation of new communications technologies, the perceived homogenization of culture, and the erosion of the borders and sovereignty of the nation-state—derive from the United States' encounter with the growing power of Japanese corporations in the 1970s and 1980s. The discourse of Japan-as-globalizer was the reverse side of the coin of Japan revisionism. If so-called Japan-bashers saw Japan as a potential danger, globalists saw the country as an opportunity and its Morita-Honda phenomenon as a model to be emulated.

Below I weave an interpretive thread through three figures—Akio Morita, the founder of the Sony Corporation; Kenichi Ohmae, at the time a brilliant and well-connected McKinsey analyst; and Theodore Levitt, a professor at

Japan Won the Cold War, and Other Strange Ideas

Harvard Business School and editor of the *Harvard Business Review*—and then I conclude with a central economic policy maker in the 1990s, Robert Reich. These figures represented an optimistic transpacific dialogue about the promises of a globalized future, a dialogue that stood in sharp contrast to the era's gloomy polemics of Japan-bashing. Above the nationalistic noise, some Japanese and Americans envisioned a "borderless" future of economic prosperity and technological transformation, and in their conversation we find the origins of our contemporary concept of globalization.

Beginning in the 1970s, Japanese corporations assumed a greater presence in the daily lives of most Americans. Honda, Toyota, and Nissan sold automobiles that were inexpensive and fuel-efficient compared with their American counterparts, an advantage in the market after the oil crises of 1973 and 1979. Matsushita, through a variety of brand names like Panasonic and Quasar, distributed a wide range of consumer electronics. At the beginning of the 1980s a hundred-year-old Japanese card game manufacturer, Nintendo, was virtually unknown in the United States; it would be a household name by the end of the decade. Arguably the consumption of foreign goods had not had such a radical impact on the ways that Americans went about their daily lives since the first decades of the Republic.[63]

The most iconic Japanese company in the American imagination was and continues to be Sony. Since 1961, when Sony became the first Japanese corporation to have its stock traded on the New York Stock Exchange, the company has managed to sell an image of global success and superior quality, consistently ranking at the top of "Best of" consumer surveys. (A 1990 poll found that Sony was also the most recognizable brand name in the Soviet Union.)[64] Sony has also successfully marketed and sold another image: the global corporation, the company without borders or a distinct ethnic or national identity. As *Business Week* said in 1987, Sony was "the most international of companies."[65] No one better cultivated the image of the global corporation than Sony's charismatic cofounder Akio Morita. Morita was self-consciously performative in the way he presented Sony's global identity to U.S. audiences.

Morita embedded the company's narrative of globalization within the story of how he crafted the name "Sony." Morita claimed to have revised his vision of the company—the tongue-twisting Tokyo Tsushin Kogyo Kabushiki Kaisha ("Totsuko" for short)—after a visit to the European home of the respected Dutch electronics manufacturer Philips. If Philips could design and sell products from a small Dutch village, then Morita could do the same coming from a small Japanese village.[66] But what he needed, he said, was "a new name that could be recognized anywhere in the world, one that could be pronounced the same in any language." The catchiest product names were short and easily recognizable—Ford, NBC, IBM, Sears. He recounted combining the Latin word for sound, *sonus*, with the English word "sonny" (as in "sonny boy"), which sounded bright and optimistic. "The new name," Morita later said, "had the advantage of not meaning anything but 'Sony' in any language." Further, since nations in the postwar era were teaching their citizens the world's new lingua franca, English, everyone with the resources to purchase Sony products would be able to read the name. "Because it was written in roman letters," Morita recalled, "people in many countries could think of it as being in their own language."[67]

Morita had to explain to his countrymen the unprecedented decision to write the brand name in roman lettering instead of Japanese characters, a decision resisted by many employees and Totsuko's loaning bank. "It'll enable us to expand worldwide," he claims to have told the bankers.[68] The story reveals the extent to which Morita believed early on that being recognized as Japanese put his company at a disadvantage in the global marketplace, whether because of ill feelings remaining from World War II, the stereotype of Japanese products as cheap and poorly made, or anti-Asian racism dating back to the "yellow peril" fears of the nineteenth century. The name Sony "de-Japanized" Morita's company and, because its two syllables were easily pronounced in nearly any language, simultaneously globalized it.

By the early 1970s Americans already used Sony as shorthand to express two related ideas: in the "first world," Sony meant cosmopolitanism; in the "third world," Sony meant modernization. To illustrate how connected the "barefoot peasants" in Guatemala were in 1964, for instance, one journalist noticed that they strolled "along the dusty roads with $40 Sony transistor radios slung over their shoulders." Also, "along South Viet Nam's roads . . . little Sony radios are to be seen everywhere." And to show the malleability of even Communist Cuba's economy to the larger forces of globalization, one journalist provided evidence for Havana's connections to capitalism by noting that "a video room with Sony TVs" adorned the streets of Cuba's capital.[69]

As his company grew, he recounted in his English-language memoir, Morita "was struck with the idea that our company had to become a citizen of the world, and a good citizen in each country where we did business," and he told a reporter that he envied younger Japanese individuals for growing up in the postwar era of global citizenship.[70] While the notion of "world citizenship" had grown in popularity from the eighteenth century to the postwar era, Morita's late twentieth-century conception was unique for its vision of a world of shared global consumer identities. With products like the Walkman,

Sony aimed to create a market of globalized consumers with uniform cultural identities. Morita's world citizenship concept was rooted in a vision of homogeneity, whereas older notions were based on pluralism. National identities, he believed, would melt away, leaving a vacuum for corporate identities to fill.

While many observers of U.S.-Japan relations fretted that companies like Sony were amassing troubling amounts of influence over individual consumers and nations, a cohort of intellectuals in the field of international business believed Akio Morita's innovations, and those of his counterparts at a range of successful Japanese corporations, pointed the way toward a globalized future. One of those intellectuals was Kenichi Ohmae, a partner in the global consulting firm McKinsey and Company (and later dean of UCLA's Luskin School of Public Affairs) who regularly crossed lines between business, academia, and government in both Japan and the United States. He served as a bridge between national cultures and economies. Ohmae shared his acquaintance Morita's belief that becoming "a truly global citizen" was more important than being Japanese.[71] His sober attention to the U.S.-Japan relationship gave him insight into Japan's globalizing of America. He also contributed to the earliest conversations about the concept of contemporary globalization, giving Japan a central place in the story. Like Morita, he consciously presented Japan and its corporations to U.S. audiences as part of a postnational, globalizing future.

In his efforts to be "a truly global citizen," Ohmae spent much time explaining to American audiences the increasing tension between the United States and Japan and how both sides could overcome it.[72] He wrote editorials for the *Wall Street Journal* preaching conciliatory approaches and arguing that the U.S. trade deficit was "fiction."[73] He contended that "outmoded concepts of nationality and traditional antagonisms between nations and ethnic groups" stood in the way of the real work of the late twentieth century— global trade—and he shocked crowds of Washington insiders in the 1980s when he told them that corporations, not countries, mattered.[74] The titles of three of his English-language books—*Beyond National Borders, The Borderless World,* and *The End of the Nation-State*—highlight a mind attuned to the first rumblings of the concept of globalization. Anticipating the themes of Thomas Friedman's 2005 bestseller, *The World Is Flat,* Ohmae argued that the spread of corporations around the world created a vast redistribution of wealth that would ultimately end in greater global economic equality ("flattening," according to Friedman).[75] The global spread of corporations (many of them Japanese) and rapidly improving communications technologies would transform the developed world into a giant homogeneous market where all consumers' tastes were identical, regardless of national identity. This meant that in the United States, Western Europe, and Japan, a market of more than 600 million consumers existed—"a single race of consumers with shared needs and aspirations," he said, erasing even naturalized racial distinctions between nations.[76] The opportunities this market presented made it imperative for producers to see beyond their petty national differences and recognize that the growth of global corporations meant that measuring wealth on a national scale was obsolete.

Power in the international arena had a new master: the global corporation. Ohmae argued that "lines on a map mean little" to "companies without countries." "The world economy is now ruled by manufacturing and trading corporations, not nations," he declared.[77] Power would flow to those individuals who could take advantage of the "borderless world" by reigning over the corporate behemoths that had replaced the nation-state. The Japanese, Ohmae believed, were in a prime position to wield international power because they were rich in the one resource that really mattered in the borderless world: human capital. "Japan, with 120 million well-educated and hardworking people," he maintained, "is better endowed with the resources vital to success than any other nation in the world." This resource would enable Japan to reach the heights of global power "without wielding military might."[78] Ohmae was one of the earliest and most influential prophets of globalization, and in the way he presented it to U.S. audiences, Japan was blazing the trail to a new borderless world.

Ohmae developed many of his ideas about Japan's centrality to globalization in conversation with a group of intellectuals associated with the *Harvard Business Review* in the 1980s.[79] It was in that journal in 1983 that Theodore Levitt, Edward W. Carter Professor of Business Administration at the Harvard Business School, wrote the first article to use the word "globalization" in its title: "The Globalization of Markets."[80] Levitt's article today reads like a neoliberal manifesto. First, he made even more explicit Ohmae's point about the homogenization of the world market: "The products and methods of the industrialized world play a single tune for all the world, and all the world eagerly dances to it." Levitt then quickly turned to Japanese companies as exemplars of the "emergence of global consumer markets for standardized consumer products."[81] The Japanese had been so effective, Levitt argued, because they created high-quality products at low cost by selling the same product in every market without alteration for national differences. Japanese corporations recognized the homogenization of the world economy and culture better than anyone. In short, Japanese corporations did the most to speed the "globalization of markets." Instructively, Levitt subtitled one section of

Japan Won the Cold War, and Other Strange Ideas

his article "The earth is flat," anticipating the title of Friedman's best seller by more than two decades and providing further evidence that various understandings of contemporary globalization were shaped by the encounter with Japanese corporations through the 1980s. In Levitt's article (and subsequent book) we see an early narrative of contemporary globalization. At the center of that narrative was not the United States or the "West" but, just as Akio Morita and Kenichi Ohmae would have it, Japan.

The image of Japan as a "borderless nation" and the transnational economic and cultural behaviors of Japanese corporations decidedly mapped power in a globalized world. Earlier in the postwar era American mass culture products proliferated across the globe and brought with them specifically American imagery. McDonald's sold not only cheeseburgers but also an authentically American experience—fast food; Marlboro and Levi's sold not only cigarettes and blue jeans but also the iconography of freedom in the American West. Sony and its Japanese competitors changed that practice. They consciously worked to eliminate any trace of the national origin or ethnic identity of a corporation and its products. Levitt and others were excited about the possibilities. Japanese corporations promised a future of global markets with homogenized desires attuned to the sounds of transnational capital. A decade before globalization had its popular moment in the 1990s, the future looked bright—and Japanese.

CONCLUSION: AMERICAN AND GLOBAL FRONTIERS

In the heat and light of contentious U.S.-Japan relations in the early 1990s, it was difficult to see the rhetoric of revisionists and globalizers in a broader historical context. One of the United States' most sober historians of Japan, John Dower, wrote at the height of the Japan Panic,

> Japan's emergence as an economic superpower is inseparable from America's decline as the hegemon of the capitalist world. For the first time in modern history, a nonwhite nation has challenged the West by the very standards of wealth and power which for over four centuries have been associated with Western—and white—supremacy. This unprecedented development has been accompanied by rising tensions on both sides, and it is important to recognize that these tensions are rooted in the transformation of power relationships in the contemporary world. They are not irrational. They do not derive from "cultural differences." They are not fundamentally racist.

Rather, the fear and tension we see today exists because the United States and Japan are competitors in a high-stakes, high-tech global economy that no one really understands or controls anymore.[82]

Dower stated the point differently later in the same piece: "The rhetoric of 'Japan as Number One'... captures a central fact of our times—not that Japan is in fact 'number one,' but rather that the structure of global power and influence is in the midst of a historic transformation, and no one can foresee what the outcome will be."[83] The Japan Panic was the manifestation of revisionist fears about the unknown changes taking place in the global economy; globalist prophets, on the other hand, saw not fear but opportunity.

Those prophets had a few prominent champions before globalization as a concept grasped the national imagination in the mid-1990s. Perhaps no supporter was more important than Robert B. Reich, an economist at Harvard University's Kennedy School of Government who had served in the Ford and Carter administrations and would serve as secretary of labor for all four years of the first Clinton administration. From that position he helped institutionalize the concept of globalization as a grand strategy for the United States' role in the world—whereas containment once sought to construct borders, globalization aimed to bring them down.

In two books, *The Next American Frontier* and *The Work of Nations*, Reich laid out his explanation for U.S. decline and his prescriptions for confronting the changed conditions of global economic power. The first book tackled decline at the height of the "Reagan recession" of the early 1980s. The answer to foreign competition was not to shut the world out, Reich argued, but to embrace the new global economy. Standardized high-volume production would in the future flow to the cheapest labor markets. The United States, therefore, should invest in the only resource that could not physically leave the country: its people, its "human capital." "Japan understands this future," he noted, in that Japan used state power to invest in educating and training human capital.[84]

In his later and best-known book, *The Work of Nations*, Reich reiterated the imperative to invest in human capital. Every aspect of national economies as policy makers understood it had slipped the moorings of national attachments, and economic indicators floated free in a global economy. "Americans are no longer in the same economic boat," he wrote. "Yet the prevailing image remains fixed in our heads. The old picture gives comfort, suggesting national solidarity and purpose." But "the very idea of an American economy is becoming meaningless, as are the notions of an American corporation, American

Japan Won the Cold War, and Other Strange Ideas

capital, American products, and American technology." "So who is 'us'?" he asked. "Us" was no longer the material accumulations of an advanced capitalist society. Instead, "us" was the skills and abilities that American workers could contribute to a global economy.[85]

Like other globalizers, Reich thought the heated rhetoric of Japan-bashing was missing the point. A significant chunk—he estimated half—of the trade between the United States and Japan took place *within* global corporations, as when, for example, IBM's Japan operations delivered components to the company's U.S. operations. Chiding the U.S. fixation on trade deficits, Reich counseled, "The truth is that these days no one knows exactly, at any given time, whether America's (or any other nation's) trade is in or out of balance, by how much it is out of balance, or what the significance of such an imbalance might be."[86] The Japan obsession, he speculated, was bigger than trade deficits and extravagant real estate purchases. In short, it was about the ways globalization, not "Japanization," was transforming the United States. "As the 21st century approaches," he wrote as he surveyed more than thirty-five books written on Japan in 1991–92, "we can see, I believe, a profound unease about the coherence of American society. . . . The global economy is tightly linking our citizens to the citizens of other nations," creating fear for the loss of a national identity to accompany the loss of a true national economy. Earlier in the twentieth century, he observed, Europeans used the specter of Americanization "to distract public attention from domestic problems. Japan plays a similar role for us today."[87]

Reich made an implicit point that historians can develop more explicitly: much like the way Europeans from 1900 through the 1960s used "Americanization" as a catchall for everything they disliked about the changes wrought by modernization, Americans in the 1980s and early 1990s used the prospect of a "Japanization" of the United States as a scapegoat for processes that more accurately characterized contemporary globalization. Historian Richard Kuisel, for instance, demonstrates how postwar French intellectuals blamed Americanization for consumerism, mass production, and other aspects of modern life that had less to do with American influence than with modernization in general.[88] Similarly, as Reich suspected, Americans used Japanese success as a convenient explanation for the failures of U.S. industry to adapt to contemporary globalization in its earliest stages. The markers of Japanese success—corporations with ambiguous national identities, the global flow of finance capital, the proliferation of new media products, and even transnational popular culture like anime—did not "constitute a vicious plot," as Reich said, but instead were indicative of a new way of thinking about the world: globalization.

Thus when President-elect Bill Clinton selected his longtime friend Reich to head the Department of Labor, Clinton signaled that economic policy in the 1990s would reject the revisionism that had generated so much anti-Japanese heat since the mid-1980s. Support for the creation of the North American Free Trade Agreement (1994) and the World Trade Organization (1995), among other bedrock institutions of economic globalization, marked a victory for the globalist outlook that bridged the center-left and center-right of U.S. politics and a defeat for protectionists further to the left or right. The end of the Japan Panic, then, hinged not only on the Japanese recession of the early 1990s but also on the coming to power of policy makers unsympathetic to economic nationalism in a changed world. It took elite accommodation to new economic realities in order for Americans to begin to write new stories of U.S. power in a globalized world.

TWO

Wakarimasuka

Shifting Images of Japan from Shōgun *to* Rising Sun

While commentators both qualified and dubiously so penned libraries worth of articles and books on Japan's meteoric postwar rise, popular culture increasingly used Japan as a source of entertainment. As the 1980s came to a close, influential cultural creators found less to admire, or even giggle over, and more to fear. One distressed reviewer of Michael Crichton's wildly successful 1992 novel, *Rising Sun*, worried that the controversial nationalistic work of fiction, a murder mystery replete with shadowy Japanese corporate conspirators, "could be the only book about Japan that many Americans will ever read."[1] That was a distinct possibility, based on the novel's popularity, which ballooned when a film adaptation arrived a year later. But more than a decade earlier many Americans had also read James Clavell's 1975 novel, *Shōgun*, which sold more than seven million copies before an even more popular 1980 television reproduction aired. "*Shōgun* is . . . most Westerners' introduction to Japan," Clavell once said of his epic tale of an Englishman marooned in seventeenth-century Japan. "That's an appalling responsibility!"[2]

There were many nonfiction books published between 1975 and 1993 that tried to teach Americans something about Japan, a task that became a national imperative when Japan ascended to the number two position among the world's economies. But for every American who read one of these revisionist books, like Ezra Vogel's moderate *Japan as Number One* or Clyde Prestowitz's sharply critical *Trading Places: How We Are Giving Our Future to Japan and How to Reclaim It*, exponentially more received their images of Japan from popular media like television, movies, and literature—fictional representations of Japan. This chapter examines images of Japan in popular entertainment media from the mid-1970s through the early 1990s, using the multimedia narratives of *Shōgun* and *Rising Sun* as bookends to highlight changing U.S. attitudes toward and understandings of this new economic challenger.

Both *Shōgun* and *Rising Sun* entered the world as best-selling novels; both reached even greater audiences when put on television or film. In addition both went to great lengths to serve not just as entertainment but as instruments of cross-cultural consumption and education. Clavell, a British-born author who spent much of his career writing novels and Hollywood screenplays, and Crichton, an American medical doctor turned popular novelist, were both well read in the contemporary nonfiction literature on Japan and tried to expose their audiences to something of the "real" Japan in the process of entertaining. These two narratives played a critical role in shaping popular American attitudes toward Japan.

Despite the similarities, their respective representations of Japan could not have differed more. Separated by less than two decades, they appeared to come from two different centuries, and their contrasting representations serve as a window onto shifting U.S. images of Japan and its people during two decades of rapid global change. Clavell's novel offered a stereotypical yet respectful and admiring portrait of Japan, one that Americans could use to position Japan comfortably in their collective mental map of Western-style modernity. In contrast, Crichton pleaded with his American readers to see Japan as a challenge to the very existence of modernity, a conceptually *post-modern* threat to the sanctity of a "Western" (that is, American) cultural tradition. Whereas Clavell's Japan deserved Americans' respect for reaching modernity by way of its unique historical and cultural characteristics, Crichton's Japan aggressively sought the annihilation of U.S. culture and society through economic, racial, and technological conquest. *Shōgun* and *Rising Sun*, therefore, illustrated that ideas about modernity were central to the ways that Americans gazed beyond their borders.[3]

The American vision of modernity seemed secure when Emperor Hirohito visited the United States—the first time a Japanese emperor had done so, and only the second time a sovereign had ever left Japan—in October 1975, the year *Shōgun* hit bookstore shelves. The living embodiment of a people Americans had learned to hate during World War II expressed his regret for that conflict and pledged "everlasting friendship" with the United States. A few weeks after Japan's surrender in September 1945, a famous image had circulated of Hirohito's meeting with Supreme Allied Commander Douglas MacArthur—the two men stood facing the camera, emotionless and

Shifting Images of Japan from Shōgun *to* Rising Sun

awkward, separated by a space that could not have been more than two feet but that might as well have been the Pacific Ocean. Thirty years later, Hirohito visited the grave and the widow of this man he remembered as a friend, the architect of a stable Japanese government, a flourishing civil society, and a booming economy. Later that week the emperor dropped in at Shea Stadium to see the New York Jets and the New England Patriots smash helmets together. He found it all amusing but struggled to follow the action. "You got a lot of guts coming here after everything that's happened!" one fan shouted. "Hats off!"[4]

Taking public enthusiasm about the visit as his cue, historian and former ambassador Edwin Reischauer prepared a booklet, on behalf of the Japan Society of New York, to educate Americans about the emperor. It is an artifact of a moment when Americans were comfortable with Japan's place in the postwar world.[5] While Hirohito descended from the world's oldest imperial line, he and his predecessors were merely symbols of the Japanese nation, never men to wield political power or even to have any political opinions at all. In twentieth-century Japan, politics was best left to democratically elected leaders and state bureaucracies. Reischauer aimed to humanize the emperor, to create empathy for him—Hirohito was a gifted marine biologist who by necessity lived a quiet life of isolation, and as a consequence "he cannot be regarded as an easy conversationalist" (the MacArthur image returns), but he was nevertheless personally warm and sincere. Historians would later challenge Reischauer's claim that the "only political decision" the emperor ever made was to surrender to the Allies, but the former ambassador's characterization was powerful and intentional: modern Japan reveres tradition but not living deities, and the representative of this wholly un-American monarchical tradition lives an existence not unlike that of a bald eagle at the National Zoo. Hirohito's visit was a reminder that the United States and Japan "face the problems of the world together from the shared basis of a common devotion to an open, free society and democratic institutions of government."[6]

The public mood was notably more tense two decades later when Emperor Akihito, Hirohito's son, visited for the first time. His father had died in 1989, and Reischauer a year later, both passing at a moment when popular attitudes toward Japan in the United States had devolved to mistrust and fear. Unlike the 1975 visit, press reports focused not on friendship and reconciliation but on World War II anniversaries and conflicts over their meanings. Akihito's handlers had planned a visit to Pearl Harbor but quietly canceled when Japanese conservatives complained that it would give the appearance of an apology. If the United States would not apologize for Hiroshima and Nagasaki, reasoned some Japanese critics, why should Japan apologize for Pearl Harbor? In 1975 the press reported only scattered minor protests by environmentalist groups upset with Japanese whaling practices. This time Japan's wartime empire in East Asia drew the attention of the Chinese American community in San Francisco, which aimed to raise awareness of the "Forgotten Holocaust," Japan's invasion of China, and especially its brutality in Nanjing in 1937. Nearly a thousand protesters greeted the emperor and empress with a burning Imperial Japanese flag. According to script and tradition, Akihito delivered brief, vague expressions of remorse for the war— but never an apology—in various public ceremonies.[7]

War with Japan was on Americans' minds much more so in 1994 than in 1975. The perception of the security of modernity shifted with the rise of Japanese power in the mid-1970s. Coinciding with Hirohito's visit, the representation of Japan in *Shōgun* serves as a starting point for illustrating that Americans were comfortable with Japanese power in 1975 because it fit neatly into their vision of modernity—according to an orthodox view shaped by modernization theory, Japan was a capitalist, democratic, rationally governed Cold War client-state that imitated the United States. *Rising Sun* serves as the other bookend, demonstrating how the rise of Japan through the 1980s jolted the American vision of modern world power such that commemorations of World War II were more contentious than they had been two decades earlier. Persistent references to Japan as the society of the future, not only in *Rising Sun* but also in such popular films as Ridley Scott's *Blade Runner* and *Black Rain*, revealed Japan as a *post*modern threat to the fabric that held together Western global supremacy.

Following the discussion of postmodernity in the introduction, I use the word again with its contextual origins in mind. The concept emerged out of the 1970s, a period in which perceived U.S. decline manifested in numerous political, economic, and military ways. Postmodernity would be a post-American age, one in which the United States held neither political hegemony nor a monopoly on the credulity of a global vision of liberal democratic capitalism. To see Japan as a postmodern nation in the eighties meant to see it as having transcended, for better or worse, the need for a metanarrative that promised universal human liberation in the form of some to-be-arrived-at future telos. In the case of those business leaders who saw Japanese corporations generating a denationalized global culture, it was for the better, as Japan's lack of a big story meant that ideology would not get in the way of commerce. For Crichton, a student of the cultural revisionists, it

Shifting Images of Japan from Shōgun *to* Rising Sun

was for the worse: Japan's postmodernity meant that in the future, economic and political power would rest in the hands of a foreign nation unattached to absolute truths and universal values. Democratic ideals, human and civil rights, guaranteed individual freedoms—modern Western "culture," as the revisionists generally articulated it—Japanese postmodernity threatened the sanctity of it all. Postmodern Japan was Roland Barthes's "Empire of Signs," with no fixed meanings, and Fredric Jameson's sublimation of culture into commerce.[8] For Americans the thought of Japanese power was ideologically discomforting and disorienting because it seemed to leave a vacuum in place of the American-style promises of modernity.

In *Shōgun* James Clavell provided an appropriate metaphor for Japan's shifting position in the American imagination. Protagonist John Blackthorne's education in Japanese language and culture is encapsulated in the phrases *wakarimasuka* ("Do you understand?"), *wakarimasen* ("I don't understand"), and *wakarimasu* ("I understand"). Early in the narrative Blackthorne repeats the phrase *wakarimasen* with uncomfortable frequency, revealing to his Japanese captors and to the audience his struggle to come to terms with his new surroundings. As the story progresses, though, not only does Blackthorne regularly use the phrase *wakarimasu*, but also his knowledge of Japanese language and culture enables him to live among the Japanese as no Westerner ever had—he becomes the first European inducted into the samurai class, in fact. Blackthorne's reconciliation with Japanese power is a metaphor for Americans' acceptance and understanding of Japan's position in the modern world of the mid-1970s, the culmination of its journey from World War II enemy to Cold War ally.

The irony of Blackthorne's transition from *wakarimasen* to *wakarimasu* is that it is the inverse of the American experience with Japan from the mid-1970s to the early 1990s. American popular attitudes went in the opposite direction of the Englishman-turned-samurai's. By 1993, when *Rising Sun* was a best-selling novel and a blockbuster summer movie, American perceptions of Japan reflected a powerful insecurity about each nation's respective place in the world that did not exist when Clavell's novel first reached the best-seller lists and Hirohito struggled to make sense of the Jets smashing helmets with the Patriots. Whether they had any direct experience with Japan or not (most did not), Americans in 1975 were confident they understood Japan; by 1993, all of that was in flux. A shift from *wakarimasu* to *wakarimasen*, from confidence in American modernity to fear of a Japanese postmodernity, serves as an apt metaphor for American attitudes toward Japan during this period.

On the night of 15 September 1980, 70 million Americans—more than 43 percent of the U.S. population—tuned their televisions to the NBC network for three hours of transpacific cultural education.[9] That Monday, and for the remainder of the week, they consumed twelve hours of a $22 million production of James Clavell's *Shōgun*, an epic novel about a British sailor's experience in Japan circa 1600. The viewing audience was the second largest in television history to that point, ranking only behind the premiere of ABC's adaptation of Alex Haley's *Roots*. "When it first aired, the whole country stopped," recalled director Jerry London. "The movie theaters lost tons of money and the restaurants lost tons of money." One of *Shōgun's* producers tried to celebrate the miniseries' final night by serving Japanese cuisine at a party at his home. When he went to retrieve the food, though, he found that both patrons and staff had abandoned the restaurant—anyone who had any interest in Japan was home watching the final three hours. The miniseries "set off a wave of Shogun chic," *Newsweek* reported. "Bars sold out of their supplies of sake, boutiques reported runs on kimonos.... Pop-culture trendies began sprinkling their conversation with words like arigato (thank you) and wakarimasu (I understand)."[10]

Shōgun served as a beginning and an ending: it was the last exemplary representation of an orthodox interpretation of Japan and the first to acquiesce to Japan's new role as a world power. Both the 1975 novel and the 1980 miniseries exhibited common postwar tropes that pervaded Western representations of Japan. They reflected many ideas about Japan and the Japanese that the anthropologist Ruth Benedict had popularized in *The Chrysanthemum and the Sword*, ideas that had dominated the ways Americans thought about Japan through the first three decades of the postwar era. This "orthodox" interpretation that revisionists targeted in the 1980s was best identified in the previous two decades with Reischauer and like-minded scholars and politicians.[11] Benedict's and Reischauer's Japan was that of traditional cultural icons like geisha, painting, calligraphy, and the tea ceremony (the "chrysanthemum" side); it also included samurai, seppuku (ritual suicide), and Bushido (the "sword" side). Anthropologist Sheila Johnson, one of the more sober (and thus largely neglected) voices in the Japan debate of the 1980s, noted that the Benedict/Reischauer line "promoted a dangerously antiquarian and exceptionalist image of the Japanese" through the 1970s.[12]

Benedict's and Reischauer's Japan was James Clavell's Japan. Clavell came to admire Japanese history and culture through cathartic experience—the eighteen-year-old British artillery officer had been captured by the Japanese in Java in 1942. He spent the remainder of the war in prison camps throughout Asia, including the notorious Changi camp in Singapore, which provided the basis for his first novel, *King Rat* (1962). "I started reading about Japan's history and characteristics," he later said, "and then the way the Japanese treated me and my brothers became clear to me. . . . They thought we were dishonored, because it's totally wrong in their culture to be captured, while we believe that by surviving we live to fight another day. I came to admire greatly certain characteristics of the Japanese."[13] Clavell's influential popular representation of Japanese and Western cultural interaction was born of the violent encounter between Japan and the West in World War II, yet he bore no animosity because Clavell saw Japanese behavior as a product of a cultural system and not as a result of individual malice. Difference was to be respected, not condemned, in Clavell's vision of modern Japan.

Clavell's *Shōgun* is the story of John Blackthorne, a British sea pilot whose ship runs aground in "the Japans" in 1600. Clavell used William Adams for inspiration: according to legend, after shipwrecking in Japan, Adams became the first European inducted into the samurai class, though historians doubt the title was ever more than honorary.[14] Over the course of 1,150 pages, or a condensed twelve hours of television, the fictional Blackthorne struggles to adapt to a new life in this exotic land. At first the European curses his captors as "heathens," "monkeys," and "savages," especially when the Protestant finds that Japan's previous experience with Europe had been mediated by equally barbaric Catholic Jesuit priests from Portugal. The Japanese reciprocate by casually referring to Blackthorne and his European shipmates as the "barbarians," which was how Clavell translated the Japanese word *gaijin*. The samurai in the village where Blackthorne lands torture and kill one of his crewmen—they boil him alive in a giant cauldron—and imprison the rest, treating the Europeans cruelly and feeding them rotten fish. On first arriving Blackthorne witnesses what seems like a spontaneous and arbitrary beheading of a peasant who offends a samurai by refusing to bow deeply. When Blackthorne curses the same samurai, he suffers the indignity of being urinated upon. (Here, assured the producers of the NBC adaptation, was a television first.)

Eventually Blackthorne, renamed Anjin (from the Japanese word for "pilot"—the audience learns that Japanese have difficulty with *l*s, *th*s, and *r*s, as in Blackthorne's European name), ends up in the care of Lord Toranaga, one of the two most powerful daimyo, or feudal lords, in all of Japan.[15] Clavell modeled Toranaga on Ieyasu Tokugawa, founder of the shogunate that would rule Japan from the early seventeenth century until the middle of the nineteenth. Blackthorne has landed in the middle of a complicated political

ILL. 2.1. In *Shōgun* (1980), John Blackthorne (Richard Chamberlain) accepts the responsibilities and privileges of being a samurai, a rank he receives from Lord Toranaga (Toshiro Mifune). (Paramount Pictures, 2003)

showdown between Toranaga and his rival for the position of shogun, Lord Ishido, and Clavell went to great lengths to describe in detail the political machinations of dozens of major and minor characters. Toranaga and his competition both come to realize that Blackthorne is an experienced sailor with unrivaled knowledge of the world outside Japan, and he also offers an important non-Portuguese perspective on the world beyond Japan's shores.

Meanwhile, Anjin-san spends a great deal of time with Lady Toda Mariko, a Christian convert who speaks Portuguese and Latin (as does, conveniently, Blackthorne) and who translates for Toranaga. Naturally, Blackthorne falls in love with Mariko. As Mariko tutors Blackthorne in all things Japanese, the Englishman comes to respect this exotic land's beliefs and practices. He also becomes so valuable to Toranaga that the daimyo makes Blackthorne the first non-Japanese initiate into the samurai class. By this point, Blackthorne speaks Japanese with some fluency and is no longer uncomfortable with Japanese norms and behaviors. The Englishman's assistance helps elevate Toranaga to the position of shogun as the story ends. The narrative was the sort that would appeal to many Americans: a strong-willed Anglo male in a strange

Shifting Images of Japan from Shōgun *to* Rising Sun

land is forced to survive and adapt, learning and teaching along the way. Since the story was relatively commonplace, the cultural representations took on greater significance in what *Shōgun* meant for its American readers and viewers. Three representations in particular are important: that of the Japanese, that of Westerners, and that showing Japanese-Western interactions.

First, the Japanese in *Shōgun* were stereotyped according to Benedict's and Reischauer's notions of what the Japanese think and how they behave. Clavell explains the behavior of Japanese men throughout the novel in passages like this one: "*Bushido,* the Way of the Warrior, . . . bound samurai to fight with honor, to live with honor, and to die with honor; to have undying, unquestioning loyalty to one's feudal lord; to be fearless of death—even to seek it in his service; and to be proud of one's name and keep it unsullied."[16] Indeed, samurai eagerness to die by way of seppuku left the reader wondering how such a population could be self-sustaining. Clavell's lively dialogue provided an introduction to both the sword and the chrysanthemum, revealing the persistent ambivalence that Americans felt toward the Japanese. Instructing Blackthorne, the Portuguese pilot Rodrigues says:

> Of course all Jappos are different from us—they don't feel pain or cold like us—but samurai are even worse. They fear nothing, least of all death. Why? Only God knows, but it's the truth. If their superiors say "kill," they kill, "die," and they'll fall on their swords and slit their own bellies open. They kill and die as easily as we piss. Women're samurai too. . . . They'll kill to protect their masters, that's what they call their husbands here, or they'll kill themselves if they're ordered to. They do it by slitting their throats. Here a samurai can order his wife to kill herself and that's what she's got to do, by law. . . . The women are something else, though, a different species . . . , nothing on earth like them, but the men. . . . Samurai're reptiles and the safest thing to do is treat them like poisonous snakes.[17]

In this passage Clavell shows the reader much of the sword (the Japanese as brutally violent and indifferent to human mortality) and hints at the chrysanthemum (the "something else" that is Japanese women). Blackthorne discovers this "something else" to be their femininity, lax attitudes toward sex, and devotion and subservience to their husbands. Clavell illustrated Benedict's point that the violent and the gentle aspects of Japanese "culture" were not mutually exclusive; this ambivalence existed in each individual, like Mariko's husband, one of Toranaga's most vicious samurai generals, who delicately performs the Japanese tea ceremony to make amends for offending her.

Clavell represents Westerners in two ways. On the one hand are the Jesuit priests, for whom Clavell can hardly hide his disdain, striking a chord with historical Protestant distrust of the Catholic Church. The Jesuits embodied a premodern, pre-Lutheran West in which church fathers dictated morality to Europe's commoners. In the novel the priests are conspiratorial, opportunistic, and blinded by their hatred of Blackthorne's heretical loyalty to England's Protestant queen Elizabeth. Japanese characters repeatedly note the priests' terrible "smell," implying that not only did the Jesuits physically stink because they were "barbarians" but their Catholic dogmatism turned noses as well. Blackthorne initially reeks too, but as he adapts to his Japanese surroundings he loses his odor. The Jesuits never lose theirs.

Blackthorne represents another Europe—the Europe to come, the Europe of the Enlightenment and rational humanism, even the Europe of capitalism. He rejects as "impossible" the irrational Japanese belief that their emperor is a descendent of the gods. The Englishman detests the samurai elite's indifference to the sanctity of human life as if he were well versed in twentieth-century debates about human rights.[18] He distrusts Japanese intentions because they lack a profit motive. Blackthorne is the contemporary Westerner in early modern Japan. As such Blackthorne became Clavell's instrument of vicarious cross-cultural education. He processes the observations of other Europeans and the teachings of Mariko and synthesizes them with his post-Enlightenment Western sensibilities. The outcome is a profound respect for Japan, its people, and their beliefs and practices. The Englishman even comes to assess Japanese culture as superior to the West in a number of ways. Initially he is embarrassed by Japanese women's carefree attitude toward nudity, but then he finds this a more "natural" practice than the artificial shame the church attaches to the human body. At first he violently opposes the practice of taking a bath, believing baths to transmit disease, but by the end of the story he sees Japanese hygienic practices as far preferable to the filthy habits of Europeans. After several months as the only European living among the Japanese, Blackthorne reunites with his crew. He is surprised to find not his close comrades but a ragtag, smelly group of Euro-barbarians, feasting on fatty, oily animal flesh, refusing to bathe, and consorting with lower-class Japanese prostitutes. No respectable Japanese woman, Clavell notes, would touch such barbarians.

So taken is Blackthorne by Japanese culture, society, and his feminine escort that he chooses to remain in Japan (leaving a wife and child in England), where he serves as a trusted adviser to the new shogun, Toranaga. He comes to the conclusion that "much of what they believe is so much better

Shifting Images of Japan from Shōgun *to* Rising Sun

than our way that it's tempting to become one of them totally."[19] His conversion touches the core of Clavell's representation of Japan. Japan is certainly different, Clavell emphasized, but difference need not imply inequality or inferiority. The implication for the contemporary reader was that the Japanese had simply found a different path to modernity. Like the West, Japan arrived at modernity through a rich history, devotion to a sophisticated moral code, and the refinement of "civilization." Mariko rebukes Blackthorne's early accusation that, because they behave differently, the Japanese are uncivilized. She retorts, "We find ourselves quite civilized, Anjin-san."[20]

It is significant that Clavell decided to perpetuate the language of "civilization," which spoke to Americans attuned to the connections between modernization and international power and implied that there were categories of both "civilized" and "uncivilized." Including the Japanese in the favorable category of such a discourse while also pointing out the cultural disparities between Japan and the West was a way of signaling Japan's acceptance into modernity—Japan could be different *and* equal, an idea that complicated simplistic models of Western orientalism.[21]

The producers of Said's European orientalist discourse created a language of cultural and racial difference that also rested on unequal power relations. In Clavell's representation of Japan, and in other U.S. representations from the 1970s, like Vogel's *Japan as Number One*, the language of difference no longer carried with it connotations of unequal power. Clavell made this idea clear when one of his Jesuits chastises a fellow priest: "You cannot equate Japanese with Indians or with illiterate savages like the Incas. You cannot divide and rule here. Japan is not like any other nation."[22] The high-ranking Jesuit then proceeds to forbid a Portuguese captain from interfering in the internal politics of Japan, much as the Portuguese had done with regularity in the Americas. Later he tells the same captain, "How many times must you be warned? You can't treat Japan like an Inca protectorate peopled with jungle savages who have neither history nor culture."[23] Clavell wanted the reader to see Japan as outside of or invulnerable to the sort of orientalist discourse that dominated Western thinking about the non-Western world. That modern Japan could be different and equal held important implications for how Americans would come to view Japan when, a decade later, its economic power appeared relentless.

The television adaptation of *Shōgun* reached an audience ten times that of the book's and added an additional level of representation and interpretation. The most critical difference between Clavell's novel and the television adaptation is that the latter contains a great deal of dialogue in Japanese that remains untranslated and lacks subtitles. The American viewer with no knowledge of Japanese was as lost in a linguistic fog as the fictional Blackthorne. It was a bold gamble on the part of the screenwriter, Eric Bercovici—an act of "*kimot-tama*," one reviewer put it, which is "Japanese for chutzpah."[24] Bercovici aimed to "take his [Clavell's] story, turn it inside-out, and tell the whole tale of *Shōgun* from Blackthorne's point of view, where we understand what he understands, where we see what he sees, and whenever he gets confused, we are equally confused."[25] Describing Blackthorne's experience of being lost in a different culture in the seventeenth century, director Jerry London said, "It's equivalent today to landing on an alien planet."[26] One television critic wrote at the time that the $22 million production "may be the world's costliest language lesson." "The use of untranslated Japanese is a ludicrous impediment to comprehension," he asserted. "Granted, after watching this 12-hour production, I now know 'dozo' means 'please,' and 'domo' means 'thank you.' But there must be an easier way."[27] Other critics from prominent media sources, many of whom screened the miniseries before its public broadcast, predicted wrongly that audiences would be confused and abandon *Shōgun* before its finale.[28] One even rebuked critics and industry analysts who banked on the miniseries' urban appeal, discounting its popularity with "allegedly 'less sophisticated' rural audiences."[29]

The result of the screenwriter's decision was that, perhaps even more than the novel, the miniseries served as twelve hours of mediated cross-cultural education for its American viewers. Like the perturbed reviewer and so many "pop-culture trendies," twelve hours of *Shōgun* really did impart knowledge of basic Japanese language phrases. In addition to simple phrases for greeting, expressing gratitude, and so on, viewers learned that attaching *ka* to a sentence converts a statement to a question; they learned that Japanese verbs end in *-masu* (with the *u* virtually silent); and they learned than *-san* is a polite suffix attached to a person's name, while the suffix *-sama* is reserved for great reverence. Americans acquired a sense of Japanese cultural practices like bowing and removing one's shoes when going indoors. They also learned of attitudes, however stereotyped, toward everything from hygiene to food.

Clavell's "research" into Japanese language and cultural practices gave the nonspecialist reader the sense that the text had an air of authenticity. So, too, did the television producers' decision to use "authentic" Japanese actors (as opposed to, say, Japanese Americans). Nearly the entire cast was Japanese. Many of them spoke little or no English, requiring a small army of translators on set. Heading the Japanese cast in the role of Lord Toranaga was world-renowned actor Toshiro Mifune—the "John Wayne of Japan,"

Shifting Images of Japan from Shōgun *to* Rising Sun

according to one producer—best known to U.S. audiences for his roles in the films of legendary director Akira Kurosawa, including *Rashomon* (1950), *Seven Samurai* (1954), and *Yojimbo* (1961).[30] Mifune's powerful, imperial scowl makes the viewer wonder if Clavell wrote the part with the actor in mind. (In fact, three years before the television adaptation, scholar Sheila Johnson predicted somewhat facetiously that Hollywood would soon get its hands on the novel and put Mifune in the role of Toranaga.)[31]

Richard Chamberlain's portrayal of John Blackthorne also helped Americans visualize a metaphor for contemporary Japanese American encounters. Chamberlain was an American actor, best known for his role as the title character on the American television series *Dr. Kildare* (1961–66). James Clavell had wanted a British actor to portray the British Blackthorne, but both Sean Connery and Roger Moore turned down the role.[32] Chamberlain was "allowed to forgo completely any trace of an English accent," wrote a critic for the *New York Times*, "reducing the authenticity quotient by one significant notch" but also making him more familiar to American audiences.[33]

Shōgun was filmed entirely in Japan, the indoor scenes in Toho Studios in Tokyo and much of the rest on location in the village of Nagashima. "Fine Japanese actors and actresses like Toshiro Mifune and Yoko Shimada add an even greater flavor of authenticity to authentic Japanese locations," wrote Arthur Unger of the *Christian Science Monitor*. "In fact, a late-tuner may believe he is seeing a subtitleless revival of that Japanese classic 'Rashomon,' so convincingly Oriental is the staging."[34] Achieving an authentic "Oriental" atmosphere was not easy for the American film crew. The producers recounted stories of cultural misunderstandings and mishaps.[35] About 130 Japanese workers joined the 30 Americans who traveled to Japan. The Japanese crew declined to use American power tools as they painstakingly constructed "authentic" Japanese sets circa 1600. Once those sets were built, the Japanese crew refused to "age" them by manipulating materials to give them a worn, seventeenth-century look. Translating the director's instructions into Japanese meant that, as Jerry London recalled, scenes that "could have been shot in a few hours" instead took two full days. The conflict between the "hard-nosed, no-nonsense, pragmatic approach to filmmaking of the American production staff" and the "more subdued, painstaking, almost philosophical methods of the Japanese crew" was among the "inherent problems of a bicultural production." By the end of filming, related the *New York Times*, the film crew felt much like the Europeans in Clavell's novel, "washed ashore in a strange, unpredictable country whose culture, customs and people they neither understood nor liked, and whose only dream was one of escape back to their native land."[36] The crew braved the dangers of filming abroad in the name of authenticity.

Those Americans best positioned to judge *Shōgun's* authenticity, professional scholars of Japan, responded with mixed feelings to the popularity of the novel and miniseries. Some were pleased that both representations increased interest in Japanese culture and history, but others were skeptical of what they saw as the perpetuation of stereotypes, both positive and negative, and exaggerated notions of Japanese thought and behavior. Wrote one historian, "Many Japan scholars were put off by countless errors of fact, anachronism, linguistic bloopers, and the continuation of an 'exotic' Japan image."[37] Henry Smith, a historian of Japan at the University of California, read the novel after his students claimed that they had "learned a good deal from it about Japanese history": "Were samurai in fact given to beheading commoners on a whim and then hacking the corpses into small pieces? Were all Japanese of that era (or any era, for that matter) so utterly nonchalant about sex and nudity? Would a peasant really have been summarily executed for taking down a rotting pheasant? Was '*karma*' in fact such an everyday word among the Japanese of the year 1600? . . . It can certainly be said that in every case Clavell exaggerates and often distorts the historical reality."[38]

Shōgun's success prompted Smith to edit a volume to aid college instructors who chose to use *Shōgun* in their classes—evidence that despite many Japan scholars' reservations, some did not object to incorporating it as a text suited for in-class analysis.[39] Most likely because it represented a Japan of the past and did so favorably, despite the stereotypes and exaggerations, *Shōgun* did not elicit the widespread protests against its representation of Japan and the Japanese that *Rising Sun* would in the early 1990s. *Shōgun* confirmed U.S. impressions about modern Japan even as it taught Americans the multiculturalist lesson of the compatibility of difference and equality.

WAKARIMASUKA: FROM COLONIZER TO COLONIZED

Less than two decades separated the publication of *Shōgun* and *Rising Sun*. Their respective representations of Japan, however, seemed to be products of two different centuries. The interim between these two texts witnessed the emergence of a cottage industry dedicated to producing critical representations of the relationships between Americans and Japanese. Of course, they were not the first of their kind in the postwar era. U.S.-Japan relations were the subject of a number of films and novels during the first two postwar decades. These included dramatizations of the Pacific War, like the films *The Bridge on*

Shifting Images of Japan from Shōgun *to* Rising Sun

the River Kwai (1957) and *Never So Few* (1959); narratives of cultural conflict and reconciliation, like James Michener's popular novel *Sayonara* (1954) and the films *The Teahouse of the August Moon* (1956) and *The Barbarian and the Geisha* (1958); and even an alternative history, Philip K. Dick's novel *The Man in the High Castle* (1962), which imagined the fate of the United States had Japan and Germany won World War II. These texts, though, confronted the Japan of the immediate postwar era, the Japan that had gone through a dramatic transformation from enemy to ally in just a few years. Postwar Japan in American eyes was a defeated, subdued nation, a quiescent and colonized Cold War ally, and the ubiquity of stereotypical icons like geisha in popular culture reaffirmed that impression.[40]

Unlike their immediate postwar predecessors, the run of popular narratives beginning in the mid-1970s first confronted the perceived challenges of Japan's "economic miracle" of the 1950s and 1960s. What *Shōgun* demonstrated was that Americans had accommodated to the reality and authenticity of modern Japanese power. With the press growing more attentive to the "trade deficit" between Japan and the United States, however, Americans increasingly perceived Japan's equality in the international realm as a threat to the very source of modernity—"Western" culture. Films like *Black Rain* and popular literature like Clive Cussler's *Dragon* helped construct a deep well of viscerally negative cultural and racial images of Japan. From this well Michael Crichton would draw on the worst nationalistic, racially charged material to produce *Rising Sun*, a novel and film with the power to exercise political and cultural agency while also reflecting existing images and ideas sloshing about in the cauldron of popular media. In the dozen years between *Shōgun's* television adaptation and *Rising Sun's* publication, American popular entertainment's representations of Japan increasingly shifted from the perspective of the powerful colonizer to the powerless colonized.

The comfortable position Japan occupied vis-à-vis Western modernity in the 1970s was expressed in two popular, albeit very different, films: *The Yakuza* and *The Bad News Bears Go to Japan*. They both tell the story of Americans journeying to the Japan of the "economic miracle," a Japan settling contentedly into its role as a modern industrial power and Cold War ally. Like *Shōgun* they show that Japan had not only attained a status of equality in modernity but also had done so on its own terms, mixing its "traditional" cultural features with what it had learned from Americans during the occupation to generate the political and economic requisites for membership in the club of Western-style liberal capitalist democracies. And like *Shōgun* both films show that the gaijin—translated, depending on the English speaker's attitude toward Japan, as "barbarian," "outsider," "foreigner," or, as only David Halberstam could put it, *"not one of us"*—could discover a "knowable" Japan, befriend the Japanese, treat them with equality, and respect the cultural differences that created two dissimilar but powerful nations.[41]

The Yakuza, directed by Sydney Pollack, starred Robert Mitchum as Harry Kilmer, a former American occupation soldier returned to Japan after a quarter century.[42] Against an homage to Japanese gangster (yakuza) films, Pollack sets Kilmer's efforts to reconnect with Eiko, a Japanese woman he had once tried to marry during the occupation. Eiko's brother, Ken, then a young yakuza (played by the omnipresent Ken Takakura), had forbidden the marriage, and she had respected his wishes. Kilmer returns to Japan because yakuza have kidnapped an American friend's daughter. To confront the yakuza Kilmer reconciles with Ken, a martial arts expert, who helps Kilmer fight the yakuza in several violent scenes. An audience accustomed to romantic endings would expect Kilmer and Eiko to live happily ever after, but a plot twist reveals that Ken was not Eiko's brother but her husband. He permitted Kilmer and Eiko's relationship because he believed that in postwar Japan she would be safer living with a U.S. soldier.

Kilmer returns to find that the woman (and the Japan) he fell in love with during the occupation has built a meaningful life in his (and the Americans') absence. To an army buddy Kilmer complains, "Everywhere I look, I can't recognize a thing." His friend responds, "It's still there. Farmers in the countryside may watch TV from their tatami mats and you can't see Fuji through the smog but don't let it fool you. It's still Japan, and the Japanese are still Japanese." The statement was intentionally ambiguous—was this "still" the treacherous Japan of wartime or the subservient Japan of the occupation?—but Kilmer's elegiac mood symbolizes his return to a Japan that has moved beyond his memories into mature modernity. No longer the country of helpless geisha or adolescent men, the Japan of 1975 needed neither Kilmer nor the Americans.

The U.S.-Japan relationship provided lighthearted source material for *The Bad News Bears Go to Japan*, the third film in the popular series about a ragtag California Little League team. Tony Curtis plays Marvin Lazar, a show-business failure with an eye for publicity and spectacle. Lazar smells a profit in fund-raising for the Bears' trip to Japan to play the Japanese Little League national champions. Once Lazar raises the money, the team travels to Tokyo for immersion into a world of cultural difference. The film tries to use racism to comical ends by way of demonstrating the uneducated players' (and general American) provincialism and narrow-mindedness. For example, the

ILL. 2.2. In *The Bad News Bears Go to Japan* (1978), the host of a Japanese variety show chastises American Marvin Lazar (Tony Curtis) for interfering with the production of American-style entertainment. (Paramount Pictures, 2002)

obese catcher responds to charges that his team is afraid to play the Japanese champions by declaring on U.S. television, "We ain't no cowards and there ain't no mother—— Nip gonna stand in our way."[43] More than three decades after the war, such antics were intended to elicit laughs.

One scene of cultural misunderstanding illustrates with unexpected poignancy the 1970s American gaze toward Japan. Lazar and the Bears attend the taping of a Japanese variety show in which the Japanese national team and its coach appear. Initially the scene shows that the Japanese simply have mimicked this staple of postwar American television, complete with Japanese couples singing "Moon River" and the theme from *Happy Days*. Lazar, the American show-business veteran, becomes uncomfortable when he sees that the charismatic host of the show is making the Japanese team's coach nervous by asking him to sing; Lazar fears the coach will be laughed offstage, victimized in the style of *The Gong Show*. With cameras rolling Lazar jumps out of his seat and onto the stage and tells the coach that the Japanese are "not professionals"; he lectures the host patronizingly, telling him that "these kinds of game shows are in my blood, I know what I'm talking about." Security guards shuffle Lazar offstage as the Japanese audience gazes in quiet discomfort. The host of the show shakes his finger at Lazar condescendingly, chiding in mixed Japanese and English, "*Iie*—no, understando?"

While the rest of the film relies on mocking American provincialism for cheap laughs, this one scene is more unnerving than comical. Marvin Lazar is the ugly American, the scorned colonizer, who fails to understand that Japanese modernity is not American modernity. Patronizing Westerners are not welcome in the Japan of the economic miracle. By the end of the film, Lazar, who eventually befriends the Japanese coach, discovers that the Japanese have reached modernity, complete with their own brand of baseball, by doing it the "Japanese way."

Both *The Yakuza* and *The Bad News Bears Go to Japan* were produced before Japanese business became a bogeyman. Ron Howard's 1986 comedy, *Gung Ho*, on the other hand, appeared just as the public discourse on Japan began to turn toward the alarmism represented in Theodore White's article "The Danger from Japan."[44] *Gung Ho* (a Chinese, not Japanese, phrase) adopts a common rust belt narrative: a fictional midwestern town struggles to survive when the local source of employment, an auto factory, closes, putting most of the town's middle class out of work. A factory foreman, Hunt Stevenson (played by Michael Keaton), travels to Japan to convince the fictional Assan Motors to purchase the factory, rehire the workers, and restart production. Hunt gets a taste of stereotyped modern Japanese life while briefly in Tokyo (including a training seminar in which weepy managers plead for their livelihood before militaristic trainers), but most of the cultural interactions take place in the fictional Hadleyville, Pennsylvania. There, a team of Assan managers arrives from Japan to ensure that the factory operates according to Assan's exacting standards.

Several years later in *Rising Sun*, the mood surrounding a Japanese company's purchase of American property was much grimmer. But in the case of *Gung Ho* the Japanese are seen almost as saviors, bringing not only their money but also their expertise to the United States. (Though the story resembles that of Marysville, Ohio—the subject of the next two chapters—the screenwriter admitted he found inspiration in the second Japanese auto plant in the United States, Nissan's facility in Smyrna, Tennessee.)[45] The Japanese managers challenge the stereotypically lazy American workers to boost production, while the Americans try to impart their laid-back sensibilities on the overworked Japanese. Cultural conflict and misunderstanding ensue. The workers believe the managers have made unreasonable production demands. Hunt lectures them on this account: "You know what you want to hear? You want to hear that Americans do things better than anybody else. They're kicking our butts, and that ain't luck—that's the truth. There's your truth. Sure, the great old American do-or-die spirit—yeah, it's alive, but they've got it. Well, I'll tell you something: we better get it back." The film concludes with the Japanese and Americans getting their hands dirty together to break production records in time to earn bonus pay. Each side recognizes that it had lessons to learn from the other, echoing early revisionist works like Vogel's *Japan as Number One*. Though Japanese economic power was a reality in *Gung Ho*, there was no racial or cultural threat attached to it, and Americans could giggle at stereotypes like militaristic corporate managers. This reflected trends in the discourse of U.S.-Japan relations during the 1980s. Nastier representations emerged only after the Japanese started buying the physical space of the United States—including real estate icons like Rockefeller Center and Pebble Beach Golf Club. *Gung Ho* did not belong to that category because it portrayed Japanese business and power not as a threat but as a healthy competitor that can teach Americans, à la Vogel, how to confront the industrial challenges of late capitalism. The film's denouement, in which everyone comes together, "riveting and spraying and putting on windshield wipers, rich and poor, yellow, black and white, white collar and blue," points toward a vision of modern multiculturalism, not the racial and cultural threats of a Japanese postmodernity.[46]

Rising Sun was not the first American popular novel or film to make the turn toward portraying Japan and the Japanese as dangerous. Two texts, Ridley Scott's film *Black Rain* and Clive Cussler's novel *Dragon*, were representative of newer interpretations of Japan as a threat to Western-style modernity. Scott had a penchant for a Japanese mise-en-scène in the 1980s; his vision of a globalized futuristic Los Angeles in *Blade Runner* was replete with Asian, particularly Japanese, imagery. For *Black Rain* Scott took his cameras to Osaka, Japan, to capture the ultramodern cityscape as a backdrop to a gaijin-in-Japan story, and his images of Osaka were eerily reminiscent of *Blade Runner*'s Los Angeles. Later he compared the imagery of both *Black Rain* and his 1980 film *Alien* to contemporary urban Japan.[47] A reviewer for the *New York Times* noted, "'Blade Runner' is set in the future. The Osaka of 'Black Rain' is a city of the future as realized today. Yet they could be the same place."[48] Another film critic stated, "We get the feeling that in Osaka we're staring the near future in the face."[49] Like the U.S. intellectuals engaged in the earliest debates about the meaning of globalization, Scott predicted a Japanese-style future. Unlike their vision, though, Scott's grew increasingly menacing over the decade.

Black Rain stars Michael Douglas as Nick Conklin, the prototypical renegade New York City police detective, the "generic Good Cop Broken Down by the World," reeking of machismo and bend-the-rules individualism.[50] Conklin and his partner spend time in Japan after yakuza dupe them into letting a dangerous Japanese gangster escape custody. Douglas's Japanese detective counterpart is Masahiro Matsumoto, played by Ken Takakura, once again typecast for American audiences as the stoic and masculine yet thoughtful Japanese man. (The "Clint Eastwood of Japan" would take on this kind of role a third time in 1992's *Mr. Baseball*, another gaijin-in-Japan story about an aging American baseball player.) In a scene mixing traditional and modern stereotypes of Japan, a motorcycle-riding, katana-wielding yakuza decapitates Conklin's partner. (Scott clearly sought to reveal cultural difference expressed in motorcycles: the Japanese models are small and quick and rev with a high-pitched screech; in contrast, Conklin's Harley-Davidson is large with a low, muscular rumble.) Conklin must work with Matsumoto to hunt down the yakuza responsible and avenge his partner's death.

Conklin's gaijin-in-Japan story takes place amid the backdrop of a yakuza counterfeiting conspiracy, which is producing millions of fake U.S. dollars intended to destabilize the U.S. economy. The *oyabun* (a yakuza boss) explains that the counterfeiting is retribution for the American "black rain" that poured down upon Hiroshima and Nagasaki. "You made the rain black and shoved your values down our throat," he tells Conklin. "We forgot who we were. . . . I'm paying you back." It is not just the "bad" Japanese characters who express anti-American sentiments. Inspector Matsumoto articulates a similar sentiment in a heated discussion with Conklin: "Music and movies are all America is good for. . . . We make the machines. We build the future. We won the peace."[51] In *Black Rain*, unlike earlier popular representations of Japan, the techno-future had a Japanese face, and it challenged, rather than complemented, American modernity.

In contrast to Blackthorne in *Shōgun*, Nick Conklin leaves Japan having learned virtually nothing of its language or cultural ideas and practices. Both characters provided the vicarious gaijin-in-Japan experience, but while Blackthorne accepted accommodation with Japanese difference, Conklin rejected the country's culture as impenetrable. In *Black Rain* the gaijin will forever remain a gaijin, unless the gaijin accepts colonization. The female protagonist in the film is Joyce (played by Kate Capshaw), who runs a glitzy nightclub that serves the insatiable appetites of Japanese businessmen. Anticipating the gender anxieties over the imagined Japanese conquest of white women in *Rising Sun*, *Black Rain* shows Joyce adapting to her new colonial subservience while Conklin refuses. When he asks her what she means by gaijin, she responds, "A stranger, a barbarian, a foreigner, me and you—more you." In the Japanized future, Americans were positioned on the outside looking in, the colonized forced to accept new realities of international power.

Black Rain tiptoed around the idea that Japan's ascendance was a threat to American culture and society. In contrast, the popular adventure writer

Clive Cussler's novel *Dragon* broached the subject with all the subtlety of a nuclear bomb. Though published in 1990, *Dragon* takes place in a near-future 1993—Cussler imagined that Japan's economic power would continue to grow unabated and in just a few years malicious Japanese corporations would have the power to challenge U.S. political institutions. The Murmoto Corporation, headed by the archetypal evil madman Hideki Suma, has been illegally assembling nuclear weapons and plans to distribute them in the United States hidden within—what else?—imported automobiles. Cussler's recurring alpha-male character, Dirk Pitt, must join a covert team of Americans to prevent catastrophe. Suma's plan is not to pour "black rain" down upon Americans but to use the bombs strategically to cripple the U.S. economy— again, Cussler eschewed subtlety in implying that the Japanese were continuing to fight the Second World War by alternative means. It is also clear, in contrast to both Clavell and Crichton, that Cussler cared not for authenticity when it came to his Japanese subjects. He invented Japanese words that phonetically could not exist (like "Murmoto") and mistakenly transliterated others (like "saki" instead of "sake" for the Japanese rice wine). Cussler's representation of the Japanese exaggerated the tone of revisionist nonfiction literature—Japan was a challenger, not a friend—but placed it in an older framework of cultural understanding, one more reminiscent of Sax Rohmer's early twentieth-century evil Asian criminal mastermind, Fu Manchu.[52]

The "bad guys" in *Dragon* find motivation not only in economic conflict but also in a blend of racial and cultural nationalism. The malignant stereotypes of "Japan 2000" echo in fictional characters, as when one of Hideki Suma's henchmen proclaims, "I bow to the emperor and our traditional culture. I believe in his divine descent and that we and our islands are also of divine origin. And I believe in the blood purity and spiritual unity of our race." Because Cussler's Japanese characters wage a race war, there are few "good" Japanese figures in the novel. Even Japanese American characters are perfidious. George Furukawa, a nisei U.S. intelligence operative, is a double agent working on behalf of the Japanese, as is Roy Orita. Furukawa's parents immigrated to the United States shortly after the war because they "hated America and its multicultures," and therefore they sought its destruction.[53]

Cussler's implication was that the racial bonds of a "unified" society were more powerful than national allegiances. Representing the U.S.-Japan clash in racial terms harkened back to the "race war" in the Pacific during World War II, and it differed sharply from the previous decade's quarrels, which, despite their frequent invocation of racial difference or the memory of the war, had proceeded from the assumption that Americans and the Japanese aspired to mutual prosperity and security. Cusslier's toxic representations were characteristic only of a very brief historical moment, barely a decade stretching from the late 1980s to the early 1990s, a span during which even the most perverse racialized images of Japan seemed fair game. In the intermingling of this revisionist-inspired nationalism with images of techno-futuristic Japan bent on a race war, popular author Michael Crichton mixed a potent brew for his controversial novel.

WAKARIMASEN: MICHAEL CRICHTON'S RISING SUN

In contrast to *Shōgun*, which asked Americans to respect Japanese modernity and power, Michael Crichton's *Rising Sun* demanded that they be fearful of a Japanese *post*modernity, a future in which the United States was no longer a superpower. Such a future also implied subservience to Japan as a new colonial master—the United States' vast natural resources, including its people, and particularly its women, were open to plunder by Japan's economic and cultural imperialists. Crichton exhorted his large audience to resist Japanese imperialism by ceasing to grant Japan inroads into the U.S. economy. One reviewer implicated the novel's relationship to political discourse, namely Paul Tsongas's 1992 economic-nationalist campaign slogans, by dubbing *Rising Sun* a "call to economic arms disguised as a police novel."[54] More than any other popular text, *Rising Sun* powerfully expressed the "Japan Panic": a widespread, intense, and ultimately fleeting moment of uncertainty about the security of the "Western" cultural tradition in the face of an assault from the "East." At the time critics made apt comparisons to the "yellow peril" panics of the late nineteenth century and the 1930s. But previous yellow peril scares played on fears of a barbaric, premodern East, the sort that produced images of conquering Mongol hordes. The Japan Panic of the late 1980s and early 1990s, which *Rising Sun* best encapsulates, instead focused the American gaze toward the postmodern, high-tech, Japan-dominated future.

If *Rising Sun* were simply the story of a corrupt corporation's efforts to cover up a murder, it would have been unremarkable. But the fact that the perpetrators are Japanese and the victim is a young white woman made *Rising Sun* a controversial statement in the heat of the Japan Panic in 1992. The novel chronicles two Los Angeles police detectives, Peter Smith ("Web" Smith in the film, an important distinction discussed below) and John Connor, as they investigate a woman's murder during an opening-night party at the Nakamoto Tower, a new high-tech high-rise built by a powerful Japanese corporation. Smith is the white American male everyman, purposefully nondescript, who struggles to adjust to the changing realities of power in Los Angeles by taking a job for which he seems entirely unprepared: he becomes the liaison between the police department and Japanese nationals living and working in Los Angeles, despite his ignorance of Japanese language and culture. As the central protagonist and the commonplace everyman, Smith exists to be the reader's eyes and ears.

The character of John Connor is considerably more provocative. Connor is an alleged expert in all things Japanese. He lived in Japan for an undetermined period, he speaks the language fluently, and he understands Japanese cultural beliefs and behaviors so well that he can manipulate the Japanese he encounters using this knowledge. Connor demands that Smith respect a *kōhai-sempai* (student-mentor) relationship if the duo is to solve the murder. In the first few pages of the novel Crichton indicates to the reader that John Connor serves as an authoritative guide to the complicated world of Japanese culture, a world that neither Smith nor presumably the reader knows. The Connor character is Crichton's fictional mouthpiece for cross-cultural education.

Through Connor, Crichton instructs the reader about a range of stereotyped Japanese customs, various sordid practices of the nefarious Japanese business community, and the collusion between U.S. politicians and their wealthy Japanese patrons. Connor is a treasure trove of pop-anthropological wisdom. In their first encounter with representatives of the Nakamoto Corporation, Connor warns Smith, "Keep your hands at your side. The Japanese find big arm movements threatening."[55] (One reviewer suggested facetiously that Crichton might have added that the Japanese "have this in common with the mountain gorillas of Rwanda.")[56] He then cautions, "For a Japanese, consistent behavior is not possible." "Basically," he tutors, "the Japanese have an understanding based on centuries of shared culture, and they are able to communicate feelings without words," implying that racial bonds run so deep as to permit telepathic communication. Connor's cynical vision of multiculturalism takes shape in statements like, "Behavior that seems sneaky and cowardly to Americans is just standard operating procedure to Japanese."[57] A reviewer for the *Nikkei Weekly*, a Japanese English-language publication, described these dozens of cultural lessons as "a parody of anthropology guides to Japan."[58]

Crichton's cultural lessons added a pessimistic revisionist spin to the orthodoxy of Ruth Benedict's descriptions of Japanese culture. But unlike Benedict, who sought to remove physiological conceptions of race from cultural discourse, Crichton placed race at the center of U.S.-Japan relations and mingled it with ideas about insurmountable cultural differences. The omnipotent Connor, growing increasingly weary of dealing with the Japanese as the novel reaches its climax, declares that "the Japanese are the most racist people on earth."[59] As the novel closes, Smith and the reader learn why Connor left Japan:

> Most people who've lived in Japan come away with mixed feelings. In many ways, the Japanese are wonderful people. They're hardworking, intelligent, and humorous. They have real integrity. They are also the most racist people on the planet. That's why they're always accusing everybody else of racism. They're so prejudiced, they assume everybody else must be, too. And living in Japan . . . I just got tired, after a while, of the way things worked. I got tired of seeing women move to the other side of the street when they saw me walking toward them at night. I got tired of noticing that the last two seats to be occupied on the subway were the ones on either side of me. I got tired of the airline stewardesses asking Japanese passengers if they minded sitting next to a *gaijin*, assuming that I couldn't understand what they were saying because they were speaking Japanese. I got tired of the exclusion, the subtle patronizing, the jokes behind my back. I got tired of being a nigger.[60]

Crichton's ideas about Japan and race evolved out of cultural revisionist arguments. He had read the work of *Atlantic Monthly* editor James Fallows, for instance, who argued that the United States' tolerance for ethnic heterogeneity was actually one of its strengths in the face of alleged Japanese racism and ethnic homogeneity.[61] The ideological construct of a racist Japan permitted American commentators concerned with economic decline to marginalize racial disunity in the postwar era.

Crichton's "research" into revisionist literature lent an air of authority to the Connor character's pronouncements. The author acknowledged that *Rising Sun* was a work of fiction, but he nevertheless included a bibliography at the end of the book as evidence of his extensive background reading and to entice the reader to learn more about the Japanese role in the U.S. political economy. "Although this book is fiction," he declared, "my approach to Japan's economic behavior, and America's inadequate response to it, follows a well-established body of expert opinion."[62] The list included some of the more vituperative published works of Japan revisionism, like Clyde Prestowitz's *Trading Places* and Pat Choate's unsubtly subtitled *Agents of Influence: How Japan's Lobbyists in the United States Manipulate America's Political and*

Shifting Images of Japan from Shōgun *to* Rising Sun

Economic System. For Crichton it was important that his readers believed his criticisms were grounded in contemporary economic realities.

As with *Shōgun*, translating Crichton's novel into a visual medium—in this case, a feature film with an expensive marketing campaign and a summer "blockbuster" premiere—added a layer of representation that provided the film's larger audience with visceral images of the U.S.-Japan conflict. The television adaptation of *Shōgun* had portrayed the Japanese in a way that encouraged a healthy, if guarded, respect for Japanese modernity and power. Renowned Japanese actors portrayed Japanese characters with depth and diversity, even if those characters did evolve from persistent Western stereotypes. Those stereotypes, however, came from an earlier period when Americans saw Japan as an emergent modern capitalist democracy and a junior partner in the Cold War. The clichés that Michael Crichton borrowed and helped to refine were of a more malevolent sort. By 1992 popular stereotypes had moved beyond Japan-as-modern-competitor to the more dangerous Japan-as-postmodern-colonizer. As such, director Philip Kaufman's *Rising Sun* showed the Japanese in the United States as harbingers of an Asianized future.

The new images of Japan as a colonizing force struck the viewer from the film's outset.[63] A group of Japanese men hang around a karaoke bar at midday singing the Cole Porter classic "Don't Fence Me In," symbolic of the Japanese effort to ride over the United States' "wide open country." One of the Japanese men, whom the audience later discovers is Eddie Sakamura, a Japanese playboy with an influential businessman father, roughly handles an attractive young blonde woman, the soon-to-be-murdered Cheryl Austin. Eddie forces Cheryl into his ostentatious sports car while reprimanding her. From the beginning the viewer sees that Japanese men have conquered white American women. The representation of Eddie Sakamura is crucial, too, because he is played by Cary-Hiroyuki Tagawa, an actor with a muscular, masculine physical presence, a sharp contrast to the persistent representation of Japanese "little men" and a return to the wartime image of physically superior Japanese "supermen."

In his novel Crichton had included references to relationships between Japanese men and white women, but the author more often focused his criticism on Japanese economic behavior. Film provided Kaufman with a canvas for emphasizing Japanese efforts to conquer and colonize American women. The effect of the images of these relationships is meant to be both comically grotesque and disturbing. In an early scene depicting the opening-night party at the Nakamoto Tower, short-statured Japanese executives (here, a return to the "little men" image) stand in front of their dates—white models who tower

ILL. 2.3. In *Rising Sun* (1993), Eddie Sakamura (Cary-Hiroyuki Tagawa) serves as the physical embodiment of the Japanese threat to the United States. Here, he threatens his soon-to-be-murdered lover (Tatjana Patitz). (20th Century Fox, 2002)

over their escorts; white men are permitted only the emasculated gaze of the conquered colonial subject. The Japanese conquest of American women is meant to be less amusing than menacing when Smith and Connor visit a *bettaku*, a "love residence," a glorified brothel where Japanese businessmen house their American mistresses. In the novel, one mistress exposes the domination of American women and the perversity of their Japanese patrons:

> These guys come over from Tokyo, and even if they have a *shokai*,
> an introduction, you still have to be careful. They think nothing of
> dropping ten or twenty thousand in a night. It's like a tip for them.
> Leave it on the dresser. But then, what they want to do—at least,
> some of them.... And to them ... their wishes, their desires, it's just
> as natural as leaving the tip. It's completely natural to them. I mean, I
> don't mind a little golden shower or whatever, handcuffs, you know.
> Maybe a little spanking if I like the guy. But I won't let anybody cut
> me. I don't care how much money. None of those things with knives
> or swords.... But they can be ... A lot of them, they are so polite, so
> correct, but then they get turned on, they have this ... this *way*....
> They're strange people.[64]

The Japan Panic, the fear that the Japanese were systematically dissecting the Western cultural tradition, is most powerfully expressed in *Rising Sun*'s representation of the relationships between Japanese men and white women. The conquest of American women represents the ultimate attack on Western power.

Shifting Images of Japan from Shōgun *to* Rising Sun

ILL. 2.4. In an early scene in *Rising Sun,* Japanese businessmen show off their dates at an inauguration party for a new Japanese-owned high-rise in Los Angeles. The film emphasizes the particular threat Japan poses to white women. (20th Century Fox, 2002)

Three other character representations in the film are also significant: Smith, Connor, and Cheryl Austin's killer. The Peter Smith of the novel became "Web" Smith in the film. Peter Smith's ethnic identity was ambiguous, but most readers probably assumed he was Caucasian. Web Smith was portrayed by Wesley Snipes, a well-known black actor. This added a third dimension of racial tension to that already existing between the white Americans and the Japanese. The viewer understands the implications when Connor tells Smith that the Japanese are "the most racist people on the planet." Using the metaphor of "nigger" to describe his feelings of isolation in Japanese society also had more meaning in the context of the film.

The representation of John Connor on film was meant to contrast sharply with that of Smith. The veteran Scottish actor Sean Connery portrayed Connor. As an older, seemingly wise white man, complete with a distinguished silver beard, Connery could deliver the most outlandish characterizations of the Japanese and make them believable for American audiences. One critic who gave *Rising Sun* a positive review wrote, "The film gets a lot done simply by making use of Connery's authoritative presence. . . . It's the quiet gravity of his stance, the comprehension in his eyes" that made Connery the physical manifestation of Crichton's efforts to teach his audience about Japan.[65] Even Web Smith, who is initially skeptical of the knowledge and power of this older white man, eventually accedes to Connor's wisdom.

In Crichton's novel Cheryl Austin's killer is a Japanese character named Ishiguro, an executive assistant with the Nakamoto Corporation. Philip

Kaufman changed this in the film, making Austin's murderer a white man. Some commentators noted that this meant Kaufman intended to tone down the racism of the novel. As one reviewer put it, "The image of an Asian choking an American woman would have been inflammatory."[66] That is, of course, one possible reading. On the other hand, Kaufman's American killer is Bob Richmond, a lawyer and lobbyist working on behalf of the Nakamoto Corporation. Richmond is one of the Americans responsible for "selling" America to Japan. When he is fingered for the crime at the end of the film, he flees, only to meet a grisly demise. Though viewers can read this scene as downplaying racial hostility between Americans and the Japanese, they can also see it as the American traitor—indeed, a race traitor—getting just what he deserved.

Some professional reviewers bought into Crichton's jeremiad, while others saw *Rising Sun* as racism and propaganda masquerading as benign fiction. A few celebratory reviews included comparisons to Upton Sinclair's *The Jungle* or Harriet Beecher Stowe's *Uncle Tom's Cabin* in the sense that, like those two classics, it would have an immediate ideological and political impact. "Every so often," wrote Robert Nathan in the *New York Times Book Review*, "a work of popular fiction vaults over its humble origins as entertainment, grasps the American imagination and stirs up the volcanic subtext of American life."[67] Other reviewers remained unstirred. Kunio Francis Tanabe, reviewing the book for the *Washington Post*, wrote that "even as fiction, it all seems too callous and irresponsible."[68] (Crichton shrugged off this negative review because it was "written, I believe, by an Asian-American.")[69] Generally, reviewers who gave the book or the film positive reviews used it to reaffirm their preexisting perceptions of the U.S.-Japan economic conflict; critics, however, saw *Rising Sun* as a malevolent step in the direction of racism and purposeful cultural obfuscation.

More important than the opinions of professional reviewers were the perspectives of the reading and viewing public. Comments posted on early Internet message boards offer a unique glimpse into how non-elite Americans—those with no weekly column in a high-profile newspaper or magazine, talking in ways that might be heard around a water cooler—consumed Crichton's work as political and cultural commentary.[70] His bibliography and "research" apparently persuaded readers to accept his critique as more than a fanciful crime drama. "My own opinion," wrote one poster, "is that the majority of the comments made by the characters in the book are true and it made me aware of what kind of position the US is in with respects [sic] to Japan."[71] Another admitted that reading *Rising Sun* inspired him to

Shifting Images of Japan from Shōgun *to* Rising Sun

learn more by reading Pat Choate's highly critical *Agents of Influence*.[72] Yet another believed that "Mr. Crichton has the right idea about inspiring economic nationalism." He wrote, "I can pretty much agree with all of Crichton's harsh assertions about Japanese manipulativeness and U.S. disintegration."[73] Finally, one poster affirmed Crichton's representation of Japanese racism: "A friend of mine (black man in his 40's) . . . used to say all these wonderful things about Japan/etc, but after he read this book he came up to me and said 'you know what, those japanese are XXXXXXXs, they may smile at you during the day but plot against you during the night. . . . They're all XXXXXXs.'"[74]

The critical reaction against Crichton was even more powerful on these message boards than the chatter praising *Rising Sun*. A series of lengthy and heated debates erupted after one poster, apparently a Japanese man living in the United States, wrote a message titled "Fuck Michael Crichton" on a discussion board for Asian American social and cultural issues:

> It would take a white man to do this. But, I strongly object to an individual taking this book to[o] seriously (unless, you like revenge). Revenge and Scapegoating, that's what this book is about. It is far below my personal honor and intelligence to go back to Nippon and write novels toward the dislike of the American People. Anti-Americanism is not my thing, but anti-japan is Mr. Crichton. To spread hatred and discord based of imagination. The white people is [*sic*] a master at doing this. . . . Mr. Cric[h]ton you[r] book is only doing well among the Americans whose intelligence is as low as yours. It is not my pleasure to mass distribute my imagination about your culture be it British or American. If I chose to write anti-white American garbage as you have chosen to do . . . all of Asia would hate me! Your kind treat you like a hero.[75]

The anger inspired by Crichton's representation of the Japanese is palpable in this post, amplified by the author's struggle to translate his fury into a non-native language. Many fellow subscribers to the newsgroup responded to the accusations by initiating a discussion, which quickly devolved into a "flame war," over which society was more racist, the United States or Japan. Each side could muster up evidence for its arguments; some participants even used Crichton's work to support their claims about Japanese racism. What is most striking about this exchange, though, is that a single fictional text helped to shape decisively the way some people perceived a divisive political, economic, and cultural issue. Americans continued to understand—and misunderstand—Japan through the mediation of culture.

A trio of films in the early twenty-first century demonstrated that, in the wake of Japan's "Lost Decade" of the 1990s, attitudes in the United States had come full circle back to postwar understandings of Japan's past and present. Absent a Japanese economic or cultural menace, Benedict and Reischauer archetypes reemerged. A popular story of a young girl turned famous geisha reminded Americans of Benedict's chrysanthemum, while a Meiji-era epic of war and politics evoked the sword. Finally, a tale of two self-searching Americans lost in Tokyo offered a thoughtful critique of the post–Cold War, post-bubble American gaze, presenting an alternative to the *wakarimasu-wakarimasen* dichotomy and the possibility of a respectful *wakarimasuka* attitude.

The 2005 film *Memoirs of a Geisha*, directed by Rob Marshall and based on the best-selling book by Arthur Golden, manages to recount a young girl's transformation from peasant to renowned geisha during the most tumultuous period in Japan's history—the 1930s and 1940s—while only vaguely alluding to Japan's imperial conquests and subsequent devastation at the hands of the U.S. Army Air Force.[76] Despite the dramatic setting, most of the action takes place in the last days of the *ukiyo*—the "floating world"—of Japanese urban nightlife, and the melodrama of the internal worlds of geisha defines the narrative more than the surrounding political and military context. As the story begins, nine-year-old Chiyo's family sells her and her sister into servitude. The young girl devotes herself to becoming a geisha—living in virtual slavery, it is the most she can hope for—after encountering a kind businessman called the Chairman. Chiyo, renamed Sayuri when she becomes an apprentice geisha, dedicates her life to securing the Chairman as a *danna*, or wealthy patron.

The film sparked controversy on multiple fronts.[77] Producers cast actors of Chinese descent—Zhang Ziyi, Gongi Li, Tsai Chin, and Michelle Yeoh—to play the main female characters, prompting criticisms in Japan. The government of China then banned the film for what it believed were representations of Japanese prostitution, a sensitive subject in light of the sexual abuse that Japanese armies inflicted on China's population during the war. In the United States, audiences did not care about East Asian politics or debates about cultural authenticity, according to Roger Ebert, but instead wanted "to see beauty, sex, tradition and exoticism all choreographed into a dance of strategy and desire." Moviegoers also went unstirred by the film's central conceit of sexual servitude; had the film been set in the West, Ebert wrote, "it would be perceived as about children sold into prostitution, and that is not nearly as wonderful as 'being raised as a geisha.'"[78] Japan's cultural differences no longer threatened the contemporary United States, which could once again gaze disinterestedly at Japan's exoticized past without evoking an anxiety-filled present.

An unthreatening Japan also appears in *The Last Samurai*, a sprawling epic starring Tom Cruise as Nathan Algren, a U.S. Army officer and Civil War veteran who ends up fighting on behalf of a samurai rebellion against the Meiji emperor's new European-style modern army.[79] Algren, who once served under George Armstrong Custer, drinks heavily to forget his complicity in the slaughter of Native American populations in the American West. He has an aptitude for learning new languages and a sensitivity to cultural differences not found in his white male peers. The Japanese government has hired Algren to train its soldiers in Western weaponry and tactics—"The ancient and modern are at war for the soul of Japan," Algren's British translator explains. The endgame is competitiveness with the West, but in the meantime the emperor's government struggles to subdue a revolt modeled on the real 1876 Satsuma Rebellion, which was the last armed uprising against the Meiji government, led by samurai displeased with the rapid push toward modernization and Westernization. Algren finds himself a captive of the samurai leader Katsumoto (played by Ken Watanabe, who would also play *Memoirs of a Geisha*'s Chairman). In Katsumoto's commitment to preserving "traditional" Japanese ways, Algren hears echoes of the Native American societies—Westerners describe samurai as "savages with bows and arrows"—being erased by his own government across the ocean. He fears modern weapons will once again cut down a proud, ancient culture, and he takes up arms on behalf of the rebellion.

Nathan Algren is John Blackthorne, a vehicle of cross-cultural communication, transported from the beginning of the Tokugawa era to the early years of the Meiji. Like Blackthorne, Algren comes to admire and understand the ways of these "savages," finding many of their traditional beliefs and practices superior to the West's modern values, which ungraciously invade this society in transition. Like *Shōgun*, *The Last Samurai* argues that those cultural elements that mark Japan as different from the West make it neither inferior nor threatening. If anything, it is the West that threatens the cultural sanctity of an essentialized Japan. The film displayed attitudes that would have found sympathetic audiences forty years earlier, while it would not have made sense at the height of the Japan Panic.

Finally, Sofia Coppola's 2003 film *Lost in Translation*, starring Bill Murray and Scarlett Johansson, presents a rare American perspective on Japan, one that leaves the viewer only with the question *wakarimasuka* rather than with definitive statements like *wakarimasu* or *wakarimasen*.[80] Bob (Murray) is a Hollywood star a couple of decades past his prime who has come to Tokyo to take advantage of lucrative advertising opportunities, while Charlotte (Johansson) is a recent college grad and newlywed looking for purpose in everything from New Age spiritualism to Buddhism. Alongside these two Americans treading water in their personal lives stars the Tokyo of the twenty-first century, a neon metropolis as bright as Ridley Scott's Osaka but drained of all the menace—the most dangerous thing Bob and Charlotte encounter on the streets of one of the world's safest cities is an angry bartender wielding a stun gun. Japan's hypermodern future is no longer a threat. Its motorcycle street gangs have morphed into pachinko addicts and teenagers in arcades, all enjoying the common luxuries of a contemporary society with a high standard of living. The Japanese are exceedingly polite and accommodating, but they do not exist to serve Americans except in the most superficial ways. Tokyo is a Japanese playground, and the most that Bob and Charlotte can do is confusingly observe from a distance. At the end of the film the two depart Japan as confused as when they arrived, because Japan and its people do not exist to help Americans find themselves. After decades of representations that effaced the Japanese present, *Lost in Translation* proved to be an uncommonly honest perspective on the American gaze toward Japan.

THREE

Ohayō I

(Good) Morning Again in Marysville

At least one viewer noticed the irony: interspersed during the commercial breaks of the NBC network's 1980 airing of its epic miniseries of seventeenth-century Japan, *Shōgun*, Lee Iacocca told Americans just what he thought of the Japanese. The former president of the Ford Motor Company left the Detroit giant in 1978 after a bitter public feud with the grandson of the firm's legendary founder. Now he was on television pitching Chryslers, having joined the failing company as president and CEO. He successfully lobbied Congress for a bailout package in 1979, pushed Chrysler to build smaller fuel-efficient cars, and took aim at the competition: Japanese automakers. "Every 10 minutes he came on with his Drop Dead Datsun and Toyota commercials," wrote Tony Kornheiser in the *Washington Post*—"a real first in point-counter-point programming."[1]

If Bob Spinelli was watching, he might have noticed the irony too. Spinelli was just a teenager when he got a job at the Ford assembly plant near Edgewater, New Jersey, a small community nestled against the Hudson River facing New York City. In 1955 Spinelli was one of the first workers to walk through the doors of the majestic new Mahwah assembly plant, Ford's largest North American facility to date. Twenty-five years and four and a half million cars later, amid rumors that the Japanese company Nissan (known as Datsun in the United States until 1983) might buy the soon-to-be mothballed facility, he and his coworkers watched as the final car, a Ford Fairmont, rolled off the line. Like a mourner at a funeral delivering an impromptu soliloquy, Spinelli declared, "This is an American plant, built by Americans, and American cars should be coming out of it."[2] On national television and in countless local moments echoing Mahwah's woes, the popular conversation about nationalist rivalries shaped the tone of what the U.S. media had dubbed the "auto wars."

Yet three years later and 500 miles away, in a similarly small town not far from Columbus, Ohio, a very different scene was playing out. Drivers traveling northwest on U.S. Route 33 outside of Marysville could not have missed the new billboard: at the very top was the name Honda, one of the three largest Japanese automobile manufacturers that had stormed the U.S. market since the mid-1970s. The billboard played on a passerby's cognitive dissonance—beneath the Japanese company's logo was a giant personalized Ohio license plate with the letters "HM GRWN." A driver also might have noticed the bumper stickers on locally owned Hondas proclaiming "Made in USA." The message was as clear as Iacocca's and Spinelli's, but it told a different story: in rural Union County, Ohio, population 29,540, the American hands assembling cars defined the products' national identity more than the Japanese name on their rear ends.[3]

The national identity distinction was more than a word game for the automobile industry in the early 1980s. It meant jobs, livelihoods, and sometimes even lives. The "Big Three" U.S. automakers (General Motors, Ford, and Chrysler) laid off more than a quarter of a million autoworkers in the early 1980s, most of them concentrated in the Midwest, which began living up to the moniker "rust belt" in earnest. Detroit's woes rippled across dozens of related supplier industries, threatening several jobs regionally for each that the auto manufacturers eliminated. At its worst the national unemployment rate hovered near 11 percent in late 1982, and in scattered cities throughout the Midwest it exceeded 20 percent.[4] For some men, unemployment challenged not only their ability to provide financially for their families but also their sense of manhood and self-worth. Eugene Pfeiffer had been making $430 a week at the Mahwah plant. "When you're working, you have more respect from the family," he said. "All of a sudden I feel like a piece of furniture around the house. I feel less than a man, less than a father."[5] For laid-off autoworkers the success of Japanese auto companies in the United States threatened both U.S. industrial supremacy and American masculinity.

The feeling that Japanese industry was emasculating the American worker had the potential to translate into tragedy. On 19 June 1982, at the height of the worst U.S. recession since the Great Depression, a recently laid-off Chrysler foreman and his stepson beat to death a young Chinese American named Vincent Chin. Encountering Chin as he left a bar on the night of his bachelor party, Ronald Ebens and Michael Nitz mistook Chin for Japanese and used a baseball bat to express their own feelings of emasculation. "It's because of you little motherfuckers that we're out of work," Ebens reportedly said during the confrontation. Outrage over the incident grew when Ebens and Nitz received only probation and a fine through a plea bargain. Chin's murder revealed the deadly power of anti-Japanese sentiment in the auto industry, permeated as it was by century-old imagery of a "yellow peril" and stereotypes of "little men" working to outfox American competitors.[6]

At the height of the Japan Panic, the numbers looked grim for Detroit's automakers. Japanese cars accounted for roughly three out of every four dollars of the trade deficit. Japanese brands' market control climbed from the single digits in the early 1970s to more than 30 percent a decade later.[7] Anxieties extended beyond simple import data, though. As David Halberstam put it, Detroit feared "not only that the Japanese made better autos, that they had newer plants, that the relationship between workers and managers was better, but that Japanese society, with its greater harmony, with its greater belief and discipline in basic education, its more limited personal freedoms, was better prepared for the coming century."[8] Having taken the U.S. steel and television industries, the Big Three argued, Japanese companies, abetted by powerful government ministries like the Ministry of International Trade and Industry, now targeted the biggest prize of all, the icon of midcentury American industrial power. Thus Bob Spinelli, the 5,000 employees at the Mahwah Ford plant, and the hundreds of thousands laid off in just a half decade all interpreted the auto wars through Detroit's lens. When Iacocca bashed Japan on TV, when autoworkers smashed Toyotas with sledgehammers at union picnics, when the unemployed murdered Asian Americans, and when Michigan congressman John Dingell blamed the industry's troubles on "those little yellow people," Detroit established the national tone of the auto wars.[9]

While they dominated the story, the Big Three and the United Automobile Workers (UAW), one of postwar America's most powerful industrial unions, were not the only storytellers. Dingell's oft-repeated "little yellow people" line came to symbolize Detroit's anti-Japanese racism, but put back in its context, it reveals a contested narrative about the meaning of Japan's global corporate expansion. Dingell uttered those words before a group of Democratic colleagues. When startled fellow representatives questioned what he said, Dingell repeated, "The little yellow people. You know, Honda." "There is something you have to understand, John," responded Albert Gore Jr., a young congressman from Tennessee. "Those little yellow people have built a plant in my district that is giving jobs to a lot of white and black people."[10] Gore represented Smyrna, Tennessee, where Nissan was building a truck assembly plant that would employ thousands of local residents. Smyrna's would be the second Japanese-owned assembly plant in the United States. Honda would build the first in a small town in rural central Ohio called Marysville.

In the context of persistent anxiety about Japan, the residents of Marysville welcomed a Japanese company to their town as a salve for the wounds of economic recession. The consequences likely exceeded the most optimistic expectations. The fears Halberstam described proved partly valid—this Japanese company did, indeed, do things better than its U.S. competitors—but the future that Detroit foresaw unfolded not half a planet away in Tokyo but fewer than 200 miles south in central Ohio. The case of Honda's arrival in Marysville illustrates that the globalizing of Japanese capital and culture worked not only to the benefit of a particular nation-state but also to the benefit of those local communities that connected to global transformations taking place largely independent of the borders of the nation-state. Honda brought thousands of jobs to central Ohio while linking the local community to global commerce and culture in ways much of the rest of the country would notice in the coming decades. The Japanese company spoke not the language of national, racial, or ethnic communities but of transnational corporate communities. When the defenders of the old postwar industrial order, the representatives of the UAW, presented their grievances to the Marysville community, they seemed petty, bitter, and vestigial compared to what Marysville had already tasted and to what Honda's future promised.

Honda's Marysville operation was the first of what would be called the "transplants," Japanese auto manufacturers that set up production facilities in the United States to take advantage of proximity to markets and to bypass complicated and increasingly restrictive barriers to trade, ad hoc stopgap measures created in Washington for short-term political gains.[11] As a rule, the transplants set up shop in rural areas of the country, most often (and in this regard Marysville was an exception) in southern states lacking in legacies of industrial labor organization and activism.[12] Nissan, Japan's second largest automaker, opened its truck assembly plant in Smyrna in 1983. The similarities to Marysville were striking: like its Ohio predecessor, Smyrna was an economically depressed rural area with a largely white population thirty miles outside of a large city (in this case, Nashville).[13] The Smyrna plant would become the second non-UAW auto facility in the United States—Marysville was the first—when its workers voted against unionization in 1989. Japanese automakers Toyota and Mazda also started U.S. operations in the mid-1980s in Fremont, California, and Flat Rock, Michigan, respectively, but those were joint ventures with GM in Toyota's case and Ford in Mazda's and thus workers were UAW members.[14] (Toyota's massive plant in Georgetown, Kentucky, which operated independent of any arrangement with GM, did not begin production until 1988, and it did so as a nonunion facility.) In 1982, three of every four cars sold in the United States bore the logo of a Big Three automaker; thirty years later, fewer than half did, and almost half sold came from the transplants, foreign automakers that had established U.S. operations.[15]

Honda's arrival in Marysville, wrote Pulitzer Prize–winning industry journalist Paul Ingrassia and Joseph B. White, marked the "watershed event that precipitated Detroit's crisis and ultimately its revival. . . . It was the Japanese, ironically, who showed that American workers could build quality automobiles, and thus stripped away Detroit's excuses." Ingrassia and White described the scramble in the late 1980s to adopt "Japanese-style" management techniques in Big Three plants (and their efforts to hire away executives from Honda) and argued that the U.S. management class's eager adoption of such styles saved the industry, improving the quality and experience of working for GM, Ford, and Chrysler.[16] While Detroit executives would "relapse" into bad habits a decade later, greedy in the wake of the Japanese economic crisis of the 1990s, Honda's commitment to Ohio grew, and more generally Japan's transnational presence in the United States, driven by Americans' insatiable desire for Japanese things, continued to connect local spaces to global flows. It all started in Marysville.

"WITH HAPPY PLEASURE WE ACCEPT A GUEST": HONDA COMES TO MARYSVILLE

In October 1977 the Honda Motor Company of Japan announced its intention to build a motorcycle assembly plant six miles northwest of Marysville, the largest municipality and county seat of rural Union County. The local newspaper, the *Marysville Journal-Tribune*, noted an auspicious coincidence: "'Ohio' in Japanese means 'Good Morning,' and that's what it was for residents of Union County and central Ohio" on the day of Honda's announcement.[17] ("Ohio" derives from the Iroquois words for "great river.") Everyone in Union County was taken aback by the announcement. The mayor and the county commissioners had never spoken with Honda's people. Two months before the public announcement, James Duerk, an economic development assistant to longtime Ohio governor Jim Rhodes, dropped into Marysville to inform the local leadership of the arrangement his boss had already made. Duerk brought with him a twelve-point agreement that Rhodes had negotiated with Honda's top management. The document laid out the various commitments Rhodes had made—some of them on behalf of Marysville and

Union County—to invest millions of state and local dollars in infrastructural improvements and to offer generous tax abatements.[18] Rhodes sold Honda on the location because of its proximity to the Transportation Research Center, a several-thousand-acre compound on U.S. Route 33 built earlier in the decade to lure the Big Three down to rural central Ohio for research and development. In the wake of Detroit's post-1973 downturn, the research center sat vacant.

The entrepreneurial Rhodes was emblematic of the globetrotting governors of the 1970s, who ventured abroad to court big foreign businesses to bring back home. The Ohio governor saw himself as a job creator; he famously once planned to build a bridge across Lake Erie connecting Cleveland to Canada to promote trade and his slogan, "Jobs and Progress." Asked at the October 1977 joint press conference with Honda whether the company would build more than just motorcycles, he responded, "I wouldn't be surprised. . . . You know, these Japs are pretty smart." When the assembled press gasped at the racial epithet and paused uncomfortably, Rhodes followed up: "Of course, you know that by Japs, I mean 'Jobs and Progress'!"[19]

Over the nine years following Rhodes's and Honda's announcements, the company invested nearly $600 million in Union County as it constructed first a motorcycle assembly plant and then a much larger automobile assembly plant; by 1986 it had expanded the auto plant and built a third facility, the Anna Engine Plant, about an hour's drive west of Marysville. In 1989 it would add another massive assembly facility in East Liberty, in Logan County, adjacent to northwest Union County. The centerpiece, the Marysville Auto Plant (MAP), would be the first auto production facility in the United States owned and operated by a Japanese company when it opened in 1982. Anticipating the theme of Ronald Reagan's 1984 presidential campaign, Honda's arrival in Marysville signaled a social and economic renaissance for a rust belt community—it was "morning again" in Marysville, courtesy of the Land of the Rising Sun.

It was no wonder, then, that the residents of Union County voted for the president's reelection by a margin of nearly four to one in 1984. The dour Democratic unionism of Walter Mondale contrasted with Reagan's can-do, free-trading smile, and the latter's shiny optimism embodied local changes in Marysville. At the same time, Honda's arrival was not a product of Reaganism or Reaganomics—the company announced construction of the MAP a full year before Reagan took office for his first term, at the height of the national "malaise" that Jimmy Carter tried to articulate. It was instead part of a national trend of northern urban deindustrialization and relocation.

(Good) Morning Again in Marysville

Industries abandoned cities where labor was concentrated and well organized. Some of them relocated production overseas, others (like steel) bowed out completely, and still others moved operations to rural areas in the U.S. South, where labor was inexpensive and frequently hostile to union activity.[20] Such deindustrialization was both a cause and a consequence of the economic woes of the late 1970s and early 1980s. When Honda began building in central Ohio, it did so at a time of widespread economic instability, a condition neither initiated nor solved by the Reagan administration.

The opening of the Marysville Motorcycle Plant (MMP) in September 1979 coincided with the beginning of hard times to come for the community. Unemployment rates for Union County hovered near 6 percent throughout 1979; the jobs the MMP provided to the "Original 64" employees hardly dented that figure in a county with a labor force of 13,000.[21] Stagnant economic growth, particularly in the industrial Midwest, combined with rising consumer prices under the Carter administration's watch to put strains on everyday life in Marysville as a new decade dawned.

But the "worst hard time" was yet to come. Unemployment in central Ohio climbed dramatically during the "Reagan recession" of 1981–83, reaching levels not seen since the Great Depression. The 1982 average rate for Union County was 12.3 percent, reaching 14.5 percent as the MAP opened its doors in November 1982; just three months later, the rate was close to 16 percent. Neighboring counties, from which Honda would also draw workers, had it equally rough—Logan and Champaign Counties had 1982 unemployment rates of 12.5 and 12.7 percent respectively, while in Marion County, to Union's north, 16.9 percent of the workforce was jobless in 1982.[22]

From a devastating low in 1982, however, Marysville would reach spectacular highs in the decade following the MAP's opening, exceeding both the company's and the community's expectations. During the recession, Union County's unemployment regularly rated as one of the dozen worst of Ohio's eighty-eight counties—in a state, no less, that monthly ranked only behind Michigan for the nation's worst jobless rates. Yet by April 1986 Union County's rate of 4.4 percent was the lowest in all of Ohio, and the occasion was the first in nearly two years that the rate in any Ohio county dipped below 5 percent. By 1988 the county's average annual income of $27,000 had passed every other county in the state, and Honda's annual tax bill exceeded $5 million, two-thirds of which went to local school districts.[23] By 1992 Honda had invested $2.4 billion in several production and assembly facilities in central Ohio, where it employed more than 10,000 people—not one of whom, the company liked to boast, Honda had ever laid off, even when it cut production to account for economic slowdowns. The nearly 400,000 Honda Accords produced every year in Marysville helped propel that vehicle model to the very top of the annual U.S. best-seller lists; made Honda the fourth largest domestic automaker in the United States; and pushed it past its Japanese rivals, Toyota and Nissan, in the competition to dominate the U.S. auto market. At the beginning of Honda's second decade in central Ohio, the MAP was "the single biggest and most productive auto plant in North America," and the county's former unemployment woes were a distant memory: the rate was 3.2 percent in 1990, and the local newspaper was "bulging with help-wanted ads."[24] *Ohayō*, indeed.

Despite the tremendous growth, Honda's Marysville experiment was not without its detractors. Heading the list was the catchall of "Detroit," which included not only the Big Three U.S. automakers but also the powerful UAW. In the 1970s the automakers alleged that the unfair trade practices of Japanese companies were responsible for layoffs nationwide. While the UAW did not take its marching orders from Detroit automakers and frequently blamed the Big Three for creating their own problems, union president Douglas Fraser nevertheless condescendingly echoed Iacocca's accusations by claiming that nothing could stop continued layoffs "except for the Japanese showing some responsibility and restraining their exports."[25] The Detroit companies got what they wanted in April 1981, when the Reagan administration negotiated "voluntary export restraints" with the Japanese government, limiting exports to 1.68 million annually until 1984 and thereafter renegotiating each year until quotas were lifted in the 1990s.

Of that 1.68 million, the Japanese government allotted Honda 348,000 exports to the United States, based on its third-place sales ranking behind Toyota and Nissan. That decision spelled trouble for the export-reliant company. In 1980 Honda had shipped to the United States nearly 380,000 units, which accounted for 68 percent of its total sales (compared to 40 percent for Toyota and 46 percent for Nissan).[26] The Reagan administration's passive-aggressive protectionism threatened the continued growth of a company so reliant on global commerce. More so than its Japanese rivals, Honda had to think creatively about relocating production to the United States. As Honda executive Kihachiro Kawashima put it upon the 1980 dedication of the MMP, "It is my sincere desire that Honda of America will gradually grow as one of your neighbors. We want to become a contributor to the growth of the American society and play a small role in American history."[27] It sounded like a proverb straight from the Book of Morita.

The reality of Honda's decision-making may have been a mix of Sony-style globalism and a keen sense of the protectionist rumblings in Washington.

Honda publicly announced construction of an auto plant in January 1980, a full fifteen months before the negotiation of restraints, though the company had already decided to build an auto plant when it announced construction of the MMP a little more than two years earlier.[28] Previous U.S. business, labor, and government uproars over Japanese trade practices in the textile, steel, and television industries had been less-than-subtle signals to Japanese auto producers that they had best be prepared for a backlash against their challenge to the flagship U.S. industry. Honda's Marysville expansion may have fit naturally into the company's globalizing philosophy—the "Honda Company Principle," articulated by its founder, Soichiro Honda, in 1956, emphasized its "global viewpoint"—but it was also an expedient decision in a moment of uncertainty.[29]

Whatever the impetus for building in what seemed the unlikeliest of locations for a Japanese company, the decision proved an unqualified economic success for both Honda and central Ohio. For Honda, producing in Marysville helped it sidestep Reagan's "voluntary restraints," adding hundreds of thousands annually to its U.S. supply at a time when consumers demanded small, inexpensive, well-made, and fuel-efficient cars. Beating Toyota and Nissan in the race to assemble vehicles in the United States was the primary reason for Honda's leap to number one on the import list. For Marysville and Union County, the jobs Honda provided at a moment of economic trauma reignited business across the area. In the early 1990s Ohio development officials estimated that for every new job Honda created in Marysville, three new jobs were created elsewhere in the state, meaning that Honda was directly and indirectly responsible for roughly 40,000 Ohio jobs by the early 1990s.[30] A decade later, as the company celebrated its first quarter-century in the region, the numbers were even more startling: Honda directly employed more than 16,000 local residents with an annual payroll in excess of $1 billion; it had invested more than $6 billion in Ohio; and, according to an independent analysis, more than 128,000 jobs were "attributable to Honda's presence."[31]

Honda's arrival altered social and cultural life for the Marysville community as much as it dramatically transformed the economic landscape of central Ohio, illustrating the impact beyond economics that global commerce and culture could have on local U.S. communities. For Honda's new "associates," as the company called all of its production employees, Honda promoted a "Japanese-style" work ethic that tried to transcend the divisions between labor and management in order to invest everyone in Honda "quality" and "pride." Consequently Marysville evolved into more than a simple space of production; its very identity merged with Honda's. Local residents not employed by Honda noticed the changes in their community as well. Hundreds of new Japanese residents brought a touch of ethnic and cultural diversity to an area populated almost exclusively by white faces.

The singularly impressive growth of the area would come only after the MAP opened its doors, but the Marysville community still warmly greeted the opening of the MMP and the hundreds of jobs it promised, witnessing small changes from the influx of global capital and commerce. The MMP produced its first motorcycle on 10 September 1979 and steadily increased production until it was ready to showcase the facility to the press and the public in April 1980.[32] The *Journal-Tribune* published a special twenty-four-page insert that month welcoming Honda and informing locals about the company's products and which of their neighbors would be responsible for making them.[33] The supplement also began Union County's education in all things Japanese. It was titled *Nikkan Shimbun*, which readers learned meant "Daily Newspaper." Also, two Japanese-language characters adorned the cover; below them read, "The Two Japanese Symbols Shown Above Literally Mean 'With Happy Pleasure We Accept a Guest.'" The *Nikkan Shimbun* was littered with warm welcomes from local businesses, congratulating Honda on its launch. It contained a dozen articles on various aspects of Honda's operations, from the mythology of Soichiro Honda to the company's emphasis on teamwork and the most rigorous quality standards. It also noted Honda's significant contribution in local property taxes, expected to be more than $200,000 in 1980, despite tax abatements that were part of generous incentive packages granted by local and state officials. (By the mid-1980s, Honda's local tax contribution registered in the millions, most of it going to the local school system.)

The supplement concluded with an introduction to the plant's five managers. The top two executives were Japanese; the next three in rank were Americans. Significantly, no one was older than forty-eight years old, and none of the three Americans was even forty years old—the entire plant, as early observers frequently noted and as pictures of the first employees attest, had a young feel to it, from the managers to the workers.[34] The very last page of the supplement was nearly blank; about a third of the way down the page three brief lines stood in modestly small font, mimicking a haiku-like aesthetic:

Thank you Marysville.
You've made your town
Honda's second home.

Supplement To:

Marysville Journal-Tribune

Nikkan Shimbun
(Translation: Daily Newspaper)

歓 迎

In Translation, The Two
Japanese Symbols Shown Above Literally Mean
"With Happy Pleasure We Accept A Guest"

These Two Symbols Combine To
Offer A Warm And Friendly Welcome Which
We At The Journal-Tribune, Our Advertisers
And Our Readers Extend To Honda.

ILL. 3.1. The 17 April 1980 edition of the *Marysville Journal-Tribune* included a twenty-four-page special supplement welcoming Honda to town. (Kevin Behrens/*Marysville Journal-Tribune*)

The only other item on the page was the Honda logo, near the bottom. The minimalist aesthetic would become a Honda trademark over the years and presented Marysville with an image of an open and straightforward business grateful for the opportunity to be part of the community.

Despite the mutual goodwill, the MMP alone could not solve the economic woes to come in the three years that followed. The dissonance between optimism about Honda's growth and the darkening economic outlook was evident in the *Journal-Tribune*'s year-end wrap-up: the top Ohio story for 1980, as the Associated Press saw it, was the "slumping economy," while the top local story, according to the newspaper's staff, was Honda's announced auto plant, which broke ground in early December.[35] As residents waited for the construction of the plant, with Honda seeking to boost its payroll from 500 to 2,500 employees, a series of local business closings painted a dire economic picture. In January 1982 food producer Nestlé announced it would close a local milk-processing facility, putting 138 people on the unemployment rolls. In April truck manufacturer Rockwell International announced that it was shutting the doors on its axle production facility in Marysville; the plant employed 530 UAW members. To make matters worse, the county's largest pre-Honda employer, the agricultural supply manufacturer O. M. Scott, announced the laying off of several hundred workers.[36] All of these numbers took a serious toll on the employment picture of a county that as of January 1982 had a total labor force of about 14,000, 11.1 percent of which was already unemployed.[37] One of Nestlé's newly unemployed expressed her fears: "You lose a job and you can't believe it. I have no idea what I will do except pray and hope to God I can find a job."[38] The dark clouds of unemployment came to define daily life in central Ohio as Honda arrived.

Layoffs through 1982 and into 1983 devastated Marysville. Amid the avalanche of bad news, the *Journal-Tribune* reported that "Thousands Hope Honda Will Cure Area Unemployment Picture." For those recently laid off, "Honda could be a lifesaver." By August 1982 Honda had already received 10,000 job applications, three months before the MAP was set to start production. The *Journal-Tribune*'s editor pleaded with readers to get beyond the "negativism" plaguing the community in 1982. "Americans must think positive in times like these," Daniel Behrens wrote, in his sunny midwestern voice. "No matter how dark the picture is, it could be darker, and eventually a brighter day will return."[39]

"BABY SITTERS, STORE CLERKS AND FARM HANDS": WORKING AT HONDA

Such was the local economic picture when the press and public got their first look at the MAP in April 1983. Honda opened its doors for a week's worth of celebrations to officially inaugurate the plant that had produced its very first Accord, a slate-gray four-door model, on 1 November 1982.[40] Visiting reporters noted the hundreds of "young American workers in clean white uniforms and green and white caps." American and Japanese managers, too, wore the same pristine white coveralls as the workers, though they wore them over shirts and ties. According to the company, the goal of the uniforms was to emphasize unity and teamwork to both insiders and outsiders—a local manifestation of a management technique popularized in a flurry of recent "Japanese management" books and seminars in U.S. business schools. There was no separate executive cafeteria, workers addressed executives by first name, and management all shared the same large office space. "The entire operation here," described New York Times reporter Kenneth Noble in 1985, "has a Japanese flavor."[41] Calling both wageworkers and managers "associates," a practice adopted from the home office, illustrated that the company wanted workers to feel that they were a crucial part of the Honda experiment in Ohio. The practice, which aimed to erase the distinction between labor and management and to convince employees that their and the company's fates were one and the same, also hinted at the coming resistance to the UAW's unionization efforts.

The kinds of people Honda hired to make its cars struck observers as unlike those in similar U.S. production facilities and hinted at Honda's labor strategy for the area. Noble of the New York Times described striking homogeneity among an almost exclusively white workforce, drawn from a twenty-five- to thirty-mile radius around the plant, with an average age in the mid-twenties.[42] With so much surplus labor available in the Marysville area, much of it the product of layoffs at businesses that had been operating for many years, why would Honda hire the least experienced people from the available labor pool? Why so many young faces? Some speculated that it was a ploy on Honda's part to discourage unionization, a game plan replicated two years later at Nissan's plant in Smyrna, Tennessee. An older union sympathizer there claimed, "They hired a young, naïve workforce, the vast majority of whom had never been involved with the union, and Nissan has thrown propaganda at them from day one. . . . They really believe that this is the best place in middle Tennessee to work."[43] The same dynamic operated in Marysville. The New York Times' hypothetical twenty-five-year-old worker would have been born around 1960 to rural-working parents (that is, nonindustrial and nonunionized) and would have graduated high school in the late 1970s, just as Detroit's decline, and the concomitant troubles of national unions, made headlines. With the economic slowdown it was unlikely that he or she would have been hired in a large industrial firm in Union County before Honda's

The Honda Team.

Pictured here are a few of the growing number of people now working with Honda of America Manufacturing, Inc., in Marysville, Ohio.

Over the years they have shown that Honda can build its quality products in America. That's evident in the top-of-the-line Honda motorcycles made in America since 1979.

The reason is simple. Honda works the same way the world over.

Everyone who joins Honda becomes a member of a team sharing in a common goal. Quality.

To help achieve that goal, each person contributes individual skills and, equally important, innovative thinking.

At Honda, people are encouraged to seek out better ways of doing a job. The thought here is to instill pride in one's work.

Many of the people shown above have gone abroad to learn more about the

Honda way of teamwork at our automobile and motorcycle plant.

They will share their impressions and knowledge with their team members. That way Honda will continue to build quality products in America.

Honda motorcycles. And soon, Honda automobiles.

HONDA

ILL. 3.2. A 1982 Honda advertisement showed off the "Honda Team," the first generation of American workers hired to assemble Japanese-branded automobiles in the United States. (American Honda Motor/Logan County District Library, Bellefontaine, Ohio)

arrival. "Unemployment lines bulged with veteran autoworkers when Honda began building cars in America," noted an Associated Press article. "But the company hired baby sitters, store clerks and farm hands to assemble Accords at Marysville."[44] (The *Journal-Tribune* later criticized the author's characterization of Honda workers and Marysville in general, pointing out that the

(Good) Morning Again in Marysville

"story was written from an outsider's viewpoint," a theme that would resonate throughout Marysville's encounter with the UAW.)[45]

Fair characterization or not, the point was that the young white faces raised in rural Union County were not the UAW's traditional constituency—the national union's black membership averaged near 20 percent, for instance. Though Honda denied it, evidence indicates that the company avoided hiring workers with union experience or potential union sympathies, which would have eliminated many workers over the age of thirty from the applicant pool. Laid-off residents with union experience pointed out that they had sent résumés to Honda but had not received a call. One college-educated radio technician said, "I am reluctant to send a resume to them as I have been affiliated with unions," his assumption being that Honda was not hiring anyone with union experience.[46] The hiring process required potential associates to undergo several separate interviews with management, which included unusual questions that probed for "clues to their attitude toward work," giving managers a sense of who might sympathize with a unionization campaign. One UAW official trying to organize Honda's workers said, "You go through four screenings before they'll hire you, and they pretty well weed out anybody they don't want in those plants."[47] It was easier to find the sort of workers Honda wanted in rural central Ohio than in, say, urban northern Ohio or Michigan.

Honda explained that it preferred hiring the sons and daughters of farmers because, according to one Japanese executive, they are "extremely hard working and many are religious. They are also used to taking care of machines. In a sense, they have some better quality which Japanese workers in Japan do not possess." Honda's top American manager, Al Kinzer, echoed this sentiment: "Farm kids, kids who have grown up in a farm environment, tend to be your best workers."[48] There was a clear racial subtext to both comments, as the 1987 agricultural census showed black farmers operating a scant few farms across the entirety of Ohio. Visiting the town in the late 1980s to report on Honda's progress, journalist David Gelsanliter claimed that Japanese executives preferred the homogeneous local German American workforce because it was shaped by a "high-context culture" similar to that of Japan. "They like a high German content," one industry consultant who worked with Japanese firms said. "Germans have a good work ethic—well-trained, easy to train, they accept things."[49]

The near exclusivity of white faces at Honda led to charges of racism in hiring practices. The company decided on a hiring radius of twenty-five to thirty miles extending out on all sides of the MAP. This included all of

Union County and parts of Champaign, Logan, Hardin, and Marion Counties, but it stopped just short of the Columbus city limits, where the black population exceeded 20 percent. Honda used this radius, covering a largely rural and white area, to explain why only 2 percent of the workforce at the MAP was black. Following a 1988 study by the University of Michigan claiming that many Japanese corporations had systematically avoided establishing U.S. operations in areas with sizable black populations, the *New York Times* estimated that the MAP's black workforce was 2.8 percent while the black population of Honda's own defined hiring radius was actually 10.8 percent.[50] In 1987 a group of 370 women and African Americans filed a federal discrimination lawsuit against Honda. Each claimed that the company discriminated in either a hiring decision or an opportunity for promotion. In 1988 the Equal Employment Opportunity Commission, headed by future Supreme Court justice Clarence Thomas, negotiated a settlement worth $6 million, which awarded each of the complainants $16,000, but which also allowed Honda to sidestep acknowledgment of wrongdoing. This settlement followed an earlier one in which Honda paid $460,000 to a group of eighty-five people ages forty and older who claimed they were discriminated against based on their age.[51]

Some commentators explained that Honda's failure to hire African Americans was a result of persistent Japanese racism, most notoriously manifested in Prime Minister Yasuhiro Nakasone's comments about "lazy" African American workers.[52] But this accusation against Japanese companies, however accurate, would be missing the bigger picture. It is important to note that the Japanese were not making all or even most of the hiring decisions in Marysville; white managers, who knew the area and its residents well, were. It is difficult to imagine that the MAP's white managers would tolerate an explicitly racist hiring directive from Japanese executives. They would have been more likely, on the other hand, to follow an implicitly antiunion one. The added exclusion of older workers is significant because it suggests that management and executives identified African Americans and older candidates as potential union sympathizers. If Honda wanted to keep the UAW at bay, then there was no more effective starting place than in the hiring process, where Honda could filter out urban black workers (whose 20 percent representation in the UAW outpaced their representation in the U.S. population) and older workers (exposed to decades of union mythology, or even membership). It was an entirely unfair practice, to be sure, but one motivated as much by antiunion sentiments as racism, and explaining it only with the latter would mean acceding to the popular national discourse on the-Japanese-as-racists, echoing Michael Crichton's claim in *Rising Sun* that the Japanese were "the most racist people on earth." In the late 1980s researchers Robert E. Cole and Donald R. Deskins Jr. concluded that a location's black population was indeed one factor that Japanese firms used in site selection decisions, but they cautioned Americans to consider that there was no reason to believe U.S. companies would not make the same decisions in similar circumstances.[53]

Once workers made it onto Honda's payrolls, they encountered work on the line that differed from that in Big Three plants in important ways. In a plant operating under a UAW agreement, there were several hundred job classifications, and union contracts dictated that employers could not assign employees to work outside their classifications. At Marysville there were only two job classifications on the line: production associates and machine maintenance associates. Honda emphasized flexible training so that workers could install windshields one month, move to wheel mounting the next, and so on. The company said it valued providing workers with a holistic understanding of the production process. A Honda advertisement in the local newspaper, part of the public relations campaign of Honda's early years, told residents what work was like at the MAP: "At Honda, people are encouraged to seek out better ways of doing a job. The thought here is to instill pride in one's work."[54] Flexibility in training facilitated this goal, giving workers a sense that they understood the entire production process and were responsible for managing it. Managers encouraged workers to think about and propose ways that they could perform their tasks more efficiently. Workers received bonuses for suggestions managers adopted. This system replicated the "Japanese-style management" so lauded in business schools, and Honda's workers reported that the company valued their input in the production process. They appreciated regular meetings, for instance, with 96 percent of workers agreeing that it was "important to have meetings in which everyone's opinion is viewed in order to increase job efficiency."[55]

Another Japanese management technique made the voyage across the Pacific: the morning calisthenic exercises parodied in the 1986 film *Gung Ho*. The company reported that about 65 percent of the workers participated in the voluntary program. In Japanese plants the routine lasted five minutes; management in Ohio expected a more modest two minutes from American workers. Workers voted on the music to accompany their workout—the theme music from the popular television show *Magnum P.I.* defeated the themes from *The Rockford Files* and *Hill Street Blues*. One worker contracted his niece, an Ohio State University cheerleader, to design the routine. She brought the cheerleading squad in to perform several routines for the workers, who then voted on their favorite.[56]

Some workers were suspicious of Honda's claims of enthusiasm for these Japanese practices. "Some of the exercises are really dumb, like clapping your hands over your head," one worker told a reporter anonymously; as for Honda's claim of 65 percent participation, "it's nothing like that." Employees estimated that aerobics participation in the MMP was about 10 percent, while nearly one-third of MAP workers performed calisthenics each morning, but only because, resistant workers explained, hundreds of MAP employees had trained in Japan.[57] Of course, participation was voluntary, and the two-minute routine was just a flash in a long workday, but it nevertheless came to symbolize the different management approaches of the Japanese and Americans. Few seemed to complain about the other allegedly Japanese aspects of the operation, like the required uniforms, though in the first year workers and management battled over the right to wear hats with union logos. Most workers simply accepted these management quirks in exchange for highly coveted jobs. Even at the height of the UAW's contentious campaign to unionize Honda's workers, union supporters had to admit, as one pro-UAW welder did, that most workers were "really happy with the Japanese—they're pretty smart, and they know how to crank out cars."[58]

Much like the cars they produced, American workers and Japanese managers created a workplace that hybridized their respective labor practices and cultures. As part of her doctoral work at Ohio State University, sociologist Kinko Ito spent the mid-1980s trying to understand the ways in which the two groups adapted to each other at several workplaces in central Ohio. Her observations on communication in the Honda plant provide particular insight into the sincere efforts of both sides to connect across cultural boundaries. For instance, out of necessity managers and workers adopted linguistic shortcuts to make it easier to work with each other. American workers learned Japanese words like *wakarimasen* (I don't understand), *mah mah* (so-so), *hai* (yes), and *chotto* (a little bit). On the floor in the plant they adopted phrases like *chiri chiri on*, with *on* being the Japanese word for "sound" and *chiri chiri* an onomatopoeic phrase for the noise a misfiring engine might make.[59]

Japanese managers, on the other hand, often arrived in Ohio confident in their English language educations, but they quickly discovered they were unprepared for local nuances in pronunciation and idiomatic expression. Among their first on-the-job lessons was adjusting to the arsenal of four-letter swear words common in the vocabulary of workers on an assembly line. Workers told Ito that they learned to communicate with managers by speaking loudly and slowly, using a few simple words, avoiding informal contractions, listening carefully, using visual aids, and peppering conversations with the various Japanese words they had learned. As a rule, English was the official language in all meetings at Honda, even if there was only one American present among many Japanese. Some American workers and managers reported to Ito that they felt it was "inappropriate for the Japanese to speak in their mother tongue" and that this induced anxiety among the Americans. American managers and engineers also felt insecure when handling documents from the home office with Japanese-language characters on them. Even words the Americans understood could lead to miscommunication, as when Japanese managers used *hai* to indicate they were simply following along with a conversation while Americans interpreted the word to signal agreement.[60]

Ito also recorded revealing attitudes toward work during the anonymous interviews she conducted with Americans and the Japanese (the latter in Japanese). She received from American workers a positive impression of their experiences, hinting at some of the reasons why these same workers resisted unionization efforts. For instance, 91 percent of workers said they would recommend the job to a friend; 73 percent believed the compensation was satisfactory and 80 percent were satisfied with the benefits offered; and 68 percent wanted to work at Honda until they retired.[61] American foremen who directly oversaw the workforce and reported to Japanese managers noticed differences in work culture most acutely. One told Ito that the Japanese had to adjust to the "most spoiled labor force in the world," one that would rather go hunting or fishing than go to work, and that this contrasted sharply with the dedicated Japanese. One Japanese manager made the same observation but articulated it in a way that disparaged Japanese commitment and praised perceived American values. "I don't think Americans are selfish, or ego-centered," he said. "The Japanese sacrifice their time and family for overtime and work for the company, but the Americans do not want to sacrifice themselves. If they work, they work—because they want to."[62]

Honda used various means to inculcate "associates" with its corporate ideology, the "Honda Way," or "Honda-ism," as a 1982 corporate brochure put it.[63] Indoctrination began with Honda's screening process at hiring, through which the company created a homogenized workforce more amenable to company philosophies, according to Ito. Consequently the "majority of employees share the same attitudes, values, beliefs, and norms."[64] Then the company routinely sent workers to Japan for several weeks of training. Honda regularly advertised these trips in local newspapers with photographs of hundreds of smiling workers who had crossed the Pacific. This practice began even before production started at the MMP. Ten Marysville workers traveled to Honda's plant in Sayama, Japan, in August 1979 to, as associate Bob Simcox put it, "appreciate the quality of the product, learn mass production systems and learn the nature and customs of the Japanese people"—no small task for a mere three weeks. By September 1982, two months before the MAP's opening, Honda had already sent 130 workers to Japan for training. By the end of the decade more than 5,000 Ohio employees had visited Japan. Honda did not require workers to visit its operations in Japan, but many workers in Marysville nevertheless came to believe that making the transpacific journey was a prerequisite for promotion to managerial roles.[65]

Just as important as the skills these trips imparted to workers were the new experiences they provided—as many, both Americans and the Japanese, would note over the years, Tokyo was worlds away from central Ohio. It is likely that most of these working- and middle-class Ohioans traveling to Japan on Honda's dime would have never had the opportunity to do so without the Japanese company's support. Worker Steve Powell later said of his trip, "It was totally unreal for a country kid. You think the rest of the world lives the same way you do until you get there. It is very important to understand the culture."[66] The training trips let these workers know that they were such an important part of the Honda family that the company would spend lavishly to show them, literally and figuratively, what the new globalized world looked like. Honda benefited by introducing "country kids," who believed they had overcome a kind of provincialism, to a global perspective. Critics accused Japan of practicing a sort of economic colonialism by setting up shop in the United States; if that was the case in Marysville, it was a most benevolent sort, and it was winning workers' hearts and minds.[67]

"IN THIS ALIEN LAND THEY ARE DIFFERENT": THE JAPANESE IN OHIO

Outside Honda's gates, the company served as both an official and unofficial channel for cultural exchange between Marysville and Japanese families. When Honda announced the construction of the MAP in January 1980, it also quietly established the Honda Foundation with the purposes of promoting "youth education and U.S.-Japan cultural exchange" and building "cultural ties between the area and Japan." The Honda Foundation would provide funds for local schools where the children of Honda executives would enroll.[68] One of the foundation's first initiatives was a modest exhibit of traditional Japanese material culture. Some of Honda's Japanese employees contributed to the display, sponsored by the foundation and the Marysville Art League, featuring "children's toys, Japanese apparel, wood handicrafts, paper sculpture and tea ceremony accessories," as well as a showcase of the Japanese holiday of Kodomo no hi, or Children's Day.[69]

The Honda Foundation's more extravagant initiative entailed sending local elementary and high school teachers to Japan to "help American teachers better understand the cultural and education background of Japanese children," sensitizing teachers to the needs of the children of Honda's Japanese managers. Each year a half-dozen educators would tour Japanese schools and cultural attractions (and Honda factories) with the company paying their way. Of Honda's generosity, kindergarten teacher Betty Shipp said, "If there was anything you wanted and you asked for it . . . the next day you had it." Shipp returned to Marysville with unique experiences but also impressions of the Japanese education system that reflected pervasive American stereotypes of Japan. "The Japanese philosophy of education is that you improve yourself in order to improve the nation. . . . They consider [their knowledge] a virtue which they contribute to their nation." "Of course," she explained, "they have a more homogeneous feeling than the United States, being an island and all of one race." Marysville school superintendent Clayton Pebble spent time in Japan learning about the educational background of the twenty-five Japanese students under his care. The self-described "country boy" not only got a better sense of the experiences and expectations of Japanese schoolchildren but also had a once-in-a-lifetime tour of the country, which likely would have never happened for any of these exchangees had Honda not set up shop in Marysville.[70]

Less official channels for cultural exchange were the day-to-day interactions of the local community and Union County's new Japanese residents. In a town of roughly 8,000 people, it was difficult for locals to avoid bumping into one of their new Japanese neighbors.[71] They attended school district meetings, shopped in local stores ("It is surprising how much they spend and it is good they are spending their money in Marysville," said a local market manager), and even participated in the local choir group.[72] By most accounts the Marysville community was pleasantly accommodating to Japanese families. The Hiroshi Matsumoto family observed, "When you meet someone here walking down the street, people smile and say hi. It's a very good custom." The *Journal-Tribune* tried to introduce Japanese "transplants" to the community with personal stories and interviews, reflecting the community's interest in befriending the new residents. One article encouraged residents to put themselves in the shoes of the Matsumoto and Suzuki families: "Imagine for a moment that you have been picked up and deposited in another country. . . . Few people speak the language you were brought up with. At work, the communication barrier slows the process of expressing your thoughts, ideas and instruction. . . . Little habits and customs which you took for granted in your old home suddenly seem important to maintain, because in this alien land they are different."[73] The description echoed a *Shōgun* producer's comparison of John Blackthorne's adventure in Japan to "landing on an alien planet."

Most Japanese executives did not live in Marysville during Honda's first decade. When they arrived in the early 1980s, the town had few amenities to satisfy Japanese families accustomed to living in metropolitan Tokyo. Instead executives commuted from Columbus or the wealthy suburbs of Dublin and Worthington. More than 100 Japanese people also settled in Bellefontaine, to Marysville's northwest, where the population was about 50 percent greater than Marysville's in the 1980s (and where Ohio's first Walmart went up early in the decade). Japanese Honda families were not alone there—by the middle of the decade, 35 percent of all Honda's employees lived in Logan County (about 20 percent lived in Marysville city limits), which certainly factored into the decision to build the East Liberty plant there in 1989. Honda provided the funds for the International Friendship Center in Bellefontaine, which opened in 1986 and offered new Japanese residents a range of services, including a twenty-four-hour translator. The center also arranged hundreds of student exchanges between Ohio locals and Japanese children from Suzuka, Japan, where Honda's largest Japanese plant was located.[74]

Ironically, the growth of institutions to cater to the needs of the area's wealthy Japanese residents meant Japanese families came to rely on each other less than they had in Honda's first years. By the end of the decade it became convenient for Japanese women to call on Japanese centers in Bellefontaine, Marysville, Dublin, and Columbus rather than on each other. One wife of a Japanese executive recalled nostalgically the early years "when she and other Japanese women would take turns driving to Dayton for rice." Local stores popped up selling Japanese goods, and restaurants catered to Japanese tastes. Honda executives started calling Dublin "Honda *mura*" (town) for the unwritten corporate policy of settling new Japanese families there.[75]

While Honda executives—all men—felt pressure to produce at the plant, regularly working twelve or more hours each day, Japanese women experienced particular stresses and anxieties operating in an "alien" environment.[76] Japanese women did not work at the plant, and like most large Japanese corporations, Honda explicitly forbade executives' wives from working at all while overseas. If wives had taken English-language classes in Japanese schools, such classes were likely not adequate preparation for living in an English-only world. Once in Ohio, many felt obligated to fill the conventional role of homemaker, providing fewer opportunities for daily

(Good) Morning Again in Marysville

English-language interaction than husbands or children had. In 1992 writer Leila Philip interviewed, anonymously and in Japanese, a number of "Honda wives" and found one who admitted that even after eleven years in Ohio, she kept to her family and almost never spoke English. Executive salaries meant material comforts and free time for executives' wives, but "free time has not meant freedom, but a sense of isolation" for women who would have had no barriers to communication and opportunities to work back in Japan.[77]

Local schoolteachers noticed that Japanese mothers were often frustrated because they could not articulate their expectations for their children's educations. Betty Shipp, one of the teachers who visited Japan, used her experience to compile a list of practical recommendations for anxious Japanese mothers. School districts, flush with money from rapidly increasing tax revenues, provided special services for Japanese students. The Dublin school district, for instance, employed a full-time Japanese-language tutor for the eighty Japanese students it served in 1985.[78] Nevertheless, Japanese mothers worried their children would fall behind their peers in Japan. Ohio State University psychiatrist Hisako Koizumi studied these women and their children during Honda's first decade. She found children eager to learn English, make new friends, and adapt to new circumstances, while mothers told her of accepting their assignments in the United States with resignation. The women worried they and their children would become "too Americanized," and thus they resisted "completely assimilating." In fact, half of the Japanese women Koizumi interviewed reported that they simply did not speak to Americans at all.[79]

The educational anxieties of Japanese parents, combined with a state government mindful of Honda's success and eager for more Japanese business, led to a proposal for a special state-sponsored Japanese language school for the children of foreign executives. Japanese instructors would teach a Japanese-style curriculum to prevent an unfortunate education trend for transplant students: for every two years spent in a U.S. school, students lost one year in a Japanese school.[80] Few Japanese Honda families planned on permanent relocations; most anticipated three- to five-year stays. Parents worried that their children would miss the crucial cultural and language education they would have received in Japan. Betty Shipp explained that "parents don't want their children to forget that they are Japanese. That way, when they go back to Japan, they still have the culture."[81]

The state school never materialized, but area parents had already been working for several years to address these concerns. Several parents who had settled in nearby Columbus founded what would eventually become the Columbus Japanese Language School. In April 1980 three instructors taught fourteen children. By the second decade of the twenty-first century, more than 500 local Japanese students gathered on Saturdays "in an atmosphere close to that of their home country" that was "conducive to their becoming successful members of Japanese society." Honda executives dominated the school's board of directors.[82] The school's creation and success reflected the cultural tensions pushing and pulling on Marysville's Japanese transplants.

"I THINK YOU CAN UNDERSTAND": ANTI-JAPANESE RACISM IN MARYSVILLE

While rarely overt, anti-Japanese racism was nevertheless a persistent concern, both for the Japanese who experienced it and for the local leaders who tried to downplay it, cognizant that it could drive away Honda and its thousands of jobs. One curious reporter from Akron speculated that it only took place "quietly in the bars and in the graffiti of the Honda plant restrooms." "I'm not a Jap lover," a local bartender told him. "But I'm not a Jap hater, either." Overhearing the conversation, a patron complained that the Japanese did nothing for the community because they "don't spend their money here," a claim other accounts contradicted. "Why the hell are we doing all this for a foreign company?" one Marysville resident asked a *Wall Street Journal* reporter, who wrote about the angry local reaction to a Columbus paper publishing an image of a large Japanese flag rising behind an aerial view of the town.[83] "I think they should have stayed in Japan," said Chuck Riedmiller. "They're running the American people out of business." Riedmiller's opinion in particular carried some weight in Marysville. Japanese forces captured Riedmiller and tens of thousands of U.S. and local soldiers in the Philippines in April 1942. They then marched him and the others more than sixty miles across the Bataan peninsula and toward prisoner-of-war camps. Thousands died on the way as a result of neglect or abuse from Japanese soldiers, and later an Allied military commission would label the Bataan Death March a war crime. "I was a prisoner of the Japanese for 43 months, so I think you can understand," Riedmiller explained to a local reporter.[84]

Those of Riedmiller's generation did not accept Honda's arrival as easily as their children and grandchildren did. "You'll always have some people who spent part of their youth in the South Pacific, who just won't like the Japanese, period," Union County commissioner Glenn Irwin said in 1984.[85] One of those young people was William Leitz. He survived the Japanese sinking of a U.S. Navy destroyer and spent weeks in a hospital bed. Three decades later he would be elected mayor of Wapakoneta, Ohio, a town of some 9,000 people a dozen miles north of Honda's Anna Engine Plant. In April 1988 he resigned in

(Good) Morning Again in Marysville

protest of Honda's growing presence in Ohio. "I don't hate (the Japanese) at all," he told a local reporter, "but I just don't want to have anything to do with them personally." Leitz's fellow mayor Gene Joseph of the nearby small city of Lima sparked calls for his own resignation when he joined Leitz in voicing criticism of Honda, particularly for its policy of avoiding "communities with sizable black populations and strong union traditions."[86]

Most local leaders, however, made a point of emphasizing that their communities welcomed Japan's corporate émigrés enthusiastically, if only because leaders knew the value of the unprecedented wealth Honda brought to a region battered by the recession early in the decade. "I think Honda's done just about everything right," said Marysville mayor Thomas Kruse in 1990. "They came into the community and considered the environment, they considered our way of life." Bellefontaine mayor Richard Vicario echoed Kruse's sentiments, describing the local Japanese residents as "so gracious, so polite and so well-mannered, and the community has just opened its arms and accepted them." Vicario pointed out that British and German companies also invested heavily in the United States, but he heard no grumbling about a European invasion. "We were all something originally," he said. "I don't know of anybody who didn't have somebody come here on a boat from somewhere. We're all ethnic."[87]

If there was any lingering anti-Japanese sentiment, stemming from World War II for the older generation or from recent trade conflicts for the younger, it remained subterranean. When talking to Japanese or Marysville residents, reporters from both local and national newspapers frequently asked about racial hostility. Rarely did they uncover anything to report. Bellefontaine residents Keiko Namiki and Hitomi Maeda each reported incidents—harassing phone calls in Namiki's case and "eggs thrown at my car and mailbox" in Maeda's—but both dismissed racist motivations; "that happens to anybody," Maeda said. "It doesn't happen because I'm Japanese."[88] Such a reaction was not unexpected from a group eager to ingratiate itself to its new neighbors in an unfamiliar region. Many local residents really did seem willing to please the new arrivals, though, and within a half decade of the MAP's opening, former Honda critics were already complaining that too few of the hundreds of Japanese in the area lived within Marysville's city limits.[89]

What distinguished Japanese families migrating to central Ohio from so many immigrant groups in U.S. history was their wealth—virtually all the Japanese brought upper-middle-class incomes. The class status of Japanese émigrés thus helped mitigate anti-Japanese racism. There were other factors as well. Japanese families settling within Honda's hiring radius in the 1980s meant fewer than 1,000 Japanese people in an area with a population approaching

100,000. Even in Dublin, "Honda *mura*," where most Japanese transplants settled, they accounted for only 2.6 percent of the population by 2010, and that
same figure was less than 1 percent in Marysville.[90] The area's Japanese rep-
utation was thus out of proportion to the actual Japanese presence. There is
the additional evidence, both anecdotal and quantitative, that many Japanese
women simply chose to avoid engaging with the local white community. Local
residents also knew that Japanese transplants typically came to the region only
temporarily and most intended to return to Japan after several years.

Most important, overt anti-Japanese racism threatened real economic
opportunities. Had it been pervasive, it would have ended Honda's Ohio experiment and cost the region thousands of jobs. In that sense Honda's executives
were in a rare position of power for an ethnic minority population. Throughout U.S. history, racism functioned as more than simple prejudice against one
minority group or another. It structured institutional power. Anti-black racism,
for instance, historically worked to the material benefit of white Americans by
excluding the black population from opportunities in political, economic, and
social institutions. But while racism lingered from decades past when workers
uttered "Jap" in the plant in Marysville—"you know, anybody would say that,"
said one American foreman—the local white community recognized how costly
it would be to systematize such thinking and how doing so would end their own
access to valuable new economic institutions.[91] The calculus of anti-Japanese
racism in central Ohio never added up, and local white leaders worked to ensure
that outsiders saw any manifestation of it as marginal and vestigial.

CONCLUSION: "THE GOOD OL' U.S. OF H."

Like Sony, Honda has excelled at crafting its own globalizing mythology, and
the company embedded that narrative in its Ohio operations from the start.
"One could not put a country on him; you could not label him 'Japanese,'" said
Honda vice president Susan Insley about company founder Soichiro Honda,
echoing descriptions of Sony's Akio Morita. "He is international. He thinks
internationally. And I believe that outlook permeates Honda."[92] When the
Marysville Honda Heritage Center, a gleaming museum celebrating Honda's
U.S. and global accomplishments, opened its doors to the public in 2015, it represented the company's most recent effort to define the role it has played locally
and nationally. It has always tried to do so in its promotional materials. Honda
provoked a local reaction in Ohio in 1982, for instance, when it tried to publicize
the opening of the MAP with an advertisement that showed a map of sixteen
states condensed into one country, "The good ol' U.S. of H.," an illustration of

(Good) Morning Again in Marysville

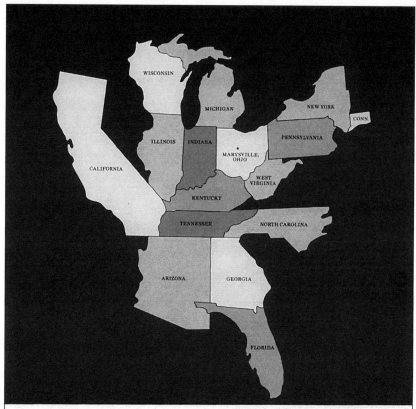

The good ol' U.S. of H.

Honda has united these states to form a network of suppliers to furnish parts and equipment to build new cars in Marysville, Ohio. Our supply lines stretch from California to Connecticut.

Right now, we're negotiating with more than forty top North American companies to provide materials for our new automobile manufacturing plant.

Whenever possible, we plan to use local suppliers. Because that's the way we like to do business.

Our first priority is quality. Because ©1982 American Honda Motor Co., Inc.

that's the way we build Honda automobiles.

Honda of America Manufacturing, Inc. invested 250 million dollars to build our first automobile plant in America. We consider it a part of our continuing American investment.

By the end of this year, we'll be spending millions on locally produced products. On steel, rubber, paint and more.

Most of the machines we will use to build Honda Accords will be made in America, too. For example, our stamping machines are made in Illinois. And our

state-of-the-art painting system comes from Michigan.

At Honda, we believe that by investing in the American economy, we become even more a part of the society we serve.

We also believe the economy is best served by investing in society.

Honda is creating jobs and putting people to work in the mid-Ohio area.

People from the good ol' U.S. of A.

HONDA

ILL. 3.3. A 1982 Honda advertisement, "The good ol' U.S. of H.," caused controversy in Marysville, where local residents were already sensitive to the recent decline in U.S. manufacturing and concurrent success of Japan. (American Honda Motor/Logan County District Library, Bellefontaine, Ohio)

the various U.S. locations that Honda's global strategy connected. "They didn't need to do that," said Marysville mayor Thomas Nuckles. "They're trying to put the American flag over Honda, and I remember something my daddy once told me: if you have to stop and tell people what you are, you probably aren't."[93]

(Good) Morning Again in Marysville

Our American dream.

Our dream began with a decision we made in 1974. To plan to build an auto manufacturing plant in America.

After all, we've always been known as American Honda. Which is an American corporation. And therefore, an American investment.

So making Honda cars in America was simply the next logical step.

Building overseas is how Honda has built its company. By joining hands with the local community, we become even more a part of the society we serve. And the economy we work in.

Being there makes us closer to people. And more aware of their needs. So we can respond to those needs as times change.

Our experience with the American worker gives us the confidence we need. We know we can build quality products here. Because we're already building them in our new motorcycle manufacturing plant in Marysville, Ohio.

Now after six years of planning and work, our dream is finally coming true.

We've broken ground for the construction of our new auto plant. Right next door to our motorcycle plant.

Honda will be the first Japanese car made in America.

And the first domestic car built like a Honda.

HONDA
Let's build together.

ILL. 3.4. A 1982 Honda advertisement, "Our American dream," demonstrated the various ways Honda would attempt to brand itself as an "American" car company in the decades to come. (American Honda Motor/Logan County District Library, Bellefontaine, Ohio)

Starting now. Made over here.

Our dream has come true. The first Honda Accords are rolling off the assembly line at our new automobile manufacturing plant in Marysville, Ohio. It has taken us eight years of planning and work, and an investment of over $250 million before we could make this announcement. From now on, they won't be made *just* over there. Now they are made over here. **HONDA**

© 1982 American Honda Motor Co., Inc.

ILL. 3.5. A 1982 Honda advertisement, "Starting now. Made over here," showcased the classic Honda aesthetic—plenty of white space, clear bold lettering, a few declarative words—in service of announcing the company's U.S. manufacturing arrival. (American Honda Motor/Logan County District Library, Bellefontaine, Ohio)

Was Honda then and is the company now "American"? That question lost much of its meaning in the late twentieth century. As early as the 1970s, each of Detroit's Big Three sourced significant quantities of parts outside the United States, sometimes even assembling vehicles beyond U.S. borders, such that by the turn of the century Honda produced models with far more U.S.-born content than many models with "American" labels like Chevrolet, Ford, and Chrysler. When Chrysler launched a new ad campaign, "Imported from Detroit," during the 2011 Super Bowl, it was met with a backlash from various organizations pointing out that the company assembled only one vehicle model in Detroit but assembled several others in Ontario—not to mention the many parts sourced from overseas. A year later the same backlash hit Republican presidential candidate Mitt Romney, a former Massachusetts governor but a native son of Detroit: he ran campaign ads in Michigan in which he drove around the state, waxing nostalgically, in a Chrysler assembled in Canada.[94]

Just outside of Detroit, housed in the Henry Ford Museum, alongside the landmark automobiles built by the Wizard of Dearborn himself, sits the four-door slate-gray 1983 Honda Accord that rolled off the production line first in Marysville on 1 November 1982—not a Japanese car, not an American car, but instead a hybrid monument to the global transformation of the U.S. economic, social, and cultural landscape in the late twentieth century.

FOUR

Ohayō II

Japanese Transplants and the UAW's Global Squeeze

By the end of the 1980s, Hondas in Ohio were Ohio-made, but that did not instill pride in all Ohioans. A statewide television game show from the era, *Cash Explosion Double Play*, produced by the Ohio Lottery, made a point of giving contestants Ohio-produced prizes. When thirty-nine-year-old Pamela Richards found herself in the winner's circle on 3 August 1990, she had a choice: she could take $1,000 and continue trying her luck on the show, or she could bow out with a big-ticket item, a 1991 Honda Accord, made in Marysville, valued at $17,600. "I don't want that Honda," she said quickly into the microphone, "I'm union."[1]

Fearing the remark might offend one of the show's sponsors and a major Ohio employer, the producers decided to edit out Richards's rejection when the show aired the next night. But word nevertheless spread, both of Richards's refusal and its censoring, which the Ohio Lottery director later characterized as "an overzealous attempt to avoid controversy." Within days Richards became a minor national labor celebrity, eventually earning the nickname "Mrs. UAW." She had worked as a member of the union for more than two decades at Toledo Precision Machining, which manufactured parts for Chrysler. "I'd do the same thing again," she told the local press. "We don't buy Honda products. The union has given me a lot through the years. A lot of benefits, wage increases, security when I retire. I feel if they could give me this all these years, I can buy union-made products." Her new notoriety led to a flood of union-made gifts. Never one to miss an opportunity to trash a Japanese company, Chrysler's Lee Iacocca gave Richards a 1991 Plymouth Acclaim, while a dealer in West Virginia loaned her a Chrysler Imperial for a year, and the AFL-CIO flew her to its headquarters in Washington, D.C., where the organization rewarded Richards with a brand-new Dodge Dakota pickup truck.

Richards struck a nerve with union members and sympathizers locally and nationally. Marysville residents were watching too, however, as she began traveling the country speaking to audiences of workers. One night a wife of a Honda worker in Marysville called with some harsh words for Richards (though, in classic midwestern fashion, she called back several hours later to apologize). "I have nothing against the people of Marysville," Richards said. "They got jobs at a time when they needed them. I'd just rather that they be union."[2]

Joseph Tomasi wanted those jobs to be union too. As Region 2B director, he was the top UAW official in Ohio through Honda's first decade in the state. The critical task of organizing the first Japanese-owned U.S. auto production facility thus fell to him. Honda repeatedly frustrated Tomasi during its first years in Marysville. The company publicly proclaimed neutrality on the union question, but its actions contradicted that pledge. It denied its "associates" the right to wear UAW hats and pins while on the job until the National Labor Relations Board ruled against Honda. After the Marysville plant's four powerhouse operators voted unanimously to join the UAW in 1981, Honda refused to recognize the union as the workers' bargaining agent. And despite the painful layoffs in the auto industry in Ohio in the early 1980s, Honda's hiring practices screened out former union members or even anyone with potential union sympathies. As the opening of the Marysville Auto Plant loomed in 1982, frustrated union leaders like Tomasi decided it was time for dramatic action.

In April, Tomasi had arranged to meet with his counterpart, Honda of America vice president Shige Yoshida, in Findlay, Ohio, a small city halfway between Tomasi's office in Toledo and Yoshida's in Marysville. The union leader drove south armed with a formidable bargaining chip: over the previous weeks the UAW had "prepared to launch the largest national labor dispute campaign in its history," an aggressive nationwide boycott of Honda, which aimed to force the Japanese company to recognize the right of all its Ohio workers to union representation. The four powerhouse operators planned to strike, and UAW members would rally outside the Marysville plant, led by President Doug Fraser, while also picketing at Honda parts warehouses and hundreds of dealerships nationwide. UAW leaders had arranged with the longshoremen's union at West Coast ports to refuse to unload Hondas from cargo ships, a potentially disastrous scenario for a company with only a couple weeks' worth of U.S. inventory. The union's $400 million strike fund stood ready to serve as a war chest for a protracted battle in the press.[3] Union leaders assembled a "coordinator kit" with detailed daily instructions that would have gone to hundreds of local boycott coordinators around the country. In his characteristic midwestern voice, Tomasi would later describe the union's plans as "probably the most massive job that has ever been done in the boycott area."[4]

The threat worked. "We were able to throw sufficient fear into the Honda people," Tomasi reported to the union's international executive board.[5] Considering he got everything he asked for—more, even—the meeting's outcome exceeded his expectations. Tomasi and Yoshida signed an agreement, the details of which the company and the union kept secret from the public, that recognized the UAW as the bargaining agent for the powerhouse workers, acknowledged workers' rights to wear union logos, and, most important, stated that the company "will advise its Associates that it is not opposed to the UAW becoming bargaining agent for its Associates and will guide the Associates to recognize the need for UAW representation."[6] In essence, Honda agreed not only to remain neutral on the question of unionization, as it had repeatedly promised in public, but also to encourage its employees to join the UAW, an agreement made and kept behind closed doors.

More than three decades later, with dozens of nonunion Japanese-owned plants dotting the American landscape, the April 1982 agreement seems lost to history. Honda certainly did not—and, if anyone even remembers it today, still does not—want to acknowledge its existence. As prospects for organizing Honda's workers dimmed in the years that followed, UAW leaders debated how best to force Honda to live up to its end of the bargain. The challenge for the UAW, however, was that revealing the precise wording of the agreement would open the union up to accusations of negotiating a "sweetheart" backroom deal with an employer without input from the employees it would represent. In the wake of the eventual failed organizing drive at the end of 1985, UAW officials considered suing Honda for violating what was essentially a signed contract. "I would dearly love to sue Honda for reneging on our April, 1982 Agreement because their conduct is so absolutely frustrating," wrote UAW associate general counsel Leonard Page to union president Owen Bieber, several months after the UAW withdrew its election petition in Marysville. But Page worried that antiunion elements from the insurgent "right-to-work" movement would use the document to embarrass the union.[7]

Union leaders debated suing Honda because by 1986 they felt they had run out of options. At the end of 1985 the union withdrew its NLRB petition for a vote on unionization, ostensibly because of an array of allegedly unfair labor practices in the weeks leading up to the election but in reality because the UAW simply did not have the support of workers at Honda. When they signed the April 1982 agreement with Honda, Tomasi and UAW leaders believed company interference had been responsible for the lack of union enthusiasm. But in the three years after Yoshida committed to helping the union organize Honda's employees, UAW leaders discovered it was in fact not an adversarial Japanese company but the local Ohio workforce that stood against unionization. Unlike Nissan, which arrived in Smyrna, Tennessee, with an aggressive antiunion agenda several years later, Honda's executives had anticipated eventually working with the union until they recognized widespread anti-UAW sentiment among their workers and the local population. A grassroots anti-UAW organization, the "Associates Alliance," successfully campaigned to reject unionization. To these workers the UAW appeared out of touch with the local transformations wrought by global capital, courtesy of a Japanese company.

Contrary to the claims of its critics, the UAW did not pursue reactionary policies in response to Japanese competition. In fact, its leadership articulated a progressive global vision of a world of transnational capital flowing across borders and into the pockets of unionized workers. The union even stood among the earliest proponents of Japanese transplants to the United States. But despite its progressive stance, the UAW experienced the squeeze of global capital and local culture in Marysville that resulted in its defeat by an unlikely alliance between a "foreign" corporation and a rural American community. Annually increasing imports from Japan (and, to a much lesser extent, Germany) were just one aspect of a "multinational squeeze-play," as the union called it in 1980, that also included excessive corporate greed in Detroit, which left U.S. companies unprepared for the smaller car market, and the Big Three's sourcing of parts abroad from producers employing inexpensive nonunion labor, a practice already well under way in the 1970s.[8] With the Big Three to blame for autoworker unemployment eclipsing 30 percent, the prospect of Japanese automakers employing tens of thousands of Americans far outweighed any cheap nationalist sentiments. Cooperating with Japan was thus central to the union's strategy at the beginning of this fateful decade.

The irony of the UAW's global squeeze of the 1980s was that the union got most of what it wanted and nevertheless continued to suffer. The Japanese transplants came—indeed, the union took credit for it—but they never hired UAW members. The Japanese government imposed "voluntary restraints" on imports in 1981, in response to pressure from the Reagan administration and the union, which had repeatedly and fruitlessly requested the same of the Carter administration, but U.S. automakers continued to lay off workers. And while the UAW's chief legislative goal of the decade, a "local content" bill that would have imposed fines on automakers whose vehicles did not contain a certain percentage (pegged to domestic sales) of U.S.-made parts, never became law, the issue was moot by the end of the 1980s, with Japanese transplants peppered across the American landscape and more planning to follow. At the beginning of the decade, Japanese automakers, including Honda, assumed they would have to cooperate with unions in the United States if they intended to produce there. But by the end of the decade, after the UAW's public failures first in Marysville and then in Smyrna, those automakers established new facilities confident they could ignore the once-powerful union.

It was not unreasonable of the UAW, then, to assume that only UAW members' hands would ever assemble automobiles in the United States. Instead, what the union failed to anticipate was the ways in which late twentieth-century globalization could produce new, unexpected political and cultural alliances between local communities and global actors independent of influential national industrial organizations. The UAW could not foresee that the residents of Marysville, a small, rural town in the American heartland, would side with a foreign corporation, let alone one transplanted from Japan, a former enemy once despised within living memory. In the wake of a crushing recession, the future promises of globalized capital proved more powerful than appeals to a fading past of national industrial glory.

"WE ARE NOT SO SURE WHO WE ARE SUPPOSED TO BE FIGHTING": THE UAW AND JAPAN-BASHING

As Tomasi sat down with Honda's Yoshida in Findlay in April 1982, he had more than a union contract on his mind. A year earlier he had written to several members of Ohio's congressional delegation, including Senator John Glenn, about the threat that Japanese auto imports posed to U.S. industry. Ostensibly prompted by the U.S. Army's purchase of forty Datsun light trucks—"I believe it is not only insensitive, stupid and asinine," Tomasi wrote, "I would even term it *Un-American*"—Tomasi connected present challenges to his past experience in World War II. "I spent 30 months in the Pacific fighting from Attu to Okinawa," he wrote, only to discover that after the war the United States "made industrial giants out of our enemies."[9]

Tomasi's letter hinted at a generational conflict in the "Battle of Marysville." Observers of Honda's growth in the town frequently commented that Honda hired young people, and the company reported that the average age of its workers was in the mid-twenties. The UAW leaders plotting the campaign in Marysville, on the other hand, like Tomasi, were old enough to be the grandparents of these young workers, members of the "Greatest Generation" that had weathered a depression and won a global war against fascism. But it was hard to forget a savage war fought for years against an intractable enemy. In meetings of the union's executive board, union leaders often drew upon their experiences in the Pacific as a way of interpreting Japanese behavior; one could expect nothing less from a generation shaped by one of history's greatest conflicts. But one also could not fault Honda for wanting to distance itself from that generation, nor could one blame the younger generation in Union County, desperate for work, for trying to dissociate from their older parents and grandparents, who risked dragging them back to a war the young had not fought.

But the war would not go away. Pearl Harbor and the atomic bombing of Hiroshima and Nagasaki lived in union conversations about how to deal with Japanese competition. The union's executive board erupted in laughter at a 1979 meeting, for instance, when one member suggested that, in dealing with Kawasaki's union-busting at a Nebraska motorcycle plant, campaign organizers should have distributed a leaflet with a simple message: "Remember Pearl Harbor."[10] A few months later, while discussing Honda's plans to build in the United States, board member Jerry Whipple was "surprised that when we talk about the Japanese, we say that we are going to take their word. If I remember, we took their word before Pearl Harbor."[11] The Japanese remained a people capable of sneak attacks. In an instance of startling unintentional irony, one union leader planning the aborted 1982 Honda boycott sketched up a possible pamphlet with several versions of a UAW Pac-Man (the world-famous video game star, a creation of Japanese game designer Toru Iawatani and the Japanese company Namco). In one version, Pac-Man gobbled up the phrase "Honda Sucks!," while another urged the Japanese company to "Pac It Up"; a third was captioned "Amer[ican] Work[ers] Eat Up Honda." On its reverse side was a simple sketch of a mushroom cloud.[12]

The persistence of war metaphors also highlighted the union's struggle to walk the tenuous line between economic confrontation and racial animosity. Instructions to boycotters cautioned them to "avoid any anti-Japanese comments or race baiting conversation." Leaders warned, "Any handbiller who makes any racial epithets should be removed immediately and sent home. We will not tolerate racism." Such instructions were necessary because anti-Japanese racism was not uncommon among the union's rank and file. In anticipation of the boycott, Lee Price of the union's Research Department

Japanese Transplants and the UAW's Global Squeeze

wrote a confidential March 1982 memo outlining a strategy to avoid both actual racist statements and policies and the perception of racist attitudes among the union's membership. In the post-1960s United States, institutional statements about race had to be managed carefully. The union could even benefit from promoting progressive attitudes, he argued. "We cannot avoid mentioning Japan in making our arguments," Price wrote. "But we need not mention race, physical features, ethnic slurs, or World War II." In fact, he speculated that it "could even be a big *plus* for the UAW to take 'affirmative action' to stem racist and chauvinist attitudes."[13]

Price pitched an argument in favor of international worker solidarity, a remarkably progressive case in the context of monthly autoworker layoffs that Detroit's Big Three blamed on Japanese imports:

> To the extent that there is an "us" versus "them," it is not Americans versus Japanese. On the one hand, Ichiro Shioji (head of the Japanese auto workers) and many in the Japanese government have supported major U.S. investment by their "Big Three" for several years. On the other hand, decisions to import into the U.S. are made by companies, all of which—U.S., Japanese, German or French—are concerned uppermost with profit. . . .
>
> We have a good economic and political case for getting companies based abroad to invest heavily here. . . . We should make every effort not to blow it by letting the UAW become associated with racism in the minds of Congress, the media, and ultimately the public. If our political effort succeeds, the public's perception of and attitude toward the Japanese will improve in the next decade, much as they have improved toward Germans in the last decade.[14]

Price's memo revealed that, in contrast to critics' charges, many in the UAW leadership not only wished to avoid antagonizing Japanese corporations but even wanted to work to improve the United States' relationship with foreign automakers.

The leadership was not the union's rank and file, however, and some critics have claimed that the union's leaders struggled to control members' baser instincts toward anti-Japanese racism, or that they even relished popular economic nationalism.[15] There are reasons to be skeptical, though, of generalizations about the attitudes of hundreds of thousands of workers throughout the country. Tommy Blackman, president of UAW Local 816 in Dallas, for example, directly challenged GM president F. James McDonald's anti-Japanese rhetoric in a lengthy 1981 letter to McDonald.[16] Blackman wrote in response to a GM pamphlet distributed to its workforce that attempted to place blame for company layoffs on Japanese imports. McDonald had warned that Japanese competition meant GM was "in a fight for our very existence" and that the solution was for management and labor to "put aside traditional adversarial relationships—the we-and-they syndrome—and join hands to meet the challenge of foreign competition together." Blackman scolded McDonald for underestimating the intelligence of GM's workers, who "see our plants packed full of General Motors parts made in Japan by Isuzu, made in Mexico by GM, made in Brazil, made in Germany . . . etc." He also noted that GM dealerships increasingly doubled as dealers for Japanese brands. "You have worked hard to convince the public and GM workers that them bad ol' Japanese workers are eating our lunches," he wrote, "but we can read between the lines"—GM's management was eager to soak up the earnings of decades of profit, but when hard times came the workers bore the burdens. "Auto Workers are ready and willing to compete," he concluded, "but we are not so sure who our aggressors are and we are not so sure who we are supposed to be fighting."[17]

Blackman was among the many union leaders and members who frequently stated that their international solidarity with Japanese autoworkers took precedence over their loyalty to greedy U.S. corporations. In the UAW's early years, wrote union member Al Davidoff from New York, Detroit's corporations had tried to divide autoworkers by race; the UAW responded by creating a "union of all colors"—a generous if not wholly accurate interpretation of the union's complicated history of racial inclusion and exclusion. The Japanese autoworkers were allies, not enemies, in creating a global system of fair trade, so it was "the multinational corporations that our anger (and our bumper stickers) must focus on."[18]

It is inaccurate, then, to characterize the UAW's response to Japanese competition as wholly nationalistic and xenophobic or to use the popular media image of the autoworker smashing a Toyota with a sledgehammer as a stand-in for the attitudes of an entire workforce. In her book *Buy American*, for instance, Dana Frank claims that the union toed the Big Three's anti-Japanese, economic nationalist line and failed to "read the global handwriting on the wall" and adjust to a new post-1960s era of global capital.[19] On the contrary, UAW records highlight that its leaders in the early 1980s were global-minded. They worked closely with their Japanese counterparts, the Jidosha Soren, the national umbrella organization for Japanese autoworkers, and they argued repeatedly that solidarity with Japanese workers was more important than loyalty to the incompetent executives managing failing U.S. auto companies. UAW president Doug Fraser told fellow members of the union's executive

Japanese Transplants and the UAW's Global Squeeze

board in 1977 that "the world is indeed getting smaller. That's not a cliché. That's what is happening in our world, and we have to give more attention to world affairs if we are going to represent our membership adequately."[20] The challenges of a globalizing world demanded greater worker solidarity across international borders.

To claim that the UAW simply reproduced the aggressively anti-Japanese rhetoric spewing from the mouths of Big Three bosses like that of Chrysler's Lee Iacocca would be unfair to the UAW. Throughout the late 1970s, Fraser articulated explanations for and solutions to the import problem that criticized corporate heads in both Detroit and Japan. He blamed Detroit for failing to make cars that appealed to U.S. consumers in an age of limits and thought haggling over high tariffs limiting U.S. auto exports to Japan, a favorite Big Three complaint, was a waste of time, since even without artificial trade barriers Japanese consumers did not want Detroit's clunkers. Fraser did not blame Japanese automakers for making cars Americans wanted to buy. Instead, as early as 1977, he and other UAW leaders urged those automakers to build production facilities in the United States. For these union bosses, a job with a Japanese automaker was as good as a job with a U.S. automaker, particularly since Fraser and his team assumed every Japanese-owned assembly plant would eventually operate under a UAW contract. In July 1977—two and a half years before Honda announced its plans for an assembly plant in Ohio—UAW vice president Pat Greathouse told an audience of Japanese industrial workers that their employers needed to build in the United States. "We at the UAW are not economic nationalists. . . . We cannot have world trade and closed borders," he said. "It is in this spirit that we strongly suggest the establishment of Japanese auto production facilities in the U.S."[21] A year later, during another regular visit to Japan, Greathouse "urged Honda to use Japanese managerial methods" when setting up U.S. operations, claiming that "this consultation method was preferable to the 'adversary' approach" that characterized U.S. labor-management relations.[22]

In short, the UAW was among the earliest and loudest boosters of the Japanese transplants, traveling to Japan and encouraging "offshoring" to the United States at the same moment entrepreneurial governors like Ohio's Rhodes courted Japanese CEOs. "Why Not a Datsun Made in Detroit? Or a Toyota from Texas?" asked the union's monthly magazine, Solidarity, in 1982. "Import Jobs, Not Cars," the ad demanded. Another, titled "Send Us Factories Instead of Cars," asked, "Will the day come when a U.S. motorist can slip behind the wheel of a new Toyota or Datsun and find the words 'Made in America' stamped on the instrument panel?"[23] By that point—just months

Why Not a Datsun Made in Detroit?
Or a Toyota from Texas?

Volkswagen builds cars in Pennsylvania and Honda will soon open an assembly plant in Ohio.

That makes sense. But it's only a beginning. Japan-based auto firms have a $13-billion market here, yet 99% of Japanese cars sold here are made in Japan. Meanwhile, over a quarter-million of our autoworkers are jobless. The Japan-based companies ought to open plants here and provide jobs and income where their market is.

That's why the UAW supports domestic auto content legislation. Content legislation would require companies that sell a lot of cars in this country to build some of them here.

Consumers still would enjoy the wide variety and choice now available, and domestic automakers still would benefit from the competitive spur of foreign-based companies.

Support for domestic auto content legislation is picking up

momentum. Over 220 Representatives and Senators in the U.S. Congress have endorsed it. it's estimated a content law could result in 868,000 jobs created or saved in this country by 1985 — jobs we need in Michigan and Missouri, Kentucky and California, and throughout the entire country.

Support domestic auto content legislation. Help put the "Made in U.S.A." tag on Datsuns, Toyotas, and other models sold here.

Auto Content Legislation: Import Jobs, Not Cars.

Support the Fair Practices in Automotive Products Act (H.R. 5133 and S. 2300).
Write your Representative (c/o House Office Building, Washington, D.C. 20015)
And your U.S. Senators (c/o Senate Office Building, Washington, D.C. 20510)
to express your support for this legislation.

ILL. 4.1. The back page of the June 1982 issue of *UAW Solidarity* encouraged union members to write congressional representatives in support of domestic content legislation. The union believed such laws would encourage more foreign-owned manufacturers to set up operations in the United States. In the case of Marysville, however, Honda used the union's support to scare employees into rejecting the union. (United Auto Workers/Walter P. Reuther Library, Wayne State University)

before the MAP began production—the union had been singing the same song for at least half a decade. It got what it wanted when Honda arrived in Marysville, or so it thought.

"WOULDN'T PATRIOTISM WORK?": THE MARYSVILLE STRATEGY

Shortly after the Marysville Motorcycle Plant started operations in 1979, Tomasi complained of trouble with the organizing effort. Honda professed neutrality, but its screening policies made it difficult for workers with UAW sympathies to get in the door. The company's hiring radius of twenty-five to thirty miles in rural central Ohio challenged the union, accustomed to organizing in more densely populated urban areas, to reach potential members. When the company hired its first workers, they were shipped off to Japan for a couple of weeks of training, which Tomasi believed made those workers invulnerable to union entreaties. After months of operation the UAW had only one authorization card signed out of a hundred employees, and the situation did not appear to be improving. "I don't know what the hell we want them here for," he said exasperatedly to union board members. "Unless we can get a better understanding, they can keep those damn cars in Japan." "Wouldn't patriotism work?" Doug Fraser asked, pointedly. Tomasi had tried. He made sure the U.S. flag adorned the union's literature, and he told employees "that the Japanese will have you out here doing exercises in the next month or two" if the union did not bargain on their behalf.[24]

By the spring of 1982 the opening of the Honda auto plant loomed and Tomasi believed the situation was "extremely serious," because failure at Honda portended a similar outcome at the planned Nissan facility in Tennessee and a rumored Toyota transplant in the works. Tomasi led an off-the-record conversation among the executive board in late March, presumably to discuss the details of the planned boycott, which union leaders always kept confidential.[25] He met with Honda vice president Shige Yoshida in Findlay two weeks later. He and the executive board were then in a celebratory mood when they convened again in June, when he reported that he had been "able to throw sufficient fear into the Honda people." The way Tomasi described the document he and Yoshida signed—"They have agreed basically to an agreement that will be in effect down there at the plant"—demonstrated both the union's confidence going forward but also the ambiguity of the agreement's legal status.[26]

As a peace offering, Yoshida invited Tomasi to the Marysville plant to tour the company's operations and to meet some of its workers. "They didn't have any qualms about letting all the employees know that we were coming down to the plant," Tomasi reported, confident that the signed agreement signaled Honda's cooperative turn. What he found in Marysville looked "a hell of a lot different from any other plant" he had toured in the United States. "You can't tell a supervisor from an employee," he explained. "You can't tell a leader from anybody else in the plant." The facility impressed him with all the "nice things" Honda did for its employees—cafeterias, break rooms, recreational facilities—"that are probably not done for workers in most of our plants."[27]

Tomasi's observations in Marysville foreshadowed the troubles to come for the union. Beyond the question of representation, the 1982 agreement addressed what might have seemed like petty issues decades earlier, when unions achieved important gains for workers on their bread-and-butter issues—wages, hours, and safety conditions. The only workplace issue the 1982 agreement solved was whether Honda's workers could wear UAW hats at work. Hats were arguably a free-speech issue but had nothing to do with the kind of economic security that labor unions had fought to achieve in the past. By its own admission, by the time the UAW called off the election at Honda at the end of 1985, the union had nothing to complain about. The "Battle of Marysville" thus was not about what the union could do tomorrow for Honda's workers; it was about the principle of the postwar bargain between industry and labor. UAW leaders expected Honda to cooperate because that was simply one of the costs of manufacturing automobiles in the United States. Japanese companies expected to cooperate too, and government agencies like the Japan Institute of Labor recommended that transplanted companies plan to work with unions and resist siding with antiunion organizations.[28] What neither big organization accounted for was local antiunion sentiment in Marysville.

Over the months that followed the April 1982 agreement, Tomasi tracked events in Marysville closely. His optimism of the summer faded by the fall to anxiety over the ways in which the auto industry's national woes could affect local organizing at Honda. In late September he noted that while he expected a contract "sometime late next year," the union "had some real heartbreaks down there," with parts manufacturer Rockwell's recent plant closings in Marysville and Bellefontaine. "That hurt us tremendously," he conceded.[29] Rockwell blamed the closings on UAW intransigence over a recent contract, which did not help the UAW in its cause in Marysville.

In addition to recent plant closings, the union's legislative campaign for a "local content" law, which would have penalized automakers that did not include U.S.-made parts in the vehicles they sold in the United States, threatened to sour its relationship with Marysville. Honda of America executives watched nervously as the bill made its way through Congress, fearing that its passage would mean, at the very least, increased local costs for the company, and possibly a reevaluation in the home office of the company's U.S. investment. Union organizers in Marysville reported Honda's anxious response back to UAW leaders in Detroit. Managers allegedly told workers that the local content bill (formally the Fair Practices in Automotive Products Act) "was threatening their jobs . . . since the passage of that bill would (according to Honda) mean that Honda would close its U.S. operations." Honda also stopped production for a day in Marysville to have a plant-wide meeting at which management discussed the threat of content legislation, a "pretty goddam treacherous" move, according to Tomasi.[30]

The UAW nevertheless pursued an aggressive public relations campaign in 1982 and 1983 to urge passage of the local content bill through Congress. While press reports often mentioned Japanese competition as the motivation for the bill, the union made clear in its publications that the local content issue was not just about Japan but about a multinational squeeze and that it was even more important to limit the extent to which U.S. automakers could purchase cheap parts from foreign firms employing inexpensive labor. In *Solidarity* magazine, the union pleaded with members to write their representatives. It warned that 1.25 million jobs would be lost without the bill's passage.[31] Though it passed the House at the end of 1982, the bill would die in the Senate, and successive incarnations would have even less success.

Union leaders failed to see how this most important national legislative goal of the early 1980s threatened to thwart the UAW's most significant local organizing goal, winning over Honda's workers. The law pegged domestic parts requirements to production levels. In its 1983 version, for instance, a vehicle had to include 1 percent of locally produced content for every 10,000 vehicles sold domestically, so selling 700,000 vehicles meant 70 percent of the content of those vehicles would have to be produced in the United States. Failing to meet these benchmarks would mean penalties for each vehicle sold over quota. Based on Honda's projected sales, the company would have needed 70 percent U.S.-made parts in each vehicle to avoid penalties.[32] The first Accords off the line at the MAP had about 50 percent local content. Within ten years that figure increased to 75 percent, which in 1992 was a higher percentage of local content than that of any equivalent Big Three models, making Accords produced in Marysville "more American" than a Ford Taurus or Chevy Cavalier.[33] Undoubtedly the local content law would have cost Honda money, but the idea that it would cause Honda to walk away from the hundreds of millions of dollars it had already invested in central Ohio was farfetched. Still, what Honda workers heard from management, and likely in countless conversations on the shop floor and in local bars, was that the UAW was pushing for a law that threatened their jobs. It did not help to attract them to the big national union just as it geared up for a major organizing campaign.

The union battle intensified in October 1985 when Honda announced it would move forward with plans to increase the MAP's size from 1 million square feet to 1.7 million (making room for a new assembly line to produce the subcompact Honda Civic) and it would build a second auto assembly plant in central Ohio (what would eventually be the East Liberty plant, opened in 1989). The expansion meant an additional 2,000 workers in the area.[34] UAW officials saw this as the time to act—it would be easier to win a vote among Honda's existing workforce of 2,800, nearly all of whom had already been exposed to the union's message, than to wait for thousands of new, inexperienced workers to join the payrolls. In late October 1985 the UAW sent Honda a letter requesting union recognition without a vote. Typically, the UAW withheld such requests until it had received signatures on union cards from at least 30 percent of the workers. Tomasi told the press the union had signatures from at least half of Honda's production employees, but that was an exaggerated estimate, at best—confidentially he told union colleagues he had authorization cards from only about a quarter of the workforce.[35]

Expectedly, Honda rejected the request for immediate recognition, opting instead to put the question to a vote among the workforce. Before rejecting the request, though, Honda management distributed a questionnaire to its workforce in order, they claimed, to gauge the union's appeal. The questionnaire asked workers to note whether they agreed or disagreed with a number of arguments for and against unionization. The company reported that more than 73 percent who responded would "advise the company to reject the union request" for immediate recognition. Another 44 percent reported "some pressure or harassment" from union supporters who wanted signed authorization cards. The UAW, in turn, called the questionnaire "p.r. and propaganda" and charged Honda with intimidating its employees by asking them to give their opinions toward a union with supervisors observing. While the practice of surveying employees may have constituted a form of intimidation, the actual language of the survey did fairly represent the arguments of pro-union workers.[36]

Once a vote was set for 19 December 1985, an intense campaign ensued. "The union told us they're pretty sure they'll win," said an anonymous associate. Union sympathizers distributed literature on Friday afternoons as the day shift departed and the night shift arrived. Union organizing campaigns earlier in the century had focused on wages, hours, and workplace safety, but those were virtually nonissues in Marysville. Base wages at Honda were about eleven dollars an hour, while they were closer to thirteen dollars for UAW members in Ford and GM plants. Still, eleven dollars was far more than most of Honda's young workforce was accustomed to. "We're dealing with people who have been baling hay for $2 an hour," said Bill Woodward, in his UAW hat. "They don't understand us." "Most of my friends make $5 an hour," said one associate, acknowledging the reality of economic circumstances in the community outside Honda's gates.[37] Relatively high wages for the area, coupled with Honda's record of safety (aimed at maximizing efficiency, if anything—happy, healthy workers work better), meant that unions' historical bread-and-butter issues were moot in Marysville.

The UAW opted for a different strategy: it praised Honda for bringing many jobs to the area—praise with which few could disagree—and told the community that it would push the company for even more. Workers, the union claimed, had complained of line speed, that is, the number of vehicles that the line produced per hour. In advertisements the union argued that the current speed was "inhumane" and left employees "exhausted by the end of every day."[38] The UAW would negotiate with Honda not to slow the line—which would, theoretically, slow production and thus slow profits—but to hire more people to produce the same amount of vehicles. Hiring forty more people per shift, the union argued, would give Honda's workers break time equal to that of employees in GM and Ford plants. "People in the community need jobs," said one ad, tugging at the community's sensitivity to unemployment. "For its size, Honda is one of the most profitable companies in the United States. It can easily afford to hire more employees."[39] Besides line speed, the UAW also pledged to negotiate for job postings based on seniority, shift and job transfer rights, and an effective mechanism for articulating shop floor grievances to management.

Workers content with Honda and unwilling to cede ground to the UAW did not watch passively. A twenty-seven-year-old associate named Lonnie Howard joined several other antiunion workers in founding the "Associates Alliance." Howard claimed he was harassed at work for opposing the union. "You're an idiot if you hand out literature for Honda, but you're a hero if you hand out literature for the UAW," he told a reporter. "This whole thing really makes me wonder who we're going to be working for—Honda or UAW."[40] The AA aimed to be a counterweight to the UAW and its expensive campaign: "We don't have the big UAW $$$$$$ from collecting union dues," so they placed advertisements in the newspaper to spread the word that they were selling hats to raise funds for their organizing efforts. Their hats also had UAW logos on them, but superimposed atop the logo was a red circle with a strike through it, akin to a "No Smoking" sign.[41]

The AA's message was clear: "We Think for Ourselves." The alliance not only lobbied for "no" votes but also wanted guarantees that employees would not be forced unwillingly to join the union should the UAW win the election. "I'll tell anybody right now that they're not going to get a dime out of me," warned Howard. Fellow AA founder Steve Barker said, "My belief that the UAW should not be at Honda is strong enough to put my money behind my mouth." Howard cautioned that unionizing would cost Honda an additional $450 million—it is unclear how he calculated that figure—and the company would sooner fold its Ohio operations than sustain such a financial blow. AA advertisements also pointed out that the UAW had been found in several court cases to have failed to provide adequate representation to its own members and that if a member did not follow "union law" as enshrined in the UAW's hundred-page constitution, he or she could be fined, even for "crossing a picket line to work during a strike in order to support one's family."[42]

UAW leaders struggled to make sense of the AA. First they believed Honda management was behind the organization—that the company was trying to establish the AA as an alternative, non-UAW union, an "employer controlled labor organization." Then when the AA admitted it received donations from Marysville businesses, they saw the alliance as a front for all variety of local antiunion elements. Antiunion attorneys from outside the community must be advising the AA and writing its advertisements, they reasoned. Union counsel Leonard Page suggested suing the AA for trademark infringement, based on its use of the UAW logo in its advertising. Page saw this as a potential back door to uncovering links between Honda's management and the alliance but ultimately decided a legal battle would also disclose the 1982 agreement the UAW signed with Honda, a public revelation the union wanted to avoid.[43]

The unionization debate played out on the op-ed page of the local newspaper, the *Marysville Journal-Tribune*, in late 1985. Howard again defended his cause, acknowledging the UAW's positive contributions to labor early in the postwar era but noting that "as times changed and the Union became larger it has failed to recognize that the boom of the post WWII era is all but a fading memory with today's young workforce who quite frankly could care less about organized labor's 'proud' history." "We are not naïve," he continued. "We know that the UAW today is big business, and we are well aware of its alleged ties to organized crime." Howard concluded grandiloquently that a "no" vote on unionization would mean an "era in which all will share equally in the future of not only Honda but will inspire a nation that was founded on liberty, justice and freedom for all."[44]

Howard's allies helped bring the debate to the public sphere. Alliance member Charles Sessor asked, "If you have a good working relationship with your company, salary satisfaction, good benefits package, bonus packages and pension and retirement plan, then ask yourself, 'Why do we need union representation?'" Based on his previous experience as a union member, he cautioned, "You will soon feel that the union is managing the plant, company rules become 'just words' and the only law is what your union rep says."[45] Employees attacked and defended Honda's responses to work injuries—one said the company was negligent, while another said there was no evidence to contradict his own positive experience with Honda's attentive medical staff.[46] The *Journal-Tribune* followed up these letters by surveying a grand total of ten residents of Marysville, six of whom disapproved of the UAW. The newspaper reported the results with the potentially misleading headline "Majority Opposed to UAW Takeover."[47]

Ultimately the weeks of debate were all for naught. Signs that the UAW would attempt to postpone the vote first appeared when UAW lawyers sent letters to members of the AA, and to newspaper editors who published the alliance's advertisements, threatening suit over use of the UAW trademark.[48] On Friday, 14 December, five days before the scheduled election, the UAW filed charges with the NLRB against Honda. The union accused the company of interrogating and intimidating employees with its questionnaires, increasing benefits and vacation time to discourage union enthusiasm, and permitting the Associates Alliance to operate as an "employer controlled labor organization." A Honda spokesperson said, "Since the charges were filed late, we can only conclude UAW took this step because it knew it did not have enough support to win." The NLRB filing effectively forced a postponement of the vote. In response to Honda's accusations, UAW's Tomasi countered, "I look forward to the day there can be an election at Honda in a truly neutral and legal atmosphere."[49]

That day never came. On 31 January 1986, the NLRB dismissed the union's charges, and Honda demanded that the election be rescheduled immediately, though the UAW threatened to appeal the ruling. Some six weeks later the union completely withdrew its petition for an election, effectively ending the organizing campaign. Union officials publicly cited the "spread of misinformation" and "a rapid influx of new hires" as their reasons for canceling—Honda was growing exponentially, having hired some 800 new employees between October 1985 and March 1986, an expansion of nearly 25 percent in six months.[50] The UAW was correct when it assessed late 1985 as a do-or-die moment for unionization, yet its efforts still fell short. Union leaders privately admitted that they had no chance of winning an election at any point in late 1985 or early 1986. For the next two years they debated strategies for winning in Marysville, but when the four powerhouse operators—the only workers at Honda that the UAW ever actually represented—notified the UAW that they were "hell bent on decertifying" with the union when their contract expired, leaders admitted that "we have no unfair practices to complain about" and the "organizing effort is not getting anywhere in Marysville anyway."[51]

CONCLUSION: "A TOWN SOMEWHERE IN THE HINTERLANDS"

Why did the UAW, one of the most powerful industrial organizations in the postwar United States, fail to organize the workforce at Honda of America? There are several possible explanations. Most visibly, Honda was the central element to Union County's economic turnaround well before the scheduling of the election. Throughout late 1985 and into late 1986, economic news was generally on the positive side, with unemployment steadily declining nationally and statewide and dropping dramatically in Union County. While Honda's wages fell short of those in UAW-organized GM and Ford factories, they were very good by Union County standards. There was an undercurrent of concern among workers and in the community that rocking the Honda boat might send it sailing back to Japan. Double-digit unemployment rates were too recent of a memory for anyone to risk such an outcome. The UAW's most potent issue of the past, the economic well-being of the laborers it represented, was a nonissue for Honda's workforce.

The Marysville community's previous disappointments with the UAW may have also factored into its rejection. The Rockwell International plant that shut down operations just as the MAP powered on the line had employed more than 500 UAW members. In 1982 the plant had suffered a slowdown concurrent with the recession, and as a consequence management asked employees to approve a new contract that reduced wages and benefits. Management threatened to close the plant if the union rejected the contract; 96 percent of workers voted against it, and the plant closed.[52] Though the workers essentially voted to resist attempted industrial blackmail, many in the local community nevertheless blamed the UAW for forcing Rockwell's hand. The memory of all those lost jobs was still fresh in 1985. Al Kinzer, plant manager at the MAP, remembered that moment as the UAW vote approached. "Nobody wants to work for a loser," he said, and a majority of his employees agreed.[53]

Antiunionism was hardly a local phenomenon. Across the country in the 1970s and 1980s, Americans were increasingly likely to think of unions generally as losers. Many cheered when Ronald Reagan crushed PATCO, the air traffic controllers' union, during a 1981 strike. Decades of antiunion propaganda and negative cultural imagery portrayed the movement as dangerous, corrupt, anti-American, and flush with mobsters and power-hungry autocrats. In the context of these decades' "pervasive antiunion culture," in historian Lawrence Richards's estimation, many working people viewed unions with deep-seated suspicion.[54]

Thus Honda arrived with antiunion sentiment already in the air in Marysville and in many similar places across the United States. The company then set about hiring a homogeneous workforce that would quickly adopt the "Honda way," which meant seeing the individual worker's and the company's fate as one and the same. Eventually Union County's rising fortunes became linked to Honda's fate as well. That handpicked workforce made a difference, and absent a document from Honda wherein management explicitly directed "Hire antiunion workers," historians can only argue based on circumstantial, albeit convincing, evidence—the limited hiring radius in a rural area; the overrepresentation of young people; the lack of ethnic or racial diversity; and the repetition of all these decisions in antiunion, transplanted Japanese facilities to come—that Honda intended to create a workforce resistant to a unionization campaign. The company's actions in its first years indicated that it simultaneously anticipated having to work with the union and wanted to hire workers who lacked sympathy for unions.

Ultimately, then, the "Battle of Marysville" proved that the context of the auto industry's woes in the early 1980s was inescapable. The same heated context responsible for the UAW's planned aggressive boycott of Honda in 1982—a boycott that was only in part about Honda but was also an expression of the union's frustrations with an entire industry's failings—was responsible for attitudes in Marysville that aimed to limit the extent to which the union could threaten Honda's operations. Rattle the company too much, Marysville residents believed in the first half of the decade, and you may spook it enough to send it packing. Those residents read the newspaper as much as the UAW's leadership did. The leadership could not divorce its union from the ailing industry it served, an industry that, in Doug Fraser's own words, appeared to be "almost disintegrating by the day" in 1982.[55] The very thing that made the UAW so successful and powerful—its postwar "grand bargain" with Detroit's Big Three, the faith that what was good for General Motors was good for union members—made it anathema to Honda's workers when it appeared that all of Detroit was set to burn. Marysville's workers did not think of the UAW as just a union; they thought of the UAW as a *Detroit* union, and that made all the difference.

That distinction contributed to a stark "insider-outsider" discourse in Honda's relationship with the community and the rest of the state and country. The jobs were welcome in 1980, but the national spotlight was not. Reporters from big cities who knew nothing of Marysville based their stories on preconceived notions about small-town life and how such a community would respond to a Japanese company. James Risen covered the MAP's first years for the *Detroit Free Press*, a newspaper with a vested interest in guarding Detroit's monopoly over the narrative of the U.S. auto industry. Risen repeatedly reproduced a dichotomy between a "sleepy little postcard village" tucked away in "corn and soybean farmland" on the one hand and "highly educated, affluent," and "high-powered Japanese businessmen" on the other.[56] *Journal-Tribune* editor Daniel Behrens later attacked a *New York Times* "yellow journalist" for his description of Marysville as "a one-horse backward community" and his largely unsuccessful effort to unearth anti-Japanese sentiment. "It's clear these so-called journalists represent areas which covet the fact that Honda located here," wrote Behrens. "Their biased reporting reflects the jealousy." It would not be the first time Behrens found fault with a national news organization's reporting on the relationship between Honda and the community.[57] Marysville resident Donald Robinson denounced the *Wall Street Journal* for "pretend[ing] to tell us (and the entire nation) our mood and thoughts about the Honda project.... We cannot allow a few out-of-state journalists to cause a cancer of distrust and hate."[58] Mayor Thomas Nuckles also defended his town, criticizing national media for portraying Marysville as a "down-in-the-dumps hamlet of 8,800." "They say all we're going to get from [Honda] is jobs," Nuckles said. "Well, what else do you want with an unemployment rate of 12.5 percent?"[5]

Honda's efforts to make itself part of the Marysville community not only through commerce but also through culture endeared it to residents. Townspeople jumped to the company's defense because it had done more than any outsider to bandage local economic wounds and because Honda's actions made evident its multifaceted commitment to Marysville. National media and the UAW had done little for the community, and sometimes even worked against its interests. Quickly the community lumped the two into the general category of "outsiders." The response to an unassuming 1985 AP article about Honda's rise to number four on the list of U.S. auto producers— due entirely to production in Marysville—demonstrated the insider-outsider dichotomy. The article repeated the backwater characterization of the town: "When trucks hauling auto parts and livestock aren't whizzing by on U.S. 33, the clip-clop of horses pulling the black buggies of the Amish resounds on back roads near the plant. The skyline is church steeples, grain silos— and Honda." It then discussed the unionization effort, portraying antiunion workers as young and naive hicks while painting union sympathizers as experienced industrial workers trying to drag the ignorant into the twentieth century. After interviewing several pro-UAW workers about the "Honda way" of managing a plant, the author made his assessment: "After five years, many workers in blue [UAW] hats have concluded that the Japanese-style workplace democracy is a sham."[60]

The *Journal-Tribune* followed up at the end of the week with a cartoon mocking the article's depiction of Marysville: two hillbillies drank beer and rested under a money-growing tree while an Amish man rode a buggy—an occasional sight in rural central Ohio—in the background. Behrens asked angry readers to remember "that the story was written from an outsider's viewpoint." He then turned his attention to what he saw as the real issue: "American car industry experts had better take notice of the Marysville-Honda phenomenon, as it fortells [sic] a new world in manufacturing." He echoed the Associates Alliance when he observed that autoworker unions were relics of a bygone era: "Years of ever-increasing union demands and decreased attention to quality of work were a significant factor in the downfall of Detroit's worldwide automobile dynasty." Behrens concluded by mentioning GM's new Saturn initiative, an attempt to take a page out of the Japanese playbook by using sophisticated automated manufacturing techniques to produce small, efficient, inexpensive vehicles. If GM was wise, he said, it would not locate its new factory in Detroit, with its "polluted landscape and dispirited labor force." "No," he snapped, "GM will take its jobs to a town somewhere in the hinterlands where the people will work, and where government and unions do not conspire to extract blood from an anemic industry."[61] (Perhaps GM was listening—Saturn landed in Spring Hill, Tennessee, not far from Nissan's operations in Smyrna.)

Ultimately the UAW's issues with line speed sounded like the past. Squeezed between collapsing U.S. industrial giants and Honda's promise of a prosperous globalized future, the union struggled to stay relevant. Marysville's rejection of the UAW, a major beneficiary of the unprecedentedly powerful national economy of the first two postwar decades, in favor of a global corporation from Japan was indicative of the globalizing of America. In a world where national boundaries, both real and imagined, appeared to grow increasingly irrelevant, Honda connected a local community to global economic flows that bypassed the national level. Through its relationship with Honda, the Marysville community experienced globalization in an intensely local way. At the same time, the local-global connection empowered the community to mobilize against forces deemed "outsiders," namely, the UAW and the national media. It was the processes of contemporary globalization that facilitated Japan's transformative role in the American heartland.

FIVE

A Medium but Not a Message

The VCR and Cultural Globalization

On its first run, history is tragedy, Marx wrote; the second time around, it is utter farce. The second Battle of Poitiers was likely just what the famous philosopher had in mind. For customs officials in this small landlocked French town a hundred miles from the coast, the number of both tragedy and farce was 732: that was the year in which Charles Martel repelled an invading North African army at a battle of world-historical importance in that very location; 1,250 years later, that was also the code number assigned to all imported goods from Japan. With the French government's 1982 decision to dam the flood of Japanese consumer electronics, particularly videocassette recorders (VCRs), however, the number came to represent in both instances resistance against a foreign invader. On the frontlines in 732 it was the Frank warlord Martel and his medieval army; in November 1982, it was customs director Pierre Galliot and his band of eight inspectors. These nine men, the French government decided, should inspect every VCR that entered France, even if it took them the rest of their lives.[1]

Galliot grinned wryly as he explained his troops' task: the special inspectors, "hand-picked for slowness," had to "thoroughly examine" all documentation to ensure it was sound and, more important, written in French; they had to open every container and remove "a substantial number" of VCRs from their packaging to check serial numbers; and to be certain that the documentation did not lie, inspectors had to dismantle select VCRs to certify that they were made in Japan. In just the ten months it took to implement the new regulations and assign Poitiers as the sole customs entry point for VCRs in all of France, 642,000 units had entered the country, nearly three times as many as in all of 1981. Thereafter Galliot's inspectors had struggled to clear

10,000 units each month, consigning hundreds of thousands to warehouses throughout the town.[2] The bottleneck created by *la Résistance* at Poitiers severely limited Japanese VCR imports and made those available to French consumers considerably more costly.

To be sure, the French state had economic motives. It had recently nationalized the country's largest electronics firm, Thomson. In 1982, fears of increased foreign competition motivated Thomson to bid unsuccessfully for a controlling interest in the West German electronics giant Grundig. Thomson also sought, again fruitlessly, an alliance with Europe's largest consumer electronics manufacturing, the Dutch firm Philips, to produce VCRs for the European market. Curtailing the flow of cheaper—and many consumers would claim higher quality—Japanese VCRs would encourage French consumers to buy products made in the European Economic Community (EEC). Japan had exported nearly 5 million VCRs to the EEC in 1982, and Japan's Ministry of International Trade and Industry had conceded to an annual quota of 4.55 million in discussions with EEC negotiators in February 1983. European consumers wanted VCRs and Japanese companies had plenty of them, but European companies wanted a piece of the action in the exploding consumer electronics industry. European governments, in contrast to the United States, were willing to enact measures to protect their national industries. As industrial policy, the second Battle of Poitiers was pragmatic, if not shameless, economic protectionism.[3]

The French response to Japan's consumer electronics boom also hinted at the cultural significance of the VCR's proliferation—this was France, after all, the bastion of *civilisation*. "France is not going to keep out Japanese VCRs no matter what they've done," said the early prophet of globalization Theodore Levitt. "It will come in underneath, sideways, over borders, through piracy, through smuggling. It will come in because people want it. They want the quality; they want the price. Somebody will have it; just like drugs it comes in."[4]

For a relatively expensive product—costing anywhere from $300 to $5,000 in 1985, depending on whether one bought one legally in Moscow, Idaho, or on the black market in Moscow, Russia—the global demand for the VCR was unprecedented. The number of people worldwide who knew what a VCR was in 1976, let alone owned one, was negligible; just ten years later, some estimates put the number of VCRs in operation worldwide at 100 million.[5] Neither radio nor television could compare with the VCR in the scope and intensity of its proliferation over such a short period of time. The global desire for a VCR was extraordinary, and acquiring one held promises

The VCR and Cultural Globalization

of increased status and independence. A journalist told the story of a small village outside of Islamabad, Pakistan, where residents lived without running water or electricity. "In the middle of the cluster of baked-mud houses is a gleaming new concrete and brick room in one corner of which is stacked a 22-inch television set, an unpacked videocassette recorder and a stereo tape-recorder," she wrote. "We are waiting for the government to put in electricity," said one of the residents, "but even without it we feel rich with all these goods around us."[6]

Of course, while Japanese electronics gadgets could make a poor village feel rich in spirit, sales also made Japanese companies like Sony and Matsushita rich in hard currency. They also helped to drive up many national trade deficits with Japan, including France's, prompting economic nationalist reactions in Western Europe and the United States. But the money consumers spent, the extensive black market networks established, and the stories told of people in underdeveloped areas desiring to acquire, trade, and use VCRs all demonstrated that this consumer electronics product that benefited Japan economically also had significant cultural meaning for users as an icon of the global imagination.

For the journalists and social scientists writing about it in the 1980s, the Japanese VCR signified the potentials of a new era of cultural globalization, both in the United States and around the world.[7] The VCR granted liberatory power to its users. American users defined their liberation in the language of what Lizabeth Cohen calls the "Consumer's Republic," that is, consumers believed democracy meant the freedom of consumer choice, autonomy from national corporate media, and independence from the shackles of rigid scheduling blocks.[8] In the non-Western world, where VCRs were often harder to find, the device signaled democratic liberation from political repression, poverty, and the evils of underdevelopment. Both in the United States and abroad, the VCR was tangible evidence that new processes of interconnectivity were breaking down borders of all kinds. As a result, the hundreds of millions of people with access to these Japanese products could choose to be exposed to previously inaccessible content, most of it innocuous but some of it threatening to powerful economic or political interests. In multicultural countries like the United States, such opportunities opened new vistas of cultural experience; in countries like France, mindful of a mythical cultural legacy, they unnerved officials; in authoritarian states like the Soviet Union, they threatened the guardians of political power.

In short, the VCR was the iconic object of contemporary cultural globalization in the 1980s, yet by the end of the decade it was so ubiquitous—so ordinary—that it blended into a cacophonic landscape of sounds and images. By consuming VCRs many millions of Americans participated in the intensification of cultural globalization enabled by new media technologies. As a device in the home, the VCR gave users the impression of being in control of an expanding media universe. Yet the hundreds of millions of devices circulating worldwide by the early 1990s placed Americans within a larger global cultural transformation that they could never hope to control. The Internet would later refine the ways that consumers could access information anytime and anywhere, independent of physical and legal state borders and often in opposition to them. In a clumsier way, the VCR enabled ideas and images to traverse the globe with greater autonomy from the people and institutions that produced cultural content than any previous communications technology had allowed. It was a dramatic evolution in the "age of mechanical reproduction" that Walter Benjamin described, a further step away from a text's "parasitical dependence on ritual," permitting mass global audiences to apply their own meanings to cultural images.[9]

The meaning attached to the VCR thus broadened from its introduction in the mid-1970s as just another consumer electronics product for affluent Westerners to a ubiquitous tool of global social and cultural consequence by the mid-1980s. By the end of the eighties, the VCR's meaning for its consumers around the world was divorced from the intentions of the corporations that first produced and marketed the device a decade earlier. It was a tabula rasa onto which different groups could project their hopes and fears about rapid global changes. In the globalizing world of the 1980s, the VCR took on a life of its own.

What often got lost in the attention paid to the transformative effects of the VCR was that the devices were exclusively Japanese in origin. Whereas global consumers embraced or rejected American products for their "Americanness," the iconography of the VCR was often devoid of images of Japaneseness. Many French dismissed American products like McDonald's, Levi's, and Hollywood films for being too American in the 1960s and 1970s (while plenty of their compatriots welcomed the same products). The second Battle of Poitiers, though, did not revolve around rejections of Japaneseness so much as it did around the conditions of global capitalism. The French state recognized the money to be made in the domestic and global VCR market in ways that it did not for the fast food or blue jeans market, because there were no objections to the VCR as a cultural object. After all, the VCR presented the opportunity for viewing French films (or Indian, or Chinese) as well as American. To some, McDonald's was a symbol of Americanization in France

The VCR and Cultural Globalization

and Toyota was a symbol of Japanization in the United States, but the VCR was not a symbol of Japanization anywhere, even though virtually every VCR sold on the world market before the late 1980s was produced in Japan. Even when U.S. congressmen smashed Toshiba products with a sledgehammer on the front steps of the Capitol, they did so not because Toshiba (a major VCR producer) was selling too many products in the United States but because the company illegally sold advanced military technology to the Soviet Union.[10] Thus while the VCR became a cultural icon with a variety of meanings in its first decade, rarely did it mean "something Japanese," and rarely did its being Japanese affect consumption patterns. VCRs crossed national borders without the stigma of national identity.

Japanese VCRs also helped define the notion that the world had entered a new, "postmodern" condition. "If there is any single technological watershed of the postmodern," writes the Marxist historian Perry Anderson, it was "the arrival of color television" in the early 1970s.[11] Color television could represent "reality" to viewers in ways that black-and-white television could not. As a device that could replicate those representations of reality at the ready, the VCR provided an additional level of representation, infinitely reproducible. In working to define the contours of the postmodern age, thinkers like Anderson, Fredric Jameson, and David Harvey all saw the VCR as a harbinger of a future in which "the machinery of images"—what Anderson called "perpetual emotion machines"—was capable of "transmitting discourses that are wall-to-wall ideology."[12] Again, as with the articulation of the concept of globalization, Japanese corporations provided the tools that defined a new era. Yet they figured only tangentially into explanatory narratives of cultural and ideological change. If the VCR contributed anything to the Japaneseness of postmodernity, it was to emphasize that Japan's future was devoid of metanarratives—the VCR was a device that could transmit narratives but was seemingly devoid of its own, a medium but not a message.

This chapter first explores VCR consumption in the United States as a symbol of the nationwide cultural shifts changing the ways Americans lived their lives. The marketing of VCRs in the United States demonstrated an imperative for consumer education as companies tried to convince consumers of the necessity of the VCR and its ability to transform everyday life. In trying to attract customers through an acculturation process, the demands of capital drove the earliest cultural meanings of the VCR. Slick advertising sold the VCR as a device of individual consumer liberation. Scholars, journalists, and commentators adopted this vocabulary as they tried to come to terms with the cultural transformations affecting the United States and the world. In the second section, I examine the VCR's global impact, which observers perceived to be even more transformative than its U.S. reception. VCRs spread across the planet at a rate unprecedented for a consumer electronics product, even surpassing the proliferation rates of television. Researchers projected their hopes for global cultural change onto the device as they examined its impact on underdeveloped and authoritarian societies. Western travelers traversing the globe in search of exotic experiences always seemed to stumble across the VCR, shattering their notions of non-Western cultural purity. Much as the Internet would be by the late 1990s, the VCR became the 1980s icon of cultural globalization.

From a vantage of more than three decades later, a reading of the VCR's cultural life span reveals curious continuities with our present moment. When the latest iteration of the iPhone, iPad, or Apple Watch promises to remake our lives, or when a social media technology like Twitter enables a political and social revolution against an authoritarian regime, it echoes an earlier era when Japanese goods were responsible for Americans' global anxieties and millenarian expectations.

CONSUMER LIBERATION: THE VCR IN THE UNITED STATES

The videocassette recorder's prehistory dates to the 1950s, when an array of American and Japanese companies began experimenting with the placement of images onto videotape.[13] The first iteration, produced for industrial use by the U.S. Ampex Corporation, meant that television broadcasters no longer needed to air programs live; Ampex machines allowed viewers on the West Coast to watch programs at the same hour as viewers on the East Coast.[14] It was not until Japan's Sony released the U-Matic unit in 1972 that a viable videotape recorder (VTR, a generic category to which VCRs belonged), weighing in at a "portable" sixty pounds, entered the market, but it was intended for professional use and priced well out of most consumers' budgets.[15] Sony used what it learned from the U-Matic experience to develop, produce, and market the first commercially successful consumer VTR, and the first VCR available, the Sony Betamax.

As electronic media inundates the United States of the early twenty-first century, where instantaneous information gratification is only mouse clicks away, it is difficult to appreciate what the Betamax did when it arrived on the U.S. market in 1976. Unless a consumer was connected to an early cable or satellite television service—both still very much in their infancies—the television viewing options were mostly limited to what the three major networks

The VCR and Cultural Globalization

offered. Missing a favorite program, movie, or live event like a sports game because of inconvenience or a scheduling conflict meant maybe never seeing it again. By connecting the forty-five-pound Betamax to a television, viewers could overcome such problems. The device recorded sound and video from a broadcast signal onto videocassettes about the size of a paperback book. The 1976 model permitted viewers to record only one hour's worth of programming, but subsequent models allowed for up to three hours of recording.

The Betamax's recording function was the real trick. Throughout the 1970s several U.S. manufacturers had introduced VTR units to the U.S. market, but they all failed to catch on like VCRs would because they performed only playback functions and did not allow users to record. Avco's Cartrivision, RCA's Selectavision, and MCA's Discovision formats gave consumers the option to watch prerecorded material from a limited catalog, but these companies stopped short of including recording functions for fear of antagonizing copyright holders. The Japanese companies that developed the various VCR formats did not accept such limitations.[16] The divergent national paths of VTR development stood as a metaphor for two countries moving in opposite directions: manufacturers in the United States, turning inward in the 1970s, clung to a system of media governed tightly by national laws; producers in Japan, beginning with the Betamax, developed products for a still-to-be imagined future.

Just two years after Betamax's U.S. introduction, more than twenty different brand-name companies offered VCRs to the consumer market. Prices ranged from $1,000 to $1,300, putting the VCR in the "luxury goods" category until spikes in demand and supply led to significant price drops in the early 1980s.[17] Producers were split between two formats that performed the same functions but were incompatible: Betamax and VHS ("video home system"). On the Betamax side sat, among others, Sony, Toshiba, Pioneer, and Zenith; on the VHS side were JVC, Panasonic, Sharp, Mitsubishi, and RCA. This VCR "format war" has been of interest to scholars writing about the VCR for two reasons: first, because most histories concentrate on VCR production (rather than on consumption); second, because the field's great innovator, Sony, eventually lost.[18] In telling the story of VCR consumption, though, one important point emerges: whoever won (VHS did), the winner was guaranteed to be Japanese. "Today the superiority of the Japanese in the home VCR field is so overwhelming," wrote journalist James Lardner in 1987, "that no American manufacturer even bothers to try making such a product."[19] Seven years into the VCR's life cycle, at the beginning of a run of several years in which VCR sales doubled annually in the United States,

Japanese companies accounted for more than 95 percent of global VCR production.[20] (European manufacturers Philips and Grundig, producing almost exclusively for the European market, largely accounted for the rest, while several Korean and Taiwanese manufacturers produced negligible quantities.) Americans could visit local appliance dealers and see VCRs branded with the names of "American" companies like Zenith, General Electric, and RCA, but they would not find a single VCR produced in the United States on those shelves—all were manufactured in Japan for distribution by U.S. labels.[21] So whether a VCR was Betamax or VHS, Sony, Panasonic, or RCA, expensive or budget-priced, if it was purchased in the United States, or almost anywhere else in the world, it was Japanese.

Sony's campaign to market the Betamax was successful because the company was selling more than just another electronics gadget. The company pushed the Betamax "as a tool of consumer empowerment."[22] Sony founder Akio Morita promoted the mythology of the Betamax's origins in his 1985 autobiography: "In the fifties and sixties . . . I noticed how the TV networks had total control over people's lives. . . . It was that control of people's lives that I felt was unfair." Thus when he and Sony brought the Betamax to the market, they pushed its ability for "time-shifting," a futuristic-sounding phrase that Morita claimed to have coined.[23] "Time-shifting" simply meant the ability to watch at 11:00 P.M. a program that had aired at 8:00 P.M. Looked at narrowly, the Betamax gave consumers more flexibility in their television viewing habits. In Morita's conception and in Sony's influential marketing campaign, which invented language that a cohort of academic researchers, commentators, and even the Supreme Court would later adopt, the Betamax bestowed on users the power to control time itself.

Since consumers would not inherently understand the operations of a VCR, early Betamax and VHS marketing campaigns educated consumers in the language of empowerment. Sony provided local retailers with template newspaper and magazine advertisements into which they could insert the names of their businesses. They all showed a sharp, simple image of a Betamax machine under different headlines like "How to Wake Up to Late Night Talk Shows" and "How to Take a Summer Vacation and Never Miss Your Favorite Shows." A brief paragraph beneath the image explained in simple language just what the Betamax did—what, when, how, and how long it recorded. The ads finished by evoking the image of empowerment: "You're always stuck watching what the networks want. Why not watch what you want instead?"[24]

Of course, television was a natural medium to advertise the Betamax, show off its features, and introduce consumers to the language of VCR

The VCR and Cultural Globalization

empowerment. Powerhouse advertising agency Doyle Dane Bernbach designed several television commercials for the Betamax's launch. The most notable featured Dracula, who returns home from "work" and says to the camera, "If you work nights like I do, you miss a lot of great TV programs. But I don't miss them anymore, thanks to Sony's Betamax deck."[25] In another, a cab driver ending his night shift says to his colleagues, "Good morning, gentlemen, I'm going home to watch the late show." The narrator informs the viewer that with "Sony's revolutionary Betamax deck . . . now you can automatically videotape your favorite show, even when you're not home, and watch it any time you want."[26] The introduction to a VCR lifestyle continued at local retailers. Brochures sought to comfort the consumer who might have felt overwhelmed by the confusing advanced technology. Retailers could provide customers with a copy of *Daddy, What's a Betamax?*, a "beautifully illustrated booklet that answers every child's (and adult's) questions about Betamax." (After all, what parent has not had to answer the question, "If I record a show, will it stay recorded forever?") The booklet served the dual purpose of educating customers and assuaging their insecurities about complicated new technologies.[27] For hesitant retailers, Sony offered a booklet titled *How to Sell Betamax (as If You Needed Help)*, which suggested ways to approach both inexperienced electronics customers as well as the "Sophisticated Customer." Along with educational literature, customers would find a "Demonstration Center" at retailers that showcased a Betamax on a Sony television, displayed on two pedestals that informed the consumer of the Betamax's various basic recording and playback features.[28] While it did not push the boundaries of consumer marketing, the Betamax campaign successfully introduced the U.S. public to the ways that VCRs could affect their daily habits, evidenced by the tremendous boom in VCR sales in the product's first decade. (That the VHS format ultimately outpaced Betamax did not mean that Sony's marketing campaigns failed; on the contrary, Sony's competitors in the "format war" adopted Sony's advertising techniques for their own VCRs. Betamax's failure was instead a result of Sony's many Japanese competitors, particularly the giant Matsushita, allying against the innovative company.)[29]

It was not just shoppers who noticed Sony's calls for consumer empowerment in the "largest ad campaign ever put behind a single Sony product." The week before NBC broadcast the classic film *Gone with the Wind* in November 1976, a full nine months after the Betamax went on sale, electronics retailers saw their shelves wiped clean of blank Betamax cassettes. For executives at MCA, the parent company of NBC and Universal Studios, the cause was obvious: as many as 25,000 Betamax owners were taping the film for their private collections. This practice, said MCA president Sidney J. Sheinberg, was blatant copyright infringement at a cost "almost impossible to estimate."[30] MCA, joined by Disney, filed suit against Sony in an attempt to stop the company from marketing and selling the Betamax. Japanese companies had given consumers recording features when U.S. companies feared to do so. Predictably, Betamax rattled Hollywood's cage, and the ensuing court battle became a showdown between Japanese hardware and American software.

Sony's plan was simple: stall the court decision long enough to sell so many units that enforcing an MCA-Disney victory would be nearly impossible. In this effort it was aided by its VHS competitors, who were outselling Sony by a three-to-one ratio at the beginning of the 1980s.[31] The legal battle bounced from court to court following a number of decisions and appeals until it finally reached the U.S. Supreme Court, which issued a 5–4 ruling in Sony's favor in January 1984 in *Sony Corp. of America v. Universal City Studios, Inc.* Sony and its VHS competitors had already won a de facto victory at that point anyway—an estimated 8 million VCRs were in use in American homes at the beginning of the year, and enforcing a ruling against VCR manufacturers would have proven to be a Sisyphean task.[32] The Court certified the legality of what millions of Americans already did on a daily basis. "Time-shifting for private home use must be characterized as a noncommercial, nonprofit activity," wrote Justice John Paul Stevens. Stevens rejected MCA-Disney's claims and adopted the language of VCR culture created by Morita and Sony—one executive's "time-shifting" was another's "copyright infringement"—acquiescing to the vocabulary of consumer transformation that sustained the VCR's popularity. Stevens continued, "Time-shifting merely enables a viewer to see such a work which he had been invited to witness in its entirety free of charge."[33] If a program was free to watch the first time, why should it cost anything to watch again?

Washington Post television critic Tom Shales intoned the victory cry: "Citizens! Hear me! We are free! Free to tape as we choose!" Shales carried on, "It transpires that even in a technocracy ruled by vast conglomerates, there is a sixth freedom: The freedom to tape. . . . Without such freedoms, life in a video age is nothing. This was not a victory for Sony. This was a victory for the human race." Shales's tone was facetious, but he nevertheless hit a sincere note: the VCR provided users with a kind of freedom that Hollywood and its congressional allies threatened to deny. Through satire Shales struck the moment's Orwellian overtones. "One giant step for man, one giant kick in Big Brother's pants," he wrote. "No more stuffing the Betamax machine under the

The VCR and Cultural Globalization

bed at every unexpected ring of the doorbell. . . . No more midnight meetings of Time-Shifters Anonymous."[34]

In repeatedly sounding the cry of freedom, Shales was poking fun at a real trend: a wide array of media scholars, technology and lifestyle journalists, and representatives of the electronics industry (if not VCR users themselves) followed Sony's lead in praising the VCR as a tool of consumer empowerment and as a bellwether of future media liberation. Placed in the broad sweep of U.S. history, replete with African Americans, women, immigrants, and other groups struggling to broaden the horizons of the ideal of freedom, some of the words used to describe the VCR's effects appear almost comical in retrospect. For example, in a study of the ways VCR users sought to avoid watching commercial advertisements, two researchers put their findings in historical context with no detectable irony: "The 1960s and the 1970s witnessed a number of profound social movements—civil rights, antiwar, counterculture, and women's liberation. As for the 1980s, historians might consider another—the television viewer's liberation movement. For the first time in the history of the medium, a majority of viewers have taken control of what they watch, when they watch, and how they watch television. Indeed viewers throughout the world are uniting behind the liberating technology of the video cassette recorder."[35]

Such language could have been dismissed as scholarly tunnel vision had it not been so common. One scholar who published a book and a number of articles on the VCR "heralded . . . [the VCR] as the technology that could liberate viewers from both the rigors of television scheduling and from the relative narrowness of television content."[36] Yet another researcher, this one studying the Turkish reception of the device, viewed "the VCR as a liberating technology that allows viewers a range of taste in media content never before possible."[37] A scholar studying audience behavior gushed that it was "the introduction of the VCR that emancipated the TV audience from being a *passive viewer* to an *active viewer*."[38] The greatest hyperbole came from a publication that synthesized general trends in communications research. It claimed that "all the evidence says that this time we are in the presence of a real revolution and that we should call it by its name": "As a true revolution, the emergence of video has been like an explosion, full of energy and even passion, provoking divisions, inflicting wounds, destroying, upsetting and, also, raising hopes and promising new riches in the so-called 'television wasteland.' . . . The video revolution has taken the world by storm, caught the popular imagination with incredible speed and set itself up as the universal entertainer of the future."[39]

It was not just scholars who waxed profoundly over the VCR's transformative effects. As it tracked the explosive annual growth in VCR sales, industry publication *Consumer Electronics Annual Review* noted early in the technology's life cycle that the "video revolution" provided consumers genuine "viewer liberation." Two years later it expounded on the industry's sense of the trend: "A transformation which is both evolutionary and revolutionary is now under way—changing not only the nature of the consumer electronics industry but the American home and the American lifestyle. The key word is 'video'—and the changes involved in our basic sources of information, entertainment, education and communication. The video revolution with its potential effects has already been compared to the revolution of the early 20th Century brought about by the automobile."[40]

The anodyne *Consumer Reports* labeled the earliest line of VCRs the "Key to a New TV World" and pondered the democratic possibilities: "For more than a generation, television has been changing the way people live. . . . We the people have a chance to change television—or at least soften its dictates to us. The instrument of blessed change may well be the video cassette recorder." Like advertisements, which shifted their focus from educating consumers about the basics of a VCR to promoting quality, value, or features, *Consumer Reports'* coverage of VCRs shifted from describing the basics in 1977–78 to extensive testing of the advanced features available on nearly four dozen models in 1983.[41] The magazine, which was usually guarded in assessing product claims, had accepted the VCR as part of every consumer's media experience. It even adopted the language that advertisements provided, the language of liberation.

The earliest marketing campaigns for the Betamax and other VCRs in the 1970s showed that the hyperbole of media transformation surrounding the VCR *preceded* the technology's extraordinary growth in the 1980s. So when media scholars did take note of the VCR boom beginning in 1982, Sony and the Japanese competitors that followed had already placed a descriptive vocabulary at their disposal. It was Sony, after all, who told consumers that the VCR could emancipate them from the shackles of broadcast television, setting the tone and framework for critical commentary on its success. The VCR thus became a self-fulfilling prophecy for industry types and researchers, as import and sales figures skyrocketed from the early 1980s on. In 1976 the Betamax was the only VCR model available on the U.S. market, and Americans purchased 30,000 of them.[42] Sales increased by nearly 700 percent in 1977, with VHS entering the market under several brand names. Still, the 200,000 units sold and the $141 million in VCR imports remained a pinprick in a consumer electronics industry on which Americans annually spent $12 billion in the late 1970s.[43] But soon that 30,000 became 200,000, then 400,000, and two years later, 800,000. Annual sales jumped another 70 percent to 1.36 million in 1981. That year VCR imports from Japan were valued at $1 billion, surpassing for the first time the value of U.S. television imports, previously the crown jewel in Japan's export-oriented consumer electronics industry. Thereafter annual sales growth rates were 49 percent in 1982, 102 percent in 1983, 86 percent in 1984, 41 percent in 1985, and 10 percent in 1986, at which point annual U.S. sales plateaued at roughly 11 million per year. They valued just under $4 billion in a consumer electronics market worth more than $40 billion annually.[44] Whatever the subjective assessments of observers, the material reality of VCR proliferation was nothing short of phenomenal.

And it all came from Japan. In the VCR's first decade, Japanese companies regularly shattered their own monthly export records. It took nearly four years for monthly exports to the United States to reach 100,000 units. Monthly figures then skyrocketed to the half-million mark by June 1983 and surpassed 1 million just one year later.[45] Annual U.S. VCR imports hit a high of 17.6 million in 1986, at which point the U.S. market was clearly saturated; prices dropped and demand leveled off. Imports nevertheless remained above 10 million units into the 1990s until the end of the decade, when VCRs ceded to the next-generation technology of DVD players.[46]

As a result, the acquisition and use of VCRs was increasingly becoming part of the experience of American life in the 1980s. There were an estimated 3 million VCRs in operation in the United States at the beginning of 1982, or roughly one for every 77 people in the country. Americans would buy some 60 million units in the seven years to follow, and by 1989 VCRs were in 61 percent of the roughly 90 million U.S. households.[47] At about 2.5 persons per household, that meant that nearly 140 million Americans had regular access to VCRs in their homes. The device was ubiquitous outside the home too, populating schools, workplaces, and waiting rooms in dentists' offices. That the VCR could do what it did—transmit information and images at the whim of users—signaled that a majority of Americans had connected to a world transformed by new media by the end of the 1980s.

This development was not lost on enterprising social scientists tapped into shifts in American social and cultural life. They surveyed and interviewed users, combed through video rental stores, and queried time-shifters about their habits as if they were conducting an ethnographic study of a remote Pacific island village. Articles and book chapters appeared in academic publications—not marketing journals—on such topics as VCR users' knowledge of the various advanced features of their devices (the authors of this particular work were disappointed that users incapable of performing the simplest operations—like setting the VCR's clock—undermined their intuition that the VCR signaled some kind of global revolution); whether people rewatched programs they had already recorded and viewed (yes, yes they do, concluded this author); and how Israelis made decisions about what videocassettes to rent (it seemed that Israelis did not put nearly as much thought into their decisions as the author had).[48] Perhaps novelist Don DeLillo had in mind these scholars, obsessed as they were with making "a formal method of the shiny pleasures" of American life, when he created the "American environments" department of a generic midwestern college in *White Noise*.[49] The arcane attentiveness to the transformational potentialities of the VCR seems curious in retrospect, but only because the transformations these researchers eyed in the 1980s have since become central facets of the globalized media experience of the developed world. Today much of the connected world has unprecedented access to information and entertainment, "freedom" of media choice, and, as researchers found when they looked beyond U.S. borders, the ability to exchange media globally and often independent of the power of the nation-state.

There were reasons for excitement. Still, there were other reasons to think that the American VCR experience was less substantial than the device's global impact. "Freedom of choice has not opened up a whole new vista," wrote one of the few dissenting voices; "it has only given viewers a greater opportunity to watch what they want to when they want to. What they want to watch is the same as they always have watched."[50] Virtually all middle-class Americans with televisions could access at least a half-dozen broadcast television stations by the early 1980s; by that point, too, many millions had already subscribed to cable television systems providing access to dozens more channels. In short, what the VCR could do—provide access to a variety of programming, or more simply, to information—was not as significant in a country where viewers already experienced the sensation of choice in the form of competing broadcast networks and cable television. So VCR owners in the United States largely used their devices to record and watch programming to which they had already been exposed.

In fact, for the first half decade of the VCR's market life span, the option to view anything other than recorded programming from broadcast or cable television was limited. Video rental operations, which would become ubiquitous in strip malls across the country by the late 1980s, were still a relatively new and sparse phenomenon early in the decade. There were 2,500 rental stores nationwide in 1980, each charging roughly seven dollars per cassette rental, equal to about twenty dollars in 2015. (Purchasing prerecorded feature films was prohibitively expensive, too, generally costing in 1980s dollars between $80 and $100 each; content producers priced cassettes so high to make up for profits lost to rental businesses.) By 1989 there were 30,000 rental stores in the United States, and the cost of rentals dropped to just over two dollars per cassette.[51] Also, only about 15 percent of "early adopters" used their VCRs in conjunction with a video camera, though the number of camera owners would increase significantly in the late 1980s with the availability of "camcorders," which contained both a VCR and a camera in one compact unit.[52] In short, while the VCR promised big things—cross-cultural global communication, empowerment against powerful corporate media—most Americans did not take advantage of what scholars saw as the product's vast potential. Instead, they recorded, watched, and rewatched episodes of *Dallas* and *Star Trek: The Next Generation*, hardly revolutionary acts of cultural resistance but nevertheless a new kind of consumer empowerment.

The VCR's apotheosis in the United States was the portable consumer electronics embodiment of what journalist Tom Wolfe called the "'Me' Decade," or what the historian Christopher Lasch labeled, with just a bit more cynicism, the "Culture of Narcissism."[53] A generation of baby boomers had matured in the turmoil of the second half of the 1960s. During those years they had learned that "revolutionary change" meant challenging the state's monopoly over the exercise of violence at home and abroad, and "liberation" meant supporting nationalist movements against imperialism in the "third world." In the 1970s, according to Wolfe and Lasch, that generation turned inward and sought individualistic "change" and "liberation." As a well-educated generation entering the workforce, newly flush with expendable income, baby boomers looked to companies like Sony to provide them with "change" and "liberation" without leaving the house. Marketing that played off baby boomers' self-representations as a generation acculturated to revolutionary change won over the young, wealthy, upwardly mobile urban professionals who would come to be called yuppies in the 1980s. The VCR put a new world in yuppie hands. Whether they took advantage of it was a different story.

THE GREAT FACILITATOR: JAPANESE GADGETS GO GLOBAL

Americans disappointed researchers with their mundane VCR habits. Around the world, however, populations unspoiled by unrestricted access to television content more fully took advantage of the revolutionary opportunities that scholars had foreseen. Japanese corporations, for their part, made certain that VCRs were available. By the end of 1984 they were already producing nearly 30 million units annually, only about half of which either stayed in Japan or went to the United States.[54] Increasing production and imports meant that as many as 200 million units were in operation worldwide by the end of 1988.[55]

Governments and researchers paid close attention to the social and cultural significance of global VCR proliferation. The material reality of 200 million VCRs was momentous enough for UNESCO to commission "a study on the international flow of video hardware and software." The UN cultural agency mandated that researchers chronicle "the creation in the blinking of an eye a whole new medium of communication, which is fundamentally individualistic, anarchic even, almost beyond institutional organization. . . . As such, it is a medium profoundly worrying to many governments as it dances with ease around their efforts to control the directions of their cultures." The resultant report noted the VCR's tremendous growth in the "video rich" areas of North America, Japan and Southeast Asia, the Arab countries, and Western Europe. While the United States and Japan expectedly had high levels of VCR "penetration," fifteen other countries had rates over 50 percent. They were as diverse as Ireland, Nigeria, and Kuwait, the last of which had the world's highest penetration rate at near 90 percent, with many households owning two units.[56] VCRs were in greatest demand, the report and others like it concluded, where citizens had money but did not have access to an abundant media environment like that in the United States.[57] So while Americans used their VCRs to watch programming that most U.S. citizens with a television could already access, people in countries like Kuwait and Nigeria used the VCR to watch cassettes with content that was difficult to find. Much of it, of course, was American or Western European in origin. (It was later in the 1990s that Nigeria would start to develop the world's second largest film industry behind India and ahead of the United States, dubbed "Nollywood," providing local content to play on global gadgets.)[58]

The potential for unlimited access to new and previously scarce content was what most troubled governments, particularly authoritarian ones in Eastern Europe, China, Iran, and elsewhere. Both the illicit trade of untaxed, unauthorized VCRs and the viewing of prohibited content threatened authoritarian control over media, information, and culture. "Despite widespread bans on both VCRs and videocassette programming," noted a Harvard study, "people globally are viewing at present almost whatever they choose to," and governments were unsuccessfully taking disciplinary action.[59] The UNESCO report, for example, claimed that the Iranian government instituted a death penalty policy for anyone caught trafficking in VCRs. It did not, however, cite a specific case, and the practice continued to flourish. This juxtaposition suggests that researchers exaggerated such claims to highlight the VCR as a tool of political resistance.[60] True or not, rumors that repressive governments were cracking down on VCR trafficking illustrated how seriously observers interpreted the VCR's potential for global social, cultural, and even political transformation. "Because VCRs and cassettes travel so rapidly and relatively inconspicuously, they penetrate even the most closed societies," wrote the authors of a study of VCRs in the underdeveloped world. "The result is that national and ideological policies imbued in the people for years without much outside interference now must cope with polished, contrary views brought into homes by videos."[61] Where information was hardest to access, the VCR thrived, promising a future free of authoritarian limitations.

Atop the list of entities most prone to crack via video was the Soviet Union and its Eastern European empire. Like all "luxury" imports, VCRs were accessible only to a small fraction of elite Communist Party members. Nevertheless, units flooded into the country through a number of black market channels, and by 1984 VCRs could be found "in a growing number of apartments inhabited by members of the large Soviet elite," reported the *Washington Post*. "The electronic revolution offers numerous threats to a system that has been based on government monopoly of information and unrestrained censorship."[62] In 1985 the Soviet government acknowledged its inability to stem the tide of illegal units and consequently committed to producing 60,000 Soviet-made VCRs by 1990.[63] But nobody wanted the $1,500 Soviet-made units, marred, as all Soviet-made versions of Western consumer goods were, by shoddy craftsmanship. The black market $5,000 Japanese-made devices represented real foreign luxury.

Software was as difficult to come by as hardware. Videocassettes followed the underground flow of black market goods in cities like Moscow and Leningrad. Overdubbed versions of Western films produced on the cheap would often have just one Russian voice narrating the action and summarizing dialogue rather than multiple voice actors playing different parts. In Romania, a single woman employed by the government, Irinia Margareta Nistor, clandestinely translated and overdubbed dialogue for more than 3,000 films smuggled into the country from 1985 to 1989. Hers became the "most well-known voice in Romania after Ceausescu's."[64] The most effective pipelines for smuggling in Western material were the official state artists and athletes who could travel abroad, make purchases, and pass through customs checkpoints with few restrictions. Underground political activists also adopted VCR technologies for their purposes, giving rise to the word "Magnitizdat," the video equivalent of samizdat underground literature. "The single issue that most exercised the Soviets was not the nuclear arms race, or the war of espionage, or Afghanistan or Nicaragua or Cuba, or even the rising confidence of China," wrote Pico Iyer in 1988, "but simply the resistless penetration of video." "What a blow to the Bolsheviks!" cried an elderly Soviet citizen upon first seeing a VCR.[65]

Authoritarian governments everywhere saw the VCR as an icon of the social and cultural transformations indicative of a new, unstable global age in which borders became increasingly porous. "Where controls have been rather rigorously attempted, they have usually been ineffective . . . even in those countries where information suppression is a high art," noted a Harvard study. VCRs represented changes greater than the individual, yet changes in which the individual could partake and changes that transcended state power. "VCRs and videocassettes represent the fulfillment of some of the world's wildest fantasies," noted the same study. "They symbolize the usurpation of control by private individuals over a mass source of information, a control that many governments consider their domain."[66] Never before had so many governments dedicated so much attention to the proliferation of a consumer electronics product. Repressive governments did not need to worry about the subversive potential of television broadcasts because governments held monopolies over the tools that transmitted signals. The same can be said for radio, though U.S.-funded programs during the Cold War like Radio Free Europe and Voice of America sought to undermine the legitimacy of the Soviet government, and a television equivalent was in its infancy in the 1980s.[67] Japanese VCRs gave individuals intimate access to content in ways that U.S. information programs could not. They operated independent of state control over the means of their use (except, of course, access to electricity). That made governments worry.

The groups most interested in moving VCRs and videocassettes across relatively porous state borders were smugglers, who sought potentially lucrative profits, and migrants, who wished to stay connected to the cultures of their homelands. Smugglers would purchase VCRs where they were relatively inexpensive and easy to move and bring them into countries with high import tariffs. Such movement often inflated statistics: in Panama, for instance, it seemed that every resident of the country owned several VCRs, if the sales statistics were to be believed. Thus Panama served as a hub of VCR smuggling throughout Latin America. Arab states, to which South Asian immigrant labor flooded in the oil boom of the 1970s, functioned as similar distribution points for VCRs smuggled by laborers returning to India, Pakistan, Thailand, and the Philippines, where tariffs were intentionally high, part of a broad pattern of import-substitution industrial policy in the developing world. Returning émigrés also brought VCRs home for the use of families, introducing the devices at the popular level in ways that would not have been possible without global labor migrations.[68]

The promises of profit drove smuggling, as the worldwide black market for videos was already worth $1 billion in 1983, but the practice also served a utilitarian purpose: it provided popular access to media and content that were either prohibitively expensive or simply unavailable. In the Philippines, an estimated 99 percent of videocassettes on the market were pirated, but that phenomenon existed because illegal copies were exponentially cheaper than legal imports from the West—a crooked but nevertheless effective form of import-substitution policy. In other countries, like Pakistan, where import tariffs were 100 percent of the VCR's value, as much as 80 percent of VCR hardware was smuggled into the country illegally.[69]

The profits that smugglers made usually came from indigenous consumers who wanted content unavailable in their home countries. Also profitable, however, was supplying immigrants and diaspora communities around the globe with tools and content that helped them stay connected to the homes they left. An Indian immigrant to the United States described his relationship to video: "There is a small but tightly knit [Indian] community here. We regularly gather to watch the films together. We eat Indian foods. We wear traditional Indian clothes, which we don't always wear. It reminds us all of home, and of how we are Indians in another land." Another Indian explained, "We left [India] because things were very bad. But when we watch the movies, we see only what was good." Connecting with home through video also facilitated resistance to assimilation or homogenization efforts in countries receiving immigrants. Malaysia's minister of information complained that Chinese immigrant laborers preferred to watch videos illegally smuggled from China rather than government-sponsored programming about national development on one of the two state-run television networks.[70]

The cross-border exchange was even more remarkable because it happened despite the different national standards developed for television systems. The United States, Japan, much of Latin America, and several other countries adopted the NTSC system for displaying images on a television; many more countries used the PAL system, including most of Western

Europe; France and the Soviet Union used a third system, SECAM. The three systems were essentially incompatible without extensive knowledge of how VCRs operated. Yet so much exchange, particularly from the NTSC United States to PAL regions in the Middle East and most of Asia, still occurred. Part of this was possible because the only multisystem units that Japanese companies made were shipped to the Middle East, a major distribution point for global smuggling. In the United States, immigrants who wanted to watch incompatible content from home could turn to a small company like Instant Replay in Miami, which operated on the borders of legality by modifying standard Japanese VCRs to play recordings from any of the three systems. The company promised that their "Image Translator" VCRs were "Your Passport to World Communication."[71]

Governments did not fret about the Japanization of their societies, even though virtually all of the devices they sought to ban were designed and produced in Japan. The threat came, they believed, from potential Western or American ideas embedded in software that countered government efforts to define the limits of national cultures. An estimated 60 percent of videocassettes available globally in 1985 were American in origin.[72] The VCR created a cacophony of images from around the planet. More often than not, images from dominant Western culture were "hybridized" with indigenous cultural imagery; that is, they mingled imagery from several cultural sources to create new "hybrid" cultural products.[73] It was in light of this reality that Pico Iyer, one of the most prolific travel writers of the last quarter century and an informal ethnographer of early contemporary globalization, referred to the United States as the "Great Communicator." His stories, however, also implicitly reflected the presence of Japan as the Great Facilitator.

The British-born, Indian American Iyer set out across the globe in search of "the brand-new kinds of exotica thrown up by our synthetic age, the novel cultural hybrids peculiar to the tag end of the twentieth century." His travels took him to places as varied as Hanoi and Havana, Kyoto and Kathmandu. As a U.S. citizen, he was sensitive to the "allure and immediacy" of the popular culture of the "Pax Americana" everywhere he visited. People in seemingly remote Nepal were as familiar with Michael Jackson's *Thriller* as mall-dwelling teenagers in Los Angeles; Vietnamese knew Meryl Streep's face from posters lining the streets of Ho Chi Minh City, even if her eyes were creatively "orientalized"; and the trendiest spots to hang out in downtown Reykjavík had names that offered to transport their patrons to Southern California or Texas. To be sure, Bollywood movies had audiences in Southeast Asia (even if nobody understood the language), but "when it came to movies and TV, the

The VCR and Cultural Globalization

United States remained the Great Communicator. And if pop culture was, in effect, just a shorthand for all that was young and modern and rich and free, it was also a virtual synonym for America."[74]

Yet what was so surprising about Iyer's stories of hybrid cultural encounters was not the extent to which he expected to find and subsequently found America everywhere; it was the extent to which he did not realize that he just as often found Japan everywhere. Where he found American software, it inevitably was transmitted on Japanese hardware. He saw Sony Walkmans, televisions, and radios; the "holy trinity of the New China" happened to be Sony, Sanyo, and Seiko.[75] For Iyer, though, it was VCRs that had the most transformative impact:

> Not only had distances in time and space been shrunk but the latest weapons in cultural warfare—videos, cassettes and computer disks—were far more portable than the big screens and the heavy instruments of a decade before. They could be smuggled through border checkpoints, under barbed wire fences and into distant homes as easily, almost, as a whim. In the cultural campaign, the equivalent of germ warfare had replaced that of heavy-tank assaults. . . . More important, the video revolution was bringing home the power of the Pax Americana with greater allure and immediacy than even the most cunning propaganda.[76]

Smugglers and entrepreneurs took advantage of the demand for Japanese VCRs in unexpected locations. Iyer recalled a plane full of Indians flying home from Bangkok loaded down with VCRs to be sold in India. He met a young Indian man whose "great dream . . . was to be hired as a VCR importer, one of those black-money makers who paid men to go to Singapore and Bangkok to bring back video machines they could sell for vast profit."[77] Iyer found in Kathmandu, tucked away in the Nepalese Himalayas, more than fifty video clubs, where entrepreneurs with $3,000 VCRs admitted dozens of viewers, for a couple of rupees each, into dimly lit inner sanctums where they might watch Hindi, kung fu, or American films.[78] Whereas one VCR in an American household might affect the lives of a half-dozen people on average, a VCR in an underdeveloped region could potentially reach hundreds of people.

When Iyer journeyed to the loneliest places in the world, his out-of-place traveling companions always seemed to be Japanese businessmen. They smiled nervously at attendants on flights to North Korea where the in-flight literature accosted them as "heinous Japanese marauders." In the "Hidden Kingdom" of Bhutan, they huddled together in hotel restaurants in dark blue suits braving the foreign food for the good of the company. *Sararimen* populated the expensive new condominiums popping up in Shenzen, China—blazing a trail, in retrospect, for U.S. and Western European businesspeople two decades later.[79] It was as if the preexisting presence of Japanese commerce had already thrust these regions into Western-style global connectivity. For fellow world traveler Gary Jennings, who retraced the steps of Marco Polo, the Japanese presence brought on a sense of despoiled premodern innocence. After "I bribed my way into a camel caravan of smugglers," he wrote, "some of the romance rubbed off . . . , because you would think a desert caravan would be smuggling spices, perfumes and slave girls. Do you know what they were carrying? They had Sonys and VCRs dangling on the humps of camels."[80] It was as if Japan had already beaten the West to those locations that had yet to be globalized.

If the United States was the "Great Communicator" of the global age, then Japan was its Great Facilitator. It provided the tools by which populations around the world could access American content. Without Japanese consumer technologies like the VCR, the post–Cold War world—the era in which "globalization" became a discourse-defining paradigm—would have never developed an American face, for better or worse. Anti-globalization forces coalescing in the second half of the 1990s chastised Hollywood for cultural imperialism and attacked mega-corporations like Nike for economic imperialism without acknowledging that neither would have been possible without Japanese corporations' giving U.S. companies the tools to do so. The attention paid to the VCR's transformative potential, which grew in inverse proportion to the attention devoted to the VCR's "Japaneseness," defined the device as the first icon of cultural globalization.

Why was the VCR's Japaneseness of relatively little importance? In the discussion of the U.S. automobile industry in the previous two chapters, Honda's Japanese identity was central to the debate about its arrival in Ohio, where participants in Honda's growth built walls to deflect the national media's insistence that what was happening in Marysville was part of the story of Japanese ascendancy. In the chapters that follow, the national identity of Japanese sushi and animation—their Japaneseness—was central to those goods' appeal throughout the United States. As for the VCR, however, it was rarely consumed as something particularly Japanese, and there were both economic and cultural reasons for that national ambiguity.

Economically, the Japanese VCR did not fall prey to the assorted groups vocally protesting Japanese economic growth. In all of the previous industries that Japan's planning ministry, MITI, singled out for growth, the United

States had an equivalent industry with plenty of political clout. The textile, steel, television, and automobile industries were all important contributors to the U.S. postwar economic boom, and each was part of the story and image of the productivity and ingenuity of American labor. When all four industries began reeling under the combined stresses of stagnating production, rising inflation, and increasing foreign competition in the late 1960s (for textiles and steel) and 1970s (for televisions and automobiles), industry leaders targeted Japan as a convenient explanation for a host of industrial and managerial failures. There was no equivalent in the U.S. VCR industry because there was no U.S. VCR industry; consequently there were no jobs to lose or unemployed VCR assemblers to organize protests. Japanese corporations created the industry, and those U.S. companies that sold VCRs simply slapped their brand labels on Japanese- (and then Korean- and Taiwanese- and eventually Chinese-) made units. Economically, the VCR boom posed no threat to any powerful U.S. industry, and if anything, it created jobs for Americans in the distribution, marketing, and retailing of consumer electronics, a market in which Americans annually spent more than $43 billion by the end of the 1980s.[81]

Consumers did not identify the VCR culturally as something Japanese because, as anthropologist Koichi Iwabuchi puts it, the VCR did not "smell" Japanese. Iwabuchi, who has written on the transnationalism of Japanese popular culture, argues that certain Japanese products, specifically the "three Cs" of consumer electronics, cartoons, and computer/video games, flow through global cultural networks with no recognizable national or ethnic Japanese identity, no detectable "cultural odor." He writes, "The cultural impact of a particular commodity is not necessarily experienced in terms of the cultural image of the exporting nation."[82] In other words, just because the VCR was not consumed as something Japanese, in the way that sushi, anime, or even a Toyota could be, does not mean that it did not have a cultural impact. The political scientist Joseph Nye argued at the end of the 1980s that it was the United States' "soft power" in the form of popular culture that supposedly transmitted a universalist ideology of liberal democratic capitalism that made people around the world sympathetic to American power.[83] The VCR's more ambiguous cultural influence points to the nature of transnationalism in a world of decentralized power. As a unique product, one that was not just a text for consumers to read but a commodity that could "mediate between texts, spaces, and audiences," the Japanese-made VCR introduced Americans to processes and experiences that they would come to associate with globalization in the 1990s.[84]

SIX

Authenticity in a Hybrid World

Sushi at the Crossroads of Cultural Globalization

For *New York Times* senior editor Jack Rosenthal, the arrival of sushi at the Harvard Club in 1981 signaled a shift in American cultural life. The staid and stuffy New York institution, long a bastion of upper-class northeastern gentility stoically braving waves of trendy popular fads, now served the chic culinary delicacy that defined the emerging, and presumably distasteful, yuppie class. In telling readers about this shift, Rosenthal recounted an increasingly familiar scene, one taking place just two city blocks from the Harvard Club: "In Times Square, the huge signs used to flash Camel (with a puff of smoke), and Planters Peanuts, and Maxwell House. Look at them now: Panasonic, Sony and JVC electronics, Seiko and Casio watches, Midori liqueur, Canon cameras, Fuji film. You have to look around before spotting non-Japanese names like Coca-Cola and Castro Convertibles."[1]

At that point, Rosenthal's readers may have expected the editor to break into his best Howard Beale impersonation, mimicking the *Network* (1976) protagonist's popular tagline, "I'm mad as hell, and I'm not going to take this anymore," railing against the growing influence of America's once-and-potentially-future enemy. Instead, Rosenthal's tone took an unexpected turn. The Harvard Club's new offering was evidence that Americans were experiencing not a commercial invasion, another blow to a nation reeling from the economic uncertainty of the early 1980s, but something else, something constructive.

> Space on a building for neon signs can be rented. Cars or cameras can be expressly designed to appeal to the American taste. But there's a difference between Americans buying products made in Japan

for the American market and Americans reaching out for things as authentically Japanese as food.

The presence of a sushi bar at the Harvard Club suggests something more than tolerating Japanese manufacturers; it suggests a genuine curiosity and welcome for aspects of Japanese culture. In a small way, it signals a new cultural convergence.[2]

To be sure, the worst rhetorical excesses of the Japan Panic lay a decade in the future. Nevertheless, at this stage astute observers of U.S.-Japan relations recognized that trade-deficit calculations and war metaphors did not define the complicated scope of how Americans engaged with Japan. At a moment when it felt like new global economic flows and technological innovations were transforming American life, Rosenthal recognized that when people willingly mix culture, culture gets complicated.

Not all members of the chattering class, however, appreciated the cultural diversity that sushi's arrival signaled. Several years later Chicago's Pulitzer Prize–winning Mike Royko—a cantankerous and confrontational columnist if ever there was one—sounded the warning bell for his readers:

> In a couple hundred years, when historians study the decline and fall of the once-great nation known as the United States, they will pinpoint April 1989 as being the beginning of the end.
>
> The fall began with the deterioration of traditional values, the rejection of our heritage, the plunge into cultural decadence and effeteness.
>
> And historians will be able to look to Southern California to see where it all began. . . . They will find that in April 1989 the San Diego Padres became the first major-league franchise in history to sell—brace yourselves—sushi to the fans.[3]

Royko stretched to make the American consumption of sushi both a class issue—"the preferred snack of the yuppiest of the yuppies"—and a gender one. He described the feminization of boys whose first culinary experiences at a traditionally masculine baseball game would be light, delicate, healthy sushi instead of a boiled flesh-stick of processed pig by-products that had always served as a rite of passage for the American man. Twenty years later, "when they have grown to what passed for manhood," the same boys would recall for their own sons, "I remember my dad buying me my first sushi and Perrier." Royko concluded by comparing the masculinity of sluggers like Babe Ruth—the legendary man-beast had reportedly consumed twenty hot dogs in a single sitting—with the yuppified players of the effeminate sushi age.[4]

Sushi at the Crossroads of Cultural Globalization

The contrast between Rosenthal's and Royko's interpretations of sushi's cooptation into traditional U.S. institutions, both elite and popular, reflected much of the ambivalence Americans felt toward all things Japanese in the 1970s and 1980s. In that sense, sushi—defined not, as many Americans believe, by raw fish but by a particular preparation of vinegared rice—was just another Japanese thing: a product of a culture to be feared, admired, or both. It was at once both *Shōgun* and *Rising Sun*, a vestige of a venerable past and a harbinger of a transformative future. But it also had become another part of the globalized landscape of the ordinary that surrounded Americans: by the early 1980s, hubs of sushi consumption like Los Angeles and New York had seen the number of Japanese restaurants within city limits increase by as much as a factor of ten in the previous decade and a half.[5] And it was not just cosmopolitan metropoles tapping into global cultural flows, despite Royko's midwestern-everyman masculine posturing. By the early 1990s, Japanese restaurants, with sushi as the star attraction, had conquered the American culinary landscape. The number of sushi bars in the United States increased by 400 percent between 1988 and 1998, and by the second decade of the twenty-first century, more than 20,000 Japanese restaurants operated across the country. Since the 1980s sushi has climbed down the ladder of social hierarchy. In many supermarkets today, one can buy a dozen pieces of pre-made sushi for less than $5, while at Urasawa in Los Angeles requesting one's sushi meal *omakase*—in essence, chef's choice—costs upwards of $250.[6] Where I live in Ruston—an enclave of 22,000 in sparsely populated Bible Belt north Louisiana, hundreds of miles from both a major metropolis and the sea—you will find sushi in no less than three locations.

Like the other Japanese goods in this book, by the 1980s sushi not only had established a noticeable material presence across the United States but also had entered the American popular imagination. John Hughes's iconic 1980s teen drama *The Breakfast Club* used sushi to highlight class distinctions among its detention-bound students. The snobbish wealthy girl explains to the troublemaking boy that she's eating sushi—"rice, raw fish, and seaweed"— and the working-class delinquent responds churlishly, "You won't accept a guy's tongue in your mouth, and you're going to eat that?"[7] Hughes used the scene to demonstrate the expanding global cosmopolitanism of wealthy Americans, even to poke fun at the quickness with which the upper class adopts chic cultural fads, and to contrast it with the provincial sensibilities of working-class Americans. Similarly, to communicate the meteoric rise in status of protagonist Bud Fox in his film *Wall Street*, Oliver Stone included a montage of Fox making sushi with his upper-class girlfriend in his expensive new Manhattan apartment. A few shots of actors Charlie Sheen and Daryl Hannah slicing raw fish and rolling sushi rice effectively conveyed the characters' class-climbing yuppie sensibilities. Several years later, however, in the midst of the worst rhetoric of the Japan Panic, two movies used sushi in a more disturbing way. In both the crime-thriller *Rising Sun* and the action-comedy *Showdown in Little Tokyo* there are scenes portraying the obscure practice of *nyotaimori*, which uses a naked woman as a serving tray for sushi.[8] Abandoning all subtlety, sushi for the directors of these films served to showcase the Japanese colonization of the United States, in particular its white women, who became not just servants but objects of servitude. By the early 1990s cultural producers could rely on sushi, in ways both lighthearted and menacing, as a set piece for communicating ideas about consumption, class, and culture.

Several quality accounts of sushi's contemporary U.S. and global impact exist.[9] Journalist Sasha Issenberg has written about the globalization of the sushi economy. He claims sushi is the exemplary globalized product, and he tells a fascinating story of getting fish caught on one side of the planet onto dinner plates on the other. "Eating at a sushi bar," Issenberg writes of his twenty-first-century observations, "is not so much an escape from fast-paced global commerce as an immersion in it."[10] On the academic side, nobody has written more prodigiously and thoughtfully about sushi's globalization than anthropologist Theodore Bestor. His groundbreaking study of Tokyo's Tsukiji Market is a landmark in understanding the interactions between the local and global.[11] Sociologist James Farrer has written extensively on the global appeal and proliferation of Japanese cuisine.[12] Typically these scholars are concerned with how sushi has fit into the increasingly complex globalizing economy and culture of the twenty-first century. No scholar has yet to return to sushi's U.S. arrival and interrogate what this curious new delicacy meant for its first American consumers.

This transpacific exchange is all the more fascinating in the context of the United States' broader encounter with Japan in the 1970s and 1980s, when it was the engagement with Japanese goods that defined that relationship for the average American more so than disputes over trade imbalances and high-tech defense contracts. As Americans ate sushi for the first time, they engaged in a particular kind of global exchange, serving as intermediaries between two societies separated by an ocean and a history of political, economic, and military conflict and cooperation. Japanese restaurants and sushi bars in big cities and small towns alike became cultural "middle grounds," spaces where American expectations met Japanese and global realities and where miscommunication and misunderstandings of customs and tastes on both sides often led to creative reworkings—new hybrid forms—of culinary practices that diners labeled authentic.[13] Alternatively, James Farrer has proposed the concept of "culinary contact zones," "spaces of cultural friction and creativity," like the kitchens and dining rooms of Japanese restaurants in the United States and elsewhere outside Japan.[14] In what ways did Americans use their consumption of sushi in such culinary contact zones to imagine Japan and understand its place in the rapidly changing world of the late twentieth century? What did it mean for U.S.-Japan relations that sushi for many Americans came to embody essential "Japaneseness"? To answer these questions, we must first consider the changing ways in which culture traveled around the world in the second half of the twentieth century and what sushi tells us about Rosenthal's global "cultural convergence."

CONSUMING AUTHENTICITY IN GLOBAL AMERICA

For such a globalized delicacy, varieties of sushi in the United States are often rooted in local places—the California roll, with avocado and crab; the Tampa roll, with fried grouper; the Texas (or Dallas) roll, with beef and spinach; and the greatest nightmare of the sushi purist, the Philadelphia roll, which features the very non-Japanese cream cheese. While raw fish, rice, and dried seaweed seem distant from cream cheese's comfortable pairing with the bagel, that latter relationship was not predestined either. Through a process of transatlantic cultural exchange and hybridization beginning with Polish Jews in the seventeenth century, crossing the ocean in the early twentieth, and reaching the supermarkets of the postwar era, the bagel became a staple of U.S. popular cuisine. Murray Lender's mass-produced culinary wonder, which tried to bring a taste of ethnic New York to heartland freezers, seemed the ideal medium for the marketers at Kraft Foods. Its Philadelphia Cream Cheese was a mass-produced derivative of several French soft cheeses, sweetened to appeal to the taste buds of Americans consuming increasing quantities of processed sugar. The bagel with cream cheese accompanied by lox (itself an import from Scandinavia by way of Jewish immigrants), the "quintessential New York brunch," was one American variant of the "other Sunday trilogy," competing for table time with bacon, eggs, and toast. It was, according to historian Donna R. Gabaccia, one of the "ways that the production, exchange, marketing, and consumption of food have generated new identities—for food and eaters alike."[15] Like a bagel with cream cheese, the Philadelphia roll is a truly American food: a hybrid cuisine of global culture remixed in North American kitchens.

Decades after it first hit supermarket coolers, cream cheese found sushi. Or more precisely, enterprising and creative American sushi chefs—curious hybrids in their own right—experimented with available North American ingredients and flavors to localize Japan's most notable contribution to global cuisine. The Philadelphia roll, which varies according to location but always includes cream cheese combined with fish and/or vegetables rolled in vinegared rice and nori (the black seaweed paper essential to the architecture of *makizushi*, or sushi rolls), is exemplary of cultural globalization—rooted in a specific time and place, it is nevertheless a product of the transplanetary interaction of ideas, customs, and foodways.

The Philadelphia roll is, in short, a tangible, edible sort of cultural globalization, a taste of the global cultural shifts of the last several decades that have sent Madonna to Malaysia and brought Bollywood back to Bakersfield. Cultural globalization contrasts with economic globalization, which has caused political conflict around the world and claimed countless headlines in the last two decades. More challenging to quantify than trade deficits and foreign direct investment, cultural globalization often has a feel of "I know it when I see it." Like the VCR, sushi enabled Americans to engage with global transformations in local contexts. To be sure, the experience of consuming sushi changed, as global experiences always do, as it crossed the Pacific in the hands of cultural intermediaries, but the end result was the same: new global experiences mediated by the technological transformations of the age of globalization. Technology and money brought Japanese food to the United States; culture demanded that it adapt to local tastes.

Thinking about local responses to globalization means thinking about the various ways people respond to the exotic and new. Local responses to the globalizing of culture are multifaceted and run along a continuum from resistance to embrace of both the passive and active sort. Those who embrace global culture do so in different ways: some seek an "authentic" cultural experience, one that transports them to an unfamiliar place and time—seekers of the global authentic, we might call them. Their counterparts are seekers of the global hybrid, adventurous consumers desirous of the new for difference's sake; they relish the remix, the mash-up, and the purist's sacrilege. The U.S. encounter with sushi since the late 1960s provides a perspective on how local consumers engage with both the global authentic and the global hybrid.

That hybridized American rolls like the California and Philadelphia have come to represent sushi in the United States today is not indicative of the delicacy's first two decades in the country after its initial transpacific journey. Central to the earliest U.S. conversations about sushi, and Japanese food in general, was the expectation of authenticity. When food writers and cultural commentators wrote about sushi, they cared most about what they defined as an "authentic" Japanese culinary experience, one that extended beyond the plate and to the larger environment of the table, the bar, and the restaurant. Diners read "Japaneseness" in their meals and surroundings, even when their qualifications for determining such characteristics seemed to be based on stereotypes and clichés.

Like the sociologist David Grazian in his thoughtful study of blues clubs in Chicago, I am not interested in "what is or is not authentic" so much as I am struck by the "*search for authenticity*" among sushi's first U.S. consumers.[16] Grazian's definition of authenticity warrants noting at length because it is as utilitarian as it is insightful:

> Broadly speaking, the notion of authenticity suggests two separate but related attributes. First, it can refer to the ability of a place or event to conform to an idealized representation of reality: that is, to a set of expectations regarding how such a thing ought to look, sound, and feel. At the same time, authenticity can refer to the credibility or sincerity of a performance and its ability to come off as natural and effortless. When we take vacations to faraway and exotic locales . . . we desire to inhabit what we imagine to be the typical, everyday worlds of our hosts, and we want to experience that world without the sense that it has been manufactured for our own benefit.[17]

Grazian observes that authenticity is always an artificial construct, a contrived performance regardless of whether or not it matches our expectations for realness. And in an observation relevant for trying to understand how Americans view foreign otherness and Japaneseness in particular, Grazian argues that "the search for authenticity incorrectly presumes that people typically observe highly predictable, customary patterns of behavior—a conceit that tricks us into thinking that cultural worlds other than our own are homogenous and unchanging, rather than complex and contradictory." Ultimately, authenticity is "based on a mix of prevailing myths and prejudices invented in the absence of actual experience."[18]

Sushi consumption in its first two decades was complicated by its foreignness. Grazian's authentic jazz seekers were often Americans searching for an authentically American art form. Sushi seekers, on the other hand, privileged sushi for its otherness and thus expected from their experiences "highly predictable, customary patterns of behavior" that were nevertheless different and foreign. This is reminiscent of the consumers whom philosopher

Sushi at the Crossroads of Cultural Globalization

Lisa Heldke calls "food adventurers," diners (she includes herself) actively looking for new, exotic eating experiences that they consider authentic—the "foodies" among the seekers of the global authentic. In critiquing the concept of authenticity, she argues that food adventurers "tend to operate from the assumption that we really can sort out the authentic from the inauthentic—that we have clear, unambiguous criteria with which to do the sorting." For Heldke's adventurers, authenticity is often a matter of expecting the unexpected: "We expect the food of the other to be distinctly different from our own foods, and we tend flat-footedly to identify the unfamiliar elements *as* the authentic ones." The criteria for difference and thus authenticity is often a matter of performance, of expecting foods "prepared the way it would be in its culture of origin—using the same methods and the same ingredients insiders would."[19] For sushi's cultural intermediaries—the restaurateurs and chefs—meeting cultural expectations demanded a delicate dance of predictable exoticism, of performing the unexpected.

To avoid a perspective that Heldke calls "food colonialism," observers might see sushi in the United States not as a one-way transmission of global culture but as a product of American cultural expectations meeting Japanese realities, a cultural middle ground. The real creativity in the relationship came not from adventurous eaters but from keen chefs attentive to global trends and cultural tastes. Grazian argues that the production of hybridity—"attempts to meld together otherwise disparate cultures in a self-conscious manner in order to generate new possibilities for creative expression"—is one of the ways in which cultural producers resist claims to authenticity.[20] Sushi's producers within the United States actively hybridized their goods under the assumption that it was the only way Americans would eat them. Passive seekers of the global authentic might assume that their *makizushi* with the backwards construction of the rice wrapped around the nori was authentic—unless, of course, it was named something like a California roll or a Philadelphia roll. In those cases, consumers actively embraced the global hybrid. But even when it was clear they were eating a hybrid product, sushi eaters still sought the global authentic in the establishments where they ate their sushi, at least in its first two decades. Those food writers well aware of the heretical role that avocado and cream cheese played in authentic sushi still demanded a Japanese experience when they went to Japanese restaurants and sushi bars—they wanted spaces and faces that met their expectations of Japaneseness. The blending of authenticity and hybridization took place on a middle ground where U.S. diners' expectations for Japaneseness met global realities of cultural exchange and local material realities of available food resources. Japanese restaurants and sushi bars became transnational spaces of negotiated cultural exchange between chefs, critics, and diners. In short, the push-and-pull between the global authentic and the global hybrid was always messy, and it is what shaped the subjective experience of cultural globalization in local places amid the United States' encounter with Japan in the 1970s and 1980s.

The search for the global authentic and the global hybrid roughly aligned with the notion of Japan as both a premodern and a postmodern society. Consuming sushi, so often identified as "raw fish," seemed sensually barbaric, the product of a delicate and effete civilization with a genuine connection to "nature" and a darker, wild, violent streak. Sushi was simultaneously the chrysanthemum and the sword. Warnings of the danger of eating raw fish were common in sushi's first years in the United States (warnings that remain in effect for pregnant women) and food writers assuaged fears of perennial parasite scares, a persistent reminder of sushi's exoticism.[21] To unadventurous diners, "an indecent display of raw fish and octopus legs" at a sushi bar could appear primitive, if not downright medieval, a scene they might imagine at home in the pages of *Shōgun*, despite the anachronism—the sushi of the twentieth century did not exist in the seventeenth, in Japan or anywhere else.[22] On the other hand, sushi could also point to a postmodern Japan, one where the most seemingly bizarre combinations could produce new global hybrids, images as disorienting as "HM GRWN" Hondas in Ohio and Michael Jackson's *Thriller* in the Himalayas, combinations of cultures that only the technologized future permitted—food Frankensteins like the Philadelphia roll.

RICE SANDWICHES

The Philadelphia roll is a curious descendant of the first and most famous (or infamous, depending on one's disposition toward national culinary authenticity) of American sushi mutations, the California roll. The latter—a concoction of crab, avocado, and mayonnaise—originated in the first U.S. sushi restaurants in the 1960s, and its creation was a microcosm for the United States' engagement with sushi. Journalist Alex Renton claims that "the key moment in sushi's crossover from native cuisine to global snack is the invention of the California roll. It's the spaghetti bolognese of sushi now.... It is an international cliché, but it was the crossover hit that took sushi out of Japan and on the path to global dominance."[23] The California roll is the embodiment of the globalization of sushi.

Sushi at the Crossroads of Cultural Globalization

Several chefs claim to have invented the roll in the late 1960s, including Yuzo Sasaki, owner of Yu-san Sushi in El Cerrito, California, and Ichiro Mashita, sushi chef at Los Angeles's Tokyo Kaikan. Hidekazu Tojo, a Japanese chef brought to Vancouver in the late 1960s to satisfy increasing local appetites for sushi, also claims to have created both the California roll (which he named the "Tojo roll") and the "inside-out" roll, which reverses the order of seaweed paper (nori) and rice in the construction of a sushi roll. With multiple claims for its origins, it is likely that multiple chefs were experimenting with local seasonal ingredients when "authentic" ingredients like fresh tuna were costly or thousands of miles away. Avocados, indigenous to Mexico and plentiful in Southern California since the nineteenth century, piled up in local supermarkets, and after some experimenting, chefs found that the fruit's smooth, buttery taste proved an inexpensive and effective substitute for tuna.[24]

In addition to the economics of sushi ingredients, the California roll's genesis was rooted in Japanese sushi chefs' impression of American culture. Years later an executive for Tokyo Kaikan's Japanese owners recounted the corporate mythology of the origins of Americans' favorite sushi morsel to journalist Issenberg. The company's owner suggested to the restaurant's chefs, "Why don't you make sushi for the Caucasians?," and the previously untested combination of king crab legs and avocado seemed the natural fit.[25] Chef Sasaki recalled upon leaving Japan, "My sushi master told me that Americans wouldn't be able to appreciate sushi. He advised me to put it on skewers."[26] Japanese perceptions of the American palate led to the creation of the California roll and colored Americans' encounters with sushi at the time and since. The same perceptions led to the reversed construction of typical *makizushi*, with the nori wrapped inside the rice instead of outside. Chefs assumed that provincial and picky American eaters would not find eating paper appetizing, so they buried the nori inside the rice. Thus from the very beginning the sushi that Americans ate, epitomized by the California roll, was not "authentic" in the sense that it resembled its Japanese counterpart; instead, it was created by cultural producers conscientious of the particular tastes of local consumers.

Of course, sushi was not Americans' first encounter with Americanized Japanese food either. The charismatic founder of the U.S.-based restaurant chain Benihana, Rocky Aoki, summed up American attitudes toward foreign food succinctly: "Americans enjoy eating in exotic surroundings but are deeply mistrustful of exotic foods"—thus the success of the chain he founded in New York as a twenty-five-year-old former Olympic wrestler in 1964.[27] No single individual did more to shape American perceptions of Japanese food in the 1970s than Aoki, who had no training as a chef but saw the commercial potential in providing Americans with what they perceived to be an authentic Japanese dining experience. The key to Aoki's success, according to anthropologist Katarzyna Cwiertka, was "the culinary entertainment it provided, without really challenging the customers' taste buds."[28] Most Americans today are familiar with the routine at Benihana, or any of the many "hibachi"-style restaurants throughout the country: on a teppanyaki grill before assembled customers, who expect to be awed by the chef's culinary acrobatics, a chef prepares a meal of nonthreatening ingredients found in most American homes, tossing shrimp into diners' mouths and creating smoking volcanoes from sliced onions. As Sasha Issenberg puts it, "Aoki had invented a restaurant version of hiring a karate expert to preside over a Memorial Day barbecue."[29] For most Americans in the 1960s, as long as the chef looked Asian, the waitresses dressed in kimonos, and the decor matched their media-inspired expectations, the food did not matter: the experience still translated as Japanese. Aoki's advertising even mocked traditional Japanese food to let eaters know they could feel comfortable bringing their American-sized appetites to a restaurant with a foreign-sounding name, with one advertisement stating, "No exquisitely carved carrot slices. No wispy vegetables arranged in perfect flower patterns. Instead, solid food in abundance."[30] While there was no place for effeminate sushi in Mike Royko's vision of America, Benihana fit comfortably.

As a popular chain with more than a hundred outlets by 1980, Benihana influenced widespread American understandings of Japanese food. Its growth coincided, however, with the rapid expansion of independently owned Japanese restaurants in cities great and small. Though it would be difficult to gauge quantitatively, it seems that most restaurants serving sushi by the 1980s did not originally open with the express intention of serving the pricey delicacies. Offering sushi, after all, was an expensive and risky proposition for a restaurant accustomed to making foods that Americans regularly ate. Such a venture required constructing new spaces, hiring a sushi chef (such chefs were almost exclusively Japanese in the 1970s), finding importers and suppliers for uncommon ingredients, and training a staff to understand, produce, and explain to customers a new cuisine with thousands of subtle variations. If many hundreds of reviews from the period provide an accurate picture, Japanese restaurants first opened in the 1960s and 1970s in response to the rising popularity of "ethnic food" but served foods that Americans regularly ate with small variations. Only later did many build new sushi bars as the fad began to grow in the late 1970s and early 1980s. In their first decades, Japanese

Sushi at the Crossroads of Cultural Globalization

restaurants in the United States had served Americanized, Benihana-style fare and transitioned to offering more "authentic" food experiences only when several larger cultural developments made the investment in sushi a worthwhile enterprise.

Americans, then, had been consuming a kind of Japanese food for decades before they started eating sushi. Even into the late 1970s, to write about or eat Japanese food did not necessarily mean writing about or eating sushi. One Washington reviewer in 1977 wanted to avoid Benihana's "Americanized steakhouse version" of Japanese food and so, "feeling adventurous," tried a restaurant she believed to be more authentic; she ordered only cooked food and soup but promised to "venture further afield next time." Choosing the cooked food at a Washington restaurant earlier that year, critic Susan Crowley noted, "True connoisseurs of Japanese cooking will enjoy the *sushi* bar"—but she passed on that opportunity.[31] Even at this late stage these critics felt they could review a Japanese restaurant in a major city without trying its sushi, indicating that sushi did not yet define Japanese food as it would a decade later.

Soon after, though, a food writer could not visit a Japanese restaurant without telling his or her readers something about the quality and selection of sushi. At the end of the 1970s, longtime *Washington Post* food critic Phyllis Richman commented on that decade's boom of "ethnic" food and the exploding popularity of sushi in particular: "In 1970, if a menu was in a foreign language, which was rare enough, the waiter carefully explained each dish in English. Now the menu in English has become all too rare, and nobody expects a waiter to speak English, at least to *you*. Sakura Palace once advertised 'One of the finest sushi bars in town.' Now it claims, 'We use the finest "tane" available,' assuming that everyone knows what 'tane' means."[32] Echoing similar sentiments for New York, reviewer Bryan Miller noted, "Ten years ago sushi bars were considered exotic, ethnic enclaves catering to Japanese immigrants and only the most intrepid of Americans." By 1984, however, roughly 300 Japanese restaurants and sushi bars served the residents of greater New York, a growth of more than 300 percent in less than a decade. According to Leslie Bennetts, who surveyed the "blossoming" of Japanese culture in the United States for the *New York Times*, it was a real shift to see that "hostesses are serving sushi to guests who not so long ago would have muttered unflattering asides about raw fish."[33] By the late 1980s sushi all but defined Japanese cuisine, and the image of small rice balls topped with raw fish was a visual metaphor for Japan's growing global presence.

Cookbooks paralleled popular and critical tastes. Showcasing Japanese food reflected changing cultural understandings of Japanese cuisine and demonstrated a trend of exoticization and othering through the 1980s. Like the transition from *Shōgun* to *Rising Sun*, Japanese cookbooks increasingly emphasized the unbridgeable differences between U.S. and Japanese cultures rather than looked for common ground. Prior to the 1980s, authors of books like Heihachi Tanaka's *The Pleasures of Japanese Cooking* and Aya Kagawa's *Japanese Cookbook: 100 Favorite Recipes for Western Cooks* chose to include almost exclusively recipes that would appeal to mainstream American palates. Tanaka, who served as head chef for Japan Air Lines, included a five-page section on sushi, within a larger section of appetizers, and noted, "So great is the popularity of these little 'rice sandwiches' that tiny *sushi* bars are to be found everywhere in Japan," though sushi provoked "the greatest resistance among casual Western visitors," observed cookbook author Nina Froud in 1963.[34] In the United States in the first three postwar decades, the bite-sized "rice sandwiches" received little attention relative to both their popularity in Japan and how Americans just two decades later would perceive Japanese cuisine.

Instead Japanese food cookbooks for American audiences before the 1980s highlighted those foods that had close Western analogues, with lots of grilled, broiled, or fried beef, chicken, and common seafoods, along with prominent recipes for dishes with proven Western popularity that required little adventurism, like teriyaki (grilled meat or seafood with a sweet sauce) and tempura (fried meat or seafood). As such, foods like teriyaki, tempura, and the popular sukiyaki (which even inspired a hit pop song in the 1960s)[35] never came to embody Japaneseness in the way sushi would—publishers could not, for instance, use a piece of fried shrimp on the cover of a cookbook to indicate its Japaneseness to audiences in the way they could two decades later with a piece of toro sushi. Early cookbook meals fit better than sushi into traditional Western understandings of food, that is, food was not food unless it was prepared at high temperatures. Tanaka's book, for example, followed the chapter on appetizers with ones titled "Soups," "Broiled Dishes," "Steamed Dishes," "Saucepan Foods," and "Fried Foods." The cover of the short booklet *Cooking Japanese Style* could mislead readers: it prominently featured a plate with a row of raw sliced tuna, and yet there were no recipes with raw fish anywhere within. The booklet instead began with a recipe for a "Japanese Egg Roll," which instructed enterprising cooks to blend together canned tuna with rice, eggs, onion, and curry, and then to deep-fry several hand-molded balls of the resulting concoction.[36] The Japaneseness of the

Sushi at the Crossroads of Cultural Globalization

Japanese Egg Roll was rather dubious; this dish was Japanese cuisine for the mass-produced, high-calorie consumption of postwar America.

By the early 1980s cookbooks had evolved to reflect changing understandings of Japan and its food, mirroring the broader cultural and intellectual reassessment of Japan. Almost universally, sushi assumed a place of prominence, with books devoted exclusively to it or at least expansive chapters detailing a variety of styles and ingredients. Large glossy color photos of sushi on thick, high-quality paper replaced the typical black-and-white paperback cookbooks of decades past. Books like Mia Detrick's *Sushi* were designed to appeal to the eyes as much as they aimed to acculturate Americans to new cultural experiences. Full-page, detailed color photographs decorated half the book, and not until the last few pages did Detrick provide readers with any instruction on making their own sushi. *Sushi* and similar books took up space on aspiring yuppie coffee tables as often as they sat on the bookshelf of an adventurous cook. Aesthetically, sushi held center stage. Even publications that functioned more like cookbooks, like *The Book of Sushi* and *Quick and Easy Sushi Cookbook*, took aesthetics very seriously: both were physically large with full-page glossy color photos.[37] These books were made for committed hobbyists and connoisseurs, even those who aspired to artistry in their cooking. No longer, it seemed, did publishers feel the need to fill a book with stereotypical Japanese iconography like geisha and cherry blossoms to make food of questionable origin more authentic. Sushi's Japaneseness, its foreignness, spoke for itself.

A series of broad social and cultural developments ushered in a national environment ripe for sushi's growth. First among those developments was the broadening of American cultural attitudes, especially attitudes toward food, in the wake of the upheavals of the 1960s. By the late 1970s the radicalized college students of the previous decade were cashing in on their expensive educations, evolving from rebellious youths to conspicuous consumers. Inexpensive jet travel spurred a "growing cosmopolitanism," according to food historian Harvey Levenstein, "which made people more receptive to foreign foods in general."[38] Consuming certain kinds of exotic new food connoted status among the class soon to be labeled "yuppies." Eating sushi was a mark of distinction, a way of communicating one's education, economic position, and openness toward new ideas and things. *The Yuppie Handbook*, which poked fun at the new consuming class, listed tuna sashimi among its "Things Yuppies Eat for Lunch."[39] For these conspicuous consumers, many of whom would fit into Heldke's category of food adventurers, eating exotic foods like sushi was a way of building up cultural capital. "By sampling a cuisine none of your friends has tasted," Heldke says, "you accumulate a bit of sophistication that you can bank, and invest later in a social situation in which it is important to raise your stature."[40] Sushi, with not only its novelty and exoticism but also its connections to a wealthy sophisticated global power, gave aspiring adventurers a lot of cultural capital to bank.

At the same time that socioeconomic changes were altering cultural attitudes, new groups of people were shifting the demographic landscape of the United States in the wake of the Immigration and Nationality Act of 1965, which abolished national origins immigration quotas. As critic Calvin Trillin put it, "Some serious eaters think of the Immigration Act of 1965 as their very own Emancipation Proclamation."[41] The law literally opened the doors to "ethnic" restaurants across the country, providing food adventurers with seemingly limitless opportunities for new cultural experiences created by emigrants from South and Southeast Asia, Latin America, and Africa. Sushi generally avoided the categorization of "ethnic"—in part, perhaps, because the spread of Japanese food was not connected to a wave of Japanese immigration, distinct from Chinese or Southeast Asian food in that respect—but establishments serving sushi benefited from the broader expansion of middle-class tastes. Levenstein remarked that "the adoption of new food tastes is probably facilitated by an absence of low-status people from whose homelands they originate," an observation particularly relevant to sushi's persistent status as an upper-class cuisine.[42]

As others have observed, sushi also satisfied new tastes for lighter, healthier food in the 1970s. In that decade a series of private- and government-funded studies confirmed what many Americans already suspected: diets high in fat and cholesterol posed long-term dangers to health. Sushi's most common ingredients—rice, vegetables, and seafood—fit comfortably into Americans' changing understandings of nutrition and health. A cross-section of calorie-conscious and status-conscious eaters gravitated toward sushi's "built-in health benefits," overlooking for the moment the high sodium content of the requisite accompaniment to nearly all Japanese food, soy sauce.[43]

Alongside sushi's perceived health benefits and the expanding tastes of the consuming class, understandings of Japanese food shifted in concert with broader intellectual and cultural trends. Conversations ranging from "Japan as Number One" to the "Coming War with Japan" could not help but bleed into how people talked about Japanese food. These exchanges raise the question of how power functions in global food relationships and in the creation of hybrid cuisines. Heldke urges eaters to be attentive to colonial relationships, to see foods like curry, for example, not as "authentic" Indian cuisine but as a product of the global inequalities of colonialism. After all, nothing like the curries that Europeans eat exists in that form in India, and yet Western consumers imagine it as a product of an exoticized East.[44] In other hybrid foods, the relationship between imperial power and the colonized is also unambiguous. The *bánh mì* sandwich, a delicious hybrid of Vietnamese ingredients (pickled vegetables, fish sauce, and spices) and French (pâté, mayonnaise, and a baguette), clearly wears its colonial legacy—one of the rare positive echoes of the forceful imposition of French culture on Southeast Asia.[45] But where do we locate power in a Philadelphia roll in the context of the U.S.-Japan relationship in the 1970s and 1980s?

From the end of World War II to the 1970s, Japan sat comfortably within the informal U.S. empire, enjoying the material benefits of a close partnership with the world's largest and most productive economy and the military protection of the U.S. nuclear umbrella. But Americans looked uneasily on that imperial relationship by the 1980s, both in the sense that Japanese industries benefited unfairly from U.S. protection and in that it appeared as if Japan aimed to overtake, if not destroy, the United States economically (and maybe one day militarily). Americans could eat teriyaki and tempura so easily in the 1950s and 1960s because of its familiar look, smell, and taste; but they also ate it because to consume the foods of those people enjoying U.S. global benevolence during the Cold War accorded well with the American global imagination. As the imperial subject seemed to catch up to the imperial power, it was harder to come to terms with the imposition of "real" Japanese food like sushi. Some Americans grew uncomfortable with Japanese food just as they grew uneasy with Japanese power. Others—like the neoliberal proponents of Japanese-style globalization and the Honda employees in central Ohio that we have already encountered and the anime fans we will meet in the next chapter—embraced a world of cultural diversity.

A CONSUMING EXPERIENCE

Embracing sushi did not mean abandoning persistent discourses on Japanese culture. For professional food writers, people paid to eat and critique cuisine, stereotypes of Japanese culture abounded. Clichés about Japanese emphasis on aesthetic beauty, delicacy, sensuality, eroticism, and even effeminacy made for a well of cultural images from which food writers could draw to illustrate cultural context to their North American readers. As a result, it seemed, eating sushi gave every food writer a license to wax poetic. Deconstructing their flowery prose provides another perspective on what it meant to consume Japan in the 1980s.

Writers drew upon clichéd imagery of an imagined premodern Japan to portray the exoticness and unfamiliarity of sushi's ingredients, preparation, and presentation. Sushi and sashimi (raw fish served without rice), wrote Phyllis Richman in the early years of sushi in the nation's capital, "are highly developed examples of the art of simplicity, of such beauty that it can be appreciated even in the abstract." A meal in the popular restaurant Samurai Sushiko, one of Washington's three premier sushi restaurants in the late 1970s, was "an occasion of purity and subtlety, of contrasting sharpness and intensity, almost a ceremony," "like eating in the middle of a Japanese brush painting" or "a small museum of Japanese arts."[46] Reviewing the restaurant Fuji, Richman adopted the uncommon second-person voice for the entire article, concluding, "You feel neither stuffed nor hungry. And definitely serene."[47] Another *Post* writer compared sushi to "an edible ikebana. A haiku in seaweed and translucent flesh."[48] Karen Kenyon, reviewing the restaurant Samurai in San Diego, wrote, "Walking into Samurai is like walking into a Zen poem," and she noted the "feeling of harmony [that] exists in the balance of the Samurai warrior figure and the Japanese Geisha doll who stand and wait on opposite sides of the entry."[49] Not to be outdone, the popular Philadelphia food writer Elaine Tait described meals at one new Japanese restaurant as "serenely beautiful as a placid, lily-covered pond."[50] Caroline Bates, writing about a California restaurant for prestigious *Gourmet* magazine, even found poetic inspiration in what amounted to far-from-exotic fried shrimp: "The word tempura, in one flight of poetic philology, breaks down into heaven (*tem*), woman (*pu*), and silk (*ra*), which all combine into an evocative word picture conveying the light, ethereal qualities characteristic of this category of Japanese fried food."[51] Sushi inspired uncommon flights of lyrical fancy.

Beyond simply satisfying one's hunger, sushi was a Japanese spiritual experience bordering on the erotic. The delicacy, Toronto writer Joanne Kates explained, "began with the nature worship of the ancient Japanese, and evolved with the Shinto religion (still widely practiced) which is essentially a celebration to the fertility of the land and the sea. Inari, the rice god, is still worshipped today. . . . Each bite is to be cherished, for none is to be wasted." The writer drew further connections to the premodern past by claiming, with little basis in fact, "The sushi of the 15th-century was the same as the sushi of today."[52] A year later, reviewing a new takeout sushi option, Kates wrote, "Never before has rice been so sensuous. On and on goes the wanton sushi night, I devour the dark oily mackerel, the sweetness of tuna so sinfully

Sushi at the Crossroads of Cultural Globalization

raw, the surprise delight of raw sardine. After a while, the ardor intensifies, and I fling the chopstick aside and use my fingers to pluck out the delights," concluding that "too few people are aware of the erotic potential of Taiko Sushi."[53] Even the most passive of readers could not have missed the linking of "sinful" eroticism with the "raw" character of sushi, the evocation of a night of passion in which one abandons Western puritanical norms to indulge in the forbidden delights of the East.

One would be hard-pressed to find similar rhetorical fireworks in reviews of beef Wellington or duck confit. From where did the urge come to wax poetic about sushi? What did Japanese food evoke in writers to lead to such lyricism, and just as important, what did writers expect American readers to understand about Japanese culture? Similar to the ways in which Americans described a range of Japanese products, writers drew upon a fount of images, clichés, and tropes familiar to readers for decades. And as in the past, meanings were never fixed, though they did gravitate toward certain tropes more often than others. Sushi suggested a premodern Japan, a society predating Western influence in everything from cooking techniques to sexual inhibitions. While no one claimed to be literally transported to Tokugawa Japan by a piece of toro sashimi, such imagery was nevertheless intended for audiences anxious to locate Japan and its trendy food on their cultural mental maps.

Food writers recognized that writing about an unfamiliar foreign food required teaching readers about more than simply what to eat. Eating sushi was a lesson in cross-cultural education. "Sushi-lovers are made, not born," wrote one Washington critic. "Learning to love raw fish, in a culture which prides itself on overcooking its food, takes effort."[54] There was a broad process of cross-cultural education at work, with food writers serving as (frequently misinformed) U.S. intermediaries who regularly interacted with sushi chefs, Japanese intermediaries of cultural exchange. Though still learning the ropes themselves, they often did their best to sound authoritative in teaching readers the ins and outs of sushi consumption. It was common in the late 1970s, when food critics first started frequenting Japanese restaurants serving sushi, to let U.S. readers accustomed to sitting at a private table know that "only the uninitiated sit at a table"; instead, diners in the know sat at the sushi bar, where it was "better to point at what you want and buy it by the piece." (The same writer admitted to the faux pas of sitting at a table a year earlier.)[55] Phyllis Richman cautioned Americans to be prepared to adopt new ways of doing things: "One eats with chopsticks . . . and drinks the soups rather than spoons them. One begins to acclimate to the Japanese way, to appreciate the pretty ceramic dishes that bear carefully arranged little portions." She also warned her meat-and-potatoes audiences that they "probably need to order more dishes than usual, because the portions are small in Japanese restaurants."[56] After all, as one Los Angeles critic informed, "Japanese cooking, like the Japanese language, is one of the more complex constructs in the world, a cuisine built more around many small gestures than fat roasts and grilled birds."[57]

The best way to enjoy sushi, writers advised, was to abandon one's assumptions about the mechanics of dining out. Sit at the bar, order a variety of unfamiliar dishes, enjoy the chef's performance, and chat with him. "At the sushi bar, those in the know attempt to ingratiate themselves with the chef," informed Moira Hodgson of the *New York Times*. "Favorite customers get special treats according to his whim and inspiration, and they have learned to expect the unexpected. In this gastronomical theater, a certain amount of suspense is involved."[58] Even so, a "few things are good to know before you sit down at a sushi bar," cautioned Philadelphia's Maria Gallagher. "You don't tell your troubles to the guy on the other side. Don't expect him to hold your football bets. Don't bother asking for a frozen margarita."[59] Diners should invite the challenge of cultural interaction: "Ordering requires gesticulation, repetition, over-enunciation, slowed speech, or, for some people, shouting," according to critic Rita Kempley. "All the same, you're never quite sure you've communicated with your waitress, who's sure to be obliging."[60] Sushi bars became physical spaces of transnational cultural exchange, especially since nearly all of the first generation of sushi chefs in the United States were Japanese, Japan being the only place one could train for such a position. Those chefs served as cultural intermediaries, hybridizing food to fit perceived customer tastes yet nevertheless presenting a performance of authenticity.

The act of eating sushi also required preparing for the performance of sushi consumption. "Before venturing into a sushi restaurant," advised Jeffrey Carmel of the *Christian Science Monitor*, educating Bostonians in the wake of an influx of new sushi bars in 1983, "it is a good idea to learn some sushi etiquette to avoid embarrassing yourself with soy-sauce-soaked rice balls disintegrating in your fingers and fish falling all over the place."[61] Diners could avoid such uncomfortable scenarios and show off their cultural capital by dipping a piece of sushi in a shallow dish of soy sauce, fish side down, and placing the whole morsel in their mouths. "The Japanese think it is very funny if you try to bite sushi in half," wrote *Post* critic Melissa Davis in a primer for Washington's sushi rookies. "It is rather like watching someone attack a Big Mac with a knife and fork. Not exactly gauche or rude, but amusingly

Sushi at the Crossroads of Cultural Globalization

ignorant. The first time I had sushi, the owner of the restaurant rushed frantically towards me and in sign language showed me how I was doing it all wrong."[62]

The ingredients, taste of the food, and the expected performance of Japaneseness were not the only elements diners used to determine the authenticity of restaurants serving sushi. The atmosphere—including the staff, the decorations, the sound, and general ambience—was essential too. Playing on American stereotypes of what defined Japaneseness, such as women servers resembling an American idea of geisha, helped a restaurant gain authenticity points. Phyllis Richman applauded a popular Washington restaurant because "it seems to grow continually more Japanese" by adding more cooking styles, a sushi bar, and a television showing Japanese programming via VCR.[63] Waitresses "outfitted in kimonos with bright blue obi sashes" who "moved about with tiny steps" contributed performances that validated a restaurant's authenticity.[64] The New York Times' Patricia Brooks praised Mako of Fairfield, Connecticut, for its ability to transport diners to "a bit of Japan." "Shoji-screen paneling and partitions with cherry tree posts, huge rice-paper globe lights, framed calligraphy, oversized painted fans and recorded Japanese folk music create Japanese ambience," she wrote.[65]

Japanese faces helped add to an atmosphere of authenticity. Getting a recommendation from "people who know Japan" or, even better, spotting Japanese clientele made a location appear "authentic in its décor as well as its food."[66] A new hotel and restaurant in downtown Los Angeles was "so authentic," wrote one observer, "that about half its guests are Japanese."[67] Owners of the Kazumi Sushi Bar outside of San Diego even prided themselves on how their establishment had catered to a largely Japanese audience—"70 to 80 percent"—when it opened in 1980 but by 1986 served a crowd that was "80 to 90 percent . . . Anglos."[68] Japanese patrons provided the mark of authenticity a restaurant needed while white diners provided the steady flow of paying customers necessary to keep the doors open. Writers oriented toward European food trusted in the expertise of acquaintances to verify the authenticity of a Japanese restaurant. A Sacramento critic, for example, noted that his "dining companion who travels often to Japan said the place accurately reflects the physical atmosphere if not the emotional ambiance of robatas [Japanese grills] there."[69]

Conversely, a disappointing atmosphere could ruin a critic's experience. For Elaine Tait, there was something disturbingly inauthentic about the restaurant Ginza and its location on noisy South Street in Philadelphia. Ginza broke an essential Japanese cookbook rule, Tait said: "A Japanese meal is unthinkable without a quiet, withdrawn room looking onto the garden."[70] (How did the 11 million residents of Tokyo manage this on a daily basis?) Ginza was not the first restaurant to break the rules of Japanese dining as Tait understood them. "Two key elements in the enjoyment of a Japanese meal have always been the presentation of the food and the beauty and tranquility of the setting," she wrote. "You should feast with the eyes while the understated elegance of the dining area soothes away the cares of the world." While the food at Hikaru in Philadelphia was acceptable, "the appearance of the food and the restaurant seem to lack the essential aesthetic quality." Tait must have gasped when "sushi arrived in a miniature plastic boat, plunked unceremoniously on the table."[71] Hikaru lacked performance, an essential component of cultural authenticity.

Always complicating the notion of authenticity, of course, was the persistent presence of the new Japan, Japan the global power. After a night at the Washington restaurant Yosaku enjoying the Japanese atmospherics, including a new "Japanese craze that doesn't seem to be catching on too quickly here," karaoke, critic Rita Kempley channeled Jack Rosenthal—or was it Mike Royko?—and drew readers' attentions to the globalized landscape of U.S. culture. "Japanese pop music seeps from the karaoke room as we leave, jump into our Honda and head home," she mused, "to put the Fuji cassettes on the Denon tape deck equipped with Yamaha headphones, load and set the Nikon clock/camera and then go to sleep, to dream the all-American dream."[72] For better or worse, there was no escaping Japan in 1980s America.

CONCLUSION: AUTHENTICITY REMIXED

Four decades after Americans first began eating sushi, demanding new culinary and cultural experiences from their economically emergent Cold War ally, authenticity remains contested ground in the global flows of Japanese food. And Americans are not alone in experimenting with Japan's most famous culinary export. Gastronomes in places throughout the world have applied local touches to dishes firmly rooted in Japanese history and society. Within the many sushi restaurants dotting the streets of Moscow, adventurous eaters will find concoctions such as "jellied meat sushi" and "pickled mushroom sushi," along with variations on other Japanese staples, like "miso cappuccino." Brazilian sushi frequently showcases a range of tropical fruits.[73] In the globalization of sushi, hybridity has overtaken authenticity.

Japanese officials have taken notice of hybrid monstrosities as heretical as sushi burritos. For some Japanese, authenticity is a strategy to mobilize

Sushi at the Crossroads of Cultural Globalization

in defense of the imagined notion of cultural purity that sushi represents. In 2006 Japanese officials were so "horrified with the liberties taken with their food overseas" that the Ministry of Agriculture, Forestry, and Fisheries created a "Japanese Restaurant Authentication Plan" for the more than 50,000 estimated sushi restaurants around the world. Agricultural minister Toshikatsu Matsuoka said, "What we are seeing now are restaurants that pretend to offer Japanese cooking but are really Korean, Chinese or Filipino," adding, with no intended irony, "We must protect our food culture." (Most Japanese restaurants in the United States, in fact, are owned not by Japanese or Japanese Americans but by migrants from elsewhere in Asia or by Asian Americans of non-Japanese descent.) Matsuoka stated that certification for "pure Japanese" restaurants would be awarded to those meeting standards of "'Japanese-ness' based on authentic ingredients, chef training, aesthetics and other criteria."[74] The press reacted by mocking the government's proposed "sushi police," and the ministry dropped the program a year later. It revived the idea a decade later, however, after UNESCO granted *washoku* (traditional Japanese cuisine) status as an "Intangible Cultural Heritage." Japanese chefs who prized authenticity had lobbied the cultural agency for years for such a designation. The sushi establishment in Japan had taken a protectionist attitude toward the delicacy's globalization. Over the years the hybridized global forms of sushi have had a difficult time catching on in Japan, and to some Japanese "using ingredients like cream cheese and smoked salmon is as offensive as a Westerner dressed in a samurai costume."[75]

As in many respects, however, the world has moved beyond the era of Japan's globalizing. As the ministry's "Sushi Squad" set out across the globe to "assess the provenance of ingredients"—meaning that, for the ministry, authenticity would be about food's origins, not necessarily its preparation, presentation, or atmospherics—many chefs rejected the effort as "meaningless," claiming that Japanese food had grown beyond its exoticized origins to become a global cuisine mixed, fused, and consumed eagerly.[76] Indeed, the world's most admired Japanese chefs, like Nobuyuki Matsuhisa, known globally simply as "Nobu," have succeeded not by producing dishes that meet Western expectations for Japaneseness but by creating entirely new cuisines that blend traditional Japanese ingredients or techniques with those of other societies—in Nobu's case, fusing Japanese cuisine with ingredients and styles he encountered as a young traveling chef in Latin America in the 1970s and 1980s. Just at the moment that Japaneseness had gone global, Nobu, frustrated by the hierarchy and tradition of the Japanese restaurant industry, rejected a notion of pure culinary Japaneseness and pursued a hybridized global style.

Arguably today "Nobu-style" denotes an authenticity linked not to a physical location or mythical nation but to a single innovative, globe-trotting personality.[77] Like identity and power, other significant categories of analysis, authenticity has been unhinged in the globalized world, no longer fixed to a nation but instead floating on transnational flows of economy and culture, available for global actors to mix and remix endlessly. And few groups in the United States understand this practice of cultural globalization better than the joyously transgressive communities of anime fans.

SEVEN

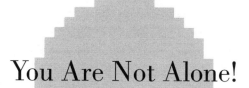

You Are Not Alone!

Anime and the Globalizing of America

The summer of 1983 was a banner season for blockbuster films. Matthew Broderick played a high school student who inadvertently brought the world to the edge of nuclear extinction in *WarGames*; John Travolta reprised his role as the iconic Tony Manero for *Staying Alive*, a sequel to 1977's *Saturday Night Fever*; and Roger Moore returned for a sixth time as James Bond in *Octopussy*. A trio of third installments of popular franchises—*Jaws 3*, *Superman 3*, and *Star Wars: Return of the Jedi*—competed for box office dollars and Monday-morning office conversations. But the 2,000 people filling "every seat in the biggest room in Baltimore" on the final night of the 1983 World Science Fiction Convention were not waiting to see any of these films, not even the final act of George Lucas's wildly popular epic. Instead, these devoted fans lingered until 1:00 A.M. to screen a film virtually unknown in the United States—the Japanese animation feature *Uchū senkan Yamato: Kanketsuhen* (Space battleship Yamato: The final chapter). Before the showing, though, the convention organizers apologetically informed the eager audience that the film's Japanese sponsors had sent the wrong film, *Saraba uchū senkan Yamato: Ai no senshitachi* (Farewell space battleship Yamato: Warriors of love), a 1978 chapter of the long-running, *Star Wars*–like "space opera."[1] Despite the blunder, despite the hour, and despite the language barrier—almost no one in the crowd spoke Japanese—the show went on and the capacity crowd remained seated and enthralled by this uncommon spectacle. One conference-goer complained that the *Yamato* crowd dwarfed even that of another 1983 Hollywood blockbuster, *The Right Stuff*, the film adaptation of Tom Wolfe's book about the first U.S. pilots to train for space missions: "The exploits of a group of militaristic Asiatics were more important than real life heroes."[2]

To the *Yamato* audience, the wrong film was still new and different. No *Yamato* film was available commercially outside Japan. Accounting for the lack of subtitles, two organizers "provided a running commentary in English," though one later admitted that his fluency in Japanese was suspect at best.[3] Yet the language barrier proved insignificant. What was important was not the message of this particular film but the audience's participation in the imaginative communal act of watching something different, something Japanese—something global. That night in 1983 the World Science Fiction Convention in Baltimore served as the front line of cultural globalization by showcasing Japanese animation, better known today as anime.

As it crossed the Pacific, anime provided the fans in Baltimore and thousands more across the United States with more than just entertainment. It presented an opportunity to participate in a global community of cultural difference. Anime looked unlike the children's cartoons of U.S. television, and it told stories that challenged viewers' emotions and worldviews more than the feel-good films of George Lucas's and Steven Spielberg's Hollywood. When anime aired at a large science fiction convention or a small fan club meeting, it offered audiences spaces where they could experience mediated cultural exchange with anime's Japanese creators and with fellow enthusiasts on the other side of the world. Across the United States the Japanese medium inspired the creation of anime fan clubs: local non-elite social communities that envisioned a world of cultural interconnectedness. The case of anime thus serves as one tangible, local illustration of the impact of Japanese cultural globalization on the United States in the last quarter of the twentieth century.

This chapter analyzes the role that the consumption of this Japanese product played in the reciprocity of global cultural exchange within the United States.[4] The impact of anime consumption on local U.S. communities began in 1977 when enthusiasts in Los Angeles established the first anime fan club. Over the next dozen years, these devotees built social communities at the local and national level around this foreign cultural product, reorienting individual and group identities according to a new awareness of transnational and global interconnectedness. Until 1989, when entrepreneurs founded the first U.S. anime import company, thus turning the corner toward anime's commercialization, fan communities existed solely because of grassroots, "do-it-yourself" initiatives. U.S. anime fandom in its first decade was a form of intercultural relations at the level of middle-class, non-elite private citizens. It was also an aspect of the U.S.-Japan relationship mediated almost exclusively through the exchange and consumption of anime texts. Like the consumption of cars, VCRs, and sushi, anime's reception demonstrated how

Anime and the Globalizing of America

the U.S.-Japan relationship was one that took place most often in the realm of consumption, and the identity most Americans assumed toward Japan was that of the consumer.

In this chapter, I examine several representative anime productions before exploring the central aspects of the fan experience that enabled non-elites to participate creatively in global cultural exchange enabled by Japanese popular culture. Exploring the activities of fan communities in the 1980s—the decade before "globalization" entered the popular lexicon—reveals not only greater depth and complexity in the U.S.-Japan relationship during this period but also how non-elite Americans at the local level engaged with the sweeping social and cultural transformations of the late twentieth century.

MUKOKUSEKI: ANIME AS JAPANESE AND GLOBAL TEXTS

The word "anime" (like all Japanese nouns, it denotes both singular and plural) refers to any and all television or film animation produced in Japan.[5] The genres of anime are as diverse as U.S. popular entertainment, if not more so. Mindlessly lighthearted and comical anime—a large segment of it, like the ubiquitous *Pokémon*, marketed to children—share the big and small screens with sophisticated philosophical treatises enjoyed by discriminating adult audiences, like Mamoru Oshii's critically acclaimed *Ghost in the Shell* (1995) and Hayao Miyazaki's Academy Award–winning *Spirited Away* (2002). In Japan, animation has never been pigeonholed as children's entertainment as it has in the United States. Its popularity in Japan is linked to the omnipresent manga, which is often translated as "comics" but which more closely resemble what Americans call "graphic novels."[6] American visitors to Tokyo often notice the many adults passing time on a train with noses buried in the latest volumes of favorite manga. Many of the most popular anime series first appear as manga.

Anime's first break on Japanese television, Osamu Tezuka's *Tetsuwan atomu*, based on Tezuka's 1950s manga of the same name, aired in early 1963.[7] Later dubbed the "godfather" of manga and anime, Tezuka credited his trademark art style to an earlier moment of cultural transfer—he adored Walt Disney cartoons like *Bambi*, and the two eponymous characters share large, endearing eyes.[8] *Testuwan atomu* signaled the birth of a popular culture phenomenon in Japan. By the late 1970s, science fiction (SF) series like *Uchū senkan Yamato*, *Kidō senshi Gundamu*, and *Makurosu* generated large and dedicated fan bases. So too did series like *Urusei Yatsura*, a comedy that mixed SF themes with a "slice-of-life" perspective on contemporary Japan. By the early

1990s the anime *otaku,* or obsessed fan, had become enough of a Japanese cultural icon to be the target of a popular spoof, the film *Otaku no video* (1991).

Some of the earliest anime on Japanese television crossed the Pacific and became familiar to U.S. children in the 1960s as *Astro Boy* (Tezuka's *Tetsuwan atomu*), *Speed Racer,* and *Gigantor,* among others. Few if any U.S. viewers, however, were aware of these programs' Japanese origins. American editors had stripped the animation of all visual and plot references to Japan. For producers like Fred Ladd, responsible for the U.S. adaptation of *Gigantor,* an early "giant-robot" anime series, Japan in the 1960s was an inexpensive source of animation that could be Americanized, or "denationalized," without great effort.[9] Ladd took for granted that the original animation's "Japaneseness" would not appeal to U.S. audiences. This assumption continued to guide the editors of commercial anime imports into the 1980s, and it would prove a perennial source of frustration to a growing grassroots fan community in the United States. It was not until after the rise of this grassroots anime fandom in the eighties that U.S. producers recognized that anime's cultural difference—its Japaneseness—had commercial potential. While producers' assumptions about mass audiences defined anime's commercial presence until the late eighties, growing fan demands for cultural authenticity defined its underground existence. The commercial boom of the 1990s was the result of several U.S. companies rectifying this tension by giving the die-hard fan community what it wanted—unfiltered, "authentic" anime.

Aside from the run of denationalized children's cartoons in the 1960s, anime was relegated to marginal status in U.S. popular culture in the 1970s and 1980s. In the early eighties Japanese anime companies had halfheartedly tested the U.S. market but concurred with Ladd's assessment that animation produced for Japanese viewers would not have wide commercial appeal.[10] The medium's fortunes shifted in the early 1990s with the founding of several U.S. companies dedicated to importing anime and manga not for Americanization but for their appeal as exotic foreign products. Films like *Ghost in the Shell* then regularly appeared on video store rental shelves with little or no editorial denationalization beyond English-language audio tracks. Children's series like *Sailor Moon* occupied coveted after-school broadcast slots. (Anime imported for the U.S. children's television market, like *Sailor Moon* or the popular *One Piece,* underwent and continues to receive extensive editing to remove "mature" content like bloodshed or alcohol consumption.) By 2000 a children's anime series, *Pokémon,* illustrated anime's exceptional U.S. and worldwide growth. As one study of the *Pokémon* phenomenon claims, it was "the most successful computer game ever made, the top globally selling

Anime and the Globalizing of America

trading-card game of all time, one of the most successful children's television programs ever broadcast, the top-grossing movie ever released in Japan, and among the five top earners in the history of films worldwide." As the franchise approached the end of its second decade, it could boast of more than 260 million video games and 22 billion trading cards sold globally, all supported by seventeen full-length feature films and more than 800 episodes of the animated series.[11]

Anime has been so successful—a major source of Japan's "gross national cool," as an oft-cited *Foreign Policy* article called it—that some scholars have suggested it is a potential "soft power" tool of Japanese foreign relations.[12] The United States is hardly the only country whose popular culture has recently experienced an infusion of "J-Pop." Anime and manga have also found receptive audiences in Italy, Germany, France, and other European countries; East and Southeast Asia; and throughout Latin America, notably in Brazil.[13] Yet, despite Foreign Minister Masahiko Komura's 2008 appointment of an "anime ambassador"—the popular animated robot cat Doraemon—Joseph Nye's political science concept is anachronistic in an era when cultural images and ideas flow independent of state power, not in support of it.[14] Indeed, the ambassadorial appointment revealed that the Japanese government recognized both the global reach and influence of anime and also the challenge of harnessing it to state ends.

Instead, by the turn of the twenty-first century, anime served as a medium for transmitting more ambiguous images of Japaneseness to hundreds of millions around the globe, images that floated untethered from traditional institutions of state power. As with VCRs, anthropologist Koichi Iwabuchi argues that anime, like much of Japanese popular culture, is "culturally odorless." Japanese products do not travel abroad loaded with ideology and symbolism as American goods frequently do. According to Iwabuchi, a product's cultural odor is also associated with "racial and bodily images of a country of origin." Thus one could assume that a product like anime, which constantly reproduces images of bodies, Japanese or otherwise, would transmit Japanese racial images as well. But this is not generally the case. Iwabuchi and other scholars cite the claims of anime directors who argue that anime demonstrates the concept of *mukokuseki*, translated as "someone or something lacking nationality" or, simply, "denationalized."[15] Indeed, the uninitiated viewer often comments that the characters in anime do not "look Japanese." Though anime today exhibits a wide range of diverse characters, a typical male protagonist drawn in the seventies or eighties might have featured cream-colored skin, brown hair, big and round blue eyes, and a nondescript face, while artists would typically add long eyelashes and a voluptuous figure for female protagonists. Limited by low budgets, anime creators used a range of wild hairstyles and colors to differentiate characters with otherwise similar faces. Anime's most celebrated director, Hayao Miyazaki, the "Walt Disney of Japan," once cryptically attributed these vaguely Western-looking characters to the fact that "the Japanese hate their own faces," while another eminent director suggested that Japanese animators "unconsciously choose not to draw 'realistic' Japanese characters if they wish to draw attractive characters."[16] Whatever the reason, anime characters have typically lacked features that non-Japanese audiences might link to ethnic Japaneseness.

Such characteristics were not lost on the earliest U.S. fans. The president of the New York chapter of a large national fan club often fielded this question from anime neophytes. She pointed to Tezuka's admiration for the West and cited Yoshiyuki Tomino, creator of the popular *Gundam* series, who echoed Miyazaki's claim that Japanese disliked their own faces and added, apocryphally, "Remember, we lost the war." She observed that one of anime's most common genre vehicles, science fiction, frequently portrayed one-world globalized futures in which national identities mattered less than planetary origins. "We can point to them and say they're 'like us,'" she wrote of anime characters, "while the Japanese can point to them and say they're 'like us, too.'"[17]

This "nonculturally specific anime style," as Japanese literature scholar Susan J. Napier calls it, appealed to American audiences in the seventies and eighties because it was aesthetically transnational—its apparent nonethnic style facilitated its diffusion across borders.[18] Like Sony VCRs and Honda Accords, anime could cross borders without carrying a distinct national identity. The *mukokuseki* style may have been ambiguous, but it also subtly adhered to Western racial and gender hierarchies in its representations of male and female bodies. The representation of characters like *Yamato*'s Nova, with her blonde hair and slim figure, or Shinji Ikari from the popular series *Neon Genesis Evangelion* (1995), with his brown hair and blue eyes, allowed these Japanese creations to be simultaneously Western and transnational. It is ironic, then, that so many fans tied their interest in anime to their fascination with its Japaneseness. The Japan that aficionados encountered on television or in club gatherings was a highly mediated one that crossed the Pacific after passing through Japan's own *mukokuseki* filter. Still, cultural odor is relative to the nose of the smeller, and what seemed denationalized to a prominent anime director could smell a lot like Japan to a young person in California. It was this complicated intersection of production and consumption, the free floating of images unmoored from authorial intent and national origins in a global age, the mingling of Japanese and Western aesthetics, genres, and racial and gender categories, that established anime's hybrid nature.

In thinking about anime's popularity in the United States, it is important to divorce American fans' fascination with its "Japaneseness" from the actual production of anime in Japan. Anthropologist Ian Condry has written skeptically of imposing a "national logic" on anime production, the assumption that there are vague forces of "Cool Japan" at work in the production of Japanese popular culture that help explain its transnational appeal. Anime producers do not simply reproduce "some generalized national culture of Japan" but rather intentionally create characters and premises that will be flexible and malleable across a range of media—not just anime but also manga, video games, toys, and so on. In that sense, anime is intentionally transmedia, not intentionally transnational—indeed, early anime creators especially seemed baffled by the idea that anyone outside Japan would enjoy the fruits of their labor. That anime did cross national borders, then, was a product not of transnational intentions but of an effort to create characters and premises that were easily transportable across a variety of media. If *Gundam's* creators designed giant fighting robots to move easily from the television screen to toy shelves, then that transportability enabled its subsequent global diffusion. Of course, by the 1990s, Japanese companies were attentive to the global possibilities, and properties like *Pokémon* were born global.[19]

Star Blazers, a 1979 U.S. television series adapted from the early-seventies Japanese version of the aforementioned *Yamato* series, is a fitting example of anime as a globalized product. It was also the most important early anime to connect fan communities. *Star Blazers* is a science fiction epic. The SF genre lends itself to themes of transnationalism because, as in *Star Blazers*, it often envisions a future in which the divisions between "races" of the Earth pale in comparison to the divisions among intergalactic races. (No better example exists than the global government—interplanetary, in fact—that is the United Federation of Planets of the *Star Trek* canon.) Centralized world governments are common SF tropes, accentuating planetary unity. *Star Blazers* also emphasizes moral values and narrative elements recognizable beyond Japanese borders—duty and sacrifice, war and peace, love and personal relationships, good and evil—which aided in its transition to non-Japanese locales.

Star Blazers tells the story of the *Yamato*, a resurrected World War II–era battleship reconstructed into a weapon and charged with saving Earth.[20] The *Yamato* launches to repel an invading alien force and then travels many light years away to acquire material essential to reviving the planet's destroyed environment. The invading alien force, the Gamilon Empire, has used nuclear-like "planet bombs" to render Earth's surface radioactive and uninhabitable. The Gamilon invasion represented two transnational challenges of the postwar era: the threat posed by nuclear proliferation and the human destruction of the natural environment. *Star Blazers* appealed to young people anxious about both.

In transforming the Japanese series *Uchū senkan Yamato* into *Star Blazers*, Westchester Films, a U.S. production company, purposefully obscured the *Yamato*'s history. To many Japanese living in the postwar era, the name *Yamato* was reminiscent of the sacrifices of World War II and a racial self-referent. The *Yamato*, the largest battleship ever built, sank near Okinawa in April 1945 in a suicide mission to prevent American forces from seizing the island. Its name derived from the mythical Yamato race from which the imperial state claimed the Japanese people descended.[21] In the U.S. overdubbed version (or "dub," with English-language dialogue replacing the original Japanese voice-acting), characters refer to the *Yamato* by name only in the first episode, and the fact that Japan built the battleship with the explicit intention of fighting Americans goes unmentioned. Editors also deleted scenes showing the *Yamato*'s final heroic moments fighting the U.S. Navy. In the original, U.S. fighter planes move in similar patterns to the enemy Gamilons, and the same ominous "bad guy" music accompanies flashbacks to World War II.[22] As the ship enters the plot, its captain tells the *Yamato*'s story: "This was a great battleship at a time when great fleets sailed the seas and there were wars among the nations of Earth. It sank in one of the last wars between countries. All wars ceased when Gamilon began bombing us."[23] American viewers saw that, whatever the *Yamato*'s checkered past, in *Star Blazers* it represented humankind's unified defense against an invading alien force. To inaugurate a new era of international peace and cooperation, the *Yamato* is renamed the *Argo*, referencing the ship of Greek mythology's Jason and the Argonauts. *Star Blazers*' U.S. producers had replaced a Japanese historical reference with a Western one.

While there was a clear process of de-Japanization at work in reconstructing the narrative, editors did not have to rework racial and bodily representations in *Star Blazers* for consumption by U.S. audiences. The series' nonethnic characters already reflected a Western racial hierarchy. Though the main protagonist received an Americanized name—Susumu Kodai became Derek Wildstar—his physical appearance remained unchanged from the Japanese original; he has long, flowing brown hair, a strong chin, and large

Anime and the Globalizing of America

round eyes. In the first episode he and his partner stumble upon a woman they describe as "beautiful"—she is tall and thin with long blonde hair, blue eyes, and pale white skin. Though drawn in a "nonculturally specific anime style," this character still reinforces the primacy of Western aesthetic categories as the embodiment of attractiveness in anime.

Star Blazers first aired in syndication in several large media markets in September 1979. It differed from its 1960s anime predecessors in the United States, like Astro Boy and Speed Racer, in that its producers aimed for an audience of teenagers and young adults instead of children. It was also serialized; like a soap opera, viewers had to watch episodes consecutively, or they would miss crucial plot developments. These two elements helped create a small but dedicated U.S. fan base for Star Blazers. Inquisitive fans found upon investigation that Star Blazers derived from the long-running Japanese Yamato series, but they had to work to discover this and then work some more to find other curious buffs with whom they could connect. Star Blazers was thus a watershed for anime in the United States, serving as the first series to entice fans to learn more about other Japanese animated products. One admirer, who later went on to a career in the nascent U.S. anime industry, said of Star Blazers, "It was my 'poison'—the series that put me beyond any turning back."[24]

Star Blazers and the anime that followed it on U.S. television continued to undergo extensive editing to erase its Japaneseness, but they retained enough difference from common broadcast fare to hint to captivated viewers that something non-American lay behind their favorite programs. Another prominent example was the popular SF series Robotech, which first aired in 1985.[25] Producer Carl Macek managed to amass enough episodes for U.S. syndication (which required a minimum of sixty-five) by combining the animation from three unrelated Japanese series, writing a new script for American voice actors, and following the editorial trend of downplaying national origin. While the Frankensteinian result divided purists from casual viewers, it nevertheless attracted a significant audience that also eagerly consumed associated product tie-ins like books and character model kits. Enthusiastic fans, like their Star Blazers compatriots, discovered the show's Japanese origins and used Robotech as something of a gateway drug to exploring other anime and connecting with fellow devotees. The dean of U.S. anime fans, Fred Patten, wrote that Robotech was "arguably the single anime title to have the greatest influence in bringing the existence of Japanese animation to the awareness of the public."[26]

Within a year of its initial release, Robotech aired in syndication in 90 percent of television markets in North America, and advertisements for product tie-ins were inescapable during after-school television hours. Ratings demographics revealed that among teenage viewers 70 percent were male, but among the coveted eighteen to forty-nine age group, 53 percent of viewers were female.[27] Likely teenage boys watched for the fast-paced action sequences, pitting giant human-piloted robots against each other, while adult women and men appreciated the mature "space opera" storylines about friendships, romance, and the tragic social consequences of war. As one fan put it, "Here was love, hate, friendship, intrigue, and interstellar warfare on a truly grand scale."[28]

Growing public awareness of the Japaneseness of this fan favorite led to demands from nascent fan communities for more accessible anime. Enthusiasts were particularly interested in what they considered "authentic" anime, untouched by the corrupting hands of U.S. editors, which was difficult to acquire in the United States unless one was connected to one of the national fan clubs. The demand for authenticity inspired *Robotech* producer Macek, assisted by animation expert Jerry Beck, to launch Streamline Pictures in 1988. Streamline was the first U.S. company created to import, translate, and subtitle or overdub anime for distribution in the U.S. theater and home video markets. One of the company's early projects, *Akira*, became the first anime released with limited distribution in theaters in December 1989.[29] *Akira* also became a cult film classic and a milestone in anime's U.S. history.

With Streamline's adaptation of *Akira*, fan communities got a more "authentic" product. The only violation of authenticity was the English-language dubbing, which Streamline produced in lieu of the subtitling preferred by fans. Otherwise, the company curbed efforts to minimize the film's Japaneseness. The main characters' names, Tetsuo and Kaneda, remain unchanged. The plot unfolds in Neo-Tokyo, and Japanese-language characters appear on street signs and store fronts in the background of many scenes. Promotional posters advertised the film as an English-language adaptation of a Japanese original, and they did not hide the director's Japanese name, Katsuhiro Otomo.[30] Streamline advertised *Akira*'s Japaneseness, linking images of futuristic Neo-Tokyo to popular images of Japan as a futuristic utopia/dystopia from U.S. films like *Blade Runner* and *Black Rain*. The film played only to small audiences on college campuses and in independent theaters, yet it gained a cult following in the early nineties thanks to a commercial release on videocassette.

Streamline marketed *Akira* specifically as a Japanese product, but the film continued to display the same transnational themes that made anime like *Star Blazers* and *Robotech* appealing beyond Japanese borders. Through the SF

ILL. 7.1. In the opening scene of *Akira* (1988), the date "1988.7.16" flashes in front of an aerial shot of Tokyo, seconds before the city is annihilated by an unexplained nuclear blast. (Geneon Entertainment, 2001)

genre, *Akira* expressed as well as any work of art the global nuclear anxieties of the eighties. Its opening scene, which flashes the date "1988.7.16" in front of contemporary Tokyo moments before an atomic explosion annihilates the city, hauntingly articulated the immediacy of nuclear holocaust. Otomo's dystopian vision also reflected anxieties about the technological transformation of the natural environment. Tetsuo and Kaneda, members of a nihilistic motorcycle gang, ride through the crumbling streets of Neo-Tokyo, seemingly drowning in mass media, corporate advertising, and buildings that reach endlessly to the sky. Neo-Tokyo's hyper-urbanism is reminiscent of director Ridley Scott's vision of a postapocalyptic Los Angeles in *Blade Runner*. (In homage to Scott, director Otomo also set *Akira* in the year 2019.)

The film climaxes in the grotesque transformation of one teenage protagonist, Tetsuo, from an adolescent outcast to a world-destroying monster. Through government experimentation Tetsuo acquires the apocalypse-inducing power of the character Akira, "the power of a god," the consequence of a top-secret military research program. Adolescent immaturity and foolish pride drive Tetsuo to wield this power to destructive ends. Tetsuo's body swells to the size of a stadium, filling the massive structure built to host the 2020 Olympics (an eerily correct prediction), generating another citywide nuclear catastrophe. The film then ends with characteristic anime ambiguity; from within a divine white light a voice whispers, "I am Tetsuo," suggesting the dialectical nature of destruction and creation. Viewers in the United States might have read these climactic

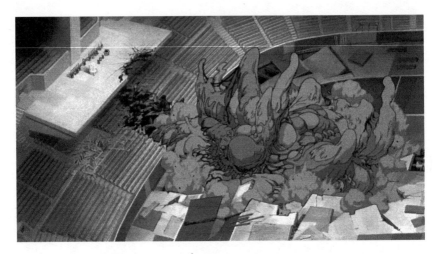

ILL. 7.2. Tetsuo, one of the protagonists of *Akira*, suffers the consequences of government experimentation with godlike powers. In the film's climax, he can no longer control his powers—a possible allegory to Japan's extraordinary economic growth in the 1980s— and his metastasizing body destroys the stadium Tokyo had built for the 2020 Olympic Games. (Geneon Entertainment, 2001)

scenes as an allegory of Japan's newly acquired global economic power in the 1980s. Tokyo's 1964 Olympics had marked the end of Japan's postwar recovery and the beginning of its rapid rise to global economic power; on the eve of 2020, according to the film, its power had metastasized beyond control. In a U.S. popular discourse that often framed Japan's postwar political and economic development in the language of maturity, one possible reading of *Akira*'s apocalyptic conclusion, once the film crossed the Pacific, was that Japan was emotionally unprepared for the consequences that accompanied extraordinary global power.[31]

Akira set a new benchmark for artistic achievement in the Japanese medium. Otomo's creative accomplishment was also significant as a commercial turning point for anime in the United States. Streamline's production marked the birth of an industry that would grow exponentially in the 1990s and profit greatly from properties like *Ghost in the Shell, Sailor Moon,* and *Pokémon. Akira* was also a triumph for the U.S. fan community, which had been growing since the late 1970s. Streamline's *Akira* and the boom of the nineties resulted from fan demands for anime that was not simplified and Americanized, anime that provided a more "authentic" Japanese cultural experience. The earlier persistence of U.S. producers to downplay anime's Japanese origins had actually intensified the fan community's insistence on the authenticity of a foreign product. Supporters were able to achieve their goals

Anime and the Globalizing of America

because they had organized into visible cultural communities that flourished in a variety of local, national, and global spaces.

"WEIRD, TOGETHER": CONSUMPTION
AND THE GLOBAL IMAGINATION

New York's WNEW started airing *Star Blazers* in 1979, but it never found a place for this animated series that looked nothing like the children's cartoons occupying afternoon and Saturday morning time slots. The program director bounced the show around different time slots, from the afternoon to the early morning, but decided in the spring of 1980 to pull it off the air altogether. For a couple of New York teenagers, Michael Pinto and Brian Cirulnick, this outrage could not stand. They began a letter and phone campaign to organize *Star Blazers* devotees to pressure WNEW to put the show back on the air. By 1981 they had founded a fan club and started compiling a newsletter. They never got what they wanted—WNEW never put *Star Blazers* back on the air—but they got so much more: within a couple of years the club had grown to several hundred strong with chapters around the United States, and the show's U.S. production company, Westchester Films, had granted club officers semi-official status. As club president Michael Pinto worked persistently to keep enthusiasts connected to a larger fandom community. For him, connecting fans meant pushing them to engage, to be more than just passive viewers of a favorite animated series. "IT'S YOUR CLUB MAKE THE DAMN BEST OF IT THAT YOU CAN!" he wrote in the August 1982 newsletter. "To be a fan you must be active. That means alot [*sic*] of things. It can mean writing a letter of comment to the club up to running a convention. Alot [*sic*] of you write in saying things like 'I thought I was the only fan of Star Blazers in the world!' Well now that you have found this club of some 250, why not make the best of that money you gave in for your membership? How?"[32]

There were many ways to answer that question. What drove anime fandom in the United States from its birth in 1977 through the commercialization of the 1990s was the varied activism of its community. Activism manifested primarily in three forms: fan clubs, conventions (or "cons"), and the creation of an underground, self-published English-language literature on anime. The demand for activism contributed to a unifying sense of community and permitted participants to experiment with new cultural identities. Active commitment also required vigorous imagination in order to envision national and transnational communities of shared experiences. As fans consumed anime texts and then organized clubs, attended national conventions, published underground literature, and eventually conversed over the Internet, they connected local communities to global cultural trends and contributed to the globalizing of America.

Fan clubs, cons, and underground literature from this period illustrated fans' conscious efforts to define anime as a distinct cultural category, to develop knowledge about the medium and its relationship to Japanese culture, and to construct boundaries to mark the territory in which legitimate fan behavior could take place. Like the "media fans" that Henry Jenkins describes in his seminal work, *Textual Poachers*, anime fans were "spectators who transform[ed] the experience of watching television into a rich and complex participatory culture."[33] Fandom maintained the "function of an interpretive community" and the "status of an alternative community," allowing participants a space in which to critically and communally engage anime texts.[34] This "work of the imagination," as anthropologist Arjun Appadurai has described it, often took place with an oppositional attitude toward mainstream U.S. entertainment media, though it would be inaccurate to assume a simplistic, binary mainstream-versus-underground tension—after all, without *Star Wars'* unprecedented mainstream success, *Star Blazers* would have found neither a producer nor an audience when it did. And, following Appadurai, that fans were not only critically engaging popular texts but also doing so across formidable cultural and linguistic boundaries made their "work of the imagination" all the more central to defining the cultural communities they created.[35]

Early anime fandom matured in a political climate frequently hostile to Japanese economic growth, yet it also bloomed in a consumer culture more ambivalent toward Japanese products like automobiles and VCRs. In this context, the promotion of anime as a Japanese object could be an act of resistance to a mainstream political culture of "Japan-bashing," though the construction of fan communities as nonpolitical spaces made such resistance largely implicit. Devotees were more likely to think of fandom as an escape from politics rather than as an implicit political statement. Rather than being indicative of a political attitude, the consumption of anime was instead, like that of cars, VCRs, and sushi, one small part of a nuanced U.S.-Japan relationship that took the form of a trade conflict at the international level but manifested in the acquisition and consumption of hundreds of millions of goods at the level of the individual consumer. The heated rhetoric of the "trade wars" obscured the fact that Americans desired Japanese products. Among all U.S. consumers of Japanese things during this period, none were as fervent in their engagement with the Japaneseness of goods as anime fans.

Anime and the Globalizing of America

Fandom began at the local level with clubs. The first club dedicated exclusively to anime was the Cartoon/Fantasy Organization (C/FO—it would be years before American fans adopted the word "anime"), founded in May 1977 by several Los Angeles–area buffs who had all previously attended meetings of the popular Los Angeles Science Fiction Society. The C/FO met monthly to watch episodes of English-language commercial anime from the sixties, like *Astro Boy* and *Gigantor,* and products of the seventies, series like *Star Blazers* and *Battle of the Planets.* Occasionally they watched videotape copies of Japanese-language anime that aired on local California cable access stations, a practice enabled by the increasing availability of inexpensive VCRs.

In 1979 the Los Angeles Science Fiction Society began to receive requests from Japanese SF fans for videotaped copies of popular U.S. series like *Star Trek* and *Battlestar Galactica.* The C/FO responded to the call by sending copies of those programs in exchange for tapes of untranslated, unsubtitled anime recorded from broadcast television in Japan. This transpacific exchange provided fans access to "pure," unedited anime. None of the C/FO members understood Japanese. Nevertheless, one fan says that interest in the videos was so high that club members "were willing to watch them and guess what the dialogue was about."[36] Far from discouraging screenings, the language barrier contributed to anime's appeal because it accentuated anime's difference from the popular U.S. media that fans were accustomed to consuming, and the shared experience of being "lost in translation" helped build a sense of community.

From humble origins the C/FO expanded by the late eighties to nearly three dozen chapters in major cities like New York and Chicago and in unexpected locations across the rural Midwest and South.[76] The locations of fans from the period demonstrated the varied places that Americanized commercial anime reached in syndication in the seventies and eighties. Of course, the California and New York markets had stations airing anime, particularly on local access Japanese-community stations where Japanese immigrant populations thrived. More surprisingly, more than one station in rural Oklahoma aired *Star Blazers.*[38] Local stations in rural areas were not motivated by a sense of cosmopolitanism to purchase syndication rights to these programs; more simply, the shows made for cheap content. But where commercial anime like *Star Blazers* spread seeds of interest, fan communities began to take root, interested in more than just the anime available in syndication. Supporters then made contact through informal networks of friends or fellow SF fans with a C/FO chapter to join or to get information on forming a new local chapter.

Many fans also participated in large and small clubs independent of the C/FO, like Rhode Island's Anime Hasshin club, which had more than 400 members on six continents at its peak and boasted that it was the "largest international anime fan club of its time."[39] The independent Boston Japanimation Society, which still meets today, also had a sizable presence in fan networks and at conventions in the Northeast.[40] What defined the C/FO, Anime Hasshin, and other similar organizations as clubs was their size and their small cadres of dutiful record-keeping officers who scheduled meetings and kept track of dues payments, membership rolls, budgets, and inventories. Countless less formal gatherings also occurred in living rooms across the country.

Some fans labeled large but informal meetings outside the scope of clubs "disorganized fandom." Many were dismayed by what they saw as the petty politics of clubs like the C/FO, which served as the largest pipeline for distribution of underground noncommercial anime. In November 1985 a San Francisco Bay Area resident founded A.N.I.M.E. (Animation of Inter-Mediary Exchange) as an informal gathering space for fans. Within two years A.N.I.M.E. grew to a "monthly barbeque-and-video-watching party of sometimes 200 fans from all over Northern California."[41] The parties were "a great departure from organized fandom," said one enthusiast, an alternative for "fans who were totally disgusted by organized fandom and its power-tripping Secret Masters."[42] (The national C/FO organization broke apart in the late eighties due to squabbles over control of and access to underground anime recordings.) Even though supporters of the "disorganized" variety chose to avoid local club politics, they nevertheless participated in the imagined community of fandom. In fact, one proud participant in disorganized fandom started the first successful anime discussion network on the Internet, a mailing list dedicated to the series *Urusei Yatsura*, a "slice-of-life" comedy that fans could acquire only through underground videotape-copying networks.[43]

The remarkable system of exchange and distribution that early anime fans utilized demonstrated the interconnectedness between local communities and the global flow of culture. One U.S.-Japan anime pipeline began with U.S. military personnel at C/FO Rising Sun, a club chapter at Misawa Air Force Base in northern Japan. The club videotaped anime broadcast on Japanese television and mailed these copies to fan acquaintances in San Francisco. A distribution network based in the Bay Area then made multiple copies and sent them to C/FO chapters throughout the United States.[44] Other similar pipelines existed. Marc Carlson acquired episodes of *Maison Ikkoku* and other anime from a friend in Japan and shared these at A.N.I.M.E.

Anime and the Globalizing of America

meetings.[45] Canadian fan Tom Edwards was so enthusiastic about building the library of his fan club, J. A. C. Victoria, that he purchased a second VCR and a computer to connect via the Internet to other anime enthusiasts at universities and began copying and distributing videotapes throughout North America.[46] Laura Whittier in Sacramento received videocassettes from a U.S. military friend stationed in Okinawa; she then duplicated and dispensed these throughout the C/FO network.[47] Tape exchange was by and large a nonprofit affair. Often only a blank videocassette and postage reimbursement were necessary, especially if a supporter was a dues-paying club member. The goal was not to violate copyright or intellectual property laws but to distribute anime and expand the U.S. fan community. "I am willing to dub anything for anyone with a blank tape and the guts to ask for it," wrote the editor of the Ann Arbor Anime Organization's newsletter.[48] Similar invitations, along with warnings against profit-seeking, appeared in almost all of the underground fan literature.

The videocassettes traded via underground networks contrasted considerably with the commercial anime that had enticed fans on U.S. broadcast television. Dialogue was in the original Japanese, there were no subtitles, and underground anime were uncorrupted by American editors and censors. While SF anime like *Mobile Suit Gundam* were among the favorites of fans hooked by programs like *Star Blazers*, non-SF underground series like *Urusei Yatsura* and *Maison Ikkoku* were popular because they dealt with daily life in contemporary Japan from comical, romantic, or nostalgic perspectives. These series attracted fans interested in anime specifically for its Japaneseness.

Despite the fact that so few of the fans understood Japanese, the appetite for these underground tapes was insatiable. Some admirers were "annoyed" by the language barrier and decided that the next logical step was "to actually try to go out and learn the language—which I did."[49] (Some of those who did so early were fortunate to launch lucrative careers when the U.S. anime industry boomed in the nineties.) But while some fans used anime as an excuse to learn Japanese, most had neither the resources nor the time to dedicate to learning a new language. Even Fred Patten, who spent decades running fan clubs like the C/FO, amassing an enormous anime and manga collection, and speaking publicly on behalf of the fan community, never learned to speak or read Japanese fluently.[50] On the other hand, while earning two engineering degrees from Johns Hopkins University, Sharon Stapleton taught herself Japanese for the noble purpose of translating anime for her fellow enthusiasts. She typed translations and distributed them through mail order, charging only

ILL. 7.3. In the 1980s a New York City chapter of the Cartoon/Fantasy Organization met in the basement of the Polish Democratic Club in St. Mark's Place. In this 1990 photo, club members are about to begin a marathon session of viewing untranslated, unsubtitled anime. (Saul Trabal)

enough to recover printing and shipping costs.[51] Once again, the emphasis was on community, not commerce.

Clubs adopted a variety of practices to deal with the language barrier. Often those familiar with a program's plot or with some Japanese language skills would shout out summaries of what was happening onscreen. "Other times," recalled one fan, "the tension or comedy would cause viewers to start 'filling in the dialog' that was missing with their own version, out-loud," which gave club gatherings a feeling of public ritual and aided the work of the imagination that enabled fans to "think up my own dialog for stories that had no translation available."[52] Henry Jenkins, observing a U.S. fan club dedicated to the live-action program *Beauty and the Beast*, noted a similar phenomenon when the club attended a French-only screening of several episodes. According to Jenkins, "mutual assistance was required to decipher the narrative content since none of the members was fluent in French. The members were encouraged to 'shout out' if they could make sense of any of the words."[53] As with anime, the act of interpreting the foreign created communal solidarities.

With linguistic obstacles placed in the way of understanding content, the medium of anime became the message. Club gatherings were as much

Anime and the Globalizing of America

about the communal activities of watching, interpreting, and participating as they were about anime's content. Viewing occurred in a social environment of like-minded individuals, not in the privacy of one's home, contributing to the social construction of a distinct community. As one fan insightfully commented, "It was . . . comfortable to view these shows with the same 'characters' in the audience constantly. There is a social aspect that can and had caused the club members to accept one another, without too much judgment. We were all being sort of 'weird, together.'"[54] More than just opportunities for entertainment, then, clubs became real communities, complete with norms and behaviors expected of members. The sense of local community embodied in clubs fostered the social cohesion necessary to envision larger national and transnational networks of shared interest, especially since connections with fans outside the United States were more imagined than real. Sharing one's couch, then, turned a domestic space into a site of global engagement, shaping creative consumers into cultural ambassadors.

The work of the cultural imagination continued at the regional and national level at cons, where anime fans congregated for one or several days' worth of interaction. One participant described cons as "a buffet/smorgasbord of ideas, philosophies and beliefs, but in a friendly environment of mutual respect."[55] During the eighties, enthusiastic fans traveled to SF and comic book conventions throughout the county with VCRs and anime tapes in hand. Anime screenings, often staged in small rented hotel rooms with a VCR and a handful of con attendees, introduced the medium to new fans. Anime buffs frequently piggybacked onto larger SF cons, which had been running successfully for decades. In 1981 a group of fans based in the New York metropolitan area established the "Gamilon Embassy" (named for the "bad guys" of Star Blazers) with the mission of traveling to cons in the Northeast and publicizing anime to SF audiences.[56] At bigger conventions, like Bay-Con '86, which boasted an eighty-hour anime marathon, anime was shown twenty-four hours a day.[57] The popular practice of cosplay, or attending a con costumed as a favorite anime character, also emphasized the participatory nature of the anime fan community. Participants could spend dozens of hours assembling elaborate homemade costumes. Cosplay owed a debt to SF fandom as well—it was the "Trekkies" (or "Trekkers," as some preferred) who dressed up like Star Trek's Captain Kirk and Mr. Spock that made cosplay a con institution in the seventies.[58]

The final facet of activist anime fandom, and another borrowed from decades-old SF fandom, was the creation of an underground literature. When I asked fans from this period, somewhat naively, what underground anime

ILL. 7.4. In the back room of the basement of the Polish Democratic Club, members of a New York City C/FO chapter could shop for hard-to-find Japanese pop merchandise during club meetings. Standing second from left is Michael Pinto, founder of the Star Blazers Fan Club. (Saul Trabal)

literature they had access to or read, I did not expect so many to respond instead with the titles of "fanzines," club newsletters, and amateur press associations (APAs) to which they *contributed*. Again, it was the active engagement of the fans at the local level—not the imperatives of global capitalism—that created and sustained the U.S. anime community. Fans provided artwork, news updates, gossip, reviews, and fan fiction, a style borrowed from SF fandom wherein authors wrote their own stories about anime (or fictional universes like that of *Star Wars* or *Star Trek*) that already existed.[59] An APA, which functioned as a precursor to Internet message boards, required that every subscriber contribute something to the publication; hence one could not receive *Bird Scramble!* if one did not participate. What Jenkins says of television fans of the period applies equally to underground anime publishing: "Undaunted by traditional conceptions of literary and intellectual property, fans raided mass culture, claiming its materials for their own use, reworking them as the basis for their own cultural creations and social interactions."[60] Participation in the creation of an English-language anime literature provided an opportunity to actively engage in creative cultural work and reinforced the social commitment and solidarity required to be a part of the fan community.

Anime and the Globalizing of America

APAs were a kind of social media before that term applied to Internet-based communities in the twenty-first century. Many an APA chose a particular favorite series for its theme. The APA *Bird Scramble!*, for instance, published fan-authored stories about characters from the late-seventies series *Battle of the Planets*, adapted from the Japanese original *Gatchaman*, while *Megalord: APA Superdimension U.S.A.* served fans of the *Macross* and *Robotech* universe. Others connected members of local fan clubs or chapters of national clubs. The contents, which could amount to several dozen to a hundred or more photocopied pages per volume, often with tiny text so as to save space and minimize page counts and mailing costs, reflected the tremendous variety of ways in which fans imagined themselves as part of a community. A single APA volume might contain a 5,000-word essay on speculative engineering in anime mecha followed by a fan fiction piece expanding on the lives of a couple of minor characters from *Star Blazers* and many pages of amateur artwork.[61] Issues also frequently contained personal narratives of fandom—the who, where, when, how, and why of individual fans and testimonies of conversion to the medium or a particular series. One mother of two young children from the suburbs of Dallas, Texas, wrote nearly a dozen single-spaced pages in a 1986 volume of *APA Hashin*, which served the San Antonio C/FO chapter, about her various interests ranging from "Bible study, drawing, softball, and of cource [sic], animation, especially Japanese." She was grateful the club and the APA gave her a chance to connect with other like-minded fans. "I'm a firm believer in if you like something someone else must also," wrote the twenty-one-year-old founder of *Megalord: APA Superdimension U.S.A.*[62] A fan's first contribution frequently took the form of these kinds of testimonies, efforts to find human connection through Japanese animated media.

The Rose, the newsletter for the Hasshin RI (of Rhode Island; later named Anime Hasshin) fan club, serves as another example of the underground literature produced in the first decade of local underground publishing.[63] The first issue of *The Rose* stated that the "purpose of Hasshin RI is to circulate information about Japanimation as it comes to us and to show Japanese animation."[64] In just three years the newsletter grew in size from ten pages to twenty-five, illustrating the concurrent growth in knowledge about anime in the United States and proving Hasshin RI successful in its original goals. The improvement in size, paper quality, artwork, and density of information from issue 1 (January 1987) to issue 19 (January 1990) was significant, and that could have happened only in a context in which enthusiasm for anime was growing consistently.

The nineteenth issue celebrated *The Rose's* third anniversary. It dedicated nearly a third of its pages to networking with the national and global anime fan community. Like other underground publications of its kind, it contained encouragement for contributions, merchandise for sale, news about other national clubs, and addresses for clubs, media, and club members.[65] Features like short synopses of various anime series (essential companion materials for watching untranslated anime at club meetings), a word puzzle, and a page with lessons on Japanese vocabulary typified the efforts of aficionados to expand the boundaries of the U.S. knowledge base. It also reflected fan interests in learning more about the culture that produced anime, as evidenced in the vocabulary lesson page from the nineteenth issue.

The May 1989 issue demonstrated explicitly the way anime fans envisioned their community through underground literature. A map, prefaced by the comforting words "You are not alone!," pinpointed the location of every known anime fan club, totaling forty-six, in the United States. The editors encouraged readers: "Don't be shy, write to these clubs . . . and make new anime friends." Through this map, an artifact of the global imagination, anime fans envisioned a national community that traversed vast open spaces to connect groups with shared cultural affinities. Japanese goods created American and global communities.

The Rose also provides insight into fans' demands for cultural authenticity. Most discussion space of particular anime was dedicated to underground, Japanese-language anime, and because of either the language barrier or the feeling of authenticity these anime provided, reviews were uncritical. Contributors reserved their venom for U.S. producers' corruption of "pure" anime. One fan, reviewing Carl Macek's post-*Robotech* union of two popular anime, *Captain Harlock* and *Queen Millennia*, melodramatically referred to the end result, *Captain Harlock and the Queen of 1,000 Years*, as an "ANIMATED ABORTION."[66] Another criticized the infamous English adaptation of Hayao Miyazaki's classic *Nausicaä of the Valley of the Wind*, titled *Warriors of the Wind*, for reducing the two-hour original to ninety minutes and for obscuring the poignancy of the environmentalist message of the original.[67] On the other hand, commercially imported anime had potential to satisfy fans, much like the English adaptation of Miyazaki's *Laputa: Castle in the Sky* (a Streamline production), if it appeared that the importers strived to maintain the integrity of the original. One contributor wrote, "The English version is uncut. None of the names were changed. The translation, as nearly as I can tell, is quite faithful to the original."[68] Like food writers evaluating the authenticity of a Japanese restaurant, it was not clear what criteria or expertise enthusiasts used to make such judgments. Nevertheless, by 1990 fans praised U.S. production companies that responded to their demands by meeting their expectations for authenticity, as Streamline did with *Akira*.

By the nineties underground newsletters like *The Rose* gave way to two trends in anime fan communication: professional magazines and, eventually, the Internet. The Usenet newsgroup rec.arts.anime signaled an important moment in the transnationalizing of U.S. anime culture.[69] As one fan stated, rec.arts.anime "was more or less a global forum," though until the early nineties access was limited to people at U.S., Japanese, and European universities linked to the Internet.[70] The newsgroup launched in January 1988 under the initiative of one of the founders of A.N.I.M.E.[71] Message traffic was slow at first, but it exploded in late 1989 with, ironically, the release of Disney's successful animated film *The Little Mermaid*. The resulting high volume of messages about U.S. animation instigated debates about the definition of anime, why it should be restricted only to Japanese animation, and why it deserved its own newsgroup distinct from all other forms of animation.

A 1988 challenge to rec.art.anime's subject matter witnessed a group of subscribers attempt to create a separate newsgroup to discuss only animation produced in the United States. They claimed that rec.arts.anime "was felt to be too biased towards Japanimation," which one contributor derisively called "Jap Warrior Robot shows." One fan also admitted that the new newsgroup had "become necessary in order to prevent friction over nationalistic issues."[72] This discussion reflected the developing perception among devotees that anime was a unique cultural category that deserved to be distinguished from dissimilar U.S. media. It also illustrated the establishment of an "other"—U.S. entertainment—that anime fans used to define the inner and outer boundaries of their own community. The more often fans discussed U.S. popular culture, the better they were able to articulate anime's expression of cultural difference. Anime appealed to so many fans precisely because it was so different from what they saw on U.S. television.

The attitudes that manifested in public debates about the rise of Japanese economic power were visible in these online arguments and ruminated within the larger anime subculture, demonstrating that fans' interests frequently ran counter not only to U.S. mainstream entertainment but also to popular political attitudes. While fans from the period recall clubs as explicitly nonpolitical spaces, fan activism on behalf of a Japanese product was an implicit statement of cultural politics at a time when companies directed "Buy American" campaigns and labor unions smashed Toyotas with sledgehammers at picnics. Such overt "Japan-bashing" was inherently incompatible with the attitudes of the enthusiasts who enjoyed anime precisely for its Japaneseness. "Buy American" campaigns were rooted in economic nationalism, while anime fandom required a more cosmopolitan, globalized worldview, one that embraced positive cultural representations of Japan at a time when such representations were more uncommon than not. The perspectives of anime fans had more in common with those of Robert Reich and the Honda associates in Marysville than it did with the worldview of Japan's many detractors.

In fact, anime fandom encouraged enthusiasts to explore Japanese history and culture more intimately. Some of the early buffs mentioned above used anime as a first step toward learning the Japanese language. (Many college students in Japanese language courses today say that anime and manga inspired them to register; tellingly, after several semesters of instruction those same students say that their interests in Japan and its culture have grown more varied and sophisticated.)[73] In August 1986 a group of thirty California fans from several C/FO chapters organized a trip to Japan, dubbed "Japanimation '86," to meet animators, visit production studios, attend the Japanese National Science Fiction Convention, and shop for anime-themed merchandise in Tokyo and Osaka.[74] Japanimation '86 was the first trip of its kind and a rare face-to-face encounter during this period between anime's Japanese producers and American consumers, and also between Japanese and American fans. The intercultural anime relationship more often took place in the mediated realm of consumption and imagination. Anime tourism like Japanimation '86 has grown significantly since the 1980s, however, with fans from across the globe flocking to the Akihabara district of Tokyo for total immersion in Japanese anime, manga, and video game culture.

CONCLUSION: GRASSROOTS GLOBALIZATION

There are several precedents to anime's U.S. expansion. It is possible to compare transpacific anime encounters to the European and American *japonisant* artists of the late nineteenth and early twentieth centuries and the American Zen Buddhists of the 1950s. For example, Lafcadio Hearn, the Greek-born American writer who fell in love with Japan in the late nineteenth century, spent the last decade and a half of his life there. Also, beat poet Gary Snyder traveled widely across Japan in the 1950s, absorbed in the study of Zen Buddhism.[75] Anime's U.S. boom, though, has become more widespread than these two instances because it has benefited from the global proliferation of inexpensive media technologies, enabling more people than ever to participate in global cultural and economic exchange. As such the U.S. anime experience has also been a highly mediated phenomenon, and most early U.S. anime fans accepted a mediated Japan through the consumption of anime texts, unlike Hearn or Snyder, who chased "authentic" experiences by actually living in Japan. Indeed, it was possible to be an anime fan and have never met a Japanese person—not an unlikely scenario considering the vast spaces between the U.S. coasts and the small numbers of Japanese immigrants relative to those from other East Asian nations. Yet contact with Japan or the Japanese has not necessarily implied cultural authenticity. As Edward Said demonstrated, traveling to "the East" did not preclude a writer from reproducing the most malevolent strains of orientalism.

Anime devotees were instead likely the cultural successors to the early twentieth-century middle-class white women whom historian Mari Yoshihara describes. Such women "embraced the East" by consuming Asian objects, making the women "agents of the culture of Orientalism without their having to physically travel to the Orient."[76] The consumption of underground anime enabled fans to adopt a representation of Japan at once unmediated by elite ideological structures of Western orientalism yet mediated through a border-crossing technology of cultural representation. Still, if Western racial and gender representations influenced anime's *mukokuseki* style, then U.S. viewers consumed texts already infused with orientalist ideology. This complicated and indistinct "Möbius strip" of representation, transmission, and consumption defined how U.S. fans consumed anime's Japaneseness.[77] If nearly three decades of scholarship on cultural globalization has taught us anything, it is that it is messy, and simplistic models of one-way transmission do not match empirical realities.

Another precedent in the history of U.S.-Japan cultural exchange is baseball. Anime is to the United States what baseball is to Japan—a transplant that has established a foothold in the landscape of a foreign national popular culture. Sayuri Guthrie-Shimizu and Thomas W. Zeiler have each chronicled baseball's journey to Japan and around the rest of the globe as one early instance of U.S. cultural globalization.[78] After more than a century of cultural exchange and adaptation, according to Zeiler, "baseball (rather than sumo) can be considered Japan's national pastime."[79] Japanese players have excelled so much in recent years that American sports fans regularly cite the names of all-stars like Ichiro Suzuki, Hideki Matsui, and Kosuke Fukudome. Perhaps in time, considering baseball's hundred-year head start, anime fandom might become a pastime of similar popularity and meaning in the United States.

The anime phenomenon in the United States is also not unique in terms of the local effects of contemporary cultural globalization. A non-Japanese example is the growing popularity of bhangra, a colorful and energetic style of Indian music and dance with roots in the Punjab region. Indian popular cultural exports like Bollywood films have accumulated increasingly larger audiences in the United States in the last two decades, even among Americans not of South Asian descent. Bhangra dancing, though, is closer in nature to the anime phenomenon in the way that its popularity hinges on active participation in the creation of new transnational cultural identities and communities. As with anime fans, some of the earliest organizing occurred on college campuses. In 1995, George Washington University in Washington, D.C., hosted a local bhangra dance competition for college teams. By the first decade of the twenty-first century, the competition had grown into the annual "Bhangra Blowout," which brings together eight "elite" college teams chosen from more than forty applicants. Though most of the competitors are children or grandchildren of South Asian immigrants, white and African American students also participate.[80] Bhangra allows Americans not of South Asian descent to "try on" South Asian cultures in ways similar to anime's mediation of Japanese culture.

Bhangra dance teams have dealt with some of the same questions of cultural globalization that anime fans have confronted. For example, what makes a global cultural product or practice "authentic"? When young people in the United States first discovered bhangra in the early nineties, they incorporated it into cultural practices with which they were already familiar, like break dancing and hip-hop. As college students started forming dance teams, however, they organized these new communities around the principle of cultural difference, highlighting the non-Americanness of bhangra and promoting its "traditional" Indian characteristics. Dance teams made it their goal to "dance as authentically and traditionally as possible," and such criteria factored into competition judging.[81] Echoing the fears of early anime fans, one college student lamented, "Bhangra has gotten so much exposure, but we kind of lose what's authentic."[82] Like anime and sushi, the popularity of bhangra shows not only that cultural globalization has created heterogeneity—the proliferation of cultural difference—but also that it has been created by the efforts of countless non-elites acting at a local level to pull the global into the United States. Bhangra dancers and anime fans in the United States have made the "production of difference," in Charles Bright and Michael Geyer's phrasing, a communal ambition within the domestic space of the very empire so often accused of practicing a homogenizing cultural imperialism abroad.[83] Of course, this does not excuse or downplay the impact of U.S. imperialism around the world, but it does show that the American experience of globalization has always been more complicated than simplistic narratives of cultural imperialism.

The examples of anime, bhangra, and other foreign products and practices help scholars draw conclusions about the ways in which cultural globalization has transformed the United States. The story of America's globalizing moment usually rests on the actions of government, corporate, or nongovernmental organizations; in the cases of anime and bhangra, however, cultural globalization would not have occurred without the ambitions and actions of local non-elites disconnected from all three conventional globalizing institutions. The important actors in anime's story were postal clerks, computer technicians, college students, and anonymous middle-class women and men with no professional training in the arts of international relations and communication. Multinational corporations play a central role in the history of globalization in the postwar era, but anime's global boom was a process driven from below, a kind of grassroots globalization.

The technological tools of contemporary globalization have facilitated bhangra's popularity as well as the attractiveness of other global products and practices. Without the Internet, many U.S. practitioners of bhangra would have no access to videos of "authentic" Indian dancing. Without inexpensive media technologies like the VCR, progenitor of YouTube, much of the world would not know of the Hong Kong action cinema of Bruce Lee and Jackie Chan or the vibrant worlds of Bollywood film. And without advancements in rapid and inexpensive air transportation, coupled with new refrigeration technologies, cosmopolitans the world over would not feast on sushi, a truly global delicacy.

Finally, anime's border crossing and its popular consequences reveal a different side of life in "Reagan's America." The simplistic narrative transition from Jimmy Carter's "malaise" to Reagan's "morning again in America" obscures the complexity of life in an era when Americans were engaging social and cultural developments independent of traditional institutions of state politics and power. Some people looked beyond the culture of the late Cold War, beyond Reagan, and even beyond the borders of the United States to the globalizing of America. No nation was more central to that project in the 1980s than Japan.

EPILOGUE

Back to the Future
in U.S.-Japan Relations

As I finish writing this book, the businessman and reality television star Donald Trump steamrolls toward the Republican nomination for the 2016 presidential election. Whatever the outcome, Trump's campaign has already been one for the proverbial history books. Whether motivated by sincerity or cynicism, he has drawn upon deep-seated fears, particularly among white American men, of a wide array of "others"—Syrian refugees, Mexican immigrants, Black Lives Matter protesters. Perhaps more effectively than any candidate in living memory, Trump has stoked racial anxieties and harnessed xenophobic rage with promises to, among other things, build a massive wall between the United States and Mexico, ban all Muslims from entering the country, and force China to pay exorbitant tariffs on the hundreds of billions of dollars of goods it exports to the United States each year.

Historians are not in the practice of predicting the future, but we are attuned to the disjunctures between present and past. As Trump lobbed rhetorical grenades at everyone and everything that angered white Americans in the age of the black president, one attack failed to stick and fell on American ears as anachronistic and out of touch. As he launched his improbable campaign in the summer of 2015, he labeled the United States a failure in international trade, and among the culprits was a bogeyman Americans had forgotten to fear: Japan. "When do we beat Japan at anything?" he asked a crowd. "They send their cars over by the millions, and what do we do? When was the last time you saw a Chevrolet in Tokyo? It doesn't exist, folks. They beat us all the time." The claim was not literally true—Chevrolet sells cars in Japan, though they account only for a tiny fraction of the Japanese automobile market— but, as Trump would prove repeatedly on the campaign trail, literal truth mattered less than the subjective feeling of American decline captured by his catchphrase "Make America Great Again." Trump continued to sprinkle mild Japan-bashing into speeches, pledging, for instance, to refuse to use Komatsu construction equipment to build his wall on the Mexican border. The rhetoric perked up the ears of Japanese Foreign Ministry officials sensitive to protectionist rumblings in the United States, but it otherwise disappeared into the cacophony of media sensationalism surrounding a campaign that embraced racism and even violence.[1]

To a generation of Americans born after 1980—the so-called millennials—Trump's Japan-bashing risen from the grave made little sense in a global context in which China's tremendous economic surge, with India not far behind, arguably presented the greatest international challenge to U.S. prosperity. Indeed, Trump's anti-Japanese economic nationalism may have received less media attention than a Republican strategist's offhand remark that Trump supporters were "childless single men who masturbate to anime," a claim intended to portray the candidate's followers as antisocial outsiders obsessed with a weird foreign subculture. The Japan of 2016 was not the Japan of almost three decades earlier, when Trump had said to Oprah Winfrey, "They come over here, they sell their cars, their VCRs. They knock the hell out of our companies."[2] Rather, it served more effectively as a punch line than as a bogeyman.

Seventy years after the end of World War II, and a quarter century after the Japanese economy entered a tailspin that would lead to a "Lost Decade" of national economic growth, Americans had forgotten the menace that defined the brief Japan Panic. More than two-thirds of them surveyed believed Japan was trustworthy, while less than one-third said the same of China. When asked to choose the most important development in U.S.-Japan relations in the last century, 31 percent said World War II; an equal number said the 2011 earthquake and tsunami in Japan; 23 percent said the postwar military alliance between the two countries; and only 8 percent responded with the "trade wars" of the 1980s and 1990s. The Pew Research Center also asked 1,000 Americans to say what came to mind when they think of Japan. Twice as many respondents mentioned sushi or food over any other answer.[3] The era when nearly seven out of ten respondents claimed Japan was a greater threat than the Soviet Union was long past, even if Donald Trump did not know it.

The idea that Japan presents a threat of any kind to the United States in the second decade of the twenty-first century belies the reality of Japan's persistently tepid economic growth, rapidly aging population, and perennial ambivalence about assuming a greater military role in East Asian affairs.

Since 2012 Prime Minister Shinzo Abe has attempted to address all of these problems, in the form of "Abenomics" reforms and a push to revise Article 9 of the Japanese Constitution, which prohibits the use of military force as an instrument of state policy. The results have been mixed at best. To be sure, it is unfair to label a failure an affluent society that provides arguably the best standard of living in the world to the widest swath of its population.[4] Japan has nevertheless lost the power to make Americans panic.

Ultimately the Japan Panic may have been just a "warm-up" for the twenty-first-century clash with China. The "trade deficit" with the behemoth of East Asia has soared to levels the most ambitious of Japanese businessmen in the 1980s could not have predicted. The consumer goods that continue to shape daily American life are made in China now; even Japan's electronics giants like Sony manufacture their products on the continent. Where Japanese leaders, even at the height of the bubble, were always reticent to translate economic superpowerdom into regional or global political influence, China has pursued it aggressively. Steve Lohr of the *New York Times* cautions against reading too much into the similarities, though. The heated rhetoric is there for sure—one need only listen to Donald Trump to hear echoes of yellow peril fears—but most analogies are superficial. Japan's government ministries worked hard to limit foreign investment in Japan, making it difficult even to this day, while the government of China has actively encouraged it. Americans have found open arms and economic incentives to develop in China that they never found in Japan. The mythical "China market," luring ambitious business leaders in the nineteenth century, remains a powerful draw for U.S. commercial interests as well. Trump's Chevrolet comments point to decades-old complaints about Japan's unwillingness to open its markets to U.S.-made goods. Though China has not been innocent of creating similar obstacles, the prospect of selling to more than a billion potential customers in the country has kept U.S. business leaders mum on "unfair" Chinese trade practices in ways they were not in the 1980s. For Lohr, hope may rest in China serving as an "economic Sputnik," spurring the U.S. government to articulate a clear industrial policy intended to make the United States competitive in a global market, a move it refused to make during the height of the trade wars.[5]

The analogy between Japan in the 1980s and China in the 2010s also fails to hold up in terms of the two countries' comparative global cultural influence. China simply isn't cool, at least not in the way Japan has been for several decades now. In fact, South Korea has become the rising cultural power of East Asia that China is not, so much so that even Japan has started to envy the outsized success a nation of 50 million has on hundreds of millions throughout the region. Korean dramas (or "K-dramas," as they are known in the West), pop music ("K-pop"), fashion, and food have collectively formed a *hallyu*, or "Korean wave," that has washed over East Asia (especially China) since the 1990s and has started to trickle onto North American shores in the last decade. A broadband Internet connection in North America gives consumers access to countless manifestations of Korean pop culture. As a result, interest in Korea grows in much the same way interest in Japan did in the 1980s: enrollment in Korean-language classes at U.S. colleges, for instance, climbed 45 percent in just a half decade, while overall enrollment in language classes dropped. In contrast to the Japanese government, which treated the global expansion of Japanese popular culture with benign neglect for decades, the South Korean government aggressively sponsored the expansion of *hallyu* in the new millennium. Noting its new rival's success, the government of Japan responded in turn in 2013 with the creation of the Cool Japan Fund, a $300 million program to promote Japanese pop culture abroad more systematically, an implicit institutional acknowledgment of the failure to capitalize on decades of cultural cool. In both cases these governments believe the nebulous concept of "soft power" promises returns on such investments, even if no one has yet to figure out how to quantify global cultural impact effectively. Whatever the outcome, at least the arms race of East Asian pop culture empires will prove more entertaining than the imperial arms races of the previous century.[6]

What that kind of rivalry portends for the future of U.S.-Japan relations or for the United States' role in the world in the twenty-first century is unclear. The narrative of globalization suffered two dramatic shocks in the first decade of the twenty-first century. First, the attacks on the United States of 11 September 2001 triggered a nationalist response that threatened the institutionalization of a Fortress America. The U.S. government reasserted the power of the nation-state in dramatic fashion just at the moment when scholars of globalization claimed such power was disintegrating. It identified the elements of a globalizing world—the increasing irrelevance of borders and the transnationalization of commerce and culture, among others—not as opportunities for economic prosperity, as the Clinton administration had, but as central causes of U.S. insecurity. The George W. Bush administration strengthened physical borders while violating others, particularly those civil boundaries outlined in the U.S. Constitution. It declared a global war on "terrorism"—a transnational ideology, a way of looking at the world and a prescription for behaving in it that regards the boundaries human beings draw as illusory.

The processes and tools of globalization had created opportunities for transnational networks like Al Qaeda to have a global impact disproportionate to their actual numbers. The Bush administration thus found monsters to destroy in the very processes that had transformed the United States and the world in the previous quarter century.

The second shock to the globalization story came in late 2008 when the globalized economy entered its worst crisis since the Great Depression—the "Great Recession." The most visible indicators of Americans' consumption of global production, levels of consumer spending, foretold troubled times. "Suddenly, our consumer society is doing a lot less consuming," wrote David Leonhardt in the *New York Times*. Drops in consumer spending during the deep but brief recession of the early 1980s affected industries that produced consumer goods throughout the country, and as a consequence many of those industries started relocating production outside the United States. Three decades later, the United States produced far fewer of such things. The goods Americans bought were made primarily in Asia or Latin America, and the stability of production in those regions hinged on U.S. consumers' unchanging appetite to spend. "It would be silly to insist that a few terrible months meant the end of American consumer culture," wrote Leonhardt. "But it would be equally silly to assume that culture could never change. It might be changing right now."[7] Three years into the crisis, historian James Livingston urged Americans to keep popular consumption at the center of the conversation about recovery. In an antitax political climate, one in which even the very richest Americans found no shortage of defenders among a battered and bruised middle class, arguments about letting the wealthy keep their money to reinvest in the economy were historically shortsighted, Livingston believed. The lesson of twentieth-century economic history was that consumer spending rather than business investment powered economic recoveries. "We have reached the point where we have to confront our fears about consumer culture," he wrote, "because the renunciation of desire, the deferral of gratification, saving for a rainy day—call it what you want—has become dangerous to our economic health."[8] In that regard, China may be more of a savior than a menace: Michael Schulman suggested in *Time* that a growing China means 1.3 billion potential customers for the world's goods, taking pressure off Americans to serve as the central consumerist node for global production. China has already become the world's largest automobile market, with the Chinese buying almost twice as many new vehicles each year as Americans do, and both General Motors and Ford are building new production facilities in the country.[9]

A quarter century after Japan's bubble burst and it began a slide from which it had yet to recover, the once-and-future superpower again served as a model for a West eager for answers. This time, however, Japan's development served as a tragic warning rather than a model for emulation. "Japan seems to have pulled into a shell, content to accept its fade from the global stage," wrote Martin Fackler in the *New York Times*. Two decades of austerity had created a "dark and subdued" young urban class, very much the opposite of their "flashy and upbeat" predecessors of the 1980s. Knowing nothing but the politics and economics of austerity, the emerging professional generation were "consumption-haters," as one Japanese marketing executive called them, drawing attention to their penchant for saving more and refusing to consume the goods that needed consuming, if Japan were ever to return to the heights of the eighties. Some economists warned of "Japanification" (the irony!), of the United States falling victim to the "same deflationary trap of collapsed demand" responsible for stagnation in Japan, a country where in 2010 the national economy was the same size it had been twenty years earlier.[10] Decades earlier Japan showed the United States what a world of globalized consumption could look like. In the twenty-first century, it had very different lessons to teach.

To conclude, I want to return to images of the consumption of Japan over the course of nearly four decades, from just before this study began chronologically to the early twenty-first century. There has always been, it seems, a certain artistry involved in representing Japan on the cover of popular U.S. weekly magazines. Design choices aside, certain themes persist—namely, Americans continue to represent Japan as a premodern-postmodern producer of desirable consumer goods.

The first cover, from the 10 May 1971 issue of *Time*, shows Sony founder and consumer electronics innovator Akio Morita inside of a portable Sony television, accompanied by the headline "How to Cope with Japan's Business Invasion."[11] Of the four covers, the oldest one, ironically, resorts the least to cultural essentialism and orientalism. It is also the only cover to show a photograph, albeit a purposefully distorted one, of an actual Japanese person. Here was a conspicuous trend: the more that Japanese economic power became a reality, the more likely Americans resorted to fantastical representations of Japanese culture and commerce. That after the early 1970s publications were much less likely to print images of actual Japanese people and much more likely to represent them in cartoon or caricatured form suggests an impulse to ignore both economic realities and actual Japanese bodies in the years of U.S. decline and Japanese ascension. It was no coincidence that even in the late 1980s, when Japan was on many Americans' minds and in their domestic spaces, most of them could not name a single Japanese person besides artist Yoko Ono, whom most knew only because of her marriage to murdered Beatle John Lennon. The only Japanese figure recognized by more than one in ten Americans was Prime Minister Yasuhiro Nakasone, while global culture shapers Morita, filmmaker Akira Kurosawa, and fashion designer Issei Miyake all polled under 10 percent.[12] When *Time* put Morita on its cover, though, Americans still imagined a Japan safely ensconced within the camp of Western-style liberal capitalist modernity, and physical Japanese bodies did not yet challenge U.S. power. Its corporations could be represented as business competitors without being characterized as cultural threats. Still, the Morita cover hinted at a theme of pre-1945 understandings of East Asia with the use of the word "invasion."

The next two covers (a *Time* cover from 1981 and a *New Yorker* cover from 2002) reveal both changing and unchanging attitudes toward Japan over two decades.[13] The first shows a traditional samurai character—a premodern icon of war, perhaps a reference to the military notion of "invasion"—bedecked in the consumer luxuries of contemporary Japan. He holds a camera, calculator, golf clubs, car keys, gold watch, briefcase, and necktie (the last four not iconic products of Japan but references to wealthy businessmen). The cover mixes images of the premodern with the cutting edge of technology and commerce. It points toward a hypercapitalist future, one in which the grand stories of human liberation inherent in modernity no longer apply and only the acquisition of wealth, driven by primal, uncivilized urges, matters. Japan as the techno-samurai appears alert and poised to strike, as it did to many Americans throughout the 1980s.

The *New Yorker* cover also mingles notions of traditional and futuristic Japan, but it defangs the threatening Japan of twenty years earlier. Instead of the warlike symbol of masculinity, the samurai, the *New Yorker* uses a symbol of docile femininity, the geisha. She wears a kimono made of Pikachu, the primary "pocket monster" character from the global anime phenomenon *Pokémon*, a figure instantly recognizable to hundreds of millions of children (and their parents). In place of the standard folding fan accessory, she holds several cellular phones. Incorporated into her intricate hair styling are earphones, likely connected to a Walkman. The geisha is not prepared to attack or invade anything. In contrast to the samurai's anxious look, she seems content with her role as unthreatening provider of popular consumer goods—a techno-servant rather than a techno-threat.

The final cover, from a December 2007 international edition of *News-week*, shows a silhouetted, katana-wielding samurai connected to—what else?—an Apple iPod.[14] In the techno-consumer world, Japan has "lost its groove," replaced, as the article explains, by U.S. powerhouses like Apple and Google. The silhouetted samurai is ready to strike, but the direction he faces is unclear. The aggressive globalizer of a quarter century earlier has become, quite literally, a shadow of its former self.

Why do U.S. media continue to represent Japan in such a way? Would an article on, say, BMW's global success fuse images of Bavarian men clad in lederhosen driving overpriced cars? Would a *Motor Trend* cover story on British car company Mini make sense to readers if it showed a family of Puritans packing into a futuristic electricity-powered vehicle? Both images seem silly. So why do Americans persist in representing another decades-long ally and trading partner, Japan, in ways that blend dissonant images of a premodern past and a consumerist future while effacing actual Japanese bodies? The answer lies in the U.S. encounter with Japan in the 1970s and 1980s. While the heated rhetoric and the idea that Japan poses a threat to U.S. economic hegemony are relics of a bygone era, the imagery of the period has been added to the deep well of representations from which Americans draw to portray Japan and the Japanese. The figure of the techno-samurai drained of color, yet still fully "wired," encapsulates the popular amnesia that has erased many earlier notions of Japan pointing the way toward a globalized future. The result is today's narrative of international power, one that is a fully de-Japanized vision of the globalizing of America.

Honda of America knows how to sell that image to consumers. In 2012 the company produced a television advertisement, "Through It All," to commemorate the company's thirtieth anniversary of assembling automobiles in the United States.[15] The first five seconds of the thirty-second commercial recreate an image I had seen dozens of times in my years working on this project: it is the Marysville Auto Plant on 1 November 1982, the day the first vehicle, a slate-gray four-door 1983 Accord, rolled off the line (illustration E.1).[16] The scene is celebratory, with silver tinsel decorating a makeshift ceremonial platform, a giant red-and-white wreath atop the car, and confetti sprinkling from the ceiling. It was obvious the ad agency had carefully studied the same image I had seen repeatedly in local newspapers and Honda promotional materials from the time. The ways the image changed from 1982, then, must have stood out to the producers as much as it did to me. A big sign behind the car, for instance, displays a counter with the number "001." In the 2012

ILL. E.1. The first seconds of the 2012 Honda television advertisement "Through It All" features a recreation of the scene in Marysville on 1 November 1982, when the company celebrated the production of the first U.S.-made Honda Accord. (American Honda Motor/YouTube)

version it sits between two U.S. flags, while in the original (illustration E.2) it is positioned between the U.S. flag and the flag of the state of Ohio—a revision perhaps motivated by the desire not to confuse viewers in forty-nine states to whom the flag would be unrecognizable. (Coincidentally, the Ohio flag has a red orb on a white field not unlike the flag of Japan.) The sign in the TV spot proclaims, "1st Accord Built in America," while the original had said, "Another product with pride!"—a clumsy phrase lacking a verb, but one that emphasized Honda's labor philosophy over nationalism. The most striking revision comes at the podium, where the 2012 advertisement shows a white man dressed in the iconic white jacket that all plant employees, whether management or worker, wear. Flanking him are other white men wearing the same uniform, smiling and congratulating each other. At the podium in the original promotional image from 1982, however, is Kiyoshi Kawashima, president of Honda of Japan, the executive who had replaced Soichiro Honda as head of the company in 1973. The only other faces in the image are a couple of teenagers from the local high school marching band, staring into the camera like deer in headlights. The story Honda wanted to tell in 1982, the story of a global corporation from Japan coming to rescue a town in the depths of a brutal recession, was no longer useful thirty years later. Honda's global success was an American triumph, and the Japanese role in the globalizing of America was once again effaced.

MARYSVILLE, Ohio, November 1—The first Japanese car built in the United States, a 1983 Honda Accord, rolls off the line at a new 1,000,000 square-foot manufacturing plant here, as Kiyoshi Kawashima, President of Honda Motor Co., Ltd., looks on.

ILL. E.2. A Honda promotional photograph from 1982 shows the same scene as the 2012 television advertisement, but some significant details have been altered: both the Ohio flag and the Japanese Honda executive, Kiyoshi Kawashima, have been replaced. (American Honda Motor/Logan County District Library, Bellefontaine, Ohio)

Notes

Note: For articles from popular periodicals not listed in the bibliography, full citations appear in the notes, with the following abbreviations for frequently cited publications.

BW	*Business Week*
CEAR	*Consumer Electronics Annual Review 1975–1990*
CSM	*Christian Science Monitor*
DAFR	UAW President's Office: Douglas A. Fraser Records, Archives of Labor and Urban Affairs, Walter P. Reuther Library, Wayne State University
DFP	*Detroit Free Press*
IEBM	UAW International Executive Board Minutes and Proceedings Collection, Archives of Labor and Urban Affairs, Walter P. Reuther Library, Wayne State University
MJT	*Marysville Journal-Tribune*
NYT	*New York Times*
OBC	UAW President's Office: Owen Bieber Collection, Archives of Labor and Urban Affairs, Walter P. Reuther Library, Wayne State University
PI	*Philadelphia Inquirer*
UAWS	*UAW Solidarity*
TDCE	*Television Digest with Consumer Electronics*
WP	*Washington Post*
WPM	*Washington Post Magazine*

INTRODUCTION

1. Williams, *Resources of Hope*, 4.
2. C. Johnson, "How to Think about Economic Competition from Japan," 417.

3. I want to clarify at the outset what this book is not: it is not a history of Japan. As much as I try to learn about Japan, and will continue learning about Japan, I claim no expertise on the country's history, language, or culture. Since I am interested in how Americans consume Japanese goods, I have titled this book *Consuming Japan* rather than *Producing Japan*. Writing the latter book would not only double the size of the current one but also demand expertise that this historian of the twentieth-century United States does not have. Besides, a cohort of very good scholars has already addressed many of the questions that a book on the production of Japanese consumer goods would attempt to answer. I have learned a great deal from them and cite their work throughout this text, but it is worth drawing the reader's attention at the outset to, among other scholars of Japan, anthropologists Harumi Befu, Koichi Iwabuchi, Anne Allison, Marilyn Ivy, Theodore Bestor, and Ian Condry; literary scholars Hiroki Azuma, Susan J. Napier, and Thomas LaMarre; and historians Carol Gluck, John Dower, and William Tsutsui. My work would not be possible without theirs, and as such I hope it contributes to an evolving conversation about the messy relationship between national production and global consumption.

4. Dower, *War without Mercy*.

5. T. White, "Danger from Japan."

6. The term "Japan Panic" comes from Morley and Robins, *Spaces of Identity*, 147, though this definition is my own adapted version. White is discussed in a number of commentaries on the period. See Hobart Rowan, "Low Point in Japan-Bashing," *WP*, 1 August 1985; Miyoshi, *Off Center*; and Barshay, "What Is Japan to Us?"

7. T. White, "Danger from Japan."

8. A useful survey of the history of consumer theory is Sassatelli, *Consumer Culture*.

9. For example, Miller's *Comfort of Things* is an empathetic investigation of how people in a London neighborhood find comfort in the seemingly innocuous material goods that surround them, but its audience is an academic one. On the other hand, Gosling's *Snoop*, while generally acknowledging the value of studying consumption, establishes a different tone, one in which consumption patterns are means to acquiring information about people to be used for different ends. It found a broader audience.

10. Putnam, *Bowling Alone*, 27.

11. One of the more creative of these critiques is Gilvary, "Skinny Jeans."

12. This definition derives from several works. Steigerwald, "All Hail the Republic of Choice," 385, defines consumption as "how Americans have acquired and used goods not strictly necessary to biological existence." I take Steigerwald's definition a step further, searching for the ways in which that acquisition and use creates cultural meaning. In this regard, I have found guidance in Bourdieu, *Distinction*, and in Douglas and Isherwood, *World of Goods*.

13. See Steigerwald, "All Hail the Republic of Choice"; Breen, *Marketplace of Revolution* and "Will Americans Consumers Buy a Second American Revolution?"; and L. Cohen, *Consumer's Republic* and "Escaping Steigerwald's 'Plastic Cages.'"

14. See Hoganson, "Stuff It," "Cosmopolitan Domesticity," and *Consumers' Imperium*, 254, 5. For an engaging theoretical contribution to the conceptualization of "domestic" and "foreign," see Kaplan, *Anarchy of Empire* and "Manifest Domesticity."

15. Rawson, "Foreign Exchange."

16. Rawson, "Foreign Exchange," 179; Stelzer, "How to Save Free Trade," 16.

17. See Breen, *Marketplace of Revolution*. Also, John Kuo Wei Tchen argues that Chinese goods played a formative role in defining U.S. national identity in the early Republic. See Tchen, *New York before Chinatown*.

18. Williams, *Marxism and Literature*, 132–33.

19. Didion, *After Henry*, 25–46.

20. For example, see H. Johnson, *Sleepwalking through History*; Noonan, *What I Saw at the Revolution*; and Wills, *Reagan's America*.

21. Cowie, *Stayin' Alive*; Stein, *Pivotal Decade*; Rodgers, *Age of Fracture*.

22. See Ritzer, *McDonaldization of Society*.

23. See Huntington, *Clash of Civilizations*.

24. Classic works in this regard are Appadurai, *Modernity at Large*; and Hannerz, *Transnational Connections*. For a recent evolution of the hybridization argument, see Pieterse, *Globalization and Culture*.

25. Hopper, *Understanding Cultural Globalization*, 10.

26. Cooper, *Colonialism in Question*, 111, 9.

27. Charles Paul Freund, "Playing the 90's," *WP*, 29 October 1989.

28. Lyotard, *Postmodern Condition*, xxiv. An important history of the concept of postmodernity is P. Anderson, *Origins of Postmodernity*.

29. Farber, "Torch Had Fallen."

30. Barthes, *Empire of Signs*.

31. Nye, *Bound to Lead*; Crichton, *Rising Sun*.

32. For example, see Miyoshi and Harootunian, *Postmodernism and Japan*.

33. Jameson, "Notes on Globalization as a Philosophical Issue," 54.

34. LaFeber, *Clash*, 326.

35. Zeiler, "Nixon Shocks Japan," 305.

36. Ferguson et al., *Shock of the Global*.

37. Robert G. Kaiser, "Sony in Alabama: A Competitor Takes Root in American Soil," *WP*, 2 December 1979.

38. Harvey, *Condition of Postmodernity*, 166; Castells, *End of Millennium*, 235; Kingston, *Japan in Transformation*, 83.

39. Kingston, *Japan in Transformation*, 233.

40. Gordon, *Modern History of Japan*, 314–17; Zeiler, "Business Is War," 243–46.

41. David E. Sanger, "Gloom Lifts in U.S. and Falls on Japan," *NYT*, 29 December 1992.

42. Zeiler, "Business Is War," 243; Castells, *End of Millennium*, 236–37.

43. Castells, *End of Millennium*, 237.

44. For instance, LaFeber, *Michael Jordan and the New Global Capitalism*.

45. See Tchen and Yeats, eds., *Yellow Peril!*

46. Dower, *War without Mercy*, 3–14.

47. Shibusawa, *America's Geisha Ally*, 11.

48. For example, see Steven Sabotta, letter to the editor, "The Japanese Are Working Themselves to Death," *NYT*, 19 March 1990.

49. "Surprising Attitudes Found in U.S.-Japan Poll," *San Francisco Chronicle*, 14 January 1987.

50. Klein, *Cold War Orientalism*, 9.

51. See LaFeber, *Clash*; Schaller, *Altered States*; and Iriye and Wampler, *Partnership*.

1. Dan Balz, "Tsongas, Clinton Top Democratic Field," *WP*, 2 February 1992; Tsongas campaign brochure is available at http://www.4president.org/brochures/paultsongas1992brochure.htm; the Clinton campaign is recounted in Patterson, *Restless Giant*, 247–52.

2. Michael Wines, "Bush Collapses at State Dinner with Japanese," *NYT*, 9 January 1992; "Job Performance Ratings for President Bush (G. H. W.)," Public Opinion Archives, Roper Center for Public Opinion Research, ropercenter.uconn.edu.

3. Quoted in LaFeber, *Clash*, 404.

4. Fukuyama, *End of History*.

5. Richard C. Leone, "Foreword," in Garten, *Cold Peace*, vii.

6. For example, see Burstein, *Yen!*; L. Anderson, *Japanese Rage*; Friedman and Lebard, *Coming War with Japan*; Dietrich, *In the Shadow of the Rising Sun*; and Choate, *Agents of Influence*.

7. Choate, *Agents of Influence*, xv.

8. "Japan's Hardening View of America," *BW*, 18 December 1989, 63.

9. For a thoughtful take on the mirror metaphor in U.S.-Japan relations, see Schodt, *America and the Four Japans*.

10. Horvat, "Revisionism Revisited."

11. An example of early alarmism over the deficit is Abegglen and Hout, "Facing Up to the Trade Gap with Japan."

12. Annual balance of payment statistics available at U.S. Census Bureau, "U.S. Trade in Goods and Services—Balance of Payments (BOP) Basis," http://www.census.gov/foreign-trade/statistics/historical/gands.pdf. Statistics specific to trade with Japan available at U.S. Bureau of Economic Analysis, "International Transactions Tables," http://www.bea.gov/international/bp_web/tb_download_type_modern.cfm?list=1&RowID=1.

13. Engerman, "American Knowledge and Global Power," 600.

14. The label was first attached by *Business Week*'s Robert Neff in a popular article, "Rethinking Japan," *BW*, 7 August 1989, 44. Neff listed who he thought were the four most prominent revisionists: Chalmers Johnson, Clyde Prestowitz, Karel van Wolferen, and Commerce Secretary Robert A. Mosbacher. The "Gang of Four," as they would be labeled in Japan, replaced Mosbacher with journalist James Fallows.

15. These are not definitive categories. Some of the less conscientious revisionists regularly crossed lines, but a dichotomy between structuralism and culturalism is helpful in sorting out the wide range of attitudes. Representative structural revisionist texts include C. Johnson, *MITI and the Japanese Miracle*; van Wolferen, *Enigma of Japanese Power*; and Vogel, *Japan as Number One*.

Representative cultural revisionist texts include Christopher, *Japanese Mind*; Wolf, *Japanese Conspiracy*; Taylor, *Shadows of the Rising Sun*; Zimmerman, *How to Do Business with the Japanese*; Alston, *American Samurai*; Fallows, *More Like Us*; and Holstein, *The Japanese Power Game*.

16. The "Gang of Four" (Chalmers Johnson, Clyde Prestowitz, Karel van Wolferen, and James Fallows) responded to accusations of racism and "Japan-bashing" in Chalmers Johnson et al., "Beyond Japan Bashing," *U.S. News and World Report*, 7 May 1990, 54.

17. See Reischauer, *Japanese Today*. The cultural process of creating this popular understanding of Japan is detailed in Shibusawa, *America's Geisha Ally*.

18. LaFeber, *Clash*, 333; A. Smith, "English-Language Historiography of Modern Japan," 648. Also indispensable for understanding the generational evolution of U.S. scholarly thinking on Japan is Gluck, "House of Mirrors."

19. Van Wolferen, "Japan Problem."

20. Carter, "'Crisis of Confidence' Speech."

21. Vogel, *Japan as Number One*, viii, ix.

22. C. Johnson, *MITI and the Japanese Miracle*, viii. Johnson's analysis of the state-market relationship in Japan serves as the basis for Walter LaFeber's concept of the "two capitalisms" of the United States and Japan. See LaFeber, *Clash*, chapter 12.

23. C. Johnson, *MITI and the Japanese Miracle*, 268–72.

24. On industrial policy debates in the 1970s, see Stein, *Pivotal Decade*.

25. Horvat, "Revisionism Revisited," 33.

26. Pyle, "Forum on the Trade Crisis," 239.

27. For instance, see Miyoshi and Harootunian, *Postmodernism and Japan* and *Japan and the World*.

28. Bruce Cumings, "CIA's *Japan 2000* Caper," *Nation*, 30 September 1991, 366–67.

29. Dougherty, "Japan 2000." The document was never published, and it is unclear how many unpublished copies remain of the nine different drafts. To clarify, throughout the chapter I put "Japan 2000" in quotation marks, following style guidelines for unpublished documents, since it remains unpublished. Writers at the time, however, often put the document in italics, since it was intended for publication as a book; I have not altered their formatting when quoting.

Also, the question of authorship is complicated. Andrew J. Dougherty is listed as the sole author, but he had no expertise in Japanese language, culture, or history. Conference attendees, however, did. My assumption is that Dougherty, Rose's executive assistant, served as a scribe during discussions with the intention of writing up the proceedings in a publishable format. And so although I cite Dougherty as the author of "Japan 2000," my assumption is that the document's ideas came directly from conference discussions. I also assume that Dougherty played a small role in these discussions. Therefore throughout the chapter I credit Dougherty with authorship in the notes, but I give the document agency throughout the text to convey that it was a group effort.

30. Ibid., 84, 69.

31. Douthwright, "Rochester Institute of Technology."

32. See ibid.; editorial, "CIA U," *PI*, 24 June 1991; William Glaberson, "College's C.I.A. Links Cause Furor, and Soul-Searching," *NYT*, 20 June 1991; and Rosenberg, "CIA at RIT."

33. The report originally had the subtitle "DEFCON 1." The version that I was able to obtain, however, no longer had this subtitle and was simply titled "Japan 2000." According to one report, the document went through nine drafts before finally being discarded. The first draft was apparently dated February 1991, while the draft in my possession is dated May 1991.

34. The extent of the CIA's involvement is unclear. Some commentators have cited the CIA as the author of the report, which is technically erroneous since only Andrew

J. Dougherty is listed as the author. Kang, "Getting Asia Wrong," lists the Central Intelligence Agency as the author, perhaps revealing less the reality of the document and more how it is remembered by the few people who actually do. Contemporary media accounts varied on the CIA's involvement. One journalist claimed that, along with the eight listed participants, "CIA personnel" also contributed, while the same journalist wrote elsewhere that the document was "prepared for the Central Intelligence Agency by outside specialists." See Paul F. Horvitz, "CIA Spurns Report that Assails Japan," *WP*, 12 June 1991; and Paul F. Horvitz, "CIA-Funded Study Says Japan Lacks Global Responsibility," *WP*, 8 June 1991. Another article made explicit that the initiative was entirely Rose's and Dougherty's, as the document was "prepared for the CIA (but not at its request)." See Rosenberg, "CIA at RIT," 30.

35. Borstelmann, *1970s*, 14–15.

36. Dougherty, "Japan 2000," 4.

37. Benedict, *Chrysanthemum and the Sword*. Benedict's book remains in print, with the most recent edition appearing in 2006, and is an important text not only in U.S.-Japanese studies but also in anthropology in general, despite its obvious flaws. For a thoughtful analysis of *The Chrysanthemum and the Sword*, see Yoshihara, *Embracing the East*, especially chapter 7.

38. Yoshihara, *Embracing the East*, 178.

39. Dougherty, "Japan 2000," 5, 17, 21–22.

40. Holstein, *Japanese Power Game*, 3.

41. Christopher, *Japanese Mind*, 21.

42. Benedict, *Chrysanthemum and the Sword*, 1.

43. Dale, *Myth of Japanese Uniqueness*; Miyoshi and Harootunian, *Japan in the World*, 3.

44. Kazufumi and Befu, "Japanese Cultural Identity"; Sugimoto, "Making Sense of *Nihonjinron*." See also Befu, *Hegemony of Heterogeneity*; and Burgess, "'Illusion' of Homogeneous Japan and National Character."

45. Kyonosuke Ibe, "It Took the Japanese to Build Japan," *BW*, 6 October 1980, 17.

46. Readers report, "Wake Up, America," *BW*, 16 December 1982, 8.

47. Dougherty, "Japan 2000," 25; Fallows, *More Like Us*, 7, 2.

48. Dougherty, "Japan 2000," 10–18.

49. Ibid., 32.

50. Rosecrance, *Rise of the Trading State*.

51. Ibid., ix.

52. Ibid., xi.

53. Kennedy, *Rise and Fall of the Great Powers*; the 225,000 figure comes from Patterson, *Restless Giant*, 202.

54. See Kennedy, *Rise and Fall of the Great Powers*, chapter 8.

55. Nye, *Bound to Lead*, ix.

56. Ibid., 188, 182.

57. Ibid., 194–95.

58. Nye, "Coping with Japan," 100.

59. Nye, *Bound to Lead*, 195.

60. Lance Morrow, "Japan: All the Hazards and Threats Of," *Time*, 1 August 1983.

61. Gibson, *Neuromancer*, 203.

62. LaFeber, *Michael Jordan and the New Global Capitalism*, 156–57.

63. See Breen, *Marketplace of Revolution*.

64. Frederick Ungeheuer, "Mr. Ambition's Biggest Bid," *Time*, 23 July 1990.

65. Larry Armstrong, "Sony's Challenge," *BW*, 1 June 1987, 64.

66. Morita, *Made in Japan*, 67.

67. Ibid., 70.

68. "Sony History."

69. "Booming toward Elections," *Time*, 6 November 1964; "The New Invasion of Greater East Asia," ibid., 2 March 1970; Cathy Booth, "Cuba: Dancing the Socialist Line," ibid., 12 August 1991.

70. Morita, *Made in Japan*, 92; Jill Smolowe, "The Challenges of Success," *Time*, 13 April 1987.

71. McKinsey and Company, *Japan Business*; Ohmae, *Beyond National Borders*, ix.

72. Ohmae has published many books in English and many more in Japanese. His most recent U.S. publisher, Wharton School Publishing, erroneously states that Ohmae coined the word "globalization" in his 1990 book, *The Borderless World*. The word itself had been around for decades before 1990. Even in the sense that Ohmae uses the word, Theodore Levitt preceded him in print in 1983.

73. For example, see Kenichi Ohmae, "Global Village No Place for Japanophobia," *Wall Street Journal*, 29 November 1989.

74. Ohmae, *Beyond National Borders*, 83; Walter S. Mossberg, "New 'One-Worlders' Are Conservatives," *Wall Street Journal*, 3 April 1989.

75. Friedman, *World Is Flat*.

76. Ohmae, "Becoming a Triad Power," 2–3.

77. Ohmae, *Beyond National Borders*, 24, 100.

78. Ibid., 1.

79. Ohmae published several articles in the journal in 1988 and 1989. These articles became the basis for his 1990 book, *The Borderless World*.

80. Levitt, "Globalization of Markets"; see also Levitt, *Marketing Imagination*. For another *Harvard Business Review* article on globalization, which also argues that American companies need to learn from their Japanese counterparts, see Webber, "Globalization and Its Discontents."

81. Levitt, "Globalization of Markets," 94, 92.

82. Dower, *Japan in War and Peace*, 262.

83. Ibid., 284.

84. Reich, *Next American Frontier*, 231.

85. Reich, *Work of Nations*, 7–8.

86. Ibid., 114.

87. Robert B. Reich, "Is Japan Out to Get Us?," *NYT*, 2 February 1992.

88. Kuisel, *Seducing the French*.

CHAPTER 2

1. Karl Taro Greenfeld, "Return of the Yellow Peril," *Nation*, 11 May 1992, 636.

2. S. Johnson, *Japanese through American Eyes*, 111; Clavell quoted in Arthur Unger, "How Japanese Can a Westerner Feel?," *CSM*, 15 September 1980.

3. For theoretical and historical perspectives on the question of modernity, see the AHR Roundtable, "Historians and the Question of 'Modernity.'"

4. Philip Shabecoff, "Hirohito Arrives for Tour in U.S.," *NYT*, 1 October 1975; Philip Shabecoff, "Hirohito Extols Japanese-U.S. Ties," ibid., 3 October 1975; Lucinda Franks, "Hirohito Samples American Ways," ibid., 6 October 1975.

5. Reischauer, *Emperor of Japan*.

6. See Gluck, "Idea of Showa," 15–16; Reischauer, *Emperor of Japan*.

7. T. R. Reid, "The Emperor Who Bowed to Change," *WP*, 11 June 1994; Ken McLaughlin, "Chinese-Americans to Protest Japanese Emperor's U.S. Trip," *San Jose Mercury News*, 10 June 1994; Merrill Goozner, "The Words Not Spoken," *Atlanta Journal and Constitution*, 10 June 1994; Michael Dorgan and Michael Zielenziger, "S.F. Fanfare, Protest Greet Royal Couple," *San Jose Mercury News*, 23 June 1994.

8. Barthes, *Empire of Signs*; Jameson, *Postmodernism*.

9. "NBC, with 'Shogun,' Gets Its Best Ratings," *NYT*, 24 September 1980.

10. "'Shogun' Ratings Second Only to 'Roots' Premiere," ibid., 18 September 1980; "The Making of *Shōgun*," *Shōgun*, DVD; "Samurai Night Fever," *Newsweek*, 29 September 1981.

11. See, for example, Reischauer, *Japan* and *Japanese*.

12. S. Johnson, *Japanese through American Eyes*, v.

13. Cynthia Gorney, "Orient Expressed: The Words of Novelist James Clavell," *WP*, 2 February 1979; Edwin McDowell, "Behind the Best Sellers: James Clavell," *NYT*, 17 May 1981.

14. Smith, "James Clavell and the Legend of the British Samurai," 6.

15. Clavell loosely modeled his characters and narrative after historical events. John Blackthorne was based on the real-life William Adams, an Englishman who became the first European inducted into the samurai class. He was granted that privilege by the real-world equivalent of Lord Toranaga, Ieyasu Tokugawa, founding shogun of the Tokugawa dynasty.

16. Clavell, *Shōgun*, 65.

17. Ibid., 134.

18. For example, see his diatribe in ibid., 351.

19. Ibid., 589.

20. Ibid., 350.

21. Said, *Orientalism*. A number of scholars have pointed out that Japan's experience complicates Said's framework. For example, Napier, *From Impressionism to Anime*, 6.

22. Clavell, *Shōgun*, 292–93.

23. Ibid., 305.

24. Harry F. Waters, "Samurai and Shoguns at NBC," *Newsweek*, 8 September 1980, 86.

25. "The Making of *Shōgun*," *Shōgun*, DVD.

26. Ibid.

27. John J. O'Connor, "'Shogun': Englishman's Adventures in Japan," *NYT*, 15 September 1980.

28. Ibid.; see also Waters, "Samurai and Shoguns at NBC"; Neil A. Martin, "NBC's $12-Million Gamble on Shogun," *NYT*, 14 September 1980; Tom Shales, "Shogun: The Bravado and Blunders of NBC's 12-Hour Samurai Saga," *WP*, 14 September 1980; and Arthur Unger, "'Shogun'—An Oriental 'Gone with the Wind'?," *CSM*, 11 September 1980.

29. Randy Shipp, "'Shogun' Extravaganza Gives NBC Rave Ratings," *CSM*, 18 September 1980.

30. "The Making of *Shōgun*," *Shōgun*, DVD.

31. S. Johnson, "Review: Images of Japan," 448.

32. "The Making of *Shōgun*," *Shōgun*, DVD.

33. O'Connor, "'Shogun': Englishman's Adventures in Japan."

34. Unger, "'Shogun'—An Oriental 'Gone with the Wind'?"

35. There are interviews with several of the people responsible for production in "The Making of Shogun," *Shōgun*, DVD. Also see Martin, "NBC's $12-Million Gamble on Shogun."

36. Martin, "NBC's $12-Million Gamble on Shogun."

37. Hearst, "Review of *Learning from Shōgun*."

38. H. Smith, "Reading James Clavell's 'Shogun,'" 39–41.

39. H. Smith, *Learning from Shōgun*.

40. See Shibusawa, *America's Geisha Ally*. A fascinating study of Hollywood's role in the reconstruction of postwar Japan is Kitamura, *Screening Enlightenment*.

41. Halberstam, *Reckoning*, 272. Emphasis in original.

42. *Yakuza*, DVD. Quotes in the next paragraph are also from this DVD.

43. *Bad News Bears Go to Japan*, DVD. This line of dialogue was censored in the film. Quotes in the next two paragraphs are also from this DVD.

44. *Gung Ho*, DVD. Hunt's quote in the next paragraph is also from this DVD.

45. Vincent Canby, "The Screen: 'Gung Ho,' Directed by Ron Howard," *NYT*, 14 March 1986.

46. Rita Kempley, "'Gung Ho': Auto Manifesto," *WP*, 14 March 1986.

47. "Black Rain: The Script, the Cast," *Black Rain*, DVD.

48. Vincent Canby, "Review/Film: Police Chase a Gangster in a Bright, Menacing Japan," *NYT*, 22 September 1989.

49. Jay Carr, "'Black Rain' Is Just an Exchange of Clichés," *Boston Globe*, 22 September 1989.

50. Russell Stamets, "'Rain' Is a Puddle of Damp Ideas," *St. Petersburg Times*, 22 September 1989.

51. *Black Rain*, DVD. Joyce's quote in the next paragraph is also from this DVD.

52. For example, see Rohmer, *Insidious Dr. Fu-Manchu*.

53. Cussler, *Dragon*, 219, 151.

54. M. R. Montgomery, "Gunning for the Japanese," *Boston Globe*, 17 February 1992.

55. Crichton, *Rising Sun*, 14.

56. Vincent Canby, "A Tale of Zen and Xenophobia in Los Angeles," *NYT*, 30 July 1993.

57. Crichton, *Rising Sun*, 59, 103, 218, 275.

58. Jorge Ribeiro, "'Rising Sun' Doesn't Rise above Bashing," *Nikkei Weekly*, 21 March 1992.

59. Crichton, *Rising Sun*, 245.

60. Ibid., 370–71.

61. Fallows, *More Like Us*, 2.

62. Crichton, *Rising Sun*, 397.

63. *Rising Sun*, DVD.

64. Crichton, *Rising Sun*, 70.

65. Jay Carr, "'Rising Sun': A Smart, Sexy, Subtle Thriller," *Boston Globe*, 30 July 1993.

66. Steve Persall, "Saving Face," *St. Petersburg Times*, 1 August 1993.

67. Montgomery, "Gunning for the Japanese"; R. Nathan, "Is Japan Really Out to Get Us?"

68. Kunio Francis Tanabe, "Crime and Bashing: Michael Crichton's Degrading Digressions," *WP*, 3 February 1992.

69. Montgomery, "Gunning for the Japanese."

70. These discussions come from Usenet newsgroup postings from the early 1990s. The Usenet e-mail distribution system was one of the earliest open communication forums on the Internet. A full Usenet archive is available at https://groups.google.com.

71. Peter Wu, "The Rising Sun by Michael Crichton," soc.culture.asian.american, 30 December 1992.

72. FJM, "Rising Sun (the book)," sci.econ, 10 December 1992.

73. Henry Robertson, "Michael Crichton," soc.culture.japan, 4 March 1993.

74. Danielle T. Wei, "The [*sic*] Rising Sun by Michael Crichton," soc.culture.asian.american, 31 December 1992.

75. Rikiya Asano, "Fuck Michael Crichton," soc.culture.asian.american, 16 July 1993.

76. Golden, *Memoirs of a Geisha*.

77. *Memoirs of a Geisha*, DVD.

78. David Gritten, "Memoirs of a Very Controversial Geisha," *Telegraph* (UK), 2 December 2005; "China Bans Memoirs of a Geisha," *Guardian* (UK), 1 February 2006; Roger Ebert, "Memoirs of a Geisha," *Chicago Sun-Times*, 15 December 2005.

79. *Last Samurai*, DVD.

80. *Lost in Translation*, DVD.

CHAPTER 3

1. Tony Kornheiser, "A Week of 'Shogun': A Retrospective from the Scene of the Occident," *WP*, 20 September 1980. On Iacocca at Ford and Chrysler, see Halberstam, *Reckoning*; and Brinkley, *Wheels for the World*.

2. Robert Hanley, "Last Ford Leaves Mahwah Plant," *NYT*, 21 June 1980.

3. Photograph with caption, "Proclaim Honda's Presence Here," *MJT*, 6 July 1983; John Holusha, "Honda Plant Brings Touch of Japan to Ohio," *NYT*, 26 April 1983; Horovitz, "Honda Not So Simple Anymore"; "Union County Population Shows over 20 Percent Increase from 1970," *MJT*, 20 February 1981.

4. Edward Cohen, "Despite a Recovery, High Jobless Rate Is Expected during the Next Two Years," *NYT*, 2 January 1983.

5. "Majority from Ford's Mahwah Plant Still Jobless," *NYT*, 25 April 1982.

6. Tim Kiska, "'Vincent Provoked the Fight,' Friend Says at Chin Trial," *DFP*, 15 June 1984; Yip, "Remembering Vincent Chin"; "Killers Stalked Vincent Chin."

7. Rauch, "Drive Shaft."

8. Halberstam, *Reckoning*, 47.

9. Francis X. Clines and Warren Weaver, "Briefing: Startling Comment," *NYT*, 16 March 1982.

10. Quoted in ibid.

11. Relevant works on "transplants" other than Honda, all written from a business perspective, include Wickens, *Road to Nissan*; Fucini and Fucini, *Working for the Japanese*; Perrucci, *Japanese Auto Transplants in the Heartland*; and Karan, *Japan in the Bluegrass*.

12. For a thoughtful discussion of the origins of Japanese business expansion in the United States, particularly in the U.S. South, see Guthrie-Shimizu, "From Southeast Asia to the American Southeast." Guthrie-Shimizu notes that Japanese companies include southern Ohio in their definition of the U.S. South.

13. John Holusha, "Japanese Faulted over Black Hiring," *NYT*, 27 November 1988, claimed that 19.3 percent of Nissan's hiring radius was black, while just 14 percent of the workforce was. Again, as with Honda in Marysville, Nissan likely defined its radius to not include most of Nashville, which had a significant black population like Columbus.

14. See John Holusha, "In Tennessee, the U.S. and Japan Mesh," *NYT*, 16 June 1983; Halberstam, *Reckoning*, 634–35; "A New Land of the Rising Sun," *U.S. News and World Report*, 9 May 1988; William J. Hampton, "Mazda's Bold Embrace of the United Auto Workers," *BW*, 17 December 1984, 40; and Maralyn Edid, "Why Mazda Is Settling in the Heart of Union Territory," *BW*, 9 September 1985, 94.

15. James R. Healey, "30 Years Ago, Honda Gambled on a U.S. Factory," *USA Today*, 3 April 2012.

16. Ingrassia and White, *Comeback*, 13, 325, 461.

17. "Honda to Build Near Marysville," *MJT*, 11 October 1977.

18. Ernie Bumgarner to Tom Nuckles, 10 October 1986, folder Honda, 1982–1988, and "Points of Agreement Between Honda Motor Company, Ltd., and the State of Ohio," August 1977, folder Union County Commissioners, 1978–1988, both in County Commissioners Records, Union County Records Center and Archives, Marysville, Ohio.

19. Quoted in Ingrassia, *Crash Course*, 63, 68–69.

20. The classic work on this subject from the period is Bluestone and Harrison, *Deindustrialization of America*; see also Cowie and Heathcott, *Beyond the Ruins*.

21. "Ohio Labor Force Estimates, by County, November 1979," *MJT*, 21 December 1979.

22. "Annual Averages for 1982," ibid., 7 March 1983; "Ohio Labor Force Estimates by County, November 1982," ibid., 28 December 1982.

23. "County Jobless Rate Lowest in State," ibid., 5 June 1986; "Personal Property Taxes Paid by Honda in 1987," folder Honda, 1982–1988, County Commissioners Records, Union County Records Center and Archives, Marysville, Ohio.

24. Scott Pendleton, "Honda Leads the 'Transplants,'" *CSM*, 30 January 1990; Zachary Schiller, "The Backlash Isn't Just against Japan," *BW*, 10 February 1992, 30; Doron P. Levin, "Auto Slump Hits Honda and Production Is Cut," *NYT*, 30 January 1991; Doron P. Levin, "Honda to Reduce Output at Auto Plants in Ohio," *NYT*, 28 July 1992.

25. "Detroit Hopes the Worst Is Over," *BW*, 21 July 1980, 62.

26. "Honda Building Overseas to Meet Demand Diplomatically," *BW*, 28 January 1980, 112; "Honda May Begin Car Production Early," *MJT*, 6 July 1981.

27. Honda press release, 18 April 1980, Standing File, Marysville Public Library, Ohio.

28. "Honda to Proceed with Auto Plant," *MJT*, 11 January 1980.

29. The 1956 "Honda Company Principle" greets visitors to the Honda Heritage Center on the grounds at Honda in Marysville.

30. Marvel and Shkurti, *Economic Impact of Development*, 18.

31. Fleeter, *Honda in Ohio*, 3.

32. "Honda Turns Key on Assembly Line," *MJT*, 10 September 1979.

33. *Nikkan Shimbun*, special supplement to *MJT*, 17 April 1980.

34. Pictures of all of the "Original 64" associates who opened the MMP are reproduced in HAM's official history; see Hensley, *Building on Dreams*, 76–79.

35. "Slumping Economy Is Top Ohio Story in 1980," *MJT*, 31 December 1980; "Honda Expansion Top Story," ibid., 2 January 1981.

36. "Nestle Plant Closing Sept. 1," ibid., 15 January 1982; "Rockwell Plant Closing Likely after UAW Rejects Contract," ibid., 27 April 1982; "Scotts Announces Cutbacks," ibid., 8 June 1983.

37. "Ohio Labor Force Estimates, by County, January 1982," ibid., 1 March 1982.

38. Pat Parish, "Nestle Employees Voice Reactions to Recent Plant Closing Decision," ibid., 19 January 1982.

39. "Thousands Hope Honda Will Cure Area Unemployment Picture," ibid., 30 August 1982; editorial, "Positive Approach Needed in 1983," ibid., 31 December 1982.

40. Ibid.; reports from the first day of production include "First Auto Rolls off Assembly Line," ibid., 1 November 1982; Warren Brown, "First U.S.-Built Honda Rolls off Line," *WP*, 2 November 1982; "Honda's First U.S.-Built Car Rolls Out," *NYT*, 2 November 1982.

41. Holusha, "Honda Plant Brings Touch of Japan to Ohio"; Kenneth B. Noble, "Auto Union Battles Uphill in Japanese Plant in Ohio," *NYT*, 10 December 1985.

42. Noble, "Auto Union Battles."

43. Kenneth B. Noble, "Union Organizers' Task Is Uphill at Nissan Plant," *NYT*, 3 April 1988.

44. "Honda Assumes Position of No. 4 U.S. Carmaker," *MJT*, 4 March 1985.

45. Editorial, "Honda and Marysville Working Well Together," ibid., 8 March 1985.

46. Clara Miller, "Newspaper Interviews Show Many Area Residents View Honda as a Positive Development Here," ibid., 18 November 1982.

47. Holusha, "Honda Plant Brings Touch of Japan to Ohio"; Peter Behr, "Honda Is Rolling Success off Its Ohio Assembly Line," *WP*, 3 May 1987, quoted in "Honda Assumes Position of No. 4 U.S. Carmaker."

48. Ito, "Organizational Adaptation of Japanese Companies," 116–17; Gelsanliter, *Jump Start*, 28.

49. U.S. Bureau of the Census, *1987 Census of Agriculture*, 97; Gelsanliter, *Jump Start*, 24–25; Cole and Deskins, "Racial Factors in Site Location," 17.

50. "Honda Assumes Position of No. 4 U.S. Carmaker"; Holusha, "Japanese Faulted over Black Hiring"; Louise Kertesz, "Japanese Rapped on Black Jobs," *Automotive News*, 29 August 1988, 1.

51. "Honda to Pay $6 Million in Rights Settlement," *NYT*, 24 March 1988; Matt DeLorenzo, "Honda to Pay $6 Million in Bias Probe," *Automotive News*, 28 March 1988, 50.

52. See James B. Treece, "What the Japanese Must Learn about Racial Tolerance," *BW*, 5 September 1988, 41.

53. Cole and Deskins, "Racial Factors in Site Location," 20.

54. Advertisement, "The Honda Team," *MJT*, 26 October 1982.

55. Ito, "Organizational Adaptation of Japanese Companies," 107.

56. "Honda Begins Exercise Practice," *MJT*, 14 October 1982; Hensley, *Building on Dreams*, 18.

57. James Risen, "Stretching It at Honda Assembly Line—Aerobics Get Mixed U.S. Reviews," *DFP*, 11 November 1982.

58. Noble, "Auto Union Battles."

59. Ito, "Organizational Adaptation of Japanese Companies," 149–50.

60. Ibid., 120, 145, 147, 151, 167.

61. Ibid., 126.

62. Ibid., 121–22.

63. Honda brochure, 1982, folder Logan County—Industry—Honda, Standing File, L4, Logan County District Library, Bellefontaine, Ohio.

64. Ito, "Organizational Adaptation of Japanese Companies," 128, 134.

65. Clara B. Miller, "Local Honda Employees Visit Plants in Japan," *MJT*, 1 August 1979; Pat Parish, "Production Slated to Begin in November at Local Honda Manufacturing Plant," ibid., 27 September 1982; Ito, "Organizational Adaptation of Japanese Companies," 100; Rich Harris, "Honda Careful to East Community Fears," *Bellefontaine (Ohio) Examiner*, 6 September 1990.

66. Quoted in Hensley, *Building on Dreams*, 18.

67. Behr, "Honda Is Rolling Success off Its Ohio Assembly Line."

68. "Honda Officers Host State, Local Officials; Confirm Construction of Auto Assembly Plant," *MJT*, 18 April 1980; "Quality of American Worker Is Best Says Honda President," ibid., 21 April 1980.

69. Scott Underwood, "Traditional Japanese Items Exhibited in Marysville Art League's Show," ibid., 21 May 1981.

70. Pat Parish, "Area Seeing Benefit of Honda Foundation," ibid., 29 November 1982; Susie Taylor, "Visit to Japan Helps Edgewood Teacher Understand Culture, Education Structure," *Union County Advertiser*, 9 January 1984; Dan Saddler, "Local Educator Learns from Trip to Japan," *MJT*, 14 December 1984.

71. There were approximately 180 Japanese Honda employees working in Marysville as of the opening of the MAP; it is likely, therefore, that Honda brought around 500 Japanese to the area by November 1982, and as the plant expanded the number of Japanese managers grew as well. See James Risen, "Honda's U.S. Debut Brings No Miracles," *DFP*, 7 November 1982.

72. Quoted in C. Miller, "Newspaper Interviews."

73. Lana Wetterman, "Japanese Families Adjusting to American Ways of Living," *MJT*, 12 October 1981.

74. Mark Hamilton, "Honda Expansion Good News for Logan," *Bellefontaine (Ohio) Examiner*, 28 February 1988; "International Friendship Center, Honda Aid Each Other," in "Honda: 25 Years of Manufacturing Leadership in America," special insert to *MJT*, September 2004.

75. Philip, "Chrysanthemum and the Buckeye," 24.

76. On Japanese executives' long hours, see Ito, "Organizational Adaptation of Japanese Companies," 123.

77. Philip, "Chrysanthemum and the Buckeye," 24–25.

78. S. Taylor, "Visit to Japan Helps Edgewood Teacher"; Saddler, "Local Educator Learns from Trip to Japan"; "English Problems Concern Board," *Columbus Dispatch*, 23 October 1985.

79. Philip, "Chrysanthemum and the Buckeye," 25–26; see also Koizumi, Farkas, and Koizumi, "Stress and Coping of Japanese Children in American Society."

80. "Ohio Considering School for Japanese Children," *MJT*, 29 July 1986.

81. S. Taylor, "Visit to Japan Helps Edgewood Teacher."

82. See the Columbus Japanese Language School's website, http://web.archive.org/web/20090805093949/http://www.columbushoshuko.com/english.htm.

83. Terry Oblander, "Honda, UAW Collide Head-On Thursday," *Akron Beacon Journal*, 15 December 1985, quoted in Douglas R. Sease, "Honda's U.S. Plant Brings Trouble, Not Prosperity, to Small Ohio Town," *Wall Street Journal*, 5 October 1982.

84. "Honda and Japanese Gain Acceptance in Central Ohio," *MJT*, 5 September 1990.

85. "Marysville High on Honda Experience," *Sidney (Ohio) Daily News*, 24 March 1984.

86. Beth Grace, "Honda Brings Economic Boom to Area," *Bellefontaine (Ohio) Examiner*, 13 June 1988.

87. "Honda and Japanese Gain Acceptance."

88. Ibid.

89. Robert W. Reiss, "Honda Has Won Over Most Critics in Marysville," *Columbus Dispatch*, 20 September 1987.

90. Holly Zachariah, "Marysville Seeks to Deepen Links to Japan," ibid., 9 December 2013.

91. Quoted in Ito, "Organizational Adaptation of Japanese Companies," 120.

92. Harris, "Honda Careful to East Community Fears."

93. Sease, "Honda's U.S. Plant Brings Trouble, Not Prosperity."

94. Aschoff, "Imported from Detroit"; Linkins, "Mitt Romney." The American Automobile Labeling Act (1994) charges the National Highway Transportation Safety Administration with maintaining data on the percentage of domestic content in each vehicle model sold in the United States.

CHAPTER 4

1. I pieced together the Richards story from the following press reports: "Lottery Prize No Accord," *Dayton Daily News*, 9 August 1990; "Lottery Winner Turns Down Non-union Car," *Cincinnati Post*, 9 August 1990; "Player Who Refused Non-union Car Has Lots of Support," *Dayton Daily News*, 12 August 1990; "Union Loyalty Puts Woman in the Driver's Seat," *Cincinnati Post*, 15 August 1990; "Refusal of $17,000 Car Is Winning Move," *NYT*, 16 August 1990; "Autoworker Heroine Leads Labor Parade," *Cincinnati Post*, 4 September 1990; "Turning Down Honda Turned Up Roses for Ohio's 'Mrs. UAW,'" *Dayton Daily News*, 12 July 1991; David Jacobs, "Woman Who Rejected Honda Irked by Japanese Remarks," *Columbus Dispatch*, 16 February 1992.

2. Jacobs, "Woman Who Rejected Honda."

3. Leonard Page to Joe Tomasi and Dick Martin, 13 April 1982, part 2, box 3, folder 26—Honda: Correspondence, 1982, DAFR.

4. "Proceedings of Regular Session of International Executive Board, UAW" (hereafter IEB Minutes), 7–9 June 1982, 180, box 26, IEBM.

5. Ibid., 178.

6. "Memorandum of Agreement between UAW and Honda," April 1982, part 2, box 3, folder 26—Honda: Correspondence, 1982, DAFR.

7. Leonard Page to Owen Bieber, 15 April 1986, box 140, folder 25—Honda: Correspondence, 1986–1989, OBC.

8. "A Multinational Squeeze-Play," *UAWS*, 1 May 1980, 6–7.

9. Joseph Tomasi to John Glenn, 17 February 1981, part 2, box 1, folder 11—Correspondence: Joe Tomasi, 1981–1983, DAFR.

10. IEB Minutes, 12–14 November 1979, 45–46, box 23, IEBM.

11. Ibid., 26–28 February 1980, 43, box 24.

12. Undated pamphlet sketches, part 2, box 3, folder 24—Honda Coordinator Kit, 1982, DAFR.

13. "Instructions for Honda Handbillers," undated photocopy, box 3, folder 24, Honda Coordinator Kit 1982, DAFR; Lee Price, "Statements about Japanese," 18 March 1982, box 58, folder 10—Foreign—Japan 1982–83, DAFR.

14. Price, "Statements about Japanese."

15. For instance, see Frank, *Buy American*, especially chapter 7; and also Caulfield, *NAFTA and Labor in North America*, 164.

16. Tommy Blackman to F. James McDonald, 8 June 1981, box 58, folder 23—Japan, Dick Martin Files, 1981–82, DAFR.

17. Undated (1981), F. James McDonald, *A Battle for Survival: Excerpts from a Film for GM Employees on the Japanese Competition*, ibid.

18. Al Davidoff, "It's Not the Japanese," *UAWS*, May 1982, 20.

19. Frank, *Buy American*, 161.

20. IEB Minutes, 29 November–2 December 1977, 72, box 22, IEBM.

21. "Remarks by Pat Greathouse to North American–Japan IMF Conference, Tokyo," 11 July 1977, part 1, box 58, folder 20—Foreign: Japan, DAFR.

22. Report, "Visit of the UAW Delegation to Japan, March 11–24, 1978," part 1, box 58, folder 19—Japan 1977–1979, DAFR.

23. "Send Us Factories Instead of Cars," *UAWS*, April 1982, 12; "Why Not a Datsun Made in Detroit?," *UAWS*, June 1982, back cover.

24. Ibid., 37; IEB Minutes, 12–14 November 1979, 43, box 23, and 14–16 September 1981, 132, box 25, IEBM.

25. IEB Minutes, 22–23 March 1982, 151, box 26, IEBM.

26. Ibid., 7–9 June 1982, 178.

27. Ibid., 179.

28. K. Tamura, K. Noguchi, and T. Hashimoto, "Labor Issues Facing Japanese Affiliates in the United States," translated unpublished report of the Japan Institute of Labor, 1980, box 58, folder 10—Foreign—Japan 1980, DAFR.

29. IEB Minutes, 20–22 September 1982, 102, box 26, IEBM.

30. Leonard Page to Owen Bieber, 10 November 1983, box 140, folder 24—Honda Correspondence, 1984–85, OBC; IEB Minutes, 19–21 September 1983, 157, box 26, IEBM.

31. "Content Bill Moves toward Showdown in Congress," *UAWS*, August 1983, 8–9.

32. David T. Cook, "Honda and Its White-Coated 'Associates': Firm's Expanding U.S. Facility Focuses Attention on Domestic Content Issue," *CSM*, 6 July 1984.

33. "Honda Announces Intention to Use U.S. Parts, Material," *MJT*, 9 June 1982; Zachary Schiller, "The Backlash Isn't Just against Japan," *BW*, 10 February 1992, 30.

34. "Honda Announces Auto Plant Expansion," *MJT*, 10 January 1984; "Honda May Build Second Auto Plant," ibid., 2 October 1985.

35. Paul Lienert, "UAW Nears Vote at Ohio Honda Plant," *DFP*, 15 December 1985. Tomasi reported signatures from 650 of the plant's 2,800 employees in March 1986. See Steve Yokich to Owen Bieber, "Honda," 14 March 1986, box 140, folder 25—Honda: Correspondence, 1986–1989, OBC.

36. "Honda, UAW Mum on Efforts to Force Union Recognition," *MJT*, 24 October 1985; "Honda Officials Not in Receipt of Letter Requesting Recognition," ibid., 25 October 1985; "Honda Rejects UAW Recognition Request," ibid., 31 October 1985. See Shige Yoshida, "To All HAM Production and Maintenance Associates," 29 October 1985, and Shige Yoshida to All Associates, 30 October 1985, box 140, folder 24—Honda Correspondence, 1984–1985, OBC.

37. "Honda, UAW Mum"; Warren Brown, "Honda Making Inroads in the U.S. by 'Doing Everything Right,'" *WP*, 14 April 1985; "Honda Assumes Position of No. 4 U.S. Carmaker," *MJT*, 4 March 1985.

38. UAW advertisement, *MJT*, 13 November 1985.

39. UAW advertisement, "Honda Should Hire More People Now," ibid., 6 December 1985. The same advertisement also ran 10–12 December 1985.

40. "Honda Officials Not in Receipt of Letter Requesting Recognition."

41. Advertisement, "The Associates Alliance," *MJT*, 22 November 1985.

42. Ibid.; "Long Campaign for UAW Nearly Over, Vote Next Month Will Determine Fate," ibid., 22 November 1985; "The Associates Alliance—We Think for Ourselves," 2 December 1985, box 140, folder 24—Honda Correspondence, 1984–1985, OBC.

43. Leonard Page to Gerald Lackey, "Re: Honda Associates Alliance," 31 January 1986, and Leonard Page to Joe Tomasi, "Honda Associates Alliance," 25 February 1986, box 140, folder 25—Honda: Correspondence, 1986–1989, OBC.

44. Letters to the editor, "Readers Oppose Union," *MJT*, 29 November 1985.

45. Ibid.

46. Letters to the editor, "Responds to Letter," ibid., 13 December 1985.

47. Joan Christy and Susie Taylor, "Majority Opposed to UAW Takeover," ibid., 5 December 1985.

48. Susie Taylor, "UAW: Stop Unauthorized Use of Organization Logo," ibid., 11 December 1985.

49. Joan Christy, "Honda-UAW Vote Postponed," ibid., 17 December 1985.

50. Susie Taylor, "With NLRB Charges Dismissed, Honda Wants Vote Date Re-set," ibid., 3 February 1986; "Election at Honda Cancelled after UAW Withdraws Petition," ibid., 18 March 1986.

51. Jim Turner to Steve Yokich, "Honda—Marysville, Ohio," 6 March 1986, and Leonard Page to Owen Bieber et al., "Honda," 26 February 1988 and 29 February 1988, box 140, folder 25—Honda: Correspondence, 1986–1989, OBC.

52. "Rockwell Plant Closing Likely after UAW Rejects Contract," *MJT*, 27 April 1982; "Explains Rockwell Union Position," ibid., 30 April 1982.

53. Michael Cieply, "Meanwhile, Back in Marysville," *Forbes*, 12 March 1984, 127.

54. On Reagan and PATCO, see McCartin, *Collision Course*; and Richards, *Union-Free America*, 5.

55. IEB Minutes, 20–22 September 1982, 280, box 26, IEBM.

56. James Risen, "Honda's U.S. Debut Brings No Miracles," *DFP*, 7 November 1982; James Risen, "U.S.-Made Honda Rolls off Line Today," ibid., 1 November 1982.

57. Editorial, "Marysville Visited by Yellow Journalist," *MJT*, 15 February 1980; see also editorial, "Honda Has Been Gracious; Associated Press Has Not," ibid., 29 April 1983.

58. Letters to the editor, "Unhappy with Honda Article," ibid., 15 October 1982.

59. Lana Wetterman, "Mayor Critical of News Media for Distorted Honda Coverage," ibid., 5 November 1982.

60. "Honda Assumes Position of No. 4 U.S. Carmaker."

61. "The Uninformed View of Union County" (cartoon) and editorial, "Honda and Marysville Working Well Together," *MJT*, 8 March 1985.

CHAPTER 5

1. Paul Lewis, "The Latest Battle of Poitiers," *NYT*, 14 January 1983.

2. Ibid.; William Safire, "The Battle of Poitiers," ibid., 22 November 1982.

3. "An Electronics Entente against Japan," *BW*, 6 December 1982, 48; "Europe Gangs Up on Japanese Electronics," ibid., 21 March 1983, 25; E. J. Dionne, "Japan Video Accord Leaves Europeans Weary but Hopeful," *NYT*, 22 February 1983.

4. "Theodore Levitt on Global Goods," *WP*, 23 September 1984.

5. Ganley and Ganley, *Global Political Fallout*, 1.

6. Ibid., 47.

7. For an overview of scholarly works on cultural globalization, see Hopper, *Understanding Cultural Globalization*.

8. L. Cohen, *Consumer's Republic*.

9. Benjamin, "Work of Art in the Age of Mechanical Reproduction," 224.

10. Editorial, "When Japan-Bashing Goes Too Far," *NYT*, 6 July 1987.

11. P. Anderson, *Origins of Postmodernity*, 88.

12. Ibid., 89. See also Jameson, *Postmodernism*; and Harvey, *Condition of Postmodernity*.

13. For a thorough technical pre-history of the VCR, see Wasser, *Veni, Vidi, Video*.

14. Dobrow, *Social and Cultural Aspects of VCR Use*, 10.

15. Wasser, *Veni, Vidi, Video*, 70–71; Lardner, *Fast Forward*, 93.

16. Wasser, *Veni, Vidi, Video*, 59–60.

17. "Home VTRs under 15 U.S. Brandnames," *TDCE*, 27 June 1977, 8–9; "Video Cassette Recorders: Key to a New TV World," *Consumer Reports*, September 1978, 506.

18. See Wasser, *Veni, Vidi, Video*, 72–75; and Lardner, *Fast Forward*, 11–22.

19. Lardner, *Fast Forward*, 11.

20. "World VCR Capacity Near 30 Million," *TDCE*, 16 July 1984, 8.

21. Alvarado, *Video World-Wide*, 128.

22. Wasser, *Veni, Vidi, Video*, 50.

23. Morita, *Made in Japan*, 231–32.

24. Sony of America, "Sony Newspaper Ad Program," retailer informational binder, undated (1978?).

25. John Nathan, *Sony*, 106.

26. Dailymotion, "Sony SL-7200 Betamax Commercial #1—1977."

27. Sony of America, "Sony Product Literature," retailer informational binder, undated (1978?).

28. Sony of America, "Betamax Demonstration Center," retailer informational binder, 1980.

29. John Nathan, *Sony*, 110–11.

30. "Why Sony's Betamax Has MCA Seething," *BW*, 29 November 1976, 29; "The Home Replay Fray," *Newsweek*, 13 December 1976, 66. For a detailed history of the ensuing court battle between Sony on one side and Disney and MCA-Universal on the other, see Lardner, *Fast Forward*.

31. "Video Cassette Recorders," *Consumer Reports*, May 1982, 230.

32. *CEAR 1984*, 23.

33. "Excerpts from Court's Majority and Dissenting Opinions," *NYT*, 18 January 1984.

34. Tom Shales, "I'll Tape Tomorrow; and So Will You, Thanks to the Court," *WP*, 18 January 1984.

35. Sapolsky and Forrest, "Measuring VCR 'Ad-Voidance,'" 148.

36. Dobrow, "Away from the Mainstream?," 193.

37. Ogan, "Worldwide Cultural and Economic Impact of Video," 245.

38. Lin, "Audience Activity and VCR Use," 75. Emphasis in original.

39. De Vera and McDonnell, "Video," 1.

40. *CEAR 1980*, 13; *CEAR 1982*, 9.

41. "Video Cassette Recorders: Key to a New TV World," 505; "Video Cassette Recorders," *Consumer Reports*, July 1983, 327–35.

42. *CEAR 1977*, 14.

43. *CEAR 1978*, 1, 14, 27.

44. Data from multiple volumes of *CEAR*.

45. "Japan Sets VCR Export Record in Sept.," *TDCE*, 3 November 1980, 10; "Japan Shatters VCR Export Record," ibid., 8 August 1983, 11; "Japan Exported Million VCRs in June," ibid., 6 August 1984, 11.

46. *CEAR 1987*, 51.

47. See *CEAR 1982* and *CEAR 1989*.

48. Cohen and Cohen, "Big Eyes but Clumsy Fingers"; Dobrow, *Social and Cultural Aspects of VCR Use*, 181–93; A. Cohen, "Decision Making in VCR Rental Libraries."

49. DeLillo, *White Noise*, 9.

50. Lindstrom, "Video," 49.

51. Wasser, *Veni, Vidi, Video*, 101.

52. Dan Bowdren Associates, *Study among Videocassette Recording System Owners*, 16.

53. Wolfe, "'Me' Decade"; Lasch, *Culture of Narcissism*.

54. "World VCR Capacity Near 30 Million," *TDCE*, 16 July 1984, 8.

55. Alvarado, *Video World-Wide*, 323. Alvarado's edited collection was the published version of the UNESCO study.

56. Ibid., vii, ix, 5, 323.

57. Boyd, Straubhaar, and Lent, *Videocassette Recorders in the Third World*; and Boyd, "Home Video Diffusion and Utilization in Arabian Gulf States."

58. "Nigeria Surpasses Hollywood as World's Second Largest Film Producer," *UN News Centre*, 5 May 2009.

59. Ganley and Ganley, *Global Political Fallout*, xi. This report was produced at Harvard University's Center for Information Policy Research, an entity itself indicative of scholarly interest in the impact of new media. The institution was founded in 1973 as the Program on Information Technologies and Public Policy and today exists as the Program on Information Resources Policy.

60. Ibid., 37.

61. Boyd, Straubhaar, and Lent, *Videocassette Recorders in the Third World*, 35.

62. Robert G. Kaiser, "Is 'Veedeyo' a Blow for the Bolsheviks?" *WP*, 9 September 1984.

63. De Vera and McDonnell, "Video," 3.

64. Ilinca Calugareanu, "VHS vs. Communism," *NYT*, 17 February 2014.

65. Boyd, "Videocassette Recorder in the USSR and Soviet-Bloc Countries," 261–62; Ganley and Ganley, *Global Political Fallout*, 24–26; Iyer, *Video Night in Kathmandu*, 6; Kaiser, "Is 'Veedeyo' a Blow for the Bolsheviks?"

66. Ganley and Ganley, *Global Political Fallout*, xi, 4.

67. See Hixson, *Parting the Curtain*, 29–56. The United States Information Agency launched its satellite television service, Worldnet, in 1985. Peter W. Kaplan, "U.S. Agency Transmits TV Programs to Europe," *NYT*, 23 April 1985.

68. Boyd, Straubhaar, and Lent, *Videocassette Recorders in the Third World*, 18; Boyd, "Home Video Diffusion and Utilization in Arabian Gulf States," 549; Ganley and Ganley, *Global Political Fallout*, 46.

69. Boyd, Straubhaar, and Lent, *Videocassette Recorders in the Third World*, 36, 40.

70. Quoted in Dobrow, "Away from the Mainstream?," 200–201; Boyd, Straubhaar, and Lent, *Videocassette Recorders in the Third World*, 34; "South-East Asian Television: A Switch-Off," *Economist*, 8 October 1983, 77.

71. Vic Sussman, "Up against the Video Wall," *WPM*, 16 August 1987.

72. Ganley and Ganley, *Global Political Fallout*, 1.

73. On cultural hybridization see Hannerz, *Transnational Connections*.

74. Iyer, *Video Night in Kathmandu*, 10, 7; Iyer, *Falling Off the Map*, 113, 76.

75. Iyer, *Video Night in Kathmandu*, 135.

76. Ibid., 5–6.

77. Ibid., 259, 277.

78. Ibid., 94.

79. Iyer, *Falling Off the Map*, 13, 100; Iyer, *Video Night in Kathmandu*, 147.

80. Quoted in Ganley and Ganley, *Global Political Fallout*, 23.

81. *CEAR 1989*, 6.

82. Iwabuchi, *Recentering Globalization*, 24–28.

83. Nye, *Bound to Lead*, 188.

84. Iwabuchi, *Recentering Globalization*, 25.

CHAPTER 6

1. Jack Rosenthal, "Sushi at the Harvard Club," *NYT*, 2 November 1981.

2. Ibid.

3. Mike Royko, "Ballpark Sushi Marks the Beginning of the End," *St. Petersburg Times*, 22 March 1989.

4. Ibid.

5. Cwiertka, *Modern Japanese Cuisine*, 182.

6. Isle, "Sushi in America"; Anthony Faiola, "Putting the Bite on Pseudo Sushi and Other Insults," *WP*, 24 November 2006.

7. *Breakfast Club*, DVD.

8. *Wall Street*, DVD; *Rising Sun*, DVD; *Showdown in Little Tokyo*, DVD.

9. For example, see Issenberg, *Sushi Economy*; and Corson, *Zen of Fish*.

10. Issenberg, *Sushi Economy*, xi.

11. Bestor, *Tsukiji*; see also Bestor, "How Sushi Went Global"; and Bestor, "Supply-Side Sushi."

12. See Farrer, *Globalization of Asian Cuisines*.

13. I have adopted the term "middle grounds" from R. White, *Middle Ground*.

14. Farrer, *Globalization of Asian Cuisines*, 8.

15. Erika Kinetz, "So Pink, So New York," *NYT*, 22 September 2002; Nathan, "Short History of the Bagel"; Gabaccia, *We Are What We Eat*, 3–4.

16. Grazian, *Blue Chicago*, 9.

17. Ibid., 10–11.

18. Ibid., 11–13. See also Grazian, "Demystifying Authenticity"; and Atkins, *Blue Nippon*.

19. Heldke, *Exotic Appetites*, 24, 27. Emphasis in original.

20. Grazian, "Demystifying Authenticity," 197.

21. For example, Jean Carper, "Sushi Scare: It's Safe Once You Learn a Few Raw Facts," *WP*, 19 November 1981; Marian Burros, "Reports of Parasites Rekindle a Debate about Raw Fish," *NYT*, 14 October 1987.

22. Detrick, *Sushi*, 12.

23. Renton, "How Sushi Ate the World."

24. Tatou Takahama, "Origin of the California Sushi Roll Offers Some Food for Thought," *Daily Yomiuri*, 10 December 1997; Renton, "How Sushi Ate the World"; Issenberg, *Sushi Economy*, 90; Yang, "California Roll Creators."

25. Quoted in Issenberg, *Sushi Economy*, 89–90.

26. Takahama, "Origin of the California Sushi Roll."

27. Quoted in Gabaccia, *We Are What We Eat*, 217.

28. Matt Schudel, "Rocky Aoki: Flashy Founder of Benihana," *WP*, 12 July 2008; Cwiertka, *Modern Japanese Cuisine*, 189.

29. Issenberg, *Sushi Economy*, 94.

30. Quoted in Cwiertka, "From Ethnic to Hip," 249.

31. Penelope Lemov, "Mikado Restaurant," *WP*, 8 September 1977; Susan Crowley, "A Weekly Guide to Family Dining," ibid., 10 February 1977.

32. Phyllis C. Richman, "Dining through the Decade," *WPM*, 30 December 1979.

33. Bryan Miller, "The Care and Handling of Fish for Sushi," *NYT*, 1 February 1984; Leslie Bennetts, "Culture of Japan Blossoming in America," ibid., 7 August 1982.

34. Tanaka, *Pleasures of Japanese Cooking*, 37; Kagawa, *Japanese Cookbook*; Froud, *Cooking the Japanese Way*, 164.

35. "Ue o muite arukou," or "I shall walk looking up," is a 1963 song by Kyu Sakamoto. It was the first Japanese-language song to chart on the Billboard 100 in the United States. The likeliest explanation for the name "Sukiyaki" in the United States is that radio DJs could not pronounce the song's actual name and instead adopted a familiar Japanese word. See "Complicated History of the Song 'Sukiyaki.'"

36. *Cooking Japanese Style*, 3.

37. Ōmae and Tachibana, *Book of Sushi*; Tohyama, *Quick and Easy Sushi Cookbook*.

38. Levenstein, *Paradox of Plenty*, 217.

39. Piesman and Hartley, *Yuppie Handbook*, 53.

40. Heldke, *Exotic Appetites*, 16.

41. Trillin, *Feeding a Yen*, 71.

42. Levenstein, *Paradox of Plenty*, 216.

43. Gerald Etter, "A Healthful Diet the Japanese Way," *PI*, 6 June 1984.

44. Heldke, *Exotic Appetites*, 39.

45. Daniel Young, "East Meets West in 'Nam Sandwich," *New York Daily News*, 25 September 1996.

46. Phyllis C. Richman, "Samurai Sushiko," *WP*, 30 April 1978; Phyllis C. Richman, "Dining Guide," *WPM*, 14 October 1979; Phyllis C. Richman, "Dining 1980," *WP*, 21 September 1980.

47. Phyllis C. Richman, "Fuji," *WP*, 26 October 1980.

48. Anne Crutcher, "The Books of Sushi," *WP*, 19 November 1981.

49. Karen Kenyon, "The Samurai," *San Diego Union*, 29 November 1984.

50. Elaine Tait, "Spirit of the East Prevails," *PI*, 29 November 1981.

51. Bates, "Specialités de la Maison."

52. Joanne Kates, "Plain and Frugal, but Very Good," *Globe and Mail* (Canada), 22 December 1979.

53. Joanne Kates, "Sensual Sushi Whips Raw Passion," ibid., 6 December 1980.

54. Marian Burros, "To Sushi or Not to Sushi," *WP*, 27 March 1983.

55. Kates, "Plain and Frugal"; Joanne Kates, "A Gourmet's Garden of Sushi," *Globe and Mail* (Canada), 25 October 1978.

56. Phyllis C. Richman, "Genji," *WPM*, 18 November 1979.

57. Merrill Shindler, "Affordable Feasts," *Los Angeles Daily News*, 19 July 1990.

58. Moira Hodgson, "Sushi and More and New Italian," *NYT*, 10 October 1980.

59. Maria Gallagher, "Hikaru," *Philadelphia Daily News*, 30 September 1983.

60. Rita Kempley, "'Yosaku' Slices the Sushi While You Play the Piano," *WP*, 2 February 1983.

61. Jeffrey J. Carmel, "Sushi: Raw Fish Is Making Waves across U.S.," *CSM*, 16 February 1983.

62. Melissa Davis, "Doing Sushi," *WP*, 27 March 1980.

63. Richman, "Samurai Sushiko."

64. Lemov, "Mikado Restaurant."

65. Patricia Brooks, "Japanese Ambience in Fairfield," *NYT*, 5 February 1984.

66. "Sakura," *WPM*, 15 May 1977.

67. Elizabeth Hartigan, "Experiencing the Japanese," *Los Angeles Daily News*, 20 June 1986.

68. Marie Combs, "Japanese Food, Culture Link," *San Diego Evening Tribune*, 19 March 1986.

69. Mike Dunne, "Japanese Delicacies Enhanced by Warm, Intimate Atmosphere," *Sacramento Bee*, 22 November 1987.

70. Elaine Tait, "Japanese Flavor for South Street," *PI*, 13 May 1984.

71. Elaine Tait, "Hikaru, a Japanese Newcomer," ibid., 16 October 1983.

72. Kempley, "'Yosaku' Slices the Sushi."

73. Joyce, "Japan Starts World Campaign"; Hideko Takayama, "Bringing Sushi to Japan," *Newsweek*, 21 January 2002; Nghiem, "Brazilian Sushi."

74. Faiola, "Putting the Bite on Pseudo Sushi."

75. Joyce, "Japan Starts World Campaign"; Farrer, "Traveling Cuisines In and Out of Asia," 11; Clare Leschin-Hoar, "Sorry, Sushi Burrito: Japanese Program Certifies Authentic Cuisine," *NPR News*, 11 February 2016.

76. Leo Lewis, "Japanese Restaurants Invited to Win Approval of the Sushi Squad," *Sunday Times* (London), 1 January 2008.

77. Imai, "Nobu and After."

CHAPTER 7

1. I have used literal translations of these titles because in 1983 no official English-language adaptations yet existed. These would both see U.S. releases in the 1990s as *Final Yamato* and *Farewell to Space Battleship Yamato: In the Name of Love.*

2. This story is recounted in R. F.'s response (15 November 2005) to a questionnaire I distributed to anime fans of the 1977–89 period. Hereafter these responses are cited in this style: R. F. response, 15 November 2005. For respondents who are not published authors, I have chosen to use initials for anonymity and have created pseudonyms for names in the text. Complaint quoted in Brian Cirulnick, "A Quick History," *Star Blazers Fandom Report*, April 1993.

3. R. F. response, 15 November 2005.

4. Recent works on other aspects of the globalizing of Japanese popular culture include Tsutsui and Ito, *In Godzilla's Footsteps*; and Yano, *Pink Globalization*.

5. In Japan, animation of any national origin, including the United States, is anime. In the United States, however, fans have worked hard to ensure that the word "anime" refers only to animation produced in Japan. Well into the 1990s Americans used the words "anime" and "Japanimation" interchangeably, but the latter died off because of the authenticity of "anime" and the potential of offensively mispronouncing "Japanimation."

6. The classic English-language work on manga culture is Schodt, *Manga! Manga!*.

7. Clements and McCarthy, *Anime Encyclopedia*, 373–74.

8. Kelts, *Japanamerica*, 44–46.

9. Fred Ladd, "Commentary," *Gigantor*, DVD.

10. Patten, *Watching Anime*, 28.

11. Tobin, *Pikachu's Global Adventure*, 3; Lien, "How Successful Is Pokémon?"

12. Napier, "World of Anime Fandom in America," 53; Allison, "Japan Fad in Global Youth Culture," 13; and McGray, "Japan's Gross National Cool."

13. See Lent, *Animation in Asia and the Pacific*; Berndt and Richter, *Reading Manga*; Jüngst, "Japanese Comics in Germany"; Pelliteri, "Manga in Italy"; and Luyten, *Cultura pop japonesa*.

14. "Doraemon Sworn In as Anime Ambassador," *Daily Yomiuri*, 21 March 2008.

15. Iwabuchi, *Recentering Globalization*, 28; Allison, *Millennial Monsters*, 20.

16. Ethan Sacks, "Hayao Miyazaki, the 'Walt Disney of Japan,' Still Does Animation the Old Fashioned Way in 'Ponyo,'" *New York Daily News*, 8 August 2009, quoted in Napier, *Anime from "Akira" to "Howl's Moving Castle,"* 25.

17. Patricia Malone, "But They Don't Look Japanese," *Anime-Zine* 3 (1988): 6.

18. Napier, *Anime from "Akira" to "Howl's Moving Castle,"* 24.

19. Condry, "Anime Creativity," 141, 160; see also Condry, *Soul of Anime*; and Allison, *Millennial Monsters*, 234.

20. *Star Blazers: The Quest for Iscandar*, DVD.

21. Dower, *War without Mercy*, 262–90.

22. Amos, "Star Blazers You Didn't See."

23. *Star Blazers: The Quest for Iscandar*, DVD.

24. A. C. response, 16 November 2005.

25. *Robotech*, DVD.

26. Patten, *Watching Anime*, 34.

27. Robotech official website, "Robotech Broadcast and Ratings History."

28. Jay Stranahan, "To my fellow members," *Megalord* 1, no. 1 (1987).

29. Patten, *Watching Anime*, 38–40. Patten mentions that Miyazaki's *Laputa: Castle in the Sky* was Streamline's first theatrical release, though it was shown only on one screen, whereas *Akira* had (very limited) national distribution on college campuses and in art house theaters.

30. Examples can be seen at "Paper Goods," BlueBlade Akira.

31. On the language of maturity in postwar U.S.-Japan relations, see Shibusawa, *America's Geisha Ally*, 5–6.

32. The origins of the *Star Blazers* fan club are recounted repeatedly through the run of the newsletter, which began in 1981 as the *Starblazers* [sic] *Fan Club News Line* and in 1982 became *Star Blazers Fandom Report*. See also the interview with Michael Pinto and Brian Cirulnick in Eldred, "Star Blazer Chronicles: The Superfans."

33. Jenkins, *Textual Poachers*, 23.

34. Ibid., 2.

35. Appadurai, *Modernity at Large*, 1–3.

36. Fred Patten response, 28 October 2005.

37. J. B. response, 2 November 2005; T. B. response, 6 November 2005; A. C. response, 16 November 2005.

38. T. B. response, 6 November 2005; B. M. response, 15 November 2005.

39. L. S. response, 14 November 2005.

40. This group is mentioned in *The Rose: Newsletter of Hasshin RI* 1, no. 1 (January 1987): 2.

41. Patten, *Watching Anime*, 35.

42. Crispin, "Brief History of rec.arts.anime."

43. Ibid.

44. This particular pipeline is recounted in Leonard, "Progress against the Law."

45. M. C. response, 1 November 2005.

46. T. E. response, 14 November 2005.

47. L. W. response, 4 November 2005.

48. *Animania* 1 (March 1988): 2.

49. R. A. W. response, 14 November 2005.

50. Fred Patten response, 28 October 2005.

51. C. S. S. response, 14 November 2005.

52. S. P. response, 13 November 2005.

53. Jenkins, *Textual Poachers*, 76.

54. S. P. response, 13 November 2005.

55. J. J. response, 16 November 2005.

56. Patten, *Watching Anime*, 29.

57. "Japanese Animation Program Guide."

58. See Geraghty, *Living with "Star Trek"*.

59. For examples of *Star Blazers* fan fiction, see Kopetz, *Visions*.

60. Jenkins, *Textual Poachers*, 18.

61. The mecha engineering essay can be found in *Nova* 12 (1987): 19–21.

62. *APA Hashin* 3 (1986); Edward C. Craddock, "Sumpo Kuso Yume," *Megalord* 1, no. 1 (1987).

63. I am indebted to Lorraine Savage, editor of *The Rose*, for providing copies of issues of the newsletter from 1987 to 1990. Increasingly, materials like these can be found archived on the Internet, as older fans dig them out of attics and closets and scan them for younger fans (and scholars). Their availability also offers interested readers opportunities to read the stories and see the fan art, which is difficult to publish because of the challenge of tracking down copyright owners. See, for instance, "Artifacts of Anime Fandom."

64. *The Rose: Newsletter of Hasshin RI* 1, no. 1 (January 1987): 2.

65. Ibid., 4, no. 19 (January 1990). Illustrations from this issue, including the "You are not alone!" map from the May 1989 issue, are printed in McKevitt, "'You Are Not Alone!'"

66. *The Rose: Newsletter of Hasshin RI* 2, no. 9 (May 1988): 5–6.

67. Ibid., 2, no. 11 (September 1988): 4–5.

68. Ibid., 3, no. 15 (May 1989): 5.

69. The website for the rec.arts.anime archive is http://groups.google.com/group/rec.arts.anime/about.

70. D. B. response, 19 November 2008.

71. Crispin, "Brief History of rec.arts.anime."

72. "OFFICIAL Proposal for creation of Rec.Arts.Cartoons," rec.arts.anime, 22 September 1988; "FINAL CALL FOR VOTES—Creation of Rec.Arts.Cartoons," rec.arts.anime, 22 October 1988.

73. This was the topic of a panel titled "Anime, Youth Culture, and Identity" at the 2006 International Conference on Asian Comics, Animation, and Gaming (York University, Toronto, Ont., 18–19 May 2006). Two papers particularly spoke to this point: Annie

Manion, "Discovering Japan: Anime and Learning Japanese Culture," and Masako Hamada, "What Anime Can Teach Us about Japanese and American Cultures." See Yoon, "Conference Review."

74. Patten, *Watching Anime*, 35–36; Blume, "David's Life Story."

75. For this comparison, see Napier, *From Impressionism to Anime*, 84–90.

76. Yoshihara, *Embracing the East*, 18.

77. Kelts, *Japanamerica*, 42, suggests the Möbius strip analogy as a way of describing the cross-cultural exchange of ideas and images in the production of animation.

78. Guthrie-Shimizu, *Transpacific Field of Dreams*; Zeiler, *Ambassadors in Pinstripes*.

79. Zeiler, *Ambassadors in Pinstripes*, 189.

80. "Traditional Folk Dance Modernized," *NPR News*, 20 February 2008.

81. S. Mitra Kalita, "Dancing between Cultures and Having a Great Time," *WP*, 12 April 2004.

82. Ibid.

83. Bright and Geyer, "Where in the World Is America?," 69.

EPILOGUE

1. Sanders, "Donald Trump"; Jonathan Soble and Keith Bradsher, "Donald Trump Laces into Japan with a Tirade from the '80s," *NYT*, 7 March 2016.

2. Lauren Orsini, "Why Getting Off to Anime Porn Is Shorthand for Supporting Donald Trump," *Forbes*, 21 January 2016; quoted in Soble and Bradsher, "Donald Trump Laces into Japan."

3. "Americans, Japanese: Mutual Respect 70 Years after the End of World War II."

4. Eamonn Fingleton, "The Myth of Japan's Failure," *NYT*, 6 January 2012.

5. Steve Lohr, "Maybe Japan Was Just a Warm-up," ibid., 21 January 2011.

6. Joo, "Transnationalization of Korean Popular Culture"; Lie, "What Is the K in K-pop?"; Larry Gordon, "Korean Language Classes Are Growing in Popularity at U.S. Colleges," *Los Angeles Times*, 1 April 2015; Kazuaki Nagata, "Cool Japan Fund Launches to Help Spread Products Overseas," *Japan Times*, 25 November 2013.

7. David Leonhardt, "Buying Binge Slams to a Halt," *NYT*, 11 November 2008.

8. Livingston, "Austerity Is Bad for Us and No Fun."

9. Michael Schulman, "Why Do We Fear a Rising China?," *Time*, 7 June 2011; Angelo Young, "China Extends Lead as World's Largest Car Market by Sales," *International Business Times*, 7 July 2014.

10. Martin Fackler, "Japan Goes from Dynamic to Disheartened," *NYT*, 16 October 2010.

11. Images of this magazine cover, as well as the three others discussed in the following, can be found easily with a search engine like Google.

12. "Surprising Attitudes Found in U.S.-Japan Poll," *San Francisco Chronicle*, 14 January 1987.

13. *Time*, 30 March 1981; *New Yorker*, 18 March 2002.

14. *Newsweek*, international ed., 10 December 2007.

15. "2012 Honda Accord 'Through It All' Commercial."

16. Honda promotional photograph, 1982, folder Logan County—Industry—Honda, Standing File, L4, Logan County District Library, Bellefontaine, Ohio.

Bibliography

ARCHIVAL COLLECTIONS

Bellefontaine, Ohio
   Logan County District Library
      Standing File, L4
Detroit, Mich.
   Wayne State University, Walter P. Reuther Library
      Archives of Labor and Urban Affairs
         UAW International Executive Board Minutes and Proceedings Collection
         UAW President's Office: Douglas A. Fraser Records
         UAW President's Office: Owen Bieber Collection
Marysville, Ohio
   Marysville Public Library
      Standing File
   Union County Records Center and Archives
      County Commissioners Records

SELF-PUBLISHED AND UNPUBLISHED SOURCES

Animania. Self-published fanzine edited by Tim Eldred, 1988.
Anime Stuff. Self-published fanzine edited by Tom Mitchell, 1987–93.
Anime-Zine. Self-published fanzine edited by Robert Fenelon, 1988.
APA Hashin. Self-published fanzine edited by Randall S. Stukey, 1986.
Dougherty, Andrew J. "Japan 2000." Unedited prepublication manuscript. 1 May 1991.
   Dudley Knox Library, Naval Postgraduate School, Monterrey, Calif.
Ito, Kinko. "Organizational Adaptation of Japanese Companies in the United States."
   Ph.D. diss., Ohio State University, 1987.
"Japanese Animation Program Guide." BayCon '86. Photocopy from private collection of
   Lorraine Savage.

Megalord: APA Superdimension U.S.A. Self-published fanzine edited by Edward
  Craddock, 1987.
Morris, Narrelle. "Destructive Discourse: 'Japan-bashing' in the United States, Australia,
  and Japan in the 1980s and 1990s." Ph.D. diss., Murdoch University (Australia), 2006.
Nova. Self-published fanzine edited by Kelli Alexander, 1987.
Panime's Image. Self-published fanzine edited by Kirk Houser, 1986.
The Rose: Newsletter of Hasshin RI. Photocopies from private collection of Lorraine
  Savage.
Sony of America. Retailer informational binder. Undated (1978–80?).
Starblazers Fan Club News Line. Self-published fanzine edited by Michael Pinto, 1981.
Star Blazers Fandom Report. Self-published fanzine edited by Michael Pinto, 1982–93.

FILMS AND TELEVISION SERIES

Akira. Directed by Katsuhiro Otomo. 1988. Long Beach, Calif.: Geneon Entertainment,
  2001. DVD.
The Bad News Bears Go to Japan. Directed by John Berry. 1978. Los Angeles: Paramount
  Pictures, 2002. DVD.
Black Rain. Directed by Ridley Scott. 1989. Los Angeles: Paramount Pictures, 2004. DVD.
Blade Runner. Directed by Ridley Scott. 1982. Los Angeles: Warner Brothers, 2007. DVD.
The Breakfast Club. Directed by John Hughes. 1985. Los Angeles: Universal Studios,
  2009. DVD.
Dr. Strangelove, or, How I Stopped Worrying and Learned to Love the Bomb. Directed by
  Stanley Kubrick. 1964. Culver City, Calif.: Columbia Pictures, 2001. DVD.
Farewell to Space Battleship Yamato. Directed by Leiji Matsumoto and Toshio Masuda.
  1978. Teaneck, N.J.: Voyager Entertainment, 2007. DVD.
Final Yamato. Directed by Leiji Matsumoto and Toshio Masuda. 1983. Teaneck, N.J.:
  Voyager Entertainment, 2005. DVD.
Gigantor. Directed by Fred Ladd. 1964. Los Angeles: Rhino Home Video, 2004. DVD.
Gung Ho. Directed by Ron Howard. 1986. Los Angeles: Paramount, 2002. DVD.
James Clavell's Shōgun. Directed by Jerry London. 1980. Los Angeles: Paramount Pictures,
  2003. DVD.
The Last Samurai. Directed by Edward Zwick. 2003. Los Angeles: Warner Home Video,
  2004. DVD.
Lost in Translation. Directed by Sofia Coppola. 2003. Los Angeles: Universal Studios,
  2004. DVD.
Memoirs of a Geisha. Directed by Rob Marshall. 2005. Los Angeles: Sony Pictures
  Entertainment, 2007. DVD.
Rising Sun. Directed by Philip Kaufman. 1993. Los Angeles: 20th Century Fox, 2002. DVD.
Robotech: The Macross Saga. Directed by Carl Macek. 1985. Houston: A.D. Vision,
  2001. DVD.
Showdown in Little Tokyo. Directed by Mark L. Lester. 1991. Los Angeles: Warner Home
  Video, 1998. DVD.
Shōgun. Directed by Jerry London. 1980. Los Angeles: Paramount, 2003. DVD.

Star Blazers: The Quest for Iscandar. 1979. Produced by Westchester Films. Teaneck, N.J.: Voyager Entertainment, 2004. DVD.

Wall Street. Directed by Oliver Stone. 1987. Los Angeles: 20th Century Fox, 2000. DVD.

The Yakuza. Directed by Sydney Pollack. 1975. Los Angeles: Warner Brothers, 2007. DVD.

ONLINE SOURCES

Note: all websites were accessible as of October 2016. For defunct websites,
the most recent version available on archive.org is provided.

Another Economic Patriot for Paul Tsongas. Paul Tsongas for President 1992 campaign brochure. http://www.4president.org/brochures/paultsongas1992brochure.htm.

"Artifacts of Anime Fandom." Flickr discussion group. https://www.flickr.com/groups/922349@N21/pool/.

Aschoff, Nicole M. "Imported from Detroit." *Jacobin*, April 2013. https://www.jacobinmag.com/2013/04/imported-from-detroit/.

Blume, David. "David's Life Story." http://web.archive.org/web/20080216212917/http://home.dlma.com/DavidBlume.html.

Carter, Jimmy. "'Crisis of Confidence' Speech (July 15, 1979)." Miller Center, University of Virginia. http://millercenter.org/president/speeches/speech-3402.

Columbus Japanese Language School. http://web.archive.org/web/20090805093949/http://www.columbushoshuko.com/english.htm.

"The Complicated History of the Song 'Sukiyaki.'" *Eurasian Sensation*, 11 October 2010. http://eurasian-sensation.blogspot.com/2010/10/complicated-history-of-song-sukiyaki.html.

Crispin, Mark. "A Brief History of rec.arts.anime." Eyrie Archives. http://archives.eyrie.org/anime/00HISTORY.gz.

D., Patrick. "Looking Back on the Anime Conventions of 2007." Anime Convention News. http://www.animecons.com/news/article.shtml/594.

Dailymotion. "Sony SL-7200 Betamax Commercial #1—1977." http://www.dailymotion.com/video/x3upd8_sony-sl-7200-betamax-commercial-1-1_tech.

Google Usenet archive. http://groups.google.com. Material cited from the following Usenet groups: soc.culture.asian.american; sci.econ; soc.culture.japan; rec.arts.anime.

Harris Interactive. "Sony on Top in Annual 'Best Brands' Harris Poll for Seventh Consecutive Year." *Harris Poll*, 12 July 2006. http://web.archive.org/web/20060718031459/http://www.harrisinteractive.com/harris_poll/index.asp?PID=682.

Imai, Shoko. "Nobu and After: Westernized Japanese Food and Globalization." In *Globalization, Food, and Social Identities in the Asia Pacific Region*, edited by James Farrer. Sophia University Institute of Comparative Culture, 2010. http://icc.fla.sophia.ac.jp/global%20food%20papers/pdf/3_4_IMAI.pdf.

Isle, Ray. "Sushi in America." *Food and Wine.* N.d. http://www.foodandwine.com/articles/sushi-in-america.

"Job Performance Ratings for President Bush (G. H. W.)." Public Opinion Archives, Roper Center for Public Opinion Research. http://ropercenter.uconn.edu.

Kopetz, Frederick P., ed. *Visions: Virtual Fanzine.* http://visions.comet-empire.com.

Leonard, Sean. "Progress against the Law: Fan Distribution, Copyright, and the Explosive Growth of Japanese Animation." Massachusetts Institute of Technology, 12 September 2004. http://web.mit.edu/seantek/www/papers/progress-columns.pdf.

Lien, Tracey. "How Successful Is Pokémon?" *Polygon*, 18 August 2014. http://www.polygon.com/pokemon/2014/8/18/6030089/Pokemon-sales-numbers.

Nghiem, David E. X. N. "Brazilian Sushi: The Magical Mixture of Japan and Brazil." *Open Salon*, 2 February 2009. http://web.archive.org/web/20130115014700/http://open.salon.com/blog/dnghiem/2009/02/02/brazilian_sushi_the_magical_mixture_of_japan_and_brazil.

"Nigeria Surpasses Hollywood as World's Second Largest Film Producer." *UN News Centre*. 5 May 2009. http://www.un.org/apps/news/printnewsAr.asp?nid=30707.

"Paper Goods." BlueBlade Akira. http://www.bbakira.co.uk/merchandise/paper/paper.htm.

Pinto, Michael. "Star Blazers Chronicles: The Superfans." http://www.michaelpinto.com/press_coverage/star_blazers_chronicles_the_superfans.ht.

Robotech official website. "Robotech Broadcast and Ratings History." http://web.archive.org/web/20081012100710/http://www.robotech.tv/info.php?id=history.

Sony Global. "Sony History." http://www.sony.net/Fun/SH/.

"2012 Honda Accord 'Through It All' Commercial." YouTube. 24 October 2011. https://www.youtube.com/watch?v=dwNSczgc004.

U.S. Bureau of Economic Analysis. "International Transactions Tables." http://www.bea.gov/international/bp_web/tb_download_type_modern.cfm?list=1&RowID=1.

U.S. Census Bureau. "U.S. Trade in Goods and Services—Balance of Payments (BOP) Basis." http://www.census.gov/foreign-trade/statistics/historical/gands.pdf.

White, Theodore H. "The Danger from Japan." *New York Times Magazine*, 28 July 1985. http://www.nytimes.com/1985/07/28/magazine/the-danger-from-japan.html.

Wolfe, Tom. "The 'Me' Decade and the Third Great Awakening." *New York*, 23 August 1976. http://nymag.com/news/features/45938/.

Yang, Lillian. "California Roll Creators." *Food Non-Fiction*, 25 February 2016. http://www.foodnonfiction.com/2016/02/california-roll-creators.html.

Young, Angelo. "China Extends Lead as World's Largest Car Market by Sales." *International Business Times*, 7 July 2014. http://www.ibtimes.com/china-extends-lead-worlds-largest-car-market-sales-gm-ford-china-deliveries-double-1621254.

PUBLISHED SOURCES

Abegglen, James C., and Thomas M. Hout. "Facing Up to the Trade Gap with Japan." *Foreign Affairs* 57 (Fall 1978): 146–68.

AHR Roundtable. "Historians and the Question of 'Modernity.'" *American Historical Review* 116, no. 3 (June 2011): 631–37.

Allison, Anne. "The Japan Fad in Global Youth Culture and Millennial Capitalism." *Mechademia* 1 (2006): 11–21.

———. *Millennial Monsters: Japanese Toys and the Global Imagination*. Berkeley: University of California Press, 2006.

Alston, Jon P. *The American Samurai: Blending American and Japanese Managerial Practices.* New York: Walter de Gruyter, 1986.

Alvarado, Manuel, ed. *Video World-Wide: An International Study.* London: John Libbey, 1988.

"Americans, Japanese: Mutual Respect 70 Years after the End of World War II." *Pew Research Center,* 7 April 2015.

Amos, Walter. "The Star Blazers You Didn't See." *Animerica,* August 1995, 10.

Anderson, Benedict. *Imagined Communities: Reflections on the Origin and Spread of Nationalism.* 2nd ed. New York: Verso, 1991.

Anderson, Leon. *Japanese Rage: Japanese Business and Its Assault on the West.* New York: Four Walls Eight Windows, 1992.

Anderson, Perry. *The Origins of Postmodernity.* New York: Verso, 1998.

Appadurai, Arjun. *Modernity at Large: Cultural Dimensions of Globalization.* Minneapolis: University of Minnesota Press, 1996.

Atkins, E. Taylor. *Blue Nippon: Authenticating Jazz in Japan.* Durham: Duke University Press, 2001.

Bailey, Beth, and David Farber, eds. *America in the Seventies.* Lawrence: University of Kansas Press, 2004.

Barnet, Richard J. *Global Dreams: Imperial Corporations and the New World Order.* New York: Simon and Schuster, 1994.

Barshay, Andrew E. "What Is Japan to Us?" In *The Humanities and the Dynamics of Inclusion since World War II,* edited by David A. Hollinger, 345–71. Baltimore: Johns Hopkins University Press, 2006.

Barthes, Roland. *Empire of Signs.* Translated by Richard Howard. New York: Hill and Wang, 1982.

Bates, Caroline. "Specialités de la Maison." *Gourmet,* July 1980, 40–42.

Baudrillard, Jean. *Simulacra and Simulation.* Translated by Sheila Faria Glaser. Ann Arbor: University of Michigan Press, 1994.

Bauman, Zygmunt. *Globalization: The Human Consequences.* New York: Columbia University Press, 1998.

———. *Intimations of Postmodernity.* New York: Routledge, 1992.

Befu, Harumi. *Hegemony of Heterogeneity: An Anthropological Analysis of Nihonjinron.* Melbourne: Trans Pacific Press, 2001.

Bender, Thomas. *A Nation among Nations: America's Place in World History.* New York: Hill and Wang, 2006.

———, ed. *Rethinking American History in a Global Age.* Berkeley: University of California Press, 2002.

Benedict, Ruth. *The Chrysanthemum and the Sword: Patterns of Japanese Culture.* Boston: Houghton Mifflin, 1946.

Benjamin, Walter. "The Work of Art in the Age of Mechanical Reproduction." In *Illuminations: Essays and Reflections,* by Walter Benjamin, 217–52. Translated by Harry Zohn and edited by Hannah Arendt. New York: Harcourt Brace Jovanovich, 1968.

Berkowitz, Edward D. *Something Happened: A Political and Cultural Overview of the Seventies.* New York: Columbia University Press, 2006.

Berndt, Jacqueline, and Steffi Richter, eds. *Reading Manga: Local and Global Perceptions of Japanese Comics.* Leipzig: Leipzig University Press, 2006.

Bestor, Theodore C. "How Sushi Went Global." *Foreign Policy*, November/December 2000, 54–63.

———. "Supply-Side Sushi: Commodity, Market, and the Global City." *American Anthropologist* 103, no. 1 (March 2001): 76–95.

———. *Tsukiji: The Fish Market at the Center of the World*. Berkeley: University of California Press, 2004.

Bluestone, Barry, and Bennett Harrison. *The Deindustrialization of America: Plant Closings, Community Abandonment, and the Dismantling of Basic Industry*. New York: Basic Books, 1982.

Borstelmann, Thomas. *The 1970s: A New Global History from Civil Rights to Economic Inequality*. Princeton: Princeton University Press, 2013.

Bourdieu, Pierre. *Distinction: A Social Critique of the Judgement of Taste*. Translated by Richard Nice. London: Routledge, 1984.

Boyd, Douglas A. "Home Video Diffusion and Utilization in Arabian Gulf States." *American Behavioral Scientist* 30 (May–June 1987): 544–54.

———. "The Videocassette Recorder in the USSR and Soviet-Bloc Countries." In *The VCR Age: Home Video and Mass Communication*, edited by Mark R. Levy, 252–70. London: Sage, 1989.

Boyd, Douglas A., Joseph D. Straubhaar, and John A. Lent. *Videocassette Recorders in the Third World*. New York: Longman, 1989.

Breen, T. H. *The Marketplace of Revolution: How Consumer Politics Shaped American Independence*. New York: Oxford University Press, 2004.

———. "Will American Consumers Buy a Second American Revolution?" *Journal of American History* 93 (September 2006): 404–8.

Bright, Charles, and Michael Geyer. "Where in the World Is America?" In *Rethinking American History in a Global Age*, edited by Thomas Bender, 63–100. Berkeley: University of California Press, 2002.

Brinkley, Douglas. *Wheels for the World: Henry Ford, His Company, and a Century of Progress, 1903–2003*. New York: Viking, 2003.

Buell, Frederick. *National Culture and the New Global System*. Baltimore: Johns Hopkins University Press, 1994.

Burgess, Chris. "The 'Illusion' of Homogeneous Japan and National Character: Discourse as a Tool to Transcend the 'Myth' vs. 'Reality' Binary." *Asia-Pacific Journal* 8 (March 2010): 1–23.

Burstein, Daniel. *Yen! Japan's New Financial Empire and Its Threat to America*. New York: Simon and Schuster, 1988.

Castells, Manuel. *End of Millennium*. 2nd ed. Malden, Mass.: Blackwell, 2000.

Caulfield, Norman. *NAFTA and Labor in North America*. Urbana: University of Illinois Press, 2010.

Choate, Pat. *Agents of Influence: How Japan's Lobbyists in the United States Manipulate America's Political and Economic System*. New York: Knopf, 1990.

Christopher, Robert C. *The Japanese Mind: The Goliath Explained*. New York: Simon and Schuster, 1983.

Clavell, James. *Shōgun*. New York: Random House, 1975.

Clements, Jonathan, and Helen McCarthy. *The Anime Encyclopedia: A Guide to Japanese Animation*. Berkeley: Stone Bridge Press, 2001.

Cohen, Akiba A. "Decision Making in VCR Rental Libraries." *American Behavioral Scientist* 30 (May–June 1987): 495–508.

Cohen, Akiba A., and Laura Cohen. "Big Eyes but Clumsy Fingers: Knowing about and Using Technological Features of Home VCRs." In *The VCR Age: Home Video and Mass Communication*, edited by Mark R. Levy, 135–47. London: Sage, 1989.

Cohen, Lizabeth. *A Consumer's Republic: The Politics of Mass Consumption in Postwar America*. New York: Knopf, 2003.

———. "Escaping Steigerwald's 'Plastic Cages': Consumers as Subjects and Objects in Modern Capitalism." *Journal of American History* 93 (September 2006): 409–13.

Cole, Robert E., and Donald R. Deskins Jr. "Racial Factors in Site Location and Employment Patterns of Japanese Auto Firms in America." *California Management Review* 31, no. 1 (Fall 1988): 9–22.

Collins, Robert M. *Transforming America: Politics and Culture in the Reagan Years*. New York: Columbia University Press, 2007.

Condry, Ian. "Anime Creativity: Characters and Premises in the Quest for Cool Japan." *Theory, Culture and Society* 26 (2009): 139–64.

———. *The Soul of Anime: Collaborative Creativity and Japan's Media Success Story*. Durham: Duke University Press, 2013.

Cooking Japanese Style. Dallas: International Publishing Company, 1979.

Cooper, Frederick. *Colonialism in Question: Theory, Knowledge, History*. Berkeley: University of California Press, 2005.

Corson, Trevor. *The Zen of Fish: The Story of Sushi from Samurai to Supermarket*. New York: HarperCollins, 2007.

Cowie, Jefferson. *Stayin' Alive: The 1970s and the Last Days of the Working Class*. New York: New Press, 2012.

Cowie, Jefferson, and Joseph Heathcott, eds. *Beyond the Ruins: The Meaning of Deindustrialization*. Ithaca: Cornell University Press, 2003.

Crichton, Michael. *Rising Sun*. New York: Ballantine, 1992.

Cussler, Clive. *Dragon*. New York: Pocket Books, 1990.

Cwiertka, Katarzyna. "From Ethnic to Hip: Circuits of Japanese Cuisine in Europe." *Food and Foodways* 13 (2005): 241–72.

———. *Modern Japanese Cuisine: Food, Power, and National Identity*. London: Reaktion Books, 2006.

Dale, Peter N. *The Myth of Japanese Uniqueness*. London: Croom Helm, 1986.

DeGrazia, Victoria. *Irresistible Empire: America's Advance through Twentieth-Century Europe*. Cambridge: Belknap, 2005.

DeLillo, Don. *White Noise*. New York: Penguin, 1985.

Detrick, Mia. *Sushi*. San Francisco: Chronicle Books, 1981.

De Vera, Jose M., and Jim McDonnell. "Video: A Media Revolution?" *Communication Research Trends* 6 (1985): 1–3.

Didion, Joan. *After Henry*. New York: Vintage, 1992.

Dietrich, William S. *In the Shadow of the Rising Sun: The Political Roots of American Economic Decline*. University Park: Pennsylvania State University Press, 1991.

Dobrow, Julia R. "Away from the Mainstream? VCRs and Ethnic Identity." In *The VCR Age: Home Video and Mass Communication*, edited by Mark R. Levy, 193–208. London: Sage, 1989.

———. "The Rerun Ritual: Using VCRs to Re-view." In *Social and Cultural Aspects of VCR Use*, edited by Julia R. Dobrow, 181–94. Hillsdale, N.J.: Lawrence Erlbaum Associates, 1990.

———, ed. *Social and Cultural Aspects of VCR Use*. Hillsdale, N.J.: Lawrence Erlbaum Associates, 1990.

Douglas, Mary, and Baron Isherwood. *The World of Goods: Towards an Anthropology of Consumption*. 2nd ed. New York: Routledge, 1996.

Douthwright, Jean A. "Rochester Institute of Technology: A CIA Subsidiary?" *Covert Action Information Bulletin*, Fall 1991, 4–9.

Dower, John W. *Japan in War and Peace: Selected Essays*. New York: W. W. Norton, 1993.

———. *War without Mercy: Race and Power in the Pacific War*. New York: Pantheon, 1986.

Du Gay, Paul, et al., eds. *Doing Cultural Studies: The Story of the Sony Walkman*. London: Sage, 1997.

Ehrman, John. *The Eighties: America in the Age of Reagan*. New Haven: Yale University Press, 2005.

Engerman, David C. "Bernath Lecture: American Knowledge and Global Power." *Diplomatic History* 31 (September 2007): 599–622.

Fallows, James N. *More Like Us: Making America Great Again*. Boston: Houghton Mifflin, 1989.

Farber, David R. *Taken Hostage: The Iran Hostage Crisis and America's First Encounter with Radical Islam*. Princeton: Princeton University Press, 2005.

———. "The Torch Had Fallen." In *America in the Seventies*, edited by Beth Bailey and David Farber, 9–28. Lawrence: University Press of Kansas, 2004.

Farrer, James, ed. *The Globalization of Asian Cuisines: Transnational Networks and Culinary Contact Zones*. New York: Palgrave Macmillan, 2015.

Featherstone, Mike, Scott Lash, and Roland Robertson, eds. *Global Modernities*. London: Sage, 1995.

Feldman, Richard, and Michael Betzold, eds. *End of the Line: Autoworkers and the American Dream*. New York: Weidenfeld and Nicolson, 1988.

Ferguson, Niall, Charles S. Maier, Erez Manela, and Daniel J. Sargent, eds. *The Shock of the Global: The 1970s in Perspective*. Cambridge: Belknap Press, 2010.

Fleeter, Howard B. *Honda in Ohio: The Economic Impact of the First 25 Years*. Columbus, Ohio: Levin, Driscoll & Fleeter, 2004.

Frank, Dana. *Buy American: The Untold Story of Economic Nationalism*. Boston: Beacon Press, 1999.

Frieden, Jeffry A. *Global Capitalism: Its Fall and Rise in the Twentieth Century*. New York: W. W. Norton, 2006.

Friedman, George, and Meredith Lebard. *The Coming War with Japan*. New York: St. Martin's, 1991.

Friedman, Thomas. *The World Is Flat: A Brief History of the Twenty-First Century*. New York: Farrar, Straus, and Giroux, 2005.

Froud, Nina. *Cooking the Japanese Way*. London: Paul Hamlin, 1963.

Fucini, Joseph J., and Suzy Fucini. *Working for the Japanese: Inside Mazda's American Auto Plant*. New York: Free Press, 1990.

Fukuyama, Francis. *The End of History and the Last Man*. New York: Free Press, 1992.

Gabaccia, Donna R. *We Are What We Eat: Ethnic Food and the Making of Americans.* Cambridge, Mass.: Harvard University Press, 1998.

Gaddis, John Lewis. *The United States and the End of the Cold War: Implications, Reconsiderations, and Provocations.* New York: Oxford University Press, 1992.

Ganley, Gladys D., and Oswald H. Ganley. *Global Political Fallout: The First Decade of the VCR, 1976–1985.* Cambridge, Mass.: Center for Information Policy Research, 1987.

Garten, Jeffrey E. *Cold Peace: America, Japan, Germany, and the Struggle for Supremacy.* New York: Times Books, 1992.

Garthoff, Raymond L. *The Great Transition: American-Soviet Relations and the End of the Cold War.* Washington, D.C.: Brookings Institution, 1994.

Gelsanliter, David. *Jump Start: Japan Comes to the Heartland.* New York: Farrar Straus Giroux, 1990.

Geraghty, Lincoln. *Living with "Star Trek": American Culture and the "Star Trek" Universe.* New York: I. B. Taurus, 2007.

Gibson, William. *Neuromancer.* New York: Ace Books, 1984.

Giddens, Anthony. *The Consequences of Modernity.* Stanford: Stanford University Press, 1990.

Gilvary, Jane. "Skinny Jeans, John Wayne, and the Feminization of America." *Philadelphia Bulletin,* 24 August 2010.

Gluck, Carol. "House of Mirrors: American History-Writing on Japan." In *Imagined Histories: American Historians Interpret the Past,* edited by Anthony Molho and Gordon S. Wood, 434–54. Princeton: Princeton University Press, 1998.

———. "The Idea of Showa." In *Showa: The Japan of Hirohito,* edited by Carol Gluck and Stephen R. Graubard, 1–26. New York: W. W. Norton, 1992.

Golden, Arthur. *Memoirs of a Geisha.* New York: Alfred K. Knopf, 1997.

Gordon, Andrew. *A Modern History of Japan: From Tokugawa Times to the Present.* New York: Oxford University Press, 2003.

Gosling, Sam. *Snoop: What Your Stuff Says about You.* New York: Basic Books, 2008.

Graebner, Norman A., Richard Dean Burns, and Joseph M. Siracusa. *Reagan, Bush, Gorbachev: Revisiting the End of the Cold War.* Westport, Conn.: Praeger, 2008.

Grazian, David. *Blue Chicago: The Search for Authenticity in Urban Blues Clubs.* Chicago: University of Chicago Press, 2003.

———. "Demystifying Authenticity in the Sociology of Culture." In *Handbook of Cultural Sociology,* edited by John R. Hall, Laura Grindstaff, and Ming-Cheng Lo, 191–200. New York: Routledge, 2010.

Guthrie-Shimizu, Sayuri. "For Love of the Game: Baseball in Early U.S.-Japanese Encounters and the Rise of a Transnational Sporting Fraternity." *Diplomatic History* 28 (November 2004): 637–62.

———. "From Southeast Asia to the American Southeast: Japanese Business Meets the Sun Belt." In *Globalization and the American South,* edited by James C. Cobb and William Stueck, 135–63. Athens: University of Georgia Press, 2005.

———. *Transpacific Field of Dreams: How Baseball Linked the United States and Japan in Peace and War.* Chapel Hill: University of North Carolina Press, 2012.

Halberstam, David. *The Reckoning.* New York: William Morrow, 1986.

Hancock, David. *Citizens of the World: London Merchants and the Integration of the British Atlantic Community, 1735–1785.* New York: Cambridge University Press, 1995.

Hanhardt, John G., ed. *Video Culture: A Critical Investigation*. New York: Visual Studies Workshop, 1986.

Hannerz, Ulf. *Transnational Connections: Culture, People, Places*. New York: Routledge, 1996.

Harootunian, Harry, and Naoki Sakai. "Japan Studies and Cultural Studies." *east asia cultures critique* 7 (1999): 593–647.

Harvey, David. *The Condition of Postmodernity: An Enquiry into the Origins of Cultural Change*. Oxford: Blackwell, 1989.

———. *The New Imperialism*. New York: Oxford University Press, 2003.

———. *Spaces of Global Capitalism: Towards a Theory of Uneven Development*. New York: Verso, 2006.

Hearst, C. Cameron, III. "Review of *Learning from 'Shōgun.'*" *Journal of Asian Studies* 41 (November 1981): 158–59.

Heldke, Lisa. *Exotic Appetites: Ruminations of a Food Adventurer*. New York: Routledge, 2003.

Hensley, Don, ed. *Building on Dreams: The Story of Honda in Ohio*. Marysville, Ohio: Honda of America, Mfg., 2004.

Hixson, Walter L. *Parting the Curtain: Propaganda, Culture, and the Cold War, 1945–1961*. New York: St. Martin's, 1997.

Hoganson, Kristin L. *Consumers' Imperium: The Global Production of American Domesticity, 1865–1920*. Chapel Hill: University of North Carolina Press, 2007.

———. "Cosmopolitan Domesticity: Importing the American Dream, 1865–1920." *American Historical Review* 107 (February 2002): 55–83.

———. "Stuff It: Domestic Consumption and the Americanization of the World Paradigm." *Diplomatic History* 30 (September 2006): 571–94.

Holstein, William J. *The Japanese Power Game: What It Means for America*. New York: Charles Scribner's Sons, 1990.

Hopper, Paul. *Understanding Cultural Globalization*. Malden, Mass.: Polity Press, 2007.

Horovitz, Bruce. "Honda Not So Simple Anymore." *Industry Week*, 4 April 1983, 45.

Horvat, Andrew. "Revisionism Revisited—The Era of Bilateral Acrimony." *Japan Quarterly* 47 (July 2000): 33–40.

Hunt, Michael H. *Ideology and U.S. Foreign Policy*. New Haven: Yale University Press, 1987.

Huntington, Samuel P. *The Clash of Civilizations and the Remaking of the World Order*. New York: Simon and Schuster, 1998.

Ingrassia, Paul. *Crash Course: The American Automobile Industry's Road from Glory to Disaster*. New York: Random House, 2010.

Ingrassia, Paul, and Joseph B. White. *Comeback: The Fall and Rise of the American Automobile Industry*. New York: Simon and Schuster, 1994.

Iriye, Akira. *Cultural Internationalism and World Order*. Baltimore: Johns Hopkins University Press, 1997.

———. "The Internationalizing of History." *American Historical Review* 94 (February 1989): 1–10.

Iriye, Akira, and Robert A. Wampler, eds. *Partnership: The United States and Japan, 1951–2001*. New York: Kodansha International, 2001.

Ishihara, Shintaro. *The Japan That Can Say No*. Translated by Frank Baldwin. New York: Simon and Schuster, 1991.

Issenberg, Sasha. *The Sushi Economy: Globalization and the Making of a Modern Delicacy*. New York: Gotham, 2007.

Iwabuchi, Koichi. *Recentering Globalization: Popular Culture and Japanese Transnationalism*. Durham: Duke University Press, 2002.

Iyer, Pico. *Falling Off the Map: Some Lonely Places of the World*. New York: Vintage, 1993.

———. *The Lady and the Monk: Four Seasons in Kyoto*. New York: Vintage, 1991.

———. *Video Night in Kathmandu: And Other Reports from the Not-So-Far East*. New York: Vintage, 1988.

Jacobson, Matthew Frye. *Barbarian Virtues: The United States Encounter Foreign Peoples at Home and Abroad, 1876–1917*. New York: Hill and Wang, 2000.

Jameson, Fredric. "Notes on Globalization as a Philosophical Issue." In *The Cultures of Globalization*, edited by Fredric Jameson and Masao Miyoshi, 54–80. Durham: Duke University Press, 1998.

———. *Postmodernism, or, the Cultural Logic of Late Capitalism*. Durham: Duke University Press, 1991.

Jameson, Fredric, and Masao Miyoshi, eds. *The Cultures of Globalization*. Durham: Duke University Press, 1998.

Jenkins, Henry. *Textual Poachers: Television Fans and Participatory Culture*. New York: Routledge, 1992.

Johnson, Chalmers. "How to Think about Economic Competition from Japan." *Journal of Japanese Studies* 13 (Summer 1987): 415–28.

———. *MITI and the Japanese Miracle: The Growth of Industrial Policy, 1925–1975*. Stanford: Stanford University Press, 1982.

———. *The Sorrows of Empire: Militarism, Secrecy, and the End of the Republic*. New York: Owl Books, 2004.

Johnson, Haynes. *Sleepwalking through History: America in the Reagan Years*. New York: W. W. Norton, 1991.

Johnson, Sheila. *The Japanese through American Eyes*. Stanford: Stanford University Press, 1988.

———. "Review: Images of Japan." *Journal of Japanese Studies* 2 (Summer 1976): 437–48.

Joo, Jeongsuk. "Transnationalization of Korean Popular Culture and the Rise of 'Pop Nationalism' in Korea." *Journal of Popular Culture* 44, no. 3 (2011): 489–504.

Joyce, Colin. "Japan Starts World Campaign to Save Sushi." *Daily Telegraph*, 23 December 2006.

Jüngst, Heike Elisabeth. "Japanese Comics in Germany." *Perspectives: Studies in Translatology* 12 (2004): 83–105.

Kagawa, Aya. *Japanese Cookbook: 100 Favorite Recipes for Western Cooks*. Tokyo: Japan Travel Bureau, 1967.

Kang, David C. "Getting Asia Wrong: The Need for New Analytical Frameworks." *International Security* 27 (Spring 2003): 57–85.

Kaplan, Amy. *The Anarchy of Empire in the Making of U.S. Culture*. Cambridge, Mass.: Harvard University Press, 2002.

———. "Manifest Domesticity." *American Literature* 70 (September 1998): 581–606.

Karan, P. P., ed. *Japan in the Bluegrass*. Lexington: University Press of Kentucky, 2001.

Kaufman, Scott. *Plans Unraveled: The Foreign Policy of the Carter Administration*. DeKalb: Northern Illinois University Press, 2006.

Kazufumi, Manabe, and Harumi Befu. "Japanese Cultural Identity: An Empirical Investigation of *Nihonjinron*." *Japanstudien* 4 (1992): 89–102.

Keller, Maryann. *Rude Awakening: The Rise, Fall, and Struggle for Recovery of General Motors*. New York: Harper Perennial, 1989.

Kelts, Roland. *Japanamerica: How Japanese Pop Culture Has Invaded the U.S.* New York: Palgrave, 2006.

Kennedy, Paul. *The Rise and Fall of the Great Powers: Economic Change and Military Conflict from 1500 to 2000*. New York: Random House, 1987.

Kenney, Padraic. *A Carnival of Revolution: Central Europe 1989*. Princeton: Princeton University Press, 2002.

"Killers Stalked Vincent Chin: Ignored Evidence Indicates Killing Was Premeditated." *Asian Week*, 28 April 1983.

Kingston, Jeff. *Japan in Transformation, 1945–2010*. 2nd ed. New York: Routledge, 2010.

Kitamura, Hiroshi. *Screening Enlightenment: Hollywood and the Cultural Reconstruction of Defeated Japan*. Ithaca: Cornell University Press, 2010.

Klein, Christina. *Cold War Orientalism: Asia in the Middlebrow Imagination, 1945–1961*. Berkeley: University of California Press, 2003.

Koizumi, Hisako, Jennifer Farkas, and Tetsunori Koizumi. "Stress and Coping of Japanese Children in American Society." In *Advances in Research and Cybernetics*, edited by George E. Lasker, 222–26. Windsor, Ont.: International Institute for Advanced Studies in Systems Research and Cybernetics, 1989.

Kroes, Rob. *If You've Seen One, You've Seen the Mall: Europeans and American Mass Culture*. Urbana: University of Illinois Press, 1996.

Kuisel, Richard F. *Seducing the French: The Dilemma of Americanization*. Berkeley: University of California Press, 1993.

LaFeber, Walter. *The Clash: A History of U.S.-Japan Relations*. New York: W. W. Norton, 1997.

———. *Michael Jordan and the New Global Capitalism*. New York: W. W. Norton, 1999.

Lardner, James. *Fast Forward: Hollywood, the Japanese, and the Onslaught of the VCR*. New York: W. W. Norton, 1987.

Lasch, Christopher. *The Culture of Narcissism: American Life in the Age of Diminishing Expectations*. New York: W. W. Norton, 1978.

Lent, John A., ed. *Animation in Asia and the Pacific*. Bloomington: Indiana University Press, 2001.

Lettow, Paul V. *Ronald Reagan and His Quest to Abolish Nuclear Weapons*. New York: Random House, 2005.

Levenstein, Harvey. *Paradox of Plenty: A Social History of Eating in Modern America*. Berkeley: University of California Press, 2003.

Levitt, Theodore. "The Globalization of Markets." *Harvard Business Review*, May–June 1983, 92–102.

———. *The Marketing Imagination*. New York: Free Press, 1986.

Levy, Mark R., ed. *The VCR Age: Home Video and Mass Communication*. London: Sage, 1989.

Lie, John. "What Is the K in K-pop? South Korean Popular Music, the Culture Industry, and National Identity." *Korea Observer* 43, no. 3 (Autumn 2012): 339–63.

Lin, Carolyn A. "Audience Activity and VCR Use." In *Social and Cultural Aspects of VCR Use*, edited by Julia R. Dobrow, 75–92. Hillsdale, N.J.: Lawrence Erlbaum Associates, 1990.

Lindstrom, Paul B. "Video: The Consumer Impact." In *The VCR Age: Home Video and Mass Communication*, edited by Mark R. Levy, 40–49. London: Sage, 1989.

Linkins, Jason. "Mitt Romney, 'Son of Detroit,' Tools around Michigan in Car Manufactured in Canada." *Huffington Post*, 16 February 2012.

Little, Douglas. *American Orientalism: The United States and the Middle East since 1945.* Chapel Hill: University of North Carolina Press, 2002.

Livingston, James. "Austerity Is Bad for Us and No Fun." *Bloomberg*, 27 November 2011.

Logevall, Frederik, and Andrew Preston, eds. *Nixon in the World: American Foreign Relations, 1969–1977.* New York: Oxford University Press, 2008.

Luyten, Sonia. *Cultura pop japonesa: Mangá e animê.* São Paolo: Ed. Hedra, 2005.

Lyotard, Jean-François. *The Postmodern Condition: A Report on Knowledge.* Translated by Geoff Bennington and Brian Massumi. Minneapolis: University of Minnesota Press, 1984.

Maghroori, Ray, and Bennett Ramberg. *Globalism versus Realism: International Relations' Third Debate.* Boulder, Colo.: Westview, 1982.

Marvel, Mary K., and William J. Shkurti. *The Economic Impact of Development: Honda in Ohio.* Working Paper Series. Columbus: Ohio State University School of Public Policy and Management, 1993.

Matlock, Jack F. *Reagan and Gorbachev: How the Cold War Ended.* New York: Random House, 2004.

McAlister, Melani. *Epic Encounters: Culture, Media, and U.S. Interests in the Middle East, 1945–2000.* Berkeley: University of California Press, 2001.

McCartin, Joseph A. *Collision Course: Ronald Reagan, the Air Traffic Controllers, and the Strike That Changed America.* New York: Oxford University Press, 2011.

McDannell, Colleen. *Material Christianity: Religion and Popular Culture in America.* New Haven: Yale University Press, 1995.

McGray, Douglas. "Japan's Gross National Cool." *Foreign Policy*, May–June 2002, 44–54.

McGrew, Anthony. "Globalization in Hard Times: Contention in the Academy and Beyond." In *The Blackwell Companion to Globalization*, edited by George Ritzer, 29–53. Malden, Mass.: Blackwell, 2007.

McKevitt, Andrew C. "'You Are Not Alone!': Anime and the Globalizing of America." *Diplomatic History* 34, no. 5 (November 2010): 893–921.

McKinsey and Company. *Japan Business, Obstacles, and Opportunities: A Binational Perspective for U.S. Decision-Makers.* New York: John Wiley, 1982.

McLuhan, Marshall. *The Gutenberg Galaxy: The Making of Typographic Man.* Toronto: University of Toronto Press, 1962.

Millard, Mike. *Leaving Japan: Observations on the Dysfunctional U.S.–Japan Relationship.* Armonk, N.Y.: M. E. Sharpe, 2001.

Miller, Daniel. *The Comfort of Things.* Malden, Mass.: Polity Press, 2008.

Miyoshi, Masao. *Off Center: Power and Cultural Relations between Japan and the United States.* Cambridge, Mass.: Harvard University Press, 1991.

Miyoshi, Masao, and H. D. Harootunian, eds. *Japan and the World*. Durham: Duke University Press, 1993.

———. *Postmodernism and Japan*. Durham: Duke University Press, 1989.

Morita, Akio. *Made in Japan: Akio Morita and Sony*. With Edwin M. Reingold and Mitsuko Shimomura. New York: E. P. Dutton, 1986.

Morley, David, and Kevin Robins. *Spaces of Identity: Global Media, Electronic Landscapes, and Cultural Boundaries*. New York: Routledge, 1995.

Nagata, Kazuaki. "Cool Japan Fund Launches to Help Spread Products Overseas." *Japan Times*, 25 November 2013.

Napier, Susan J. *Anime from "Akira" to "Howl's Moving Castle": Experiencing Contemporary Japanese Animation*. New York: Palgrave, 2005.

———. *From Impressionism to Anime: Japan as Fantasy and Fan Cult in the Mind of the West*. New York: Palgrave, 2007.

———. "The World of Anime Fandom in America." *Mechademia* 1 (2006): 47–63.

Nathan, Joan. "A Short History of the Bagel: From Ancient Egypt to Lender's." *Slate*, 12 November 2008.

Nathan, John. *Sony: The Private Life*. New York: Houghton Mifflin, 1999.

Nathan, Robert. "Is Japan Really Out to Get Us?" *New York Times Book Review*, 9 February 1992, 22–23.

Ninkovich, Frank. *Modernity and Power: A History of the Domino Theory in the Twentieth Century*. Chicago: University of Chicago Press, 1994.

Noonan, Peggy. *What I Saw at the Revolution: A Political Life in the Reagan Era*. New York: Random House, 1990.

Novick, Peter. *The Holocaust in American Life*. Boston: Houghton Mifflin, 1999.

Nye, Joseph S., Jr. *Bound to Lead: The Changing Nature of American Power*. New York: Basic Books, 1990.

———. "Coping with Japan." *Foreign Policy* (Winter 1992–93): 96–115.

Oberdorfer, Don. *From the Cold War to a New Era: The United States and the Soviet Union, 1983–1991*. Baltimore: Johns Hopkins University Press, 1998.

Ogan, Christine. "The Worldwide Cultural and Economic Impact of Video." In *The VCR Age: Home Video and Mass Communication*, edited by Mark R. Levy, 230–51. London: Sage, 1989.

Ohmae, Kenichi. "Becoming a Triad Power." *McKinsey Quarterly*, Spring 1985, 2–25.

———. *Beyond National Borders: Reflections on Japan and the World*. Homewood, Ill.: Dow-Jones-Irwin, 1987.

———. *The Borderless World: Power and Strategy in the Interlinked Economy*. New York: Harper Perennial, 1990.

———. *The End of the Nation State: The Rise of Regional Economies*. New York: Free Press, 1995.

Ohnuki-Tierney, Emiko. "McDonald's in Japan: Changing Manners and Etiquette." In *Golden Arches East: McDonald's in East Asia*, edited by James Watson, 161–82. 2nd ed. Stanford: Stanford University Press, 2006.

Okita, Saburo. *Japan in the World Economy of the 1980s*. Tokyo: University of Tokyo Press, 1989.

Ōmae, Kinjirō, and Yuzuru Tachibana. *The Book of Sushi*. Tokyo: Kodansha, 1981.

Osterhammel, Jurgen, and Niels P. Peterssen. *Globalization: A Short History.* Translated by Dona Geyer. Princeton: Princeton University Press, 2005.

Patten, Fred. *Watching Anime, Reading Manga: 25 Years of Essays and Reviews.* Berkeley: Stone Bridge Press, 2005.

Patterson, James T. *Restless Giant: The United States from Watergate to Bush v. Gore.* New York: Oxford University Press, 2005.

Pelliteri, Marco. "Manga in Italy: The History of a Powerful Cultural Hybridization." *International Journal of Comic Art* 8 (Fall 2006): 56–76.

Pells, Richard H. *Not Like Us: How Europeans Have Loved, Hated, and Transformed American Culture since World War II.* New York: Basic Books, 1997.

Perrucci, Robert. *Japanese Auto Transplants in the Heartland: Corporatism and Community.* New York: Aldine de Gruyter, 1994.

Philip, Leila. "The Chrysanthemum and the Buckeye." *Ohio Magazine,* November 1992, 24–26.

Piesman, Marissa, and Marilee Hartley. *The Yuppie Handbook: The State-of-the-Art Manual for Young Urban Professionals.* New York: Long Shadow Books, 1984.

Pieterse, Jan Nederveen. *Globalization and Culture: Global Mélange.* Lanham, Md.: Rowman and Littlefield, 2009.

Prestowitz, Clyde V. *Trading Places: How We Are Giving Our Future to Japan and How to Reclaim It.* New York: Basic Books, 1993.

Putnam, Robert D. *Bowling Alone: The Collapse and Revival of American Community.* New York: Simon & Schuster, 2000.

Pyle, Kenneth B. "Forum on the Trade Crisis: Introduction." *Journal of Japanese Studies* 13 (Summer 1987): 239–41.

Rauch, Jonathan. "Drive Shaft." *New Republic,* 13 April 1992, 15.

Rawson, Deborah. "Foreign Exchange." *Life,* Fall 1989, 176–79.

Reich, Robert B. *Locked in the Cabinet.* New York: Vintage, 1998.

———. *The Next American Frontier.* New York: Penguin, 1983.

———. *The Work of Nations: Preparing Ourselves for 21st-Century Capitalism.* New York: Vintage, 1991.

Reischauer, Edwin O. *The Emperor of Japan: A Profile on the Occasion of the Visit by the Emperor and Empress to the United States.* New York: Japan Society, 1975.

———. *Japan: Past and Present.* New York: Knopf, 1956.

———. *The Japanese Today: Change and Continuity.* Cambridge, Mass.: Belknap, 1978.

Renda, Mary A. *Taking Haiti: Military Occupation and the Cultures of U.S. Imperialism.* Chapel Hill: University of California Press, 2001.

Renton, Alex. "How Sushi Ate the World." *Observer* (U.K.), 26 February 2006.

Richards, Lawrence. *Union-Free America: Workers and Antiunion Culture.* Urbana: University of Illinois Press, 2008.

Ritzer, George. *The McDonaldization of Society: Revised New Century Edition.* Thousand Oaks, Calif.: Pine Forge Press, 2004.

———, ed. *The Blackwell Companion to Globalization.* Malden, Mass.: Blackwell, 2007.

Robertson, Roland. *Globalization: Social Theory and Global Culture.* London: Sage, 1992.

Rodgers, Daniel T. *Age of Fracture.* Cambridge, Mass.: Belknap Press, 2012.

Rohmer, Sax. *The Insidious Dr. Fu-Manchu.* New York: Dover Publications, 1997.

Rosecrance, Richard. *The Rise of the Trading State: Commerce and Conquest in the Modern World*. New York: Basic Books, 1985.

Rosenau, James N. *The Study of Global Interdependence: Essays on the Transnationalization of World Affairs*. New York: Nichols, 1980.

Rosenberg, Jim. "The CIA at RIT." *Editor and Publisher*, 18 January 1992, 30.

Rotter, Andrew J. *Comrades at Odds: The United States and India, 1947–1964*. Ithaca: Cornell University Press, 2000.

Said, Edward. *Culture and Imperialism*. New York: Vintage, 1994.

———. *Orientalism*. New York: Vintage, 1978.

Sanders, Katie. "Donald Trump: Chevrolet in Tokyo, Japan, 'Doesn't Exist.'" *PolitiFact*, 17 June 2015.

Sapolsky, Barry S., and Edward Forrest. "Measuring VCR 'Ad-Voidance.'" In *The VCR Age: Home Video and Mass Communication*, edited by Mark R. Levy, 148–67. London: Sage, 1989.

Sassatelli, Roberta. *Consumer Culture: History, Theory, and Politics*. London: Sage, 2007.

Schaller, Michael. *Altered States: The United States and Japan since the Occupation*. New York: Oxford University Press, 1997.

———. *Right Turn: American Life in the Reagan-Bush Era, 1980–1992*. New York: Oxford University Press, 2007.

Schodt, Frederik L. *America and the Four Japans: Friend, Foe, Model, Mirror*. Berkeley: Stone Bridge Press, 1994.

———. *Dreamland Japan: Writings on Modern Manga*. Berkeley: Stone Bridge Press, 1996.

———. *Manga! Manga! The World of Japanese Comics*. New York: Kodansha, 1983.

Scholte, Jan Aarte. *Globalization: A Critical Introduction*. 2nd ed. New York: Palgrave, 2005.

Schulman, Bruce J. *The Seventies: The Great Shift in American Culture, Society, and Politics*. New York: Da Capo, 2001.

Shibusawa, Naoko. *America's Geisha Ally: Reimagining the Japanese Enemy*. Cambridge, Mass.: Harvard University Press, 2006.

Smith, Alan. "The English-Language Historiography of Modern Japan." In *Companion to Historiography*, edited by Michael Bentley, 645–62. New York: Routledge, 1997.

Smith, Henry. "James Clavell and the Legend of the British Samurai." In *Learning from 'Shōgun': Japanese History and Western Fantasy*, edited by Henry Smith, 1–19. Santa Barbara: University of California Press, 1981.

———. "Reading James Clavell's 'Shogun.'" *History Today*, October 1981, 39–42.

———, ed. *Learning from 'Shōgun': Japanese History and Western Fantasy*. Santa Barbara: University of California Press, 1981.

Steger, Manfred. *Globalization: A Very Short Introduction*. New York: Oxford University Press, 2003.

Steigerwald, David. "All Hail the Republic of Choice: Consumer History as Contemporary Thought." *Journal of American History* 93 (September 2006): 385–403.

Stein, Judith. *Pivotal Decade: How the United States Traded Factories for Finance in the 1970s*. New Haven: Yale University Press, 2011.

Stelzer, Irwin M. "How to Save Free Trade—and Still Trade with Japan." *Commentary*, July 1990, 15–21.

Stiglitz, Joseph E. *Globalization and Its Discontents*. New York: W. W. Norton, 2002.

Strasser, Susan, Charles McGovern, and Matthias Judt, eds. *Getting and Spending: European and American Consumer Societies in the Twentieth Century*. New York: Cambridge University Press, 1998.

A Study among Videocassette Recording System Owners—1979. New York: Dan Bowdren Associates, 1979.

Sugimoto, Yoshio. "Making Sense of *Nihonjinron*." *Thesis Eleven* 51, no. 1 (May 1999): 81–96.

Sugrue, Thomas J. *The Origins of the Urban Crisis: Race and Inequality in Postwar Detroit*. Princeton: Princeton University Press, 1996.

Susman, Warren. *Culture as History: The Transformation of American Society in the Twentieth Century*. Washington, D.C.: Smithsonian Institution Press, 2003.

Tanaka, Heihachi. *The Pleasures of Japanese Cooking*. New York: Cornerstone, 1963.

Taylor, Jarod. *Shadows of the Rising Sun: A Critical View of the "Japanese Miracle."* New York: William Morrow, 1983.

Tchen, John Kuo Wei. *New York before Chinatown: Orientalism and the Shaping of American Culture, 1776–1882*. Baltimore: Johns Hopkins University Press, 1999.

Tchen, John Kuo Wei, and Dylan Yeats, eds. *Yellow Peril! An Archive of Anti-Asian Fear*. New York: Verso, 2014.

Thelen, David. "The Nation and Beyond: Transnational Perspectives on United States History." *Journal of American History* 86 (December 1999): 965–75.

Thomas, Daniel C. *The Helsinki Effect: International Norms, Human Rights, and the Demise of Communism*. Princeton: Princeton University Press, 2001.

Tobin, Joseph, ed. *Pikachu's Global Adventure: The Rise and Fall of Pokémon*. Durham: Duke University Press, 2004.

Tohyama, Heihachiro. *Quick and Easy Sushi Cookbook*. Tokyo: Joie, 1983.

Trillin, Calvin. *Feeding a Yen: Savoring Local Specialties, from Kansas City to Cuzco*. New York: Random House, 2003.

Troy, Gil. *Morning in America: How Ronald Reagan Invented the 1980s*. Princeton: Princeton University Press, 2005.

Tsutsui, William M., and Michiko Ito, eds. *In Godzilla's Footsteps: Japanese Pop Culture Icons on the Global Stage*. New York: Palgrave, 2006.

U.S. Bureau of the Census. *1987 Census of Agriculture: Agricultural Atlas of the United States*. Washington, D.C.: U.S. Government Printing Office, 1987.

Van Wolferen, Karel. *The Enigma of Japanese Power*. New York: Knopf, 1989.

———. "The Japan Problem." *Foreign Affairs* 65 (Winter 1986–1987): 288–303.

Veblen, Thorstein. *The Theory of the Leisure Class: An Economic Study of Institutions*. New York: Modern Library, 1961.

Vogel, Ezra. *Japan as Number One: Lessons for America*. Cambridge, Mass.: Harvard University Press, 1979.

Vogel, Steven K., ed. *U.S.-Japan Relations in a Changing World*. Washington, D.C.: Brookings Institution, 2002.

Wagnleitner, Reinhold. *Coca-Colonization and the Cold War: The Cultural Mission of the United States in Austria after the Second World War*. Chapel Hill: University of North Carolina Press, 1994.

Wasser, Frederick. *Veni, Vidi, Video: The Hollywood Empire and the VCR*. Austin: University of Texas Press, 2001.

Webber, Alan M. "Globalization and Its Discontents." *Harvard Business Review*, May–June 1985, 38–54.

Westad, Odd Arne. *The Global Cold War: Third World Interventions and the Making of Our Times*. New York: Cambridge University Press, 2005.

———, ed. *Reviewing the Cold War: Approaches, Interpretations, Theory*. London: Frank Cass, 2000.

White, Richard. *The Middle Ground: Indians, Empires, and Republics in the Great Lakes Region, 1650–1815*. New York: Cambridge University Press, 1991.

Wickens, Peter. *The Road to Nissan: Flexibility, Quality, Teamwork*. London: Macmillan, 1987.

Wilentz, Sean. *The Age of Reagan: A History, 1974–2001*. New York: Harper, 2008.

Williams, Raymond. *Keywords: A Vocabulary of Culture and Society*. Rev. ed. New York: Oxford University Press, 1983.

———. *Marxism and Literature*. New York: Oxford University Press, 1977.

———. *Resources of Hope*. New York: Verso, 1989.

Wills, Garry. *Reagan's America: Innocents at Home*. New York: Doubleday, 1987.

Wilson, Rob, and Wimal Dissanayake, eds. *Global/Local: Cultural Production and the Transnational Imaginary*. Durham: Duke University Press, 1996.

Wolf, Martin J. *The Japanese Conspiracy: The Plot to Dominate Industry Worldwide—and How to Deal with It*. New York: Empire Books, 1983.

Yano, Christine R. *Pink Globalization: Hello Kitty's Trek across the Pacific*. Durham: Duke University Press, 2013.

Yip, Althea. "Remembering Vincent Chin." *Asian Week*, 19 June 1997, 20–24.

Yoon, Ae-Ri. "Conference Review: The First International Conference on Asian Comics, Animation, and Gaming (ACAG)." *Animation* 1 (November 2006): 252–55.

Yoshihara, Mari. *Embracing the East: White Women and American Orientalism*. New York: Oxford University Press, 2003.

Zeiler, Thomas W. *Ambassadors in Pinstripes: The Spalding World Baseball Tour and the Birth of the American Empire*. New York: Rowman and Littlefield, 2006.

———. "Business Is War in U.S.-Japanese Economic Relations, 1977–2001." In *Partnership: The United States and Japan, 1951–2001*, edited by Akira Iriye and Robert A. Wampler, 223–48. New York: Kodansha International, 2001.

———. "Nixon Shocks Japan, Inc." In *Nixon in the World: American Foreign Relations, 1969–1977*, edited by Fredrik Logevall and Andrew Preston, 289–308. New York: Oxford University Press, 2008.

Zimmerman, Mark. *How to Do Business with the Japanese*. New York: Random House, 1984.

Index

Page numbers in italics indicate illustrations.

Abe, Shinzo, 206

"Abenomics," 206

Activism, of anime community, 189–200

Adams, William, 53, 222n15

Adorno, Theodore, 3

African Americans: discrimination lawsuit against Honda, 94; Honda's hiring practices and, 91–95; Japanese racism against, 94

Age, of Honda hirees, 91–95, 113–14

Agents of Influence: How Japan's Lobbyists in the United States Manipulate America's Political and Economic System (Choate), 70–71, 75

"Age of mechanical reproduction," 134

Akihito (emperor of Japan), 49–50

Akira (film), 186–89, *187*, *188*, 237n29; artistic achievement of, 188; authenticity of, 199; as commercial turning point, 188; as milestone in U.S. anime history, 186

Alabama, Sony plant in, 15

Alien (film), 65

Amateur press associations (APAs), 196–99

American Automobile Labeling Act (1994), 228n94

American imagery, vs. homogeneity, 43

Americanization: of anime, 180, 181–85; French resistance to, 134–35; global, European attitudes toward, 45–46; of

Japanese cuisine (Benihana), 163–65; in Ohio, as fear of Honda Japanese families, 101

American made: globalization and meaning of, 108; Honda's identity as, 6, 80, 87, 104–8, *105–7*, 211–12, *212*, *213*; sourcing of parts abroad vs. local content, 108, 112, 113, 116, 120–21, 228n94; UAW as booster of Japanese plants, 117–18, *118*

Ampex machines, 136

Anderson, Perry, 135

Animation. *See* Anime

Anime, 177–203; activism of community, 189–200; *Akira*, 186–89, *187*, *188*, 199, 237n29; ambassador of, 181; Americanized or "denationalized," 180, 181–85; authenticity of, 180, 186, 188–89, 198–99; birth of phenomenon in Japan, 179–80; commercial turning point in U.S., 188; communal viewing of, 191, 194–95; conventions ("cons"), 189–90, 195, 200; definition of, 179, 236n5; "disorganized fandom" of, 192; diverse genres of, 179; early U.S. television series, 180; editing for U.S. market, 180, 184–86; exchange and distribution, 191, 192–93; fan clubs, 5, 178, 189–95, *194*, *196*, 200; first U.S. import company, 178, 186; grassroots globalization of,

178–79, 180; Japaneseness of, 180–83, 186; language barrier of, overcoming, 178, 193–95; vs. mainstream Hollywood media, 177–78; manga and, 179; map of community ("You are not alone!"), 198; in opposition to Japan-bashing, 190, 199–200; overdubbing of, 184, 186, 193; precedents for, 200–203; product (toy) tie-ins, 180–81, 185–86, 196, 200; racial and bodily representations in, 181–85, 201; *Star Blazers* adaptation, 183–85, 189, 190, 191, 193, 197, 237n32; transnationalism as theme in, 183, 186; underground literature, 189–90, 195–200; "work of the imagination," 190, 195

A.N.I.M.E. (Animation of Inter-Mediary Exchange), 192–93, 199

Anime Hasshin club, 192, 197–99

Anime tourism, 200

Anna Engine Plant, 84

Ann Arbor Anime Organization, 193

Aoki, Rocky, 163–65

APA Hashin, 197

APAs. *See* Amateur press associations

Appadurai, Arjun, 10, 190

Apple/Apple products, 17, 136, 211

Associated Press, on Honda hiring practices, 92–93

Associates, Honda employees as, 87, 95, 97–98

Associates Alliance, 112, 123–25, 129

Astro Boy (anime adaptation), 180, 185, 191

Atlantic Monthly, 70

Austin, Cheryl (fictional character). See *Rising Sun*

Authenticity: of anime, 180, 186, 188–89, 198–99; of experiences with Japan, 201; Grazian's definition of, 160; search for, 160; of sushi, 159–62, 174–75

Authoritarian states, vs. VCRs, 133, 146–47

Automobile industry: American-made claims in, 6, 80, 87, 104–8, 105–7, 211–12, 212, 213; in *Gung Ho* (film), 64–65, 95; Honda in Marysville, Ohio, 79–130; Japan-bashing in, 79–81; Japanese quality in, 81, 83; Japanese-style management in, 81, 83, 87, 91, 95–98; Japanese transplants in, 82; Japan's material presence in U.S., 5–6, 39; layoffs and shutdowns by U.S.

automakers, 28, 79–80; "multinational squeeze-play" in, 112; Nissan in Smyrna, Tenn., 64, 81–82, 91, 112, 113; sourcing of parts abroad vs. local content in, 108, 112, 113, 116, 120–21, 228n94; UAW as booster of Japanese plants, 117–18, 118; unionization in, 110–30; voluntary Japanese export restraints, 86–87, 112–13. *See also* Marysville, Ohio; *specific automakers*

"Auto wars," 79–82, 86, 114–17

Avco's Catrivision, 137

"Babysitters, store clerks and farm hands," Honda's hiring of, 92–93

Bad News Bears Go to Japan, The (film), 61, 62–64, 63

Bagel, 158

Balance of payments, trade deficit vs., 26

"Ballad of East and West, The" (Kipling), 32

Bambi (film), 179

Bánh mì sandwich, 169

Banks, Japanese, among world's largest, 15

Barbarian and the Geisha, The (film), 61

Barker, Steve, 124

Barthes, Roland, 12, 51

Baseball, cultural exchange through, 201

Bataan Death March, 102

Bates, Caroline, 170

Bathing, in *Shōgun*, 56

"Battle of Marysville." *See* United Automobile Workers (UAW), and Honda

Battle of Poitiers: first, 131; second, French restrictions on VCRs as, 131–33

Battle of the Planets (anime adaptation), 191, 197

Battlestar Galactica (TV series), 191

BayCon '86, 195

Beauty and the Beast (TV series), 194

Beck, Jerry, 186

Behrens, Daniel, 90, 128–29

Bellefontaine, Ohio: attitudes toward Japanese in, 103; closing of Rockwell plant, 120; Honda Japanese families in, 100

Benedict, Ruth, 12, 32, 52, 55, 69, 76, 220n37

Benihana (restaurant chain), 163–65

Benjamin, Walter, 134

Bennetts, Leslie, 165

Bercovici, Eric, 58

Bestor, Theodore, 157

Betamax, 136–43; cassette manufacture in U.S., 15; educational material on, 139; format war, 137–38, 139; legal battle over, 140–41; marketing of, 138–39, 142; Morita on mythology of, 138, 140; recording function, as crucial component, 137

Beyond National Borders (Ohmae), 41

Bhangra, 202–3

Bieber, Owen, 111

Big Three automakers, U.S.: adoption of Japanese approaches, 83; American-made status of, 108; "auto wars" against Japan, 79–82, 86, 114–17; decline in sales, 83; Japanese quality and management vs., 81; layoffs and closing, 28, 79–80; sourcing of parts abroad vs. local content, 108, 112, 113, 116, 120–21, 228n94; UAW tainted by association with, 127–28

Bird Scramble! (anime publication), 196–97

Blackman, Tommy, 115–16

Black market, for VCRs, 132, 133, 146–53

Black Rain (film), 50, 61, 65–66, 186

Blackthorne, John (fictional character). *See Shōgun*

Blade Runner (film), 7, 37–38, 50, 186, 187

Boas, Franz, 32

Bollywood, 150, 159, 202, 203

Book of Sushi, The, 167

Borderless World, The (Ohmae), 41, 221n72

Borderless world, Ohmae's concept of, 41–43

Boston Japanimation Society, 192

Bound to Lead (Nye), 36

Bowling Alone (Putnam), 4

Boycott, threatened against Honda, 111–12, 114–15, 127

Brazil: anime in, 181; sushi in, 174

Breakfast Club, The (film), 156

Breen, T. H., 4

Bretton Woods monetary system, 14

Brezhnev, Leonid, 12

Bridge on the River Kwai, The (film), 60–61

Bright, Charles, 202

Broderick, Matthew, 177

Brooks, Patricia, 173

Bush, George H. W., 18, 21–22

Bush, George W., 207–8

Business Week, 23, 33

Buy American (Frank), 116

California roll, 158–63

Calisthenics, in Honda plant, 95–96

Call to Economic Arms, A (Tsongas's campaign brochure), 21–22, 68

Capitalism, in modernization theory, 27–28

Capitalist developmental state, 29

Capshaw, Kate, 66

Captain Harlock (anime), 198

Captain Harlock and the Queen of 1,000 Years (anime adaptation), 198

Carlson, Marc, 192–93

Carmel, Jeffrey, 172

Carter, Jimmy, 18, 28, 203

Carter administration: economy under, 84–85; Honda's plans during, 84; Reich's service in, 44

Cartoon/Fantasy Organization (CFO), 5, 190–95, 194, 196, 200

Cartoons: traditional U.S. vs. anime, 178. *See also* Anime

Carville, James, 21

Cash Explosion Double Play (Ohio Lottery show), 109–10

Catholicism, in *Shōgun,* 56

CBS Records, 22

Central Intelligence Agency (CIA): "Japan 2000," 30–37, 219n29, 219nn33–34; RIT connection with, 30–31

CFO. *See* Cartoon/Fantasy Organization

Chamberlain, Richard, 54, 59

Champaign County, Ohio: economic conditions before and in early days of Honda operations, 85; inclusion in Honda's hiring radius, 93–94

Chan, Jackie, 203

Charter Oath, 31

Children's Day, 99

Chin, Vincent, 80–81

China: economic rise and power of, 17, 206; Japan's invasion as "Forgotten Holocaust," 50; material presence in U.S., 17; *Memoirs of a Geisha* banned in, 76; Nixon's visit to, 14; potential customers in, 208; VCRs in, 146

Chinese Americans: beating death of Chin, 80–81; protests against Japan, 50

Choate, Pat, 23, 70–71, 75

Christian Science Monitor, 59, 172

joint venture with Mazda, 82; layoffs and closings, 79–80

Ford, Gerald/Ford administration, 18, 44

"Foreign Exchange" (*Life* magazine), 5–6

Foreign Policy (magazine), 181

"Forgotten Holocaust," Japan's invasion of China as, 50

Format war, VCR, 137–38, 139

Fortress America, 207–8

Foucault, Michel, 32

France: anime in, 181; import (VCR) restrictions in, 131–33; resistance to Americanization, 134–35

Frank, Dana, 116

Frankfurt School, 3

Fraser, Douglas, 86, 111, 116–17, 127

Fremont, Calif., Toyota–GM operation in, 82

Freund, Charles Paul, 11

Friedman, Thomas, 41

Froud, Nina, 166

Fukudome, Kosuke, 201

Fukuyama, Francis, 22

Gabaccia, Donna R., 158

Gaijin in Japan, in popular culture, 53, 61–62, 66

Gallagher, Maria, 172

Galliot, Pierre, 131–32

"Gang of Four," in cultural revisionism, 218n14, 218n16

Gangster (*yakuza*) films, 61–62, 65–66

Gatchaman (anime), 197

Geertz, Clifford, 32

Geisha, 6, 18–19, 52, 61; *Blade Runner* images of, 37–38; Japanese cuisine and, 167, 170, 173; *Memoirs of a Geisha* (film), 76–77; *New Yorker* cover, 210

Gelsanliter, David, 93

Gender: in American auto industry, 80–81; in anime images, 181–85, 201; in consumption, 4; in sushi consumption, 155–56, 164, 169; in World War II image of Japan, 18–19

General Motors: adoption of Japanese approaches, 83; "auto wars" against Japan, 79–82; joint venture with Toyota, 82; layoffs and closings, 80; Saturn initiative, 129

George Washington University, bhangra at, 202

Germany, anime in, 181

Geyer, Michael, 202

Ghost in the Shell (film), 179, 180, 188

Gibson, William, 37

Gigantor (anime adaptation), 180, 191

Glenn, John, 113

Globalization: as agent of change, 11; American imagery vs. homogeneity in, 43; borderless world in, 41–43; "clash of civilizations" in, 10; dystopian visions of, 7, 37–38, 186–89; "era of bilateral acrimony" vs., 21–24; first article to use word, 42; Fortress America vs., 207–8; historical context of, 43–46; historicizing concept of, 10–11, 25; human capital in, 44–45; hybridization thesis of, 10; institutionalization, in Clinton administration, 17, 24–25, 44–46; invention of, 37–43; Jameson on, 13; Japan as catalyst for, 2, 7–9, 25, 37–43; Japan as Great Facilitator in, 145–53; Levitt and, 38–39, 42–43; McDonaldization in, 10, 43, 134–35; Morita and, 38–41; Ohmae and, 38–39, 41–43; optimistic transpacific dialogue about, 39; postmodernity and, 11–13; power concept in, 12, 24–25, 37–38, 46; Reich and, 44–46; scholarly approach to, 10; "shocks of the global," in Japan, 16–17; "shocks of the global," in U.S., 14–15; UAW and, 112–13, 115–17; U.S. as Great Communicator in, 150–53; U.S. corporations as symbol of, 17

Globalization, cultural: anime and, 177–203; bhangra and, 202–3; Japan's three C's of, 153; popular culture and, 47–78; precedents for anime and, 200–203; South Korea and, 206–7; sushi and, 157; VCR and, 132–36, 145–53

"The Globalization of Markets" (Levitt), 42

Globalizing philosophy, Honda's, 87

GM. *See* General Motors

Golden, Arthur, 76

Gone with the Wind (film), VCR recordings of, 139–40

Gong Li, 76

"Good ol' U.S. of H," 104–5, *105*

Mazda, joint venture with Ford, 82
MCA's Discovision, 137
McDonald, F. James, 115–16
McDonaldization, 10, 43, 134–35
McKinsey and Company, Ohmae and, 38–39, 41–43
Mechanical reproduction, age of, 134
"Me Decade," 145
Media. *See* Popular culture; *specific media*
Megalord: APA Superdimension U.S.A., 197
Memoirs of a Geisha (film), 76–77
Metanarratives: "incredulity toward," 12; Japan's lack of, 11–13, 36–37, 50–51; postmodernity vs., 11–13
Michael Jordan and the New Global Capitalism (LaFeber), 38
Michener, James, 61
Mifune, Toshiro, 54, 58–59
Miller, Bryan, 165
Ministry of Agriculture, Forestry, and Fisheries, Japan, 175
Ministry of International Trade and Industry (MITI), Japan, 28–29, 81, 152–53
Mitchum, Robert, 62
MITI and the Japanese Miracle: The Growth of Industrial Policy, 1925–1975 (Johnson), 28–29
Mitsubishi: purchase of Rockefeller Center, 22, 65; in VCR format war, 137
Miyake, Issei, 210
Miyazaki, Hayao, 179, 182, 198
Miyazawa, Kiichi, 21
MMP. *See* Marysville Motorcycle Plant
Mobile Suit Gundam (anime), 193
Modernization, Sony as expression of, 39
Modernization theory, 36; Charter Oath and, 31; Hirohito's visit to U.S. and, 48–50; revisionism vs., 27–28, 29; *Shōgun* and, 48, 50, 52, 60, 61
Mondale, Walter, 12, 84
Moore, Roger, 59, 177
Morita, Akio, 38–41, 43; promotion of VCR mythology, 138, 140; Sony name and image crafted by, 39–40; *Time* magazine cover, 209–10; world citizenship of, 40–41
Morning calisthenics, in Honda plant, 95–96
Morrow, Lance, 36–37
Mosbacher, Robert A, 218n14
Mukokuseki style, in anime, 181–82, 201

"Multinational squeeze-play," in auto industry, 112
Murray, Bill, 77–78

NAFTA. *See* North American Free Trade Agreement
Nagasaki, atomic bomb dropped on, 50, 114
Nakasone, Yasuhiro, 94, 210
Namco, 114
Namiki, Keiko, 103
Nanjing, China, Japanese invasion of, 50
Napier, Susan J., 182
Narcissism, culture of, 145
Nathan, Robert, 74
National exceptionalism, 33–34
National Labor Relationships Board (NLRB), 110, 125
Nausicaä of the Valley of the Wind (anime), 198
NBC, and VCR recordings, 139–40
Nebraska, Kawasaki union-busting in, 114
Neoliberalism, 24, 42, 169
Neon Genesis Evangelion (anime), 182
Nepal, VCRs and popular culture in, 150, 151
Nestlé, closing of Marysville facility, 90
Network (film), 154
Neuromancer (Gibson), 37
Never So Few (film), 61
New Jersey, closing of Ford Mahwah plant in, 79–80
Newsweek, 52, 211
New York City, sushi in, 154–56
New Yorker, cover representation of Japan, 210
New York Times: on comparison of China and Japan, 206; on Great Recession, 208; on Honda's Marysville operations, 91, 94, 128; on Japan's fading presence on global stage, 209; on perceptions of Japan, 16; on *Rising Sun*, 74; on Scott's filmmaking, 65; on *Shōgun* TV adaptation, 59–60; on sushi, 154–56, 165, 172, 173
Next American Frontier, The (Reich), 44
Nigeria, VCR impact in, 146
Nihonjinron, 33–34
Nikkan Shimbun (Marysville newspaper supplement), 88–89, 89

(from *Shōgun* to *Rising Sun*), 60–68;
Japan's economic miracle in, 61, 64;
post-World War II, 60–61; *Rising Sun*
in, 18, 47–48, 50–51; *Shōgun* in, 47–48,
50–60; soft power from, 12, 36, 153, 181,
207; South Korea and, 206–7; sushi in,
156–57; VCR transmission of, 150–53. *See
also specific works*
Postmodernity, 11–13; Jameson on, 13;
malaise in U.S. and, 12; *Rising Sun* and, 48,
50–51, 68, 71; sushi and, 162; VCR and, 135
Powell, Steve, 98
Power: corporate, 37–38, 42; cultural,
Japan's, 24–25, 181, 207; cultural
revisionism and, 34–37; food and (food
colonialism), 161, 168–69; globalization
and, 12, 24, 37–38, 46; historical concept
of, 35; imperial overstretch and, 35; soft,
12, 36, 153, 181, 207; U.S. vs. Japanese, Nye
on, 36–37
Prestowitz, Clyde, 47, 70–71, 218n14, 218n16
Price, Lee, 114–15
Protectionism, Reagan-era, 28, 86–87,
112–13
Publications, on Japan's economic success,
23, 26, 47
Putnam, Robert, 4

Queen Millennia (anime), 198
Quick and Easy Sushi Cookbook, 167

Race: in anime, nonspecific, 181–85, 201;
in "auto wars," 79–82, 114–15; in *The Bad
News Bears Go to Japan*, 62–64; cultural
revisionism and, 27, 31–32, 34; culture as
replacement for, 31–32; in "de-Japanized"
Sony, 39; in *Dragon* (Cussler), 67–68; in
Honda's hiring practices in Marysville,
91–95; in Marysville (anti-Japanese
racism), 102–4; in *Rising Sun*, 61, 68–75,
94–95; role in Japan vs. role in U.S.,
34; stereotypes of Japan, 17–19; UAW's
eschewing of tactic, 114–16; World War
II and, 18–19; "yellow peril," 17–18, 27, 39,
68, 81, 206
Rashomon (film), 59
RCA's Selectavision, 137
Reagan, Ronald: age created by vs.
creation by age, 10; anime vs. America

of, 203; antiunionism of, 127; as "Fisher
King," 9; historical views of, 9–10;
"morning again" promise of, 84, 203;
unhealthy fixation with, 9; World War II
background of, 18
Reagan administration: narrative of policy
vs. policy making in, 9; voluntary
restraints on Japanese imports under, 28,
86–87, 112–13
"Reagan recession," 44, 80, 82, 85
"Reagan Revolution," 9
Real estate acquisitions, Japan's, 22, 23, 65
rec.arts.anime, 199
Recession: as election issue against Bush
(George H. W.), 21–22; Great Recession,
208; Japan (1990s), 7, 15–16, 25, 46,
205–6; "Reagan," 44, 80, 82, 85
Reich, Robert B., 44–46, 200
Reischauer, Edwin O., 27, 49, 52, 55, 76
Renton, Alex, 162
Restaurants, Japanese: in American
culinary landscape, 156; Americanized
(Benihana), 163–65; authentication plan
for, 175; expectations for environment,
173–74. *See also* Sushi
Revisionism, 25–37; aggressiveness vs.
scholarly experience in, 29; Clinton's
rejection of, 46; first important text
of, 28; historical context of, 43–46;
Japan Panic in, 3, 25–30, 43–44, 46,
216n6; modernization theory vs.,
27–28, 29; origin of term, 26, 218n14. *See
also* Cultural revisionism; Structural
revisionism
Rhode Island, anime club of, 192, 197–99
Rhodes, Jim, 83–84, 117
Rice sandwiches. *See* Sushi
Richards, Lawrence, 127
Richards, Pamela, 109
Richman, Phyllis, 165, 170, 171–72, 173
Riedmiller, Chuck, 102
Right Stuff, The (film), 177
"Right-to-work" movement, 111
Risen, James, 128
Rise of the Trading State, The (Rosecrance),
34–35
Rising Sun (anime club chapter), 192
Rising Sun (Crichton), 18, 47–48, 50–51;
bibliography and "research" for, 70–71,

Smuggling, of VCRs, 132, 133, 146–53
Smyrna, Tenn., Nissan facility, 64, 81–82, 91, 112, 113
Snipes, Wesley, 73
Snoop (Gosling), 216n9
Snyder, Gary, 200–201
Soft power: American, 12, 36, 153; Japanese, 181, 207; South Korean, 207
Solidarity (UAW magazine), 117–18, *118*
Sony Corp. of America v. Universal City Studios, Inc., 140
Sony Corporation: brand name in roman lettering, 40; crafting of name, 39–40; "de-Japanized," 39; Dothan, Ala., plant, 15; expression of cosmopolitanism in first world, 39; expression of modernization in third world, 39; as global corporation, 39; as iconic Japanese company, 39; material presence in U.S., 1, 6; Morita's vision for, 38–41; purchase of Columbia Pictures, 22; *Time* magazine cover on, 209–10
Sony VCR (Betamax), 136–43; cassette manufacture in U.S., 15; educational material on, 139; format war, 137–38, 139; legal battle over, 140–41; marketing of, 138–39, 142; Morita on mythology of, 138, 140; recording function, as crucial component, 137
Soren, Jidosha, 116
South Korea, cultural power of, 206–7
Soviet Union, VCRs in, 133, 147–48
Speed Racer (anime adaptation), 180, 185
Spielberg, Steven, 178
Spinelli, Bob, 79–81
Spirited Away (film), 179
Spring Hill, Tenn., Saturn plant, 129
Springsteen, Bruce, 22
Stapleton, Sharon, 193–94
Star Blazers (anime adaptation), 183–85, 189, 190, 191, 193, 197, 237n32
"Starting now. Made over here." (Honda ad), 107
Star Trek (TV series and films): exchanged for anime, 191; fan fiction, 196; fans and cosplay, 195; transnationalism as theme of, 183
Star Wars (film series), 177, 190, 196
State-guided market system, 29

Staying Alive (film), 177
Steel industry, 14, 15, 29, 81, 85
Stein, Judith, 9–10
Stelzer, Irwin, 6
Stereotypes, of Japan, 17–19; *The Chrysanthemum and the Sword* and, 12, 32, 52, 76, 220n37; in cultural revisionism, 30–37; in *Dragon* (Cussler), 67–68; in *Gung Ho* (film), 64–65; on magazine covers, 209–11; in post-World War II popular culture, 61; in *Rising Sun*, 69, 71; *sarariman* (salaryman), 19, 35, 152; in *Shōgun* and, 48, 52, 55, 71; in sushi consumption, 169–74; in World War II, 18–19
Stevens, John Paul, 140
Stone, Oliver, 156–57
Stowe, Harriet Beecher, 74
Streamline Pictures, 186–89, 198–99, 237n29
Streep, Meryl, 150
Strike, threatened against Honda, 111–12
Structural revisionism, 26–30, 36, 218n15
Structures of feeling, 9, 20
Student exchanges, Ohio-Japan, 100
Sukiyaki, 166, 235n35
Sushi, 154–76, 203; aesthetics of, 167, 169–71; arrival at Harvard Club, 154–56; authenticity of, 159–62, 174–75; California roll, 158–63; class and consumption of, 155, 156; cultural convergence in, 155, 158; definition of, 156; dietary/health appeal of, 168; eroticism of, 157, 169–71; as exemplary globalization product, 157; food adventurers and, 160–61, 167–68; food writers on, 169–74; gendering of consumption, 155–56, 164, 169; hybrid (cultural mix) of, 154–62, 174–76; Japaneseness of, 158, 160–62, 166, 173–74; Japanese perceptions of American palate and, 163; lessons on eating, 171–73; local–global interaction in, 158–60; Philadelphia roll, 158–61, 169; in popular culture, 156–57; postmodernity and, 162; premodern Japan and, 162, 170–71; restaurant environment, expectations for, 173–74; Royko on, 155–56, 164, 174; stereotypes and, 169–74; supermarket presence of, 156; U.S. environment

Index

Unionization: antiunion sentiment vs., 111, 120, 123–30; Honda and UAW, 82, 96, 110–30; Honda hiring practices and discouragement of, 91–95, 110, 118–19, 127; non-union auto facilities, 82; "right-to-work" movement vs., 111; union-busting by Kawasaki, 114. *See also* United Automobile Workers

United Automobile Workers (UAW): anticipated cooperation with Japanese automakers, 112, 117, 120; and "auto wars," 81; as boosters of Japanese plants, 117–18, *118*; cultural changes unforeseen by, 113; global vision of, 112–13, 115–17; international worker solidarity sought by, 115–16; local content law sought by, 113, 120–21; "multinational squeeze-play" and, 112; Ohio lottery contestant's support for, 109–10; rejection in Nissan Smyrna plant, 82, 113; struggle to stay relevant, 129–30; taint of Big Three association, 127–28

United Automobile Workers (UAW), and Honda, 96, 110–30; Associates Alliance's antiunion stance, 112, 123–25; bread-and-butter issues moot in campaign, 122–23; dispute over logo on hats, 96, 110, 111, 120; Findlay meeting and agreement, 110–12, 119; Honda's pledge of neutrality, 110, 111, 118; Honda's refusal to recognize powerhouse operators' vote for, 110; Honda's workforce questionnaire, 122, 125; insider-outsider discourse, 128–30; line speed and additional hiring as issue, 123, 129; Pac-Man pamphlet on, 114; patriotism as strategy, 118–21; race/racism eschewed as tactic, 114–16; reasons for failure, 126–30; request for recognition without vote (1985), 122; threatened boycott and strike, 111–12, 114–15, 127; withdrawal of petition for vote (1985), 111–12, 120; workers' relationship with Honda and, 82, 96, 124–26; World War II and generational divide over, 113–15

United States: Emperor Akihito's visit to, 49–50; Emperor Hirohito's visit to, 48–50; Fortress America vs. globalization, 207–8; as Great Communicator, 150–53; imperial overstretch of, 35; soft power of, 12, 36, 153. *See also specific topics*

U. S.-Japan relations: "era of bilateral acrimony," 21–24; future of, 204–12; Nixon shocks and, 14; political vs. cultural, 23; revisionism and, 25–37; security (military), 19–20; Trump and, 204–5, 206. *See also specific topics*

Universal Studios, and VCR recordings, 139–40

University of Michigan study, on Honda hiring practices, 94

Urusei Yatsura (anime), 179, 192, 193

"Us," Reich's concept of, 44–45

Usenet newsgroup, for anime fans, 199

van Wolferen, Karel, 27–28, 218n14, 218n16

VCR, 131–53; active viewers created by, 141; advertising for, 135, 138–39, 142; annual production (1984), 146; authoritarian states vs., 133, 146–47; black market (smuggling), 132, 133, 146–53; content for, acquisition of scarce or restricted videos, 146–48; content for, American culture in, 150–53; content for, video rental, 144–45; copyright issues, 137, 140–41; cultural globalization through, 132–36, 145–53; cultural life span of, 136; development of, 136; dissociation from Japaneseness, 134–35, 152–53; format war, 137–38, 139; French restrictions on imports, 131–33; Harvard study on, 146–47, 148, 233n59; immigrant communities and, 149–50; Iyer on, 148, 150–51; Japanese exports to Europe, 132; Japanese manufacture for U.S. labels, 138, 153; as "perpetual emotion machine," 135; postmodernity and, 135; price of, 137; recording function as crucial component, 137; sales growth, 142–43; social science studies of, 143–44; Sony Betamax, 15, 136–43; television national standards and, 149–50; time-shifting through, 138, 140–45; UNESCO study on, 146, 147; units in operation (1988), 146; U.S. law vs. Japanese imagination, 137; in U.S., apotheosis of, 145; in U.S., consumer liberation through, 133, 135–45; in U.S., mundane usage of, 144–45

Veblen, Thorstein, 3

VHS, 137–38, 139